Transition and Development
in India

Transition and Development in India

Anjan Chakrabarti
and Stephen Cullenberg

ROUTLEDGE
NEW YORK AND LONDON

Published in 2003 by
Routledge
29 West 35th Street
New York, NY 10001
www.routledge-ny.com

Published in Great Britain by
Routledge
11 New Fetter Lane
London EC4P 4EE
www.routledge.co.uk

Routledge is an imprint of the Taylor & Francis Group.
Printed in the United States of America on acid-free paper.

10 9 8 7 6 5 4 3 2 1

Library of Congress Cataloging-in-Publication Data

Chakrabarti, Anjan.
    Transition and development in India / by Anjan Chakrabarti and Stephen Cullenberg.
        p. cm.
    ISBN 0-415-93485-0 — ISBN 0-415-93486-9 (pbk.)
        1. Marxian economics–India.   2. India–Economic conditions–1947-   I. Cullenberg,
    Stephen.   II. Title.

    HB97.5 .C453 2003
    330.954–dc21
                                                                            2002036621

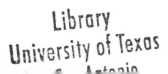

For Ajit Chaudhury, Stephen Resnick, and Richard Wolff

Contents

Acknowledgments

This is a book written by one author who as a young man grew up amid the collapse and ruin of the worldwide communist movement and the so-called then-socialist model in India and by another who was influenced by the debates of the New Left over alternative societies that were neither founded on the Anglo-American models of capitalism nor the Soviet models of socialist central planning. In the context of India this meant questioning the legitimacy of the old edifice of historical materialism (and something more) that guided the intellectual current of Indian Marxism and Marxism in general. Likewise in the context of the United States, it meant coming to terms with the Western Marxist critiques of the over-powering model of economic determinism. This is then a Marxist work, but one deeply influenced by the philosophical critiques of Marxism in the tradition of Althusser, Foucault, Derrida, and many others whom we consider to be part of the overall postmodern critique of classical Western thought, including Marxism.

Transition was and is the central development issue facing a so-called underdeveloped country such as India. The issues of transition and development dealt with in this book were present in the political and academic atmosphere of the India in the 1980s, and more so now in the present phase of the liberalization process in India since independence. The debates over the Indian mode of production and subaltern studies are the centerpiece of much of this book, and we owe an enormous amount of gratitude to the many contributors to these debates that we discuss throughout. However, the goal of this book is to take these debates in a new direction by developing an alternative model of transition and development, one that not only would displace the intellectual focus of the old debates but can also contribute to the current policy discussions over liberalization and globalization. We hope that in some small way this book will contribute to the many struggles the world over to create a new global community that is concerned with ending injustice and class exploitation.

Along the way many people have in different ways helped to shape the contours of the present work. Asha Achuthan, Pranab Basu, Ajit Chaudhury, Joseph Childers, Anirban Das, Dipankar Das, Anup Dhar, Gary Dymski, Keith Griffin, Michael Howard, Victor Lippit, Lisa Lowe, Arup Mallick, Robert Pollin, David Ruccio, Nirmal Saha, Kalyan Sanyal, and Richard Wolff were very helpful in formulating some of the fundamental ideas of this book. They have read, discussed, commented, suggested, and criticized different aspects of what we have produced. We are indebted to them all for their support and insights.

Anjan Chakrabarti
Stephen Cullenberg

CHAPTER 1

Redrawing the Boundary of Transition and Development in India

*A Prelude to an Anti-Essentialist
Conceptualization of Transition
and Development*

I am always reminded of one thing which the well-known British economist Adam Smith said in his famous treatise *The Wealth of Nations*. In it he described some economic laws as universal and absolute. Then he described certain situations which may be an obstacle to the operation of these laws. These disturbing factors are the human nature, the human temperament or altruism inherent in it. Now the economics of khadi is just the opposite of it. Benevolence which is inherent in human nature is the very foundation of the economics of khadi. What Adam Smith has described as pure economic activity based merely on the calculations of profit and loss is a selfish attitude and it is an obstacle to the development of khadi; and it is the function of a champion of khadi to counteract this tendency. (Gandhi, 1958–, CW. Vol. 59, 205–6)[1]

My own view is that evils are inherent in industrialization, and no amount of socialization can eradicate them. (Gandhi, 1958–, CW, Vol. 63, 241)

We are trying to catch up, as far as we can, with the Industrial Revolution that occurred long ago in Western countries. (Nehru, 1954, Vol. 2, 93)

Decades of development experience in dozens of countries show that a good economic environment combines the [discipline of competitive markets with efficient provision] of key public utilities. . . . Fostering an economic environment which promotes rapid, broad-based development will not be easy. [Old habits of thinking and working must be shed]. . . . Within a generation, the countries of East Asia have transformed themselves. China, Indonesia, Korea, Thailand and Malaysia today have living standards much above ours. [What they have achieved, we must strive for]. (Government of India Discussion Paper 1993, 1–2)

The above set of quotations is striking for their diverse, almost contradictory views about the transition and development of Indian society. What makes them even more intriguing is that the opinions are expressed from within the Congress party that was the dominant anti-British party and that has ruled India since independence except for the recent few years.

Opposing Gandhi, the father of the nation and the symbolic figure of the Congress party, Jawaharlal Nehru, the first Indian prime minister, was determined to industrialize India and make it a modern society. According to Nehru, the transition from a backward agricultural society to a modern industrial one was the only possible road for India to progress. In line with Nehru's wishes, India's industrialization process was propelled by the state sector, since it was argued that the private sector did not have the capacity to create the basic infrastructure and means of production needed for industrialization. In many quarters, this state involvement in industrialization came to be identified with socialism. This "Nehruvian socialism," as it is sometimes called, continued until the mid-1980s, when Rajiv Gandhi, the then–prime minister and grandson of Nehru, started a liberalization program, which, without challenging the state's dominant role in society, began the process of dismantling India's trade barriers. However, the real seismic change came in 1991 when the government of Prime Minister Narasimha Rao challenged the supremacy of the state in any input, output, and pricing decisions being taken in the economy and started an all-out war on the import substitution approach that had been the hallmark of India's industrialization process since independence. His government has initiated a series of policies packaged as the "new economic policies," which is directed toward significantly reducing the state's direct involvement in the Indian economy and has in particular emphasized the role of an export-oriented growth and industrialization strategy of development.

These policy changes do not challenge the fundamental idea of progress as growth through industrialization but they certainly contest the Nehruvian path of achieving such progress.

Yet, since independence the path of capitalist development in India via industrialization has not been easy and without compromises. Due to political considerations, the Gandhian tradition of Khadi, which, as is evident from the first quotation, is a different and diametrically opposite set of economic policies from ones directed at growth through industrialization, had to be accounted for in the Indian economic policies. And, because the Gandhian philosophy is so crucially based on the economic philosophy of Khadi, the Indian economic policies had to combine the growth-oriented "maximization" policies and the Gandhian job-oriented "benevolent" policies. The coexistence of these opposite sets of policies within the body of the state has been a source of irritation and dilemma for academic economists, both on the right and left, who are unable to find any consistent rationale in some of the decisions being made by the state agencies. This is because the economists have not paid enough attention to the complexities involved in including the Gandhian tradition in the decision-making process of the various state bodies.

Since the time of Nehru, there was no doubt in the elite circle, which includes the academic elite, that progress through industrialization is the key to growth and the eradication of poverty and unemployment. Consequently, industrialization through capital accumulation was accorded a privileged position as compared to the Gandhian policy of Khadi, which nevertheless had to be accommodated in formulating economic decisions. The problem for the Indian developmental state, then, comes down to the performance of a dual, and a seemingly impossible, act of legitimizing the rule of capital accumulation and accommodating the Gandhian tradition of Khadi (the anticapitalist set of economic policies), two fundamentally contradictory positions. This complex way of looking at the development of capitalism in India (capitalism or modernism rules by accommodating precapitalism or tradition) has been popularized by the *subaltern studies'* school of thought in recent times and is in sharp contrast to the more traditional Marxian approach summarized in the Indian modes of production debate that dominated the Indian discourse on Marxism from the late 1960s until the beginning of the 1980s.[2]

From its inception, the (traditional) Indian Marxist discourse on transition and development steeped in the Second International's historical materialistic framework was anti-Gandhian because its views on progress and on industrialization and modern civil society associated with it were totally contrary to Gandhi's antimodernist stance. The first Marxian academic debate on the Indian modes of production clearly situated itself in a historical materialistic terrain where the problem, in terms of capitalism's failure to assume its dominating form, was designated as the absence of the penetration of capital (signifying the forces of production) in Indian agriculture. This debate was based on the assumption that capitalism cannot accommodate traditional institutions that it considers to be backward or outmoded. They have to be automatically discarded with the advent of capitalism. Thus, at the conceptual level, capitalism cannot accommodate Gandhian policies of Khadi and, consequently, since it was being accommodated in the postindependent economic policies in the absence of any concerted assault on precapitalist elements, the Indian mode of production cannot be identified as capitalist. As mentioned above, the subaltern studies school challenged the fundamental premise that capitalism cannot accommodate precapitalist elements under its rule. In fact, as we shall argue, the subaltern theorists built up a general model of transition and development (one in contrast to that of historical materialism) where one moment of the transition is captured by the passive revolution of capital that roughly signifies this aspect of the appropriation of precapitalism by capitalism.[3]

However, for us, other than the substantive differences between the subaltern debate and the Indian modes of production debate, which are significant in their own right, the problem of the transition of Indian society and its development as analyzed in Indian discourses on Marxism resides at a much deeper level. It is the problem related to the conceptual thematic of Orientalism that is best summarized in Chatterjee (1984):

> At the level of thematic . . . nationalist thought accepts and adopts the same essentialist conception [as in Orientalism] based on a distinction between "the East" and "the West," the same typology created by a transcendental studying subject, and hence the same "objectifying" procedures of knowledge constructed in the postenlightenment age of Western science . . . it is vitally important to emphasize that this opposition [to the foreign rule] occurs within a body of knowledge about the East (large parts of it purporting to be scientific) which has the same representational structure and shares the same theoretical framework as Orientalism. (Chatterjee 1984, 155)

This essentialist thematic of Orientalism, which overlaps with the essentialist thematic of Western metaphysics that seems to be the basis for knowledge production, became an integral part of the postindependent Marxian tradition in India that culminated in the Indian modes of production debate.[4] A second stage in Indian Marxian thought opened with the challenge by a group of Marxist social scientists led by Ranajit Guha and Partha Chatterjee concerning the dependence of Indian Marxism on the thematic of Western metaphysics or Orientalism in producing knowledge about Indian society.[5] Unfortunately, as we will show and contrary to many misplaced views held in the West, their claim of transgressing the essentialist thematic did not materialize, at least not with respect to their theory of transition and development, with which we are concerned here.[6] One of the objectives of our book is to bring to light the problems of essentialism from within the subaltern studies, showing exactly why and how their concept of transition could not step outside the essentialist thematic of Western metaphysics.[7]

What about some of the other allegedly postmodern renditions on the evolution of Indian society? Those—often going by the name anti- or post-developmentalist—have come from essentially a cultural or (eco) feminist perspective (see the writings of Vandana Shiva and Ashish Nandy) and have called for the renunciation of the idea of "progress." They question the path of transition and the logic of development underlying the transition process. Thus they effectively abandon development as economic development. But we refuse to let either transition or development disappear, for we think that Shiva's and Nandy's renunciation of the idea of development per se is premature and counterproductive. Theorizing transition in a postmodern or disaggregated space, we rewrite the notion of progress to create development as economic development—as postmodern economic development. Postmodernism, after all, is a vast milieu constitutive of multiple imaginations in terms of historical phase, existential state, or condition, style, and critique (Cullenberg, Amariglio, and Ruccio 2001, 3–57). Working in the intersecting and compensating axis of the milieu that we constitute as postmodernism we instill new contending notions of transition and development as progress in contrast to their more orthodox and modernist counterparts. We seek the challenge of the orthodoxy in their very den and not sidestep it as do the post/anti-developmentalists by abandoning first the economic and then along with it economic development.

In this regard, it is beneficial to be aware of the rhetorical power of developmental progress as in the more modernist versions as well as its widespread functional or operative exhibition that continue to be a source of challenge to the radicals. First, at the minimum, even if we proclaimed the death of economic developmentalism, the hegemony of development as economic development is unquestionable. Development as progress still haunts the imaginary of a nation such as India and in fact the concerns over it have multiplied in recent years given the amount of literature on transition and development as well as the media coverage on the transition process. How can we ignore something that is so powerful in its deployment no matter how much we criticize or deny its presence? Second, we were and still continue to be extremely doubtful about the critiques on economic development that proclaim the death of the economic and subsequently that of economic development. Criticisms of the logic of transition and development have concentrated on pointing to the essentialism driving the notion of economic, the multiple doubts/lacks/gaps regarding its constitution and the destructive power of the notion of progress grounded on historicism that drives the economic development of society.[8] While this is commendable and has given important insights regarding the operative and universal power of economism, such critical analysis has taken the economism of economic development as secured, as if there cannot be any other conception of the economic. These theorists— mostly cultural—then parade their critique of economic development as a postmodern critique. This, again, we find unacceptable. Methodology, of whatever form, requires consistency in all axes. You don't have the option to pick and choose—being essentialist in one axis and nonessentialist in another. It is a bad theoretical move to say that a concept—such as the economic—itself is to be rejected because it belongs to a modernist frame when in fact this very concept has already been reworked within a postmodernist frame. Thus the question remains: With this renewed notion of the economic, could the concepts of transition and developmental progress be made sensible from a postmodern angle? It is not that economists have not, in recent times, tried to articulate the economic in a postmodern space (Resnick and Wolff 1987; Mirowski 1989; McCloskey 1985, 1994; Chakrabarti 1996; Gibson-Graham 1996; Cullenberg, Amariglio and Rucccio 2001, ed., to name a few). But cultural theorists have either ignored it or these developments have somehow been bypassed. Even someone as well known as Jameson, who deals with the economy, only considers it in its essentialist mould (Jameson 1991).

Another point is worth mentioning. Just as could happen with the milieu of modernity, postmodern approaches are multiple, often contradicting and viciously in opposition to one another. The projected singular postmodernity is in fact a disaggregated discursive space constitutive of multiple standpoints and political positions. The very aspect of disaggregation, heterogeneity and unevenness, temporality, and so on that postmodernists accuses modernism of failing to integrate within its framework, constitutes the very being of postmodernism as well. The confusion that postmodernism is a singular position has probably arisen because the debate has long been between modernity and postmodernity. In many instances, principally methodological, we also take recourse to such a route of analysis. But ours is also a standpoint, a—particular—story within the postmodern space. This could (and would) be in contrast and opposition to the many other alleged postmodern approaches such as the post/anti-developmental approaches some of which may take a rightist position from our standpoint.

For all of these reasons, we remain skeptical of the allegedly postmodern approaches that highlighted the Indian scenario even though these are, as it stands, few and far between as far as the economic and economic development are concerned. Our postmodern rendition of transition and development contrasts sharply with the above in the sense that we seek the renewal of transition and development, and not their disappearance.

The post/anti-development writings in India have not yet formed into a school of thought nor have they gained such prominence as to deserve to be weighed on the same scale as the Indian modes of production debate and the subaltern studies debates. In this regard, though we consider the post/anti-development school to be important (we sympathize with lots of things that they do say though we have also made our differences clear) and we will discuss/debate their positions further in the chapter on development, we are inclined to concentrate specifically only on the Indian modes of production debate and the subaltern studies debate on the topic of transition and development.

In this book, we will address three concerns associated with the theory of transition and development: (i) working within a framework that is anti-essentialist, that is, anti-Western metaphysics or, what is the same, anti-Orientalist; (ii) deconstructing the Indian modes of production debate and the subaltern studies debate on the transition and development of Indian society to bring to light the problems of essentialism and other internal problems in these literatures; and (iii) build an alternative concept of transition and development that will throw new light onto the transition of Indian society against the background of the new liberalization policies undertaken by the Indian government without slipping into the Western metaphysical thematic. Keeping these three concerns in mind, we will use an anti-essentialist postmodern Marxian framework to perform (ii) and (iii).[9] If the former concerns itself with the overall thematic then the latter two constitute our problematic. This anti-essentialist Marxian framework provides us with a micro-focused approach to conceptualizing transition from a decentered class perspective that is in stark contradistinction to the orthodox Marxian approaches to transition (to be exemplified in this book in terms of the two debates on transition in India) and that conceive of transition as what might be called a "big bang" macro theory of change. This rewriting of the concept of transition and its displacement in a postmodern space enables us to provide a new rendition of development as progress. To contest the essentialist basis of the theory of transition and development in Indian Marxism and to lay the groundwork for an alternative non essentialist approach for studying transition and development in India is the central motivation and objective of this book.

In this introductory chapter, we shall concentrate on bringing into the open the idea of "development as progress" as visualized by Marx and Engels, discuss the underlying framework of historical materialism as well as the post-Marx attempts to rationalize transition and development within that framework, and then bring to light the problems of essentialism and historicism that condition the orthodox Marxist theories of transition and development. We will concern ourselves with expressing our disquiet about the essentialist thematic of Western metaphysics (one of whose forms is orthodox Marxism) that underlies the Indian debates on Marxism and not with a discussion on the two debates per se, a task to be performed in the following chapters. In other words, this introductory chapter, which identifies and expands on the problems that underlie the orthodox Marxist theories of transition and development, should be read as a sign of our recognition of a crisis in the Marxian development field and, consequently, as a prelude to reconceptualizing a nonessentialist and nonhistoricist concept of transition and development to be carried out in the context of the Indian debates on transition.

The Evolution of the Idea of Transition and Development in Marx and Engels

Since the seventeenth century, classical political economists have been engrossed with the relation between the West and the Third World. The idea of development as linked to the concept of progressive evolution of society arose at this time. Almost all of the major classical political economists believed in the civilizing mission of the West in teaching the "backward nations" the *rules* and *norms* of civil society—encapsulating the West's mission in the idea of development or progress. Some, like Adam Smith, tried to justify the missionary roles of the West with an economic explanation, while others, such as James Mill, were more blunt. For the classical political economists, some of the "deficiencies" of the backward nations can be seen from the following quotations:

> It is "in the interest of the human species" that the advanced European nations must keep and even increase their influence in Asia . . . "with its despots and superstitions, Asia has no good institutions to lose" but "she could receive many good ones from the Europeans." (Say 1968, part 4, 311)

Independence and nationality, so essential to the due growth and development of people further advanced in environment, are generally impediments to theirs. The sacred duties which civilized nations owe to the independence and nationality of each other, are not binding towards those to whom nationality and independence are either a certain evil, or at best a questionable good. . . . (J. S. Mill, vol. x, 167–8)

The greatest of all difficulties in converting uncivilized and thinly peopled countries into civilized and populous ones, is to inspire them with the wants best calculated to excite their exertions in the production of wealth. One of the greatest benefits which the foreign countries confer, and the reason why it has always appeared an almost necessary ingredient in the progress of wealth, is its tendency to inspire new wants, to form new tastes, to furnish new motives for industry. (Malthus 1936, book II, 403)

Both nations (*meaning India and China*) are to nearly an equal degree tainted with the vices of insincerity; dissembling, treacherous, mendacious, to an excess which surpasses even the usual measure of uncultivated society. Both are disposed to excessive exaggeration with regard to every thing relating to themselves. Both are cowardly and unfeeling. Both are in the highest degree conceited of themselves, and full of affected contempt for others. Both are, in the physical sense, disgustingly unclean in their persons and houses. (J. Mill 1820, vol. II, book II, 195)

The so-called backward nations and their people lacked every aspect of what the classical political economists understood as "civil."[10] In classical political economy, West and East are separated into disparate, watertight compartments each with their specific repertoire of economic, cultural, and political attributes. The former is assumed to be superior to the latter economically, culturally, and politically. Advancement is associated with the attributes pertaining to the West and backwardness with those of the East. Because the East was unable to organically develop the "Western" attributes, progress or development must proceed from the West to the East. That is, progress would require an intervention by the West to save these nations from the labyrinth of darkness from which they were unable to rise up on their own. Also, all of these shifts signify a macro-level change in society, from its traditional *whole* to a modern *whole*. The entirety of society encompassing the economic, cultural, and political must undergo, they argued, a cataclysmic transformation.

Marx and Engels were not immune to this Eurocentric view of development. Marx's analysis of the effects of British imperialism on a backward country like that of India testifies to the Eurocentric tinge in his vision. Consider the following remark on India:

> These small stereotype forms of social organism have been to the greater part dissolved, and are disappearing, not so much through the brutal interference of the British tax-gatherer and the British soldier, as to the working of English steam and the English Free Trade. Those family-communities were based on domestic industry, in that peculiar combination of hand-weaving, hand spinning and hand-tilling agriculture that gave them self-supporting power, English interference having placed the spinner in Lancashire and the weaver in Bengal, or sweeping away both Hindoo spinner and weaver, dissolved these small semi-barbarian, semi-civilized communities, by blowing up their economic basis, and thus produced the greatest, and to speak the truth, the only social revolution ever heard of in Asia . . . we must not forget that these idyllic village-communities, inoffensive though they may appear, had always been the solid foundation of oriental despotism, that they restrained the human mind within the smallest possible compass, making it the unresisting tool of superstition, enslaving it beneath traditional rules, depriving it of all grandeur and historical energies. . . . England, it is true, in causing a social revolution in Hindostan, was actuated only by the vilest interests, and was stupid in her manner of enforcing them. But that is not the question. The question is, can mankind fulfill its destiny without a fundamental revolution in the social state of Asia? If not, whatever may have been the crimes of England she was the unconscious tool of history in bringing about that revolution. (1979, 74–6)

Engels voiced a similar opinion when he rationalized the United States's conquest of Mexico by pointing out that,

> In America we have witnessed the conquest of Mexico, which has pleased us. It constitutes progress too that a country until the present day exclusively occupied with itself, torn apart by perpetual civil wars and prevented from all development . . . that such a country be thrown by means of violence into the historical movement. It is in the interest of its own development that Mexico will be in the future under the tutelage of the United States. (1980, 183)

Following the classical political economists, Marx and Engels also understood transition as progressive macro shifts in society. However, there are three interesting points of difference as well that must be mentioned. First, unlike the classical political economists, both Marx and Engels seem to be espousing the view that the method by which the East was conquered is immoral and unjust. However, the immoral and unjust aspects are completely overridden by their emphasis on the historicity involved in the transition process of such societies, which takes us to the second point of difference.

Marx and Engels legitimize the conquest of the East by the West in terms of their theory of history—the historical materialist transition to the communist telos. All means are justified as long as they help in the progress toward communism where this progress is signified by the advanced development of the forces of production. For society to progress, and development to take place, the forces of production must be allowed to develop freely. Given the stagnant nature of the backward nations which consist of, as both Marx and Engels referred to at times, people without any history, there is no way that these societies can develop internally and organically. Because the West possesses a higher level of forces of production, development must proceed from the West to the East. The backwardness of the "backward nations" stems from the underdeveloped nature of the productive forces. Despite the brutality of colonialism, the cultural and political superstructure, which develops on the basis of the new economic structure, will in the end be far superior to the "idiocy of village life" that dominates the social space of these stagnant societies.[11] So powerful is this idea of Marx and Engels that it has percolated in different forms into the modern development literature and continues to influence the social space where actual policies are enacted and opposed.[12]

The third difference between Marx and Engels and the classical political economists relates to the fact that Marx differentiated between different types of imperialisms. The chief historical criterion for Marx was not imperialism as such but the development of the forces of production. If imperialism leads to an impediment blocking the development of the forces of production, then it is to be opposed. For example, Marx argued that the British rule in Ireland was fettering the development of the productive forces there. He called for an end to the British rule in Ireland so that capitalist development could proceed freely in that country.

The historicist idea of a rational, ordered, macro development of society depending on the state of the forces of production as developed by Marx and Engels was given an official textual form and canonical stature in the Erfurt programme of the Social Democratic Party of Germany in 1891. Its theory came to be known as historical materialism and is also sometimes referred to as the Second International or orthodox Marxism. Despite receiving extensive criticisms in recent times, both from within and outside of Marxism, this second international version of historical materialism is still important for two reasons. First, in many Third World countries, including India, it continues to enjoy a prominent place as an alternative theory of development. As will be evident in our treatment of the Indian modes of production debate in Chapter 2, this brand of Marxism dominated that discourse.[13] Second, alternative Marxian theories, such as subaltern studies, that do not accept the orthodox rendition of historical materialism take it as their point of departure, even though, as with the Indian modes of production debate, their analysis is also beset with similar problems of essentialism and historicism.

Let us now discuss in some detail the structure of historical materialism, for almost all post-Marx theories of transition and development that emphasize the macro approach to change, including the Indian modes of production debate, are situated within it.

The Theory of Historical Materialism

We begin by defining a few concepts that Marxists use to describe historical materialism, concepts that we will be using time and again in our analysis of the Indian mode of production debate and the subaltern studies debate. These include the mode of production, forces of production, relations of production, superstructure, and society (social totality).

Society or social totality in the orthodox Marxian framework is an articulation of mode of production, superstructure, and social consciousness where the mode of production (also called the economy) is given a privileged status both at the discursive and at the real (social), that is, ontological, level. The mode of production is defined as the articulation of forces and relations of production.[14] Marx mentioned five modes of production—primitive communist, Asiatic, slave, feudal, and capitalist. Society may be composed of a mixture of modes of production and the activities that tie them together, or it may be conceived in terms of only one mode of production. However, almost always, society, or the social formation, typically is reduced to a "dominant" mode of production. Thus, for example, a feudal social formation is one in which the feudal mode of production is predominant.

The modes of production are also called the economic or base of society. These terms are often used interchangeably. The other major aspect of society is the superstructure, which consists of the political, religious, cultural, and legal aspects of society. Within the category of the political, the most important components are the state and civil society. Finally, there are forms of social consciousness. Superstructure and forms of consciousness are included within the social totality but they do not have primary explanatory power so far as the reproduction, crisis, or development of social totality is concerned. According to historical materialism, the super-structure and forms of consciousness depend on and are caused/explained by the modes of production. That is, the modes of production are causally prior to all other aspects of society.

Within the structure of the mode of production, historical materialism considers technological development or the forces of production to be in-dependent of or causally prior (in order of explanation) to the relations of production. This sequential structure of causality produces a hierarchical order. At the top are the forces of production. In the second tier are the re-lations of production and then in the third and fourth tier, superstructure and forms of consciousness, respectively. All of these together constitute the complex social totality. However, this complex social totality has a cen-ter or essence (forces of production) on which every other aspect of society is in the end, or final instance as Engels put it, dependent even though the forces of production themselves are not dependent on any entity.

The theory of historical materialism appropriated the Hegelian frame-work of the historical evolution of society.[15] The crucial difference be-tween the evolutionary theory of history in Hegel and that in orthodox Marxism is that the latter replaced the idealistic notions in the Hegelian framework by materialistic elements. In Hegel, the subject (world spirit) is the essence while the object (nature) is the appearance.[16] So the subject is causally prior to the object. In historical materialism, the subject-object duality is reversed. The object (forces of production) is now causally prior to the subject (forms of consciousness). While subjects are important in the determination of historical events, their mobility is restricted and de-termined by the material structure of the economic in the first or some-times the last instance. As in Hegel, orthodox Marxian dialectics have the same mechanics—affirmation, negation, and negation of negation—but they now operate through the conflict between the forces and relations of production.[17]

The basic idea in historical materialism is that relations of production correspond to a particular stage of the development of the material pro-ductive forces. By correspondence, we mean that forces of production "select" a particular relation of production that in turn will promote the development of forces of production. Such a relation of production ob-tains because of this characteristic. No other relations of production can fulfill this role. It is important to understand that only one type of relations of production can correspond to a specific historical stage of the develop-ment of forces of production. Capitalist class society can only permit capi-talist class relations of production or, put a bit differently, capitalist society implies the absence of precapitalist class processes. In historical materialis-tic theories of transition, this aspect of uniformity of class relations of pro-duction consistent with the development of forces of production is critical, for without it the concept of mode of production and society defined in terms of mode of production would collapse. Similarly legal, political, and religious institutions correspond to the structure of the economic, or mode of production, and forms of social consciousness arise on the superstructure.[18] This *holistic* conception of society is stable if all other aspects of society, notably that of relations of production, are such that they do not impede the technological development in any manner. If they do create barriers to the free development of technology, a condition of social crisis arises, which can be resolved only with the advent of a new relation of production. This new relation of production will be so selected by the forces of production that it will provide maximum scope for the fruitful use and development of the forces of production. The change in the economic in turn brings about a change in the superstructure, and the latter in turn brings about a change in the forms of social consciousness.

The contradiction between the forces and relations of production within each complex society is resolved to give way to a new complex society—a higher moment of the original society—and subsequently a new contradiction within it. This new complex totality is a higher moment in the qualitative sense that the forces of production are freer to develop as compared to the previous complex social totality.[19]

History moves from undifferentiated unity (primitive communism) to differentiated disunity (Asiatic, slave, feudal, and capitalist society, that is, societies divided by class conflict) arriving finally at differentiated unity (communism or a society with no class and class conflict) initiated by a series of macro-level big bang shifts in the mode of production. Under communism—the telos of history—the forces of production reach their most developed stage and the relations of production can no longer act as fetters to technological development.[20] Each stage in history is negated by the next one through the operation of the dialectics of contradiction. This macro description of history was termed by Marx as the "historico philosophic theory of the general path."

The above process of transition from one mode of production to another is the theoretical core of Marxist development theory. Marxist development theory has understood transition as progress in terms of the development of the forces of production because a higher level of the forces of production signifies a higher level of society. Thus society progresses via a series of macro-level shifts in social totality, shifts that are initiated by the mode of production.

If the condition for change lies in the conflict between the forces and relations of production, the medium of change is class struggle. In traditional Marxism, each society is divided into two primary and opposed classes. The relations between the classes with respect to the means of production and the appropriation of surplus labor describe the relations of production within a society. As the relations of production become a barrier to the development of the forces of production, class conflict intensifies. The dominant class must take extreme measures to maintain the relations of production, principally through its forms of economic exploitation and intensified efforts to maintain or increase the quantity of surplus it extracts. That is, a crisis in reproducing the form of exploitation leads to an extreme form of social antagonism between the two classes. This social antagonism can only be resolved through a change that takes the form of a revolutionary class defeating the reactionary class in the long run.[21] In turn, such a resolution of the crisis leads to new class relations of production that will provide ample space for the forces of production to develop freely again.

In historical materialism, classes are assumed to represent the individual's structural position in the economy. Since the economy is the essence of the society, class as an economic relation becomes the principal, or dominant, subject position.[22] In comparison to the working class, other subject positions related to race, gender, caste, or ethnicity are considered to be less important and derivative. The working class is thereby given an ontological privileged subject position at the expense of all other subject positions.

The working class is given this ontological privilege because it is the class best suited, most able, and most disposed to preside over the development of the forces of production. Only the working class is capable of leading society to its ultimate freedom or emancipation. As we will argue, this privileged historical status of the working class is consistently accepted by the participants in the Indian modes of production debate and by the theorists of the subaltern studies.

According to orthodox Marxism, Marx (1990) understood primitive capital accumulation as the mechanism that accomplishes the specific transition from feudalism to capitalism. Primitive capital accumulation involves the process of expropriation of the individual's means of production. However, since feudal or any precapitalist system is normally dominated by the peasantry, the emphasis of such an expropriation is almost always on the peasantry. Thus the basis for primitive capital accumulation is often the expropriation of the peasantry from the land and turning them into "free" wage labor. This involves a transformation of the objective conditions of production (the linkage of the peasantry with their land) and a transformation of the subjective conditions of an individual's social existence (the linkage of the peasantry with the community). The transformation of these two conditions—expropriation of the peasantry from the land and the estrangement of the peasant from the community from which his social existence is derived—creates the mass of free wage labor. According to Marx, this creation of free wage laborers is taken as a necessary prerequisite for the birth of capitalism. A transition from feudalism to capitalism requires overcoming those elements associated with feudalism. Thus Marx writes, "The economic structure of capitalist society has grown out of the economic structure of feudal society. The dissolution of the latter set free the elements of the former" (Marx 1990, 875). This dissolution is brought about by the historical process of primitive capital accumulation. The evolutionary process could be extended to a transition from any other forms of precapitalism to capitalism or socialism without any substantial effect on the logic of historical materialism.[23] Primitive capital accumulation in the orthodox Marxian framework is understood as a single sub-moment in history within the periodization schema. There is an element of historical inevitability attached to the orthodox project. Theory is a grand metanarrative and history follows the path laid down by theory. Primitive capital accumulation, thus defined, is inevitable in the long march of history.

How is primitive capital accumulation related to the essence of historical materialism? The essence—technological development—is assumed to be freer to develop under capitalism than under feudalism. The prerequisite for the existence of the capitalist mode of production is the relationship between capital and wage labor in a commodity market. Primitive capital accumulation makes this historical possibility feasible.

The feudal serfs or simple commodity producers remain attached to their land and other means of production. The objective and subjective conditions of precapitalist society continue to provide the basis for the social existence of direct producers and other forms of precapitalist remnants. Such precapitalist relations of production constitute a barrier to the development of the forces of production. Some of these barriers can take the form of precapitalist relations of production such as debt bondage, attached labor, or feudal rent, as were pointed out and analyzed in the Indian modes of production debate. The necessary conditions for capitalist exploitation to take place without any hindrance and for the forces of production to develop freely are the two transformations that basically constitute the historical process of primitive capital accumulation.

Historical Materialism and Post-Marx Theories of Transition and Development

Earlier we discussed the evolution of the idea of transition and development in Marx and Engels. Their idea regarding the notion of "progress" culminated in the theory of historical materialism as we have explained.

But our presentation of a kind of unified theory of historical materialism may seem objectionable to some since differences and disputes among Marxists abound with regard to historical materialism. We do acknowledge the presence of these differences but our point is that all such differences melt into an abiding unity when evaluating the underlying vision and methodology governing these approaches. Especially significant is the commonly held methodological traits of essentialism and historicism by the differing approaches and the vision of developmental progress as condensed by the logic of "industrialisation through capital accumulation." In a brief discussion, we present some of the major positions on transition and development as they have historically developed and show that they share the methodological structure of historical materialism—essentialism and historicism.

Theories of transition and development in the post-Marx age can be roughly divided into three phases: (i) *The Imperialist Theories of Transition*, (ii) *The Underdevelopment Theories of Transition*, and (iii) *The Anti-Underdevelopment Theories of Transition*.[24] Despite the differences between and within the three approaches to transition and development there is an interesting convergence in their methodological basis: each continues to see the forces of production as the key to the construction of a social totality and its development as telescoping the progress of society and, despite numerous furious debates on the stages of history—bypassing some at the expense of others—none questions the telos of socialism/communism and the rationality of achieving that telos as capturing a progressive development of society. And, all view the mechanics of achieving the final destination of the rational progressive movement as being born out of the womb of "industrialisation through capital accumulation." We will briefly review the three post-Marx approaches to transition and development by keeping this concern in mind.

The Imperialist Theories of Transition

From the 1890s onward, the linkage between the Western countries and the "backward nations" became an important subject of analysis among Western European as well as Eastern European Marxists, especially the Russian Marxists. Theorists like Engels, Kautsky, Hilferding, Plekhanov, Lenin, Trotsky, Bukharin, and Luxemberg (despite their other significant differences) believed that imperialism (which they now identified with monopoly capitalism) distinguished by the export of capital, domination of finance capital, centralization of capital, formation of cartels and territorial division of the world amongst the advanced countries, led to an all-around development helping not only the imperialist countries but also the colonized countries. In the post–World War II period this idea was taken to its logical conclusion by Warren (1980), who in a provocative book declared imperialism and its modern version in neocolonialism (postindependent status of the peripheral countries) to be the pioneer of capitalism. Capitalism penetrates the Third World countries through imperialism. This penetration was justified by Warren because it helps to develop the forces of production and set up a new advanced social totality in these countries. Warren argued that even if one accepts the argument of underdevelopment theorists about international bondage, the satellites are still better off as compared to the counterfactual situation of the absence of foreign investment and international exchange relations, a point which we shall soon indicate was argued for fiercely by the underdevelopment theorists. That is, according to Warren, gains from trade far outweigh the gains from autarky and trade helps in the development of the forces of production by forcing the satellites to stay on the cutting edge of global competition. If trade takes the form of imperialism or neo-imperialism, so be it. There is no need to emphasize that Warren's defense of imperialism was a logical culmination of the essentialist role of *forces of production* in his rendition of historical materialism and the self-fulfilling rational, progressive connotation in its development. The evolution of society was to take place as per the logic of "industrialisation through capital accumulation" and that too by whatever means possible. This was also Hariss's (1986) point, which expands on Warren's proposition with the help of extensive data from the development process of the "newly industrializing countries."[25] However, unlike Marx and Engels, who differentiated between the imperialisms, Warren produced a one-dimensional representation of imperialism by arguing that all imperialisms are beneficial for the colonized countries. Warren's piece was extremely provocative because it was a challenge to the theories of underdevelopment that took off in the late 1950s with Baran's *The Political Economy of Growth*, which presented a critique of (i) the idea of development as traveling from the developed center to the underdeveloped periphery via imperialism or neocolonialism and (ii) the expressive Eurocentric content in the imperialist theories of development which failed to problematize the economy of the backward nations whose development was taken to be dependent on the penetration of capital from the capitalist countries.

The Underdevelopment Theories of Transition

According to Baran (1973), the character of monopoly capitalism changed after the Second World War, and it can no longer be conceived as monolithic so far as its positive effects are concerned. To some extent monopoly capitalism has penetrated the "backward nations" transforming them to underdeveloped countries where the term "underdeveloped" as opposed to "backward" now signifies the presence of a capitalist mode of production against its virtual absence. However, the development of capitalist mode of production in the periphery is fettered, leading to its underdevelopment vis-à-vis the developed countries (the capitalist countries in the center). According to Baran, economic growth is dependent on the size and utilization of the surplus produced in the economy. If the surplus product is utilized for productive purposes then the forces of production will develop and growth will take place. Otherwise, we will have economic stagnation. Baran gives two reasons for the underdevelopment of the capitalist mode of production in the periphery: (i) one part of the surplus generated in the periphery is repatriated to the developed metropolitan countries by the monopoly enterprises where it is thrown away in wasteful activities such as military spending and luxury consumption, since the investment outlets in the center are already clogged out and (ii) one part of the surplus that is distributed in the periphery is frittered away in unproductive uses such as luxury consumption, usury, speculation, and rent-bearing land, and they are also put in foreign banks to be used as "hedges against the depreciation of the domestic currency or as nest eggs assuring their owners of suitable retreats in the case of social and political upheavals at home" (1973, 316–17). Thus the penetration of monopoly capital, the form capital takes, helps in the "development of underdevelopment" in the periphery. According to Baran, the developed capitalist countries will never allow for the unfettered development (industrialization) of the periphery because that will threaten the established monopoly position of the foreign companies and, consequently, the growth of capitalism in the periphery will be distorted. Thus the cause of underdevelopment in the periphery is external and not generated internally. For Baran, since capitalism cannot develop on its own in these underdeveloped countries, the only way out for them is to follow the path of the socialist countries, which will again allow for the free development of the forces of production. It is useless to wait for the full development of the forces of production under capitalism in the periphery, because that will never happen.

Frank (1969) followed in the footsteps of Baran but with some important differences. While agreeing that the metropolis (center) dominated by monopoly capitalism creates the underdevelopment of the satellites (periphery), Frank departed from Baran by pointing out that the underdevelopment of the satellites leads to the gain and, hence, the further development of the metropolis. Thus, for Frank, the relation between the satellites and the metropolis is a zero-sum game where the wealth of the metropolis is a direct result of the loss of surplus from the satellites. Another crucial difference with Baran is that Frank defines capitalism in terms of market exchange. Irrespective of the modes of labor process (wage labor, serf, or slavery), whose specific existence is a result of profit maximization, a system is capitalist as long as the output is produced for the market. Because capitalism is defined by market exchange and not by the modes of production as in Baran, and because the underdeveloped countries are tied to the developed countries via an exchange relation, Frank denied the existence of any precapitalist modes of production in the satellites. Irrespective of the labor process the satellite countries are capitalist because they are tied in an exchange relationship with the metropolitan countries. The ruling class in the satellites is also tied to the ruling class in the metropolis, helping fully to perpetuate the international extraction of surplus. There is thus a chain of satellites and peripheries, each connected with the other as a result of the extraction of surplus via the market. For Frank, underdevelopment is not the pre-stage of development but rather the complement of development in the metropolis: "development and underdevelopment each cause and are caused by the other in the total development of capitalism" (Frank 1969, 240). Logically, the central struggle becomes not the class struggle but one between nations. The only way out for the satellite countries is to detach themselves from the world economy and go for a socialist revolution. However, what a socialist revolution is and how such a socialist revolution can survive in an autarkic economy is not elaborated by Frank.

Wallerstein's (1974) work was an extension of Frank and Baran. His main contribution was the concept of a world capitalist system. The world capitalist system is a trimodal system made up of the core (center), periphery, and the semiperiphery countries. In Wallerstein these countries are tied together by the zero-sum exchange relationships where capitalism is similarly defined as in Frank. The crucial difference from Frank is that Wallerstein does not consider the position of a country as fixed in the trimodal world system (that is, there can be up and down movement of countries within the world capitalist system). He considers national independence and the role of the independent state to be important for being a part in the chain of the antisystemic movement against the dominance of world capitalism, though he does not believe that an isolated movement toward Soviet-style socialism will lead anywhere. He considers the Soviet Union to be state capitalist and argues that it is not possible for any country to break out of the world capitalist system unless there is an antisystemic world revolution that overthrows capitalism at the world level. Like world capitalism, socialism can only be realized at the world level.

The unequal exchange school, whose main theorists were Arrighi Emmanuel (1972) and Samir Amin (1974), took the works of Frank and Wallerstein to a different level by producing a detailed account of the mechanisms through which surplus product is transferred from the periphery to the center. Emmanuel, the leader of this school, showed that countries are exploited at the level of market exchange through the (implicit) transfer of surplus labor hours from the poorer communities to the richer ones. While there is a tendency for profits to be equalized across the world because of international mobility of capital and commodities, there are serious differences in wages across the world since the labor market is not internationally open. Thus wages emerge as the independent variable of the system whose unequal nature becomes the source of the inequality of exchange. Emmanuel points out that a country with a lower level of wages will have a higher rate of surplus value and that wages in underdeveloped countries are much lower than the wages in developed countries. The result is a transfer of surplus value from the underdeveloped countries to the developed countries via the mechanism of exchange (where lower wages lead to lower prices of commodities produced by the underdeveloped countries in comparison to higher wages and the higher prices of the commodities produced by the developed countries). Since the rate of exploitation is presumed to be lower in the periphery as compared to the center, the workers and the capitalists in the center have a joint interest in increasing income by intensifying the rate of exploitation in the periphery. In other words, the working class in the center has been co-opted in the imperialist rule. According to Emmanuel, the major form of struggle is now that between the nations and not class struggle, which has become secondary.

Theorists did differ on the route by which to make developmental progress happen even if the telos of socialism/communism remained uncontested in all. While the imperialist theories of development saw the penetration of international capital to underdeveloped countries in positive light, the underdevelopment theories saw them as the cause of the underdevelopment of these peripheral societies. In the latter, development through industrialization (i.e., development of the domestic center) must proceed by de-linking the underdeveloped countries from their satellite center.

The Anti-Underdevelopment Theories of Transition

Underdevelopment theories were attacked from three sources: the Althusserians, Brenner's class struggle theory, and Warren's imperialism theory. The common and central point of their criticism of the underdevelopment theories, especially those of Frank, Wallerstein, and the unequal exchange school, are related to the short shrift given to class structure and modes of production. Warren, whom we have already discussed, called these theories a nationalist theory of development rather than a historical materialist theory of development since nothing in historical materialism says that autarky is preferable to free trade. Furthermore, relations of production were made secondary in these theories of underdevelopment, and it was pointed out their definition of capitalism as a market exchange relationship has nothing to do with the Marxist definition of capitalism, which is captured in terms of modes of production (Laclau 1971). The Althusserians, Brenner and Warren, questioned this point and launched an attack on the demotion of class relationships and forces of production in the underdevelopment theories.

Brenner (1977, 1985) pointed out that the motor of change was not any economic element per se but the political aspect of class struggle. Given a stage of forces of production, the outcome of crisis in a society would depend on the resolution of class struggle. Intervening in the Dobb-Sweezy debate on transition (see Hilton 1978), Brenner turned his criticism against the economic essentialism in Dobb (development of forces of production as the prime mover, Dobb 1978a, 1978b) and Sweezy (external trade as the prime mover, Sweezy 1978a, 1978b) into a criticism of the underdevelopment theories. Brenner averred that advanced countries were not dependent on the underdeveloped countries for growth or luxury consumption and that the economic plight of the underdeveloped countries should be identified in its internal class structure and not in their relationship with the developed countries. By bringing in class struggle, Brenner aspired to overthrow the privileged status of the economic and replace it with class struggle, thereby bringing in the element of subjectivity as the prime mover within the heart of historical materialism. However, Brenner's emphasis on class struggle is only a short-term measure; in the long run, in Brenner's theory, the development of society and the specific form of class struggle and, subsequently, its outcome will depend on the level of development of the forces of production. Thus, in the last instance, Brenner's political emphasis of class struggle depends on the economic, thereby undercutting his critique of economic essentialism.

The articulation of modes of production school criticizes the underdevelopment theories for demoting the mode of production. Rey (1978), the most famous of the articulation theorists, argued that capitalism is inherently dynamic and cannot be blamed for underdevelopment. According to this school, the peripheries are underdeveloped because of the precapitalist relations of production that act as a barrier to the development of capitalism. So the cause of underdevelopment resides in the social formation in the peripheral countries. Following Althusser and Balibar (1975), Rey makes a distinction between social formation and modes of production. Mode of production is composed by the real appropriation, which determines the productive forces and property relations, which determine the relations of production. Mode of production is an analytical concept while the articulatory existence of the different modes of production at a concrete historical stage constitutes the social formation. Rey points to three types of precapitalist modes of production—feudal, traditional, and colonial—but he also asserts that most underdeveloped countries are constituted by either the colonial or traditional modes of production in addition to the capitalist mode. According to Rey, the transition from precapitalism to capitalism can be divided into three stages. The first stage is when the precapitalist mode of production is dominant compared to the capitalist mode of production. The second stage is when the capitalist mode of production is dominant but it still depends on the precapitalist mode of production for food and labor power. Here, the capitalist form of exploitation is complemented by the precapitalist form of exploitation. Most underdeveloped countries are in this stage of transition. In the third stage, precapitalist modes of production are fully replaced by capitalist modes of production. According to Rey, underdeveloped countries will move toward a socialist revolution before they can reach this stage, since the transition process from the second to the third stage is painful and slow due to the considerable influence and the reactionary nature of nonfeudal precapitalist mode of production to which the capitalist mode of production is articulated. Capitalism is absolved of any role in this slow and painful transition because by definition capitalism is dynamic and hence cannot be held responsible for any drag.[26] The only way out of this impasse is violence. Capitalism will have to destroy these nonfeudal modes of production through force by expelling the peasants from the land. This violence will be counterproductive and will immediately create the conditions for a socialist revolution.

Bradby (1975) and Foster-Carter (1978) criticize the importance of violence in Rey and point out that capitalism does not necessarily require violence for its development. If violence is ruled out then Rey's explanation of capitalist development collapses, since in Rey there are no other ways for capitalism to develop. Also, Rey took a unidimensional view of capitalism by assuming that capitalism works in the same way everywhere and the differences in the social formations are only due to the types of precapitalist modes of production to which capitalism is articulated. Thus underdevelopment is blamed on the precapitalist modes of production and the specific nature of capitalism has nothing to do with it. This reductionism in identifying the root of underdevelopment was attacked by Foster-Carter, who also questioned the validity of the concept of traditional mode of production and colonial mode of production. Because a country has been colonized does not mean that its mode of production can be called colonial. There is an ad-hoc-ness in naming these modes in Rey and other theorists of this school. They do not face questions such as "What are the relations of production and class structures in the colonial mode of production" and "How and why is it different from other modes of production?" These problems had an adverse impact on the "articulation of modes of production school."[27] By early 1980s, the influence of the Althusserian school of development on Marxism waned.

Stung by the above set of criticisms, the underdevelopment theorists like Frank and Wallerstein did try to integrate aspects of class relations and modes of production in their model while Amin strove to incorporate aspects of both class struggle and productivity in unequal exchange theory but, in their corrections, the notion of class and mode of production emerged as a consequence of the international exchange relationship, leading to the loss of their discursive privilege from the Marxist paradigm. In other words, their effort to include class and modes of production did not yield any additional insights into their transition/development theories. It is indeed interesting to note that the underdevelopment theorists never questioned the central place of forces of production and its development in achieving the telo of socialism/communism as per the process of "industrialization through capital accumulation" in the present juncture. Thus while some saw their approach as departing from historical materialism, from our concern of focusing on the methodological structure, we see the underdevelopment school only as a variant of historical materialism.

Generally in post-Marxist theories of transition and development, the trajectory of development as traveling from center to the periphery is never questioned. Industrialization through capital accumulation remains the key to progressive development of society in the present juncture of history, which is essentially the transition of society forwarding the development of the forces of production. Thus the essentialism of forces of production and the historicist logic of historical materialism or some variant of the same remains unchallenged in these approaches of transition and development.

Thus, in a sense, despite the debates on Marxist concepts of transition and development within Marxism that span over a century, the unifying theme running across all of these clashing approaches seems to be the methodological structure of essentialism and historicism, where the vision of change to its final destination would follow a big-bang macro transformation of society following the process of industrialization through capital accumulation. But why is essentialism or its dynamic counterpart, historicism, a matter of concern? Whether, and if so, why, is historical materialism or any counterpart with similar kinds of features possessing the essentialist and historicist methodological traits considered problematical?[28] These are some of the questions we address in the following discussion.

A Postmortem on the Essentialist Thematic of Western Metaphysics

In this section, we will discuss the problems concerning (i) the essentialist structure of causality, (ii) the ideal of full presence or closed social totality, (iii) the problems of social totality, class, and structure of explanation in orthodox Marxism in light of the problems resulting from (i) and (ii), and (iv) the essentialist conception of history in historical materialism.[29] We will also argue for an alternative framework of postmodern Marxism taking into consideration the linkage between its epistemological position of overdetermination and anti-essentialism as developed above, its alternate concept of class, history, and the conceptualization of an alternative theory of transition. Let us begin with the essentialist structure of causality—the most elementary but important tool kit of orthodox Marxian theories of history, and which conditions the logic of such theories.

What is essentialism and why is it a problem? Both of these questions are intimately linked to the structure of causality in Western metaphysical thought, including that of historical materialism.[30] There, causality involves the elements of cause and effect. Causes produce effects: this sequential and logical order is the fundamental principle of the essentialist concept of causality. Cause is the antecedent or prior, the origin, and the effect is the consequence resulting from its dependent relation with the antecedent. This metaphysical privilege is crucial for the essentialist structure of causality. Thus, an element that causes and the element on which the effect is produced are split into a hierarchical structure where the former concept is privileged over the latter. This hierarchical structure, which differentiates between the fundamental premise, or ground, and the secondary effect has been given the name of *logocentrism* by Derrida; according to Derrida, it is the most typical and resilient conceptual structure of Western thought. Culler (1986) summarizes the definition of logocentrism well:

> Ordinary ideas about language rely on hierarchical oppositions between reality and appearance, between essence and accident, between inside and outside, between meaning and form, where the first term takes priority and the second is conceived in relation to it, as derivative and dependent. The general pattern here opposes a reality, a foundation—an order of truth, logic, reason, in short the logos (whence the term "logocentrism")—to appearances, accidents, contingencies, representations. (1986, 128–9)

This hierarchical opposition could further take the form of essence/appearance, content/form, Western/Oriental, economic/noneconomic, and so on, in the order of priority.[31] Given this logocentric structure, essentialist analysis is exemplified by

> ...the enterprise of returning "strategically," in idealization, to an origin or to a "priority" seen as simple, intact, normal, pure, standard, self-identical, in order *then* to conceive of derivation, complication, deterioration, accident, etc. All metaphysicians have proceeded thus, from Plato to Rousseau, from Descartes to Husserl: good before evil, the positive before the negative, the pure before the impure, the simple before the complex, the essential before the accidental, the imitated before the imitation, etc. This is not just one metaphysical gesture among others; it is the metaphysical exigency, the most constant, profound, and potent procedure. (Derrida 1977, 236)

There are two points to note with this procedure. First, the prior or originary element—that which causes—is autonomous and independent of other elements that are its effects. This originary element travels inexorably without being affected in any way by the other elements. Its meaning is self- or internally constituted (that is, it is intelligible, knowledgeable, and rational on its own basis) leading to its sometimes being called self-reflective or self-representative. For example, the forces of production are an inexorable element traveling in time that resists any outside determination. Second, the element that causes may or may not determine other elements on its own. For example, arguments might be put forward to the effect that the forces of production determine the elements of the superstructure on its own. A more sophisticated argument would be to say that any element of the superstructure is determined by a combination of forces of production, relations of production, and other elements of superstructures but that forces of production are not determined by any of them. However, in this case, even though the superstructure may not be solely determined by forces of production, its specific form of existence crucially depends on the stage of development of the forces of production and this dependence takes precedence over other forms of dependence.[32] Not all elements of superstructure are consistent with the prevailing stage of development of the forces of production. Thus even though many factors come together to determine the existence of any element of the superstructure, one factor (the forces of production) is accorded a privileged status of being the most important factor. The forces of production emerge as the origin—the fundamental premise—in the sense that without it the element of the superstructure would not exist in its present form. Due to the relation of dependence, the latter is derived from the former.

No such privilege is accorded to the other effects. Thus the causation of one element is privileged over the causation of other elements.

Essentialism necessarily implies some form of reductionism: that is, how the existence of an aspect of society is explained by and, henceforth, reduced to another aspect of society. What this means is that the other dimensions of the existence of the explanandum are rendered either passive or secondary in the order of explanation.

The essentialist structure of causality is problematic because the order of causality can be reversed by using the very same principle of causation. This reversal of the origin of cause and its effect destroys the sequential and logical order of causality, producing a violent disruption in its hierarchical, logocentric structure. We offer two examples to demonstrate where the cause is also the effect and hence the autonomous existence of the element causing the effect no longer holds true.

The first refers to the famous example of pin and pain by Nietzsche in *The Will to Power*. We feel a pain. Immediately, we look for a cause that turns out to be a pin. The pin is the cause while pain is the effect. Thus, the causal order says that we move from pin to pain. But the order of the event was pain to pin. Our experience of pain causes us to look for the cause (pin) and, subsequently, causes the production of a cause. Pain becomes the cause while the pin is the effect of the cause. The sequence is inverted: the cause becomes the effect while the effect is the cause. With this reversal of hierarchical order, two things have happened. First, the element as the source of cause is no longer independent and autonomous of the element that is supposed to be the source of the effect. In this context, without the pin there would be no pain and without pain there would be no pin. Second, the position of origin is destroyed. In the essentialist structure of causality, cause serves as the origin. But, as in our example, if the effect "is what causes the cause to be the cause," then it becomes the origin. Consequently, since both pin and pain can serve as the origin, the presumed origin—pin—loses its originary, metaphysical status.

The second example is from Marx in *Capital*, vol. 1. One can read in Marx the performance of a reverse move leading to a transposition of the sequential and logical order of causality that drives the structure of the traditional explanation of historical materialism. As we have explained, in historical materialism technological development (i.e., development of the forces of production) serves as the cause of the evolution and specific development of the other elements of the social totality, including that of class struggle, without in any way being affected by them. But, in Marx's discussion of transition from an absolute surplus value production process to a relative surplus value production process, a reversal of causality occurs.[33] In this transition process, along with the process of concentration of capital, a significant shift in the relation between the workers and the capitalists takes place. Different factory legislation, including the fixed working day, the increase in the power of trade unions vis-à-vis capitalists, the rise in workers' skill, and that of the reserve army of labor power significantly altered the relationship between workers and capitalists. Due to these changes, as well as the class struggles over the length of the working day and methods of exploitation, capitalists were forced to seek new methods of organization of the labor process and adopt technological innovation with the purpose of increasing the rate of exploitation through increases in the intensity of work. Thus, technological innovation is being driven by the many "other" factors we mentioned above, including class struggle, and is the cause of technological development even when simultaneously these other factors are theoretically being projected as the effect of technological development without the ability to cause technological development. The important thing to understand is that working within the logic of historical materialism, this historic change—from an absolute surplus value capitalist system to a relative surplus value capitalist system—ends up violating the very logic itself. By the essentialist structure of causality in historical materialism, such momentous historical change is to be driven by the forces of production. Yet, we find that the order of causality between cause and effect is reversed. The origin is displaced from its originary position and loses its metaphysical status, becoming dependent on others for its existence. This criticism of the logic of explanation also severely undermines the orthodox Marxian theory of transition since the logic of transition in historical materialism is only a moment of the general logic of explanation that underlies historical materialism itself.

In these two examples, we have challenged the essentialist structure of causality by reversing the hierarchical order from cause to effect and effect to cause such that the act of reversal of the sequence displaces the structure of causality by making it devoid of any metaphysical core or essence. That is, the tranquillity with which logocentrism exists is disturbed. Our critique of essentialism, then, involves three steps: (i) pointing out its hierarchical arrangement and, in the process, bringing into the foreground the fundamental premise or concept(s) of the theory; (ii) the reversal or inversion of its hierarchical status, showing the effect as the cause; and (iii) showing that (i) and (ii) produces the loss of the origin—the autonomous nature of the cause—thereby stripping the structure of its fundamental (metaphysical) premise. This three-step procedure, which occurs simultaneously at the level of application, is what we mean by deconstruction.[34]

One form that the metaphysics of logocentrism takes is that of the metaphysics of full presence or closed identity or closed totality (these terms are interchangeably used). Full presence is a self-representative entity that is not influenced or determined by outside forces. As Derrida writes, "It could be shown that [all names] related to fundamentals, to principles, or to the center have always designated the constant of a presence" (1978, 279). Full presence implies a hierarchical structure or logocentrism, because it is conceived as the superior element or the higher presence while the other elements have a lower presence, and are sometimes referred to as the domain of absences, since they are assumed not to affect the full presence in any way. The structure of a theoretical system depends on the full presence that captures the essential nature or foundation or source of the system. In the previous section, we have argued that the essentialist structure of causality runs along faulty lines. Now we ask whether in that same metaphysical framework the entity that is assumed to be the cause can conceptually exist as independent and autonomous of other elements. More generally, one can even ask the question whether it is possible for any such independent and autonomous entities to exist. In a certain way, we have grappled with this problem in our discussion of causality, but, given the critical importance given to the notion of closed totality or full presence in Marxian theories (including the ones we will be dealing with in this book), it is worth having a separate discussion on it.

The problem with the metaphysics of full presence is that the presence—the ground or origin which is also autonomous and given—is already dependent and constituted by other elements. There simply does not exist a pure, self-constituted presence at any supposed originary point. This simple presence which is also the higher presence (in the hierarchical structure) is neither the origin nor the autonomous given but is already constituted by the effects being produced on it by other elements. The order of dependency, origin, and foundation are reversed. Deconstruction is the procedure through which this reversal is made possible. This criticism overlaps with the one made on the essentialist structure of causality. We have already given one example from Marx where the moment of transition from absolute surplus value production system to a relative surplus value production system produces a reversal of the hierarchical order in historical materialism such that the origin—the forces of production—loses its originary position as it is constituted by the other elements in society at the very moment of the transition of the mode of production. Again, the cause becomes the effect and the effect the cause. Another example is from Derrida's deconstruction of phonocentrism. He deconstructs the traditional philosophical position of speech as the metaphysic of full presence, where writing is only an unnecessary representation of speech, and demonstrates that speech is in fact affected and, hence, caused in part by writing. As a result, the metaphysics of speech as full presence collapses.

What captures the process of disintegration of the metaphysics of full presence is the concept of *differance*. The French verb *differer* combines "to differ" and "to defer." "Differance sounds exactly the same as difference, but the ending "ance," which is used to produce verbal nouns, makes it a new form meaning "difference-differing-deferring. Differance thus designates both a 'passive' difference already in place as the condition of signification and an act of differing which produces differences" (Culler 1982, 97). Derrida is very particular as to what differance is not. It is not ". . . conceived on the basis of opposition presence/absence. Differance is the systematic play of differences, of traces of differences, of the spacing by which elements relate to one another" (1981, 27). Note that by presence/absence, Derrida means full presence or full absence, that is, presence or absence as a closed identity or closed totality that is self-representative and hence resists any determination from outside. Derrida starts from full presence and by a deconstructive procedure displaces the entire system by positing a *lack* in the full presence and then a lack of the lack of presence and so on. Full presence at any time is conditioned by the difference, that is, what it is not, and the deference, that is, what it stops from showing up. The simultaneous *effect* of difference and deference constitutes the full presence, thereby undercutting the proclaimed autonomous, self-representative existence of full presence. That is, *differance* signifies the spacing indicating the failure of the full presence to become the foundation, origin, or cause thereby severely undermining its self-representative and autonomous status. Derrida's framework leaves us with a social space that contains an infinite play of differences devoid of the presence of any transcendental signifier (another name of full presence). Society cannot be fixed by full presence. There are no origins, no foundations and no one-sided dependency relations in society for Derrida. For him, the essentialist structure of causality is subverted time and again.[35]

Following these anti-essentialist arguments, the social totality as described by historical materialism fails to hold its ground. The very logical structure through which social totality operates in historical materialism brings about its downfall. The sequence of causality embedded in the historicism of the historical materialistic model clearly accords a privileged status to forces of production as the engine of change. But, as we have shown earlier in an example from Marx, at the very moment of transition from backward capitalism to advanced capitalism, the forces of production become constituted (effected) by other elements in society and thereby not only violating the logical and sequential structure of causality but also bringing into fore its lack as a full presence.

The Marxist Interventions in the Anti-Essentialist Critiques

The above critique of essentialism, which can be loosely characterized as a postmodernist and poststructuralist–inspired critique, has had an enormous impact on Marxism, especially on its structure of causality, closed social totality, and class. Among Marxist theoreticians, the attack on essentialism in Marxism was first carried out principally by Althusser (1969), Laclau and Mouffe (1985), Hindess (1987), and Resnick and Wolff (1987). While Laclau and Mouffe and Hindess have, in the process of the critique, abandoned Marxism, Althusser and Resnick and Wolff tried to transform the Marxist paradigm in the process of their critique. Althusser and Resnick and Wolff's response to the crisis in the Marxian theory of causality begins with the development of a new theory of causality—encapsulated in the concept overdetermination—a theory that is thoroughly anti-essentialist.

What is overdetermination, why is it anti-essentialist, and what is the relation between deconstruction and overdetermination? To answer these important and abstract questions, let us resort to being figurative for a moment by drawing a portrait of a rainbow as seen from the spectacle of a metaphysical philosopher. In the portrait drawn up by our metaphysical philosopher, the rainbow travels from the beginning or original point to the end point. Without the original point, there would be no end point. In philosophical terms, the former is the cause and the latter the effect. Deconstruction reverses the causality by arguing that the rainbow that travels from the "original" point to the end point simultaneously also travels from the end point to the "original" point. The supposed effect is also the cause of the presupposed cause. In other words, since both serve as the origin, there can be no originary point. Deconstruction brings to light the incompleteness of the portrait drawn up by the metaphysical philosopher who had prematurely announced the closure of the portrait. In pointing out the failure of the portrait to close itself, deconstruction counterpoises how the portrait should be pictured. Let us stop and freeze the portrait from "what it should be" to "what it is"—that is, let us freeze the moment of the failure of metaphysics and begin from there. The picture, at the moment of this failure, seems one of multisided causality, cause and effect flowing back and forth between each other. In fact, we replace multi-sided causality with mutual constitutivity, because the non-essentialist logic of overdetermination is certainly not coterminous with the logic of such causality (Cullenberg 1991). The "original" point of the metaphysical philosopher is constituted by the end point and the end point by the "original" point. This spatial zone of seemingly mutual constitution of elements is one way to consider the concept of overdetermination. Deconstruction operates within the heart and soul of the metaphysical structure and finishes with its failure.[36] Overdetermination begins where deconstruction ends, at the moment of the failure of the metaphysical theoretical structure. Deconstruction is *critical* (after all, that is what it does) while overdetermination is *positive*, or *constitutive*. Overdetermination aspires to ask questions about alternative constructions of theory and society against the background of the failings of the Marxian theories based on essentialist logic. In a way, overdetermination subsumes deconstruction because its fundamental critique of essentialism (essentialist structure of causality and the ideal of full presence) is embedded in the concept of overdetermination. That is why to be a postmodern Marxist is also to be a deconstructionist. Pioneered by Althusser (1969), this concept of overdetermination is given its richest texture in the work of Resnick and Wolff (1987), where it is deployed with a dual purpose—as a nonessentialist epistemology, and which also emerges as the virtual structure of causality in their framework.

The form that causality takes in the postmodern Marxist framework is not that of separation of cause and effect but of their inalienable existence captured by the term "constitution." Overdetermination says that no process could exist on its own. Each process is "constituted" by other processes. By "constitution" we mean "being literally brought into existence." This aspect of reciprocal or mutual constitution is what is meant by overdetermination. Without other processes, the original process would not exist in the present form. Consequently, while processes are conceptually distinct, they are not autonomous and independent from one another. Overdetermination is the logic that says that each process operates as *both* the cause and the effect of other processes. Neither cause nor effect but both cause and effect—as alienable—at the same time. (Mutual) constitutivity is *not* mutual causality. Overdetermination abandons and surpasses the aspect of mutual causality because causality is no longer the basic mode uniting the parts. It is replaced by constitutivity. Constitutivity, unlike mutual causality, does not simply effect the state of *being* that is *presumed* to exist but it makes possible the very existence of the *being*. Constitutivity is that logic which brings the *being* and its state into the world.

Overdetermination also telescopes a particular notion of *difference*. The Saussarian notion of difference has been construed as A not being B or C. Overdetermination, in contrast, says that A is B, that is, B's concrete existence is brought about by A (and C, D, E, and so on). Similarly A's existence is an effect of B (and C, D, E, and so on). Thus B is both caused by and effected at the same time—both being produced and producing others at the same time. Second, if B is brought into existence or constituted by the effects of numerous other aspects then as one of these or a subset of these aspects change, they cause a change in (the meaning of) B. The aspects that constitute B thus pushes and pulls the concrete existence of B in different—contradictory—directions, leading to change in B. The state of B at one point is no longer the same state in another point. B thus becomes different from its previous state of being. B either becomes not B or another moment of B that is, say, B'in a series of never ending process. Either way B is not B. Consequently, constitutivity encapsulates a dual—overlapping—scenario whereby A is B (the first dimension) and B is not B (the second dimension). Each part of society such as B in being constituted becomes a dynamic entity and it is through this changing parts that differences between parts become mobile.

Overdetermination thus does not *presume* a state of difference (that would go with mutual causality) but rather *produces* and simultaneously *annihilates* difference as part of the logic of constitutivity. A becomes B and B becomes not B, that is, different from its previous state, through constitutivity. In the event of B not being B, B not only posits its difference from A but its previous state of difference is annihilated through the contradictory influences that produce B's difference from its previous state. Difference (under constant erasure) thus becomes dynamic, being literally brought into existence as well as its previous state taken out of existence through the process of constitutivity. For much of postmodernist thinking, negotiation between the parts is a problem to be faced which in our case is not only not a problem but rather an integral part of the logic through which an argument is constructed.

Finally because an element like B is always in a dynamic state, its *being* must be in a state of change. That is why in the postmodern Marxian theory the basic unit of analysis becomes *process* which is defined as an entity in a state of change. Within postmodern Marxism, society is a totality of overdetermined processes and all social relationships or activities or practices are subset of overdetermined processes. Since difference is dyanamised into the logic of the theory, the relevant question in postmodern Marxism is the manner and form of transition of such social relationships, a point which we will deal with later on.

As should be obvious by now, the approach of overdetermination precludes linkage of Marxist theory with essentialisms. Unlike the case with theories adopting an essentialist epistemology, the concept of theory, knowledge, truth, and reality is no longer singular but plural.[37] This implies that there exists no intertheoretic standard of truth. Overdetermination, as we mentioned, also rejects any dichotomy between two or more independent and autonomous concepts or spaces. In essentialist theories, the above dichotomy produces the result whereby one space or concept mirrors or provides the foundation for the other space(s) or concept(s). Any such mirroring is precluded by the very concept of overdetermination.

Let us now consider the other critique of Marxism related to class and social totality or society. Within Marxism, this critique reached its climatic conclusion in the work of Laclau and Mouffe (1985). The two major claims of Laclau and Mouffe are (i) the working class, as a closed entity, is a metaphysical concept and is a conceptual impossibility and (ii) society, as a closed entity, is an impossibility. These two claims follow immediately from our discussion of essentialism.

Laclau and Mouffe ask whether identity or totality of the working class contradicts the materialistic basis of the Marxist framework of historical materialism. They claim that it does because the totality of the working class could not be made consistent with the complex dialectics of the internal role and external role assigned to class in Marxian theories. By internal, we mean the pure identity of social class in which its interest is embedded as given, and by external, we mean the tasks (often alien to the internal character) that it must take upon itself. There is a hiatus between the two. For example, the working-class subjects may not know their (working-class) historical interests and consequently they would not be able to act on it.[38] The gap must be accounted for to make the theory consistent. Leninism does that by posing a concept of vanguard party. The vanguard party—mirroring the pure form of working-class consciousness—knows the historical interests of its social classes, knows the direction society and history must take. But the obvious question is how does the vanguard party know what the historical interests of the working class are, and, at a different level, how does the working class know what its historical interests are? In other words, how does this knowing come into being and what is its basis? Orthodox Marxism avoided the problem by considering knowledge and interest as autonomous, self-reflective, and pre-given. This assumption of knowing signifies a metaphysical foundation that is contrary to the self-proclaimed materialistic basis of historical materialism. We will soon discuss the problem of considering the concept of an agent or group's *interest* as a reflective given.[39] The essential point is that the hiatus between the internal and external remains unresolved. This insuperable problem results in the loss of the privileged status for class in Laclau and Mouffe. For them, the problem with class analysis is not so much the totalitarian consequences it sometimes generates but rather the logical problem that class analysis is based on a metaphysical foundation.

Hindess (1987) takes the above argument a bit further by pointing out that the concept of the working class as a subject, that is, as a homogenous group of conscious social actors, cannot exist and that the concept of a given interest is logically faulty.[40] According to Hindess, classes (such as the working class or capitalist class) cannot be regarded as social actors who struggle against each other. Unlike actors such as human individuals, and social actors such as enterprises, trade unions, political parties, and state agencies, these classes have no definite means of formulating and executing decisions, which can be considered the minimal condition required for a conceptual existence of an actor.

Furthermore, the orthodox Marxist class analysis has treated classes as social forces representing some given common (class) interest originating from the positions they occupy in the relations of production. Here the identities of classes are construed around class interests that are presumed to be pre-given. For example, the interest (of say not owning property) emanating from the economic (relations of production) is the true or real interest of the working class, and it is assumed to reflect its imputed consciousness. Hindess (1987, 1988) has argued that the assumption of real or true interest (class interest) as given or reflecting some social structural location is logically inconsistent. Interest is not something that is autonomously given but is, rather, produced contextually at the very moment at which individual or social action is being processed. He argues that,

> There is no possibility of interests (or norms or values) operating as mere transmissions between the social structure and actor's decisions. Interests have consequences only in so far as they enter actors' deliberations and contribute towards providing them with reasons for actions. Interests in this sense have to be formulated or capable of formulation by those who act on them—which is to say that the existence of interests depends on the forms of thought available to actors. There is therefore a significant element of circularity in any suggestion that actors' forms of thought reflect their interests. (Hindess 1988, 110)

The combination of these points related to (i) the conceptual hollowness of class as social actors and (ii) that of reflective interests has had a destructive impact on orthodox Marxian analyses of class. Reformulating Hindess's argument, we argue that since interests "are thought to relate to the decisions of particular actors, and therefore to their actions" and since one cannot think of class as social actors, class actors with pre-given interests are incompatible elements. Consequently, "the claim that class as a social force can be understood in terms of the representation of class interests must therefore collapse" (Hindess 1987, 112–3). This powerful critique leaves no room but to abandon the orthodox Marxian concept of class, thereby removing the agents of transition (that is, classes) from the conceptual apparatus.[41]

For the above-mentioned reasons, theorists like Hindess and Laclau-Mouffe have called for an abandonment of the concept of class, class politics, and ultimately Marxism as a discourse. We agree with their skepticism on the points regarding the concept of class as social actors, class as closed identity, and the existence of true interests but do not accept their call to abandon class analysis and class politics *tout court*.

Their critique of class takes the orthodox Marxist notion of class as a given, criticizes it, and then abandons class altogether. But what if class is conceptualized in such a way that it takes into consideration the major problems listed above? Postmodern Marxist theory does exactly that, and it comes up with a concept of class that is nonessentialist and nonreductionist.

In contrast to the orthodox Marxian approach on class as subject, postmodern Marxist theory is unique for its definition of class as process.[42] It gives class the entry-point status, the concept used to enter into a discourse. This is not an ontological privilege but, rather, a discursive privilege accorded to an aspect of society. This subtle difference in privileging class is often misunderstood by critics who conflate it with essentialism. Another way to interpret entry point is that it reflects a partisan standpoint that involves excluding other elements, such as gender, caste, and so on from becoming the initial moment of explanation only for these blocked elements to show in another moment of constitution that transforms the very initial moment from posited truism to falsity (Chaudhury, Das, and Chakrabarti 2000, 61–92). Entry point is not an independent concept that exists outside overdetermination. Quite the reverse. The logic of overdetermination makes possible the entry point. That one cannot begin a discourse without entry point within the infinitely (simultaneous) effected and causing processes making up the overdetermined social reality means that all discourses must have entry points. Through this *inalienable* relation between entry point and overdetermination a theorization of standpoint or perspective emerges: "This partisan selection is quite natural because . . . all theories have entry points, and entry-points, by definition, announce the participant standpoint of the participant" (Chaudhury, Das, and Chakrabarti 2000, 84).

Along with providing the logic and epistemology of the postmodern Marxian framework, overdetermination, unlike the postmodernism, also provides for a theory of standpoint via its inalienable concept of entry point.

In this regard, one can also contrast overdetermination with Derridean *differance* in the context of entry point. The logic of overdetermination that, as we explained earlier, encapsulates *differences as mobile* resembles the notion of *differance* where the *a* in *differance* captures the aspect of mobility in the play of differences.[43] Continuing with this theme, we further argue that overdetermination is the implicit theory that makes possible *differance* through the notion of entry point that functions within *differance* as unacknowledged, that is, as unconscious. Thus entry point brings into light the aspect of standpoint or position that is denied—suppressed—by the Derrideans. In this sense, overdetermination, while resembling *difference*, is something more than *differance*. Let us explain.

So far we have understood *differance* as difference *and* deferral. Some-times though, putting the same thing a bit differently, *differance* has also been referred to as the perpetual play of identity *and* difference—where both identity and difference are construed as constituting the other.

The classic critique of postmodernism and especially *differance* has flown primarily along the following line: because Derrida operates within the logic of *differance*, he cannot account for any entry point/position/per-spective/standpoint.

We argue that the Derridian framework has an entry point or stand-point—the only problem is that it is missed—through suppression. In Derrida, every identity is always already difference—every origin is always already trace. But the field of *differance* is impregnated with the decon-structive moments that, in turn, presume entry point(s). The work of *dif-ferance* then is also impregnated with those entry points. For example, Derrida works with the chosen entry points that mark the classical notion of speech and writing, culture and nature, bricoleur and engineer. *Differ-ance* of course abandons origin since the process of deconstruction (that destroys the moments of origin) is integrated within *differance* but the text, or more specifically the referring entry points in the text, continues to, so as to say, overdetermine the impulse of the play of difference—still writ-ing and speech, still culture and nature, still the bricoleur and engineer. The Derridean would, of course, say that this is not his entry point. But that hardly matters. His working with others' entry point does not change the fact that his system too has an entry point. An author's so-called "non position" remains overdetermined by the (entry point) position of the au-thor of the text. Tracing the trace of a (concrete) *differance*, we need to ask: How did it at all come about in the discursive horizon? What constitutes the contours of its becoming? What drives the specificity of a (concrete) *differance* and thus de-facto what makes possible *differance*? How can the play of difference function without this perspective/entry point? The fail-ure to acknowledge this moment in *differance* means that Derrida in oper-ating within the logic of *differance* forecloses the epistemological stasis, even if contingent, that a perspective demands. We criticize Derrida not because his theory lacks position/perspective/standpoint/entry point. We criticize Derrida and his brand of postmodernism because they do not acknowledge the fact that their system too has implicit within it a posi-tion/perspective/standpoint/entry point. The work of *differance* remains unconscious of the entry point that remains at the very core of *differance*. Overdetermination reminds *differance* of its own unconscious—the entry point—that remains unacknowledged.

Overdetermination is the logic that makes possible entry point and, be-cause entry point is unconsciously there in *differance*, it makes possible the existence of its structure, gives meaning to the play of difference. Overdetermination, through its alienable concept of entry point, provides a *theory* of producing knowledge. All theories must have an entry point. Because the Derridean brand of postmodernism does not explicitly acknowledge entry point even though they are operating with one (however provisional), they evacuate the possibility of a theory of standpoint within their framework. Thus they effectively evacuate the possibility of a politics of imagination. We say in contrast: it is not that a politics of imagination is impossible but that the Derridean in suppressing entry point effectively castrates the political moment of the *possible* imaginary. Not to acknowledge the concept of entry point means that one remains bound within the social imaginary that dominates since, with the disavowal of the notion of imaginary, no other (alternative) imaginary is possible. Such a process of depoliticization enabled by the theoretical absence of entry point makes the amnesia of postmodernists to social transformation complete. While appreciating much of Derrida's position, we totally reject this impulse as being theoretically problematic and politically counterproductive. In the Derridean frame what remains of politics is what we call the immobile politics of indecision or what has been called "anything goes" postmodernism. With our epistemological concept of overdetermination that has to have an entry point, we reject such a kind of postmodernism. Let it be noted that we do not reject the concept of *differance*. We only believe that *differance* has an implicit entry point whose presence needs to be theorized, which is what overdetermination provides. That is why we believe that the theory of overdetermination, though it resembles *differance*, gives something more. We operate with overdetermination because we think that it is theoretically and politically more enabling than the conception of *differance*.

In contrast to essentialist renditions, courtesy of the logic of overdetermination—the play of mutual constitutivity—explanations remain standpoint-focused but never standpoint-specific. In this context, postmodern Marxist theory analyses society from a class standpoint, where class is defined by processes relating to the performance, appropriation, distribution, and receipt of surplus labor.[44] Fundamental class processes are defined as the performance and appropriation of surplus labor. Alternatively, the processes related to the distribution and receipt of surplus labor are called subsumed class processes.[45] Postmodern Marxist theory looks for the different ways in which the fundamental and subsumed class processes are constituted (that is, overdetermined) by each other and by other aspects of society (economic, cultural, and political) at a certain time and location. Also, because each class process cannot exist without other class and nonclass processes, it does not act as the essence of society. With changes in any of the processes that constitute classes (both fundamental and subsumed), the exact specification of class keeps changing. The object of Marxist analysis is to look at the different ways in which class processes are both the cause and the effect of other social processes and how changes, resulting from such causes and effects, are produced within a society.

Consider next the thesis of Laclau and Mouffe concerning the impossibility of the concept of a closed society. Their thesis follows directly from the argument we presented earlier on essentialism. Closure of society is impossible because of the absence of any transcendental signifier. In Laclau and Mouffe, society is unhinged from its closed existence by unfixing the meaning of each element within it. Every element in society has a surplus of meanings as it cannot be located in a closed system of difference. The logic of necessity is replaced by the logic of contingency. This means that there is no transcendental signifier that has an underlying rationality and intelligibility with whose help the society could be closed. There is an infinite play of differences originating from the nonfixity of meaning and multiplicity of context. Attempts to constitute a society are made (what Laclau and Mouffe call a sutured totality), but are constantly subverted. Since social meanings are defined by moments in which elements come together, the field is open to a play of articulatory practices producing hegemonic relations. Hegemonic constructions are attempts to secure a sutured totality (that is, constructed totality) whose effort is to tie the differences together and prevent the system from collapsing. Let us briefly argue this point by slightly reformulating Laclau and Mouffe's thesis in order to incorporate our concept of class struggle within such a fragmented political space.

Laclau and Mouffe, in our view, have convincingly argued that the construction of a political identity requires a hegemonic process of enforcing unity around the issues of certain aspects of society and that any such unity (which can only be contextually produced) can only survive momentarily as the dominant unity in the political arena. Disintegration of the unity (the sutured totality) leads to a disintegration of the identity as the dominant identity. Reformulating Laclau and Mouffe, we can claim that there are multiple issues surrounding class, gender, race, caste, religion, and so on that constitute the body politic. The body politic is a fractured and disaggregated space where class struggle is only one effect among many being produced.[46] In any particular situation, one such aspect can take center stage. But to be at the center of the body politic requires a construction of political identity that is simultaneously a process of (momentary) hegemonic construction.[47] Without such construction of identity, class struggle might not take the center stage even when important decisions are being made over issues concerning class processes. In other words, contrary to the orthodox Marxian position concerning class struggle as the only important form of struggle, the postmodern Marxist perspective does not consider class struggle the dominating and universal form of struggle, even though it does emphasize the importance of forming class identity (political identity around issues over class processes) for creating the condition for conducting class struggle with the intention of producing social change. Class struggle can be understood as the politics of partial emancipation but never total emancipation.

The Twisted Face of History and the Question of Transition and Development

The principles of deconstruction also produce and are supplemented by the following results: (a) meanings are contextually produced, (b) context itself is boundless, and (c) the combination of context-based meaning and context as boundless produces indeterminacy of meaning, that is, meaning as multiple and nonfixed.[48]

These three propositions have an enormous impact on the interpretation of society and history. It is important to understand that deconstruction and postmodern Marxist theory is not against history as such but rather helps to offset the traditional meaning of history based on the "metaphysics of logocentrism," inscribing in its place a history that is context-bound, nonteleological, and where meaning is constructed and not a simple derivative of a "historico-philosophic theory of the general path."

Logocentrism in traditional Marxism operates at different levels—object, agency, and agent. The crucial object is the deus ex machina of forces of production that operates as historical materialism's full presence or closed totality. The logic of historical materialism whose explanatory mode follows the essentialist structure of causality—a point we have already criticized—gives a description of the development of society that depends on the development of the originary element or essence: the forces of production. In this progressive evolution of society, there is no logic of contingency. The only logic that operates is that of necessity. The elements that condition the ordered movement of society are predetermined and fixed by the theory of history. According to the historical materialistic theory of history, these elements *must* fulfill their projected role in history for society to travel in the right direction. For example, elements such as primitive capital accumulation are necessary for society to mirror the path laid down by the theory of historical materialism. Events that fit the schematic framework are considered important while others that do not are pushed aside.

In historical materialism, only certain types of agency, that is, certain forms of struggles related to class struggles, have been presumed to have any lasting impact on history, which produces in turn a hierarchy of struggles. For example, during the stage of transition from capitalism to socialism, only working-class struggle is considered to be of fundamental importance. Other forms of struggles (based on gender, race, ethnicity, etc.) are secondary in the grand scheme of history. The same holds true for the agents in society: the "historical" agents (for example, agents holding working-class or capitalist-class position) far outweigh the "nonhistorical" agents (say, agents holding gender or caste position) in the hierarchy of importance. Historical materialism can then be seen as a theory of exclusion. It excludes other elements in favor of the forces of production, other struggles in favor of class struggles, other agents in favor of class agents. This exclusion does not mean that these "other" aspects are not sometimes taken into consideration but, rather, in a move in tune with logocentrism, it demotes the "otherness" in favor of some chosen, autonomously pregiven privileged aspects. We have pointed out earlier the problem with the idea of an autonomously given full presence or closed identity: the full presence is neither given nor autonomous; it is as much caused as it causes.

It is indeed a twisted irony that historical materialism—a metanarrative of history—ends up as a discourse dependent on and driven by a suprahistorical and transcendental element, thereby turning (with social effect) against history itself. Postmodernism and poststructuralism can be understood in part as a reaction against this ahistorical basis of historical materialism. Following Lyotard, one can characterize postmodernism and poststructuralism as our "incredulity towards metanarratives" (1992, 138). Coming from different directions, Foucault, Derrida, Lyotard, and other critics all maintain a common suspicion of metanarrative discourses such as that of historical materialism. They argue that historical events are contextually produced and the meanings of those events, that is of history, must be generated and understood in the context that surrounds the very moment of the irruption of the event. Foucault's (1972a, 1972b) analysis of history testifies to this affirmation toward the contextual production of meaning. As we had indicated earlier, history in historical materialism illuminates the past from the present by encapsulating events in the idea of progress. Foucault contests this procedure "by freeing the chronologies and historical sequences of any 'progress-based' perspective and restoring to the history of experience a development which owes nothing to the finality of *connaissance* or the orthogenesis of *savoir*" (1972a, 138–9).[49] This counterhistory of Foucault pitches itself against the aspects of identity, certainty, order, and progression present in the orthodox Marxist notion of history.

In Derrida too one can read history as context-bound meanings surrounding the moment of irruption of events that cannot be prejudged in terms of one or more a priori aspects. The meanings produced of such events are historical and, yet, the relation of difference, differing, and deferral precludes any possibility of its becoming a foundation or a ground. History should not be reduced to some hidden a priori presumed ground or meaning that has the deleterious effect of dehistoricizing and decontextualizing the historical events. An anti-essentialist conception of history is not a procession of big-bang macro changes dependent on the whims of an autonomously given deus ex machina. As Derrida puts it, "If the word history did not carry with it the theme of a final repression of difference, we could say that differences alone could be 'historical' through and through and from the start" (1982, 141). In other words, if produced meanings are structured around differences, then those meanings will themselves be fractured by contradictory fissures—presence by absence, continuity by discontinuity, certainty by uncertainty, order by disorder, coordination by its breakdown, and so on.

Of all people, Marx, the imputed father of historical materialism, expressed grave doubts about the universal validity of the theory of historical materialism. In an ironical move that has befuddled many Marxists, Marx in his analysis of the Russian commune took up a strident anti-evolutionist position in opposition to his own evolutionist position taken in the preface to the *Contribution to the Critique of Political Economy* and parts of *Capital.* Reacting against a critic who emphasized the historicism in historical materialism and the decontextualization involved with it, he writes:

> It is absolutely necessary for him to metamorphose our historical sketch of the genesis of capitalism in Western Europe into a historico-philosophical theory of general development, imposed by fate on all peoples, whatever the historical circumstances in which they are placed, in order to eventually attain this economic formation which, with a tremendous leap of the productive forces of social labour, assures the most integral development of every industrial producer. But we beg his pardon. This does us too much honor and yet puts us to shame at the same time. . . . Thus events strikingly analogous, but occurring in different historical milieux, led to quite disparate results. By studying each of these evolutions on its own, then comparing them, one can easily discover the key to the phenomenon, but it will never be arrived at by employing the all-purpose formula of a general historico-philosophical theory whose supreme virtue consists in being supra-historical. (Marx 1975, 293–4)

What is so striking about this quotation is Marx's emphasis on the contextual production of the meaning of history and his incredulity toward metanarratives. If incredulity toward metanarrative is a definitional requirement of being a postmodernist, then Marx certainly qualifies as one, at least on this account. This aspect of Marx's challenge to the very basis of a theory of history that has been propounded the world over and helped shape history in his name is indeed remarkable and has, as we mentioned earlier, befuddled Marxists and paralyzed Marxism's analysis of the concept of transition and development in recent times. This paralytic condition is perhaps best summarized by Balibar, who, commenting on the incommensurability of two conceptions of history in Marx, remarks that,

> We can thus not avoid asking whether such a rectification does not necessarily have repercussions upon the other aspects of "historical materialism"—particularly on the way in which the 1859 Preface described the "transformation" of the superstructure as the mechanical consequence of the "changes of the economic foundations" or base. Indeed what are "milieu," "alternative," "dualism," and "political transition," if not concepts or metaphors which require us . . . they . . . indeed constitute, in certain circumstances, the very basis upon which the tendencies of the "base" operate. . . . And it is true that, a hundred years later, once again facing up to the bad side of history, Marxists are still bereaving away at this problem. (Balibar 1995 111–2)

What Balibar is saying, which is critical, is that the overturning of the orthodox conception of history by Marx is not without consequences. The disturbance it creates percolates deep down into the inner structure of the theory of historical materialism, calling into question concepts, propositions, and statements hitherto uncontested and assumed secure.

It is at the site of this disturbance and insecurity—the "bad side of history"—that we want to contribute to a theory of transition and development. The project of this book is to question the orthodox Marxist conceptions of transition and development, and its associated concepts of class, mode of production, and social totality in the context of the long-standing important debate on transition in India. We will then reconceptualize the notion of transition within a postmodern Marxist framework that is firmly located within the micro-level description of society and history and against the logocentric or essentialist logic of theory and of the history that follows from it. Furthermore, in orthodox Marxism, the concept of development is inseparable from the logic of transition: transition from one mode of production to another in a historicist manner is also reflective of the developmental path of society. The abdication of the orthodox Marxian framework and its replacement by our newly developed concept of transition that is disaggregated, heterogeneous, and uneven unhinges the fusion of transition and development. Since, following our theorization, transition is no longer grounded on the idea of progress à la historical materialism, transition becomes estranged from development as progress. In other words, along with the same for transition, a renewed and distinct problematization of the conception of development as progress from a (postmodern) Marxist perspective is called for.

Finally, let us briefly point out a theme to which we will be returning time and again. This is a point that should be obvious by now but one that needs to be made explicitly for the sake of clarification because, in a way, it is one of the more fundamental themes of our story. We will argue in the chapters that follow that, from a postmodern Marxian standpoint, historicism cannot be reconciled with class analysis.

In the theory of historical materialism, historicism is closely allied to the concept of social totality and mode of production. As we have already indicated, social totality is a closed totality defined in terms of a mode of production. Consequently, transition from one historical moment to another involves the transition of the mode of production. Now, as we will argue from a postmodern Marxist perspective, the concept of a closed social totality, such as capitalism, cannot exist. The impossibility of a closed social totality follows from the collapse of the concept of mode of production (which assumes the uniformity of class processes) as a tool of analysis because what exists as primitives are not homogenous class structures but a multiplicity of irreducible, heterogeneous, uniquely constituted class structures. In our scheme, social totalities, as a configuration of social relationships, are derived from subsets of processes that, among other things, involve a multiplicity of class processes—capitalist and noncapitalist. In other words, the orthodox notion of social totality, based on the uniformity of class processes, is contradictory to our concept of social totality and, consequently, cannot be sustained in the postmodern Marxist framework. As a result of the nonviability of the orthodox concept of closed social totality and mode of production, we cannot ground the question of transition in terms of a historicist logic. In sum, the orthodox concept of transition that is grounded on historicism is incompatible with the postmodern Marxist theory.[50]

The Trajectory of This Book

The discussion above emphasizes two things: (i) the orthodox historical materialistic theory of transition and development has deep flaws with respect to its essentialist structure of causality, closed totality, class, and history, all of which are crucial in its conceptualization of the transition and development process and (ii) many of the flaws pointed out by the postmodernist and poststructuralist theories can be overcome within a postmodern Marxist paradigm. Postmodern Marxist theory opens up new avenues with the help of which we can address the issue of transition and development from a nonessentialist and nonhistoricist class perspective. This is the central task we take up in this book. Against this background of the central task to be performed, let us now lay down the trajectory of the book. There are three parts in our story. The first part consists of a detailed textual and critical study of the theories of transition and development in the Indian modes of production debate and the subaltern studies' school. The second part deals with the production of a nonessentialist and nonhistoricist theory of transition and a similar rendition of a class-focused Marxist theory of development. The third part illustrates the concepts of transition and development in light of the recent liberalization policies adopted in India.

The Indian modes of production debate regarding the status of the Indian modes of production and hence the Indian social totality as well as its dynamics is in many ways the Indian counterpart of the worldwide debates that were raging over historical materialism as we reviewed earlier. In the second and third chapters, we unpack the Indian mode of production debate from a postmodern Marxist perspective, revealing in the process its attachment to essentialisms and historicism and insuperable problems related to its analysis of class. All of this is done with an eye to show the deep deficiencies in the theories of transition and development that were proposed in the course of the debate.

Chapters 4 and 5 will contain a similar exercise with respect to the subaltern studies debate. Performing a systematic dissection of the underlying methodology driving their theory of transition and development, we demonstrate the presence of essentialism as inhering the inner logic of its theory. This methodological underpinning then additionally flows into that representation of transition and development as proposed via the concept of passive revolution of capital. We will argue that while subaltern studies did have deep reservations about historical materialism, it did not reject the historicism embedded in the logic of historical materialism. Compounding this problem is their reduction of causal and class explanation to power relations. The essentialisms grounding their methodology including that of power essentialism and historicism that are driving subaltern studies' theory of transition and development make their theories questionable.

These two important debates on Marxism in India reveal problems with the methodological structure underlying the orthodox Marxian theory of transition and development, or some variation of it. This opens up the question as to whether transition and, subsequently, Marxist development theory can be sustained. A reformulation becomes indispensable, which we take up in chapter 6.

We will argue that, from the postmodern Marxist class perspective, a social totality consists of a configuration of social relationships derived from the subtotalities of class structures, each of which are unique and distinct. Thus every social totality encompasses capitalist and noncapitalist class processes, thereby undercutting the theoretical proposition of a closed social totality like that of capitalist society. This means that a social totality determined by a mode of production, which requires the uniform presence of class structure, cannot exist.[51] This collapse of a uniform society and mode of production follows from our displacement of the theoretical primitive of Marxian analysis to the micro-level space of class process. If transition can no longer be conceived as a macro-level change from one mode of production to another, the question then is how to reconceptualize it from the micro-level perspective of class process. That is, the task is to conceptualize transition in the presence of a multiplicity of uniquely constituted, distinct class processes. We will argue that transition, as in the case of orthodox Marxist development theory, involves a change in social totality. But the crucial difference is that the movement has been displaced from onetime big-bang change to a continuous transformation of class processes that involves no reference to historicity. As one overdetermined class structure changes, the social totality undergoes a change via a chain reaction of effects that follow from and results in disturbances percolating throughout the fundamental class process and the other processes sutured to it. Changes in society are unevenly distributed and, yet, the unevenness is produced out of a combined existence of different class processes, each affecting the others in unique ways. Transition as decentered and heterogeneous mutation of classes, consequently, captures this uneven and combined development of society.

Unlike the orthodox rendition of progress that understood a transition of society as per the logic of historical materialism or some other variant of the same, our newly developed concept of transition disconnects it from the notion of progress. This means that transition and development no longer complement one another, that is, no necessary connection between the transition of classes and its direction as developmental progress exists any longer. For example, transition of classes toward nonexploitative forms (the target of Marxist politics) may be complemented by a hideous form of distribution (a traditional developmental concern). This detachment between transition and development calls for a renewed inquiry on the meaning of progress. In that context, from a Marxist perspective, we tentatively redefine development in a (postmodern) disaggregated space as indicating progress in the form of the contraction of exploitative space along with a redistribution of the surplus in a "fair" direction. This "progress" constitutes an ethical content capturing the defining politics from a Marxist standpoint but, unlike the orthodoxy, never guided by objectivity with a finality.

One of the casualties of this theory of transition is the orthodox concept of primitive capital accumulation. Since the concept of closed social totality and mode of production has been abandoned, the old concept of primitive capital accumulation can no longer be sustained in our framework. We do not totally overthrow the concept, however, but alter it slightly to detach it from any historicist implications. We redefine primitive accumulation (dropping the term "capital" in the middle because of its historicist connotation) as reflecting the process of dispossessing people from the economic conditions of existence (affecting their current ability to be performers, appropriators, distributors, or receivers of surplus labor). Such a process of dispossession can happen in a different time and space without becoming an essential part to any inner logic of a theory. We then discuss the relation between the process of primitive accumulation and hegemony and seek to bring forth an important phenomenon that the two complement one another in effecting the rule of a particular regime/order/institution.

Finally, the discussion on transition is illustrated by using the general example of household sector to reflect the heterogeneous nature of a social totality and its uneven, decentered, and heterogeneous pattern of transition, which is then further specified with analysis of the evolving household sectors in the United States and India.

In chapter 6, we have only tentatively posed the issue of development from a postmodern Marxian perspective. In the seventh chapter, we expand on our tentative definition of development as progress to offer a full-fledged theoretical version of the same. We systematically produce a *need*-focused theory of development (within and outside the surplus economy) and then work out the details of the mutual negotiation of such a notion of development and class. *Need* is theorized as existing within two realms—one within the surplus world and the other outside of it. Working on the concept of need within the surplus world, of particular importance is our elaboration of the idea of a necessary convergence of class and developmental politics leading up to the category of expanded communism that simultaneously restricts exploitation and expands the realm of need. This fusion of the two produces a powerful ethical/political thematic that cannot be captured unilaterally by either developmental politics or class politics. Secondly, working on the concept of need outside the surplus world, it is pointed out that the expansion of certain need-based space that resides outside the operative mechanism of surplus economy may facilitate progress as defined from our perspective. In other words, the constriction of the surplus space and the expansion of the nonsurplus need-based space allude to progress. Furthermore, given a specific context, class and development politics may not always be seeking the two forms of expanded communism but could be situated in the intermediate zone. In this regard, we also lay down the various possibilities of engaging in the dual of class and developmental politics in this zone, albeit from the ethical concern of exploitation and need. Within the seeming impasse of the postmodern, maybe our conception of development from a need, that is, consumption standpoint, is something unique in offering an alternative route for understanding development.

Deploying our newly produced concept of transition, we will explain the transition process going on in India in light of the liberalization policies adopted in 1991 and whether the transition process is producing the desired effect as per the developmental logic and path put forward by the policy makers. The objective is to give a Marxist analysis of the transition process in India—to explain how policy measures, by reconstituting the prevailing class structures, are producing profound changes in Indian society and to its development route. The eighth chapter lays down the political economy of reform—the background and rationality for its adoption. The ninth chapter deals with the transition process in the agricultural sector, private capitalist sector, small-scale sector, and the state sector. The tenth chapter suggests new avenues for research and analysis.

CHAPTER 2

Confronting the Indian Modes of Production Debate

An Unhappy Encounter of a Third Kind

The first major Indian academic debate on development reflecting on the process of transition in India, which is now known as the Indian modes of production debate, began in the late 1960s and continued into the 1980s. This theoretical debate had its roots in the furious transition debate that was going on in the political arena within and between the Indian Communist parties.[1] The Communist parties took different positions on the question of transition. This difference in viewing the transition process of Indian society (positions ranging anywhere from the feudal or Asiatic mode of production to the capitalist, colonial, or semifeudal mode of production) was transplanted in the academic sphere, where it became the focal point of the debate. The debates at the two sites (academic and political) intersected, reinforced, and compensated for one another, even though, in our discussion, we will be concentrating exclusively on the academic discourse.[2] One important feature of the Indian modes of production debate was the issue of location. The agricultural sector came to constitute the site of analysis and, consequently, the debate boiled down to arguing about the modes of production in the agricultural sector.

The debate, which carried on for over two decades, dealt with many issues, and it is virtually impossible to cover all of them. We will organize our narrative and "rational reconstruction" around the *issue of transition of Indian society,* which arguably was the most important aspect of the debate.[3] In our mind, there are two major stages in the debate over the transition process. Accordingly, we will divide the debate into two parts: the first part (the present chapter) will review the debate around the issues of primitive capital accumulation, especially in the context of what was seen as either its historic failure or its success with respect to the Indian economy, while the second part (chapter 3) will deal with the question of class differentiation, class formation, and their effects on the transition process in India.

Given that almost all theorists carried out their argument within the framework of historical materialism, their goal was to discover whether India had traversed the projected historical road from precapitalism to capitalism and, if not, what were the barriers standing in the path of the transition process. In this context, the question of the accomplishment of primitive capital accumulation became crucial.

Primitive capital accumulation was considered as having two phases: (i) creation of potential "free" wage labor and (ii) incorporation of these laborers within the capitalist production process. These two conditions, it was argued, needed to be present for the process of primitive capital accumulation to fulfill its historic role in the transition from precapitalism to capitalism. The absence of a mass of free potential wage labor and their inability to be incorporated into the capitalist relations of production were regarded as a failure of primitive capital accumulation and, importantly, of capitalism to achieve its dominant position. In this context, the debate between Utsa Patnaik and Paresh Chattopadhyay was of special interest where the former emphasized productive investment as against unproductive investment for the purpose of transforming potential wage labor to actual wage labor, as the "freedom" for the wage laborer cannot be actualized without this transformation.

Another major position in the debate (the semifeudal position) argued that the reason that the pauperized peasantry could not be transformed into free wage labor and the capitalist labor market could not assume its "pure form" (meaning "free" exchange of labor power) was due to the presence of precapitalist relations of production that were inhibiting the development of the forces of production (indexed by technological development). Until and unless the precapitalist relations of production are transformed into capitalist relations of production, technological development leading to a dynamic capitalist economy will not come into existence and the capitalist labor market cannot assume its "dominant" form vis-à-vis the precapitalist labor market. Theorists looked for institutions of social arrangements (usury, sharecropping, etc.) that constitute precapitalist relations of production, thereby creating barriers to technological development in the Indian agricultural sector. This led to another round of debate between the semifeudal school and the "capitalist" school on the question of (i) whether such institutions can be termed as precapitalist and (ii) whether they are necessarily inimical to technological development.

After the initial bout of debates, many theorists came to recognize that simply naming modes of production was not leading the debate anywhere. So they shifted their emphasis to the question of class differentiation and class formation in Indian agriculture. They insisted that Indian social reality cannot be captured adequately without the application of the concepts of class (Patnaik 1987, 1990d; Bhaduri 1983; Rudra 1984, 1988). Class relationships reveal the social relationships making up the relations of production that are inhibiting the development of the forces of production. Consequently, the key to changing the relations of production and, subsequently, the key to the process of transition to capitalism or socialism lies in the evolutionary nature of class relationships. Identifying the "correct" configuration of class relationships constitutes the last phase of the debate.

However, our purpose is more ambitious than a straightforward survey of the debate. Coming from a postmodern Marxian perspective, our basic goal is to impugn the orthodox notion of transition and its surrounding concepts of primitive capital accumulation and class by divulging underlying problems (both theoretical lacunae and hidden assumptions) associated with the concepts or propositions that ground those concepts. Problems related to economic essentialism, epistemological essentialism (rationalism and empiricism), centered social totalities like capitalism, mode of production, absence of sites of class processes in the cities and household, the treatment of class as a noun, working class as an ontological privilege, reduction of agency or subjectivity to class, and so on will be brought into the limelight. These criticisms seriously undermine the orthodox concept of transition, thereby setting the stage for a discussion of the subaltern studies school and our different Marxian concept of transition.

The Initial Debate: Defining the Capitalist Mode of Production

In this section, we will critically review the debates that took place between Rudra et al. and Patnaik, and that between Patnaik and Chattopadhyay. The debates came down to the conceptual differences in defining modes of production and the empirical procedure used to identify the presence of capitalism in Indian agriculture. The first phase of the debate started off with articles by Rudra, Majid, and Talib (1990) (henceforth referred to as Rudra et al.) and Rudra (1978, 1990a). Then Utsa Patnaik (1990a, 1990b) qualified and criticized Rudra. The main objective of this debate was to determine empirically whether or not capitalist farmers existed in Indian agriculture. The conclusions were based on random sampling from surveys conducted for different parts of India. Rudra et al. examined 261 farms over twenty acres in size in Punjab (the state often referred to as the bread basket of India) in the year 1967–68. Utsa Patnaik did a survey of sixty-six "big" farmers in the year 1969 in the relatively "backward" agricultural states of Orissa, Andhra Pradesh, Mysore, Madras, and Gujarat.

Rudra et al. started the debate by trying to separate capitalist farms from big farmers by setting certain theoretical criteria for a farm(er) to qualify as a capitalist farm(er). That is, the 261 big farms they looked at had to satisfy strict criteria (which they state are both necessary and sufficient conditions) to be called capitalist. The main criteria they included are the following:

1) percentage of land rented out to total land owned (X_1);
2) wage payment in cash per acre of farm size (X_2);
3) value of modern capital equipment per acre of farm size (X_3);
4) percentage of produce marketed to total produce (X_4); and
5) cash profit per acre (X_5).

Here X_2 relates to the tendency to use hired labor, X_3 to the use of modern capital goods, X_4 to market-mindedness and X_5 to profit-mindedness. According to Rudra et al., each X_i indicates features of capitalism and their null hypothesis was that Xs in pairs (for example, X_2 and X_5 or X_3 and X_4) should have a strong positive correlation for big farms to be called capitalist. From their field data Rudra et al. found that all pairs are uncorrelated and hence capitalist farmers do not exist in India. On this basis, they concluded that the transition to capitalism has not taken place in India.

Patnaik replied to Rudra et al. with her own findings from a sample survey. Her findings showed that capitalist farms and capitalism in agriculture were emerging in India, though there are also factors that are impeding the development of capitalism. She noted that in addition to wage labor and a marketable surplus, one should add reinvestment of surplus value as an additional criterion for identifying a capitalist farmer and capitalism in general. For her, this reinvestment had to take place at the same spot from where the surplus was being generated.

Patnaik criticized Rudra et al. for ignoring the complex economic reality of India. Rudra's result would hold only if one considers modes of production in their pure, ideal form such that all the features of capitalism as outlined by Rudra will hold true. According to Patnaik, India is in a transitional state moving toward capitalism, and it is likely that during this period she would retain some precapitalist characteristics. Thus, during a transition period, a pure and idealized world with classes holding pure class attributes is only a fiction and has nothing to do with the concrete reality of India. Rudra et al. miss this point.

According to Patnaik, to understand the nature of the current transitional state in India, one should analyze the economic relations beginning in British India and show how, via a historical process, India emerged from precapitalism to capitalism. This will reveal the crucial ways in which India's development process toward capitalism was determined and consequently transformed by its articulation with the process of development in the center country—Britain. She observes that the British administration, through the land settlement act, property right policies, and systematic destruction of handicraft industries had only partly accomplished the historical process of primitive capital accumulation. The loss of land and other means of production for most of the agricultural population (the literature refers to this process as "depeasanalization") led to the creation of, as Patnaik called it, a pauperized and "semi-proletariat" group of people. According to Patnaik, the laws of primitive capital accumulation require that the depeasanalized labor force be accommodated in productive activities, most preferably that they be transformed into an industrial labor force. However, primitive capital accumulation in India has not yet been accomplished for two reasons: (i) wage labor is a necessary but not sufficient condition for capitalist development: one needs capitalist (productive) investment in addition to wage labor for capitalism to evolve in its pure, dominant form and (ii) wage labor, as it exists in India, is only formally free; in reality, it is not free. Patnaik especially emphasized the first point that is important in the context of the failure to absorb the depeasanalized portion of the agricultural population in productive activities. According to her, this failure stemmed from a lack of investment directed toward the production of surplus value, which in turn was due to the presence of precapitalist relations of production that encouraged unproductive investment over productive investment.

Assuming that there are substantial "free" wage laborers, Patnaik asked whether the social relations between the landlord and agricultural wage laborers in colonial India were capitalist in nature. Her answer was negative since she argued that even if the wage laborers were free, investment by the landlord was not directed toward producing surplus value. Instead of investing surplus value in the very spot of its appropriation, that is, in agricultural land improvements—a criterion for capitalism for Patnaik—money was diverted to such practices as trade, usury, and the purchase of land to be leased out to peasants, practices whose gains (in monetary and sociopolitical terms) far outweighed gains from investment in land. The reason for the stagnation in the agriculture sector was this emphasis on unproductive investment that was (i) due to the presence of precapitalist relations of production and (ii) a direct result of the British policy not to encourage either agricultural productive investment or industrial growth in India. Instead, the British government initiated land-settlement measures that simultaneously led to the commercialization of Indian agriculture and to a reinforcement of the precapitalist relations of production that more often took the form of share tenancy or hereditary bond-laborers. Also, due to the absence of state investment, there was a general lack of effective demand: the Keynesian idea of growth through the creation of effective demand was not given any consideration for the case of India. Patnaik considered this lack of productive investment to be the key factor that prevented the absorption of the depeasanalized labor into productive activities and, subsequently, retarded the development of capitalism in India. Thus, for capitalism to evolve in Indian agriculture, the existence of free wage labor was not a sufficient condition. The additional criterion of reinvestment of surplus for productive purposes also needs to be considered as a necessary condition for capitalism to achieve its pure form. She pointed out that capital has penetrated the sphere of circulation but it failed to gain a foothold in the sphere of production. Hence, despite the commercialization of Indian agriculture, the relations of production remained precapitalist. However, Patnaik also points out that after independence, due to massive state investment, capital began to penetrate the sphere of production in agriculture, and India is now in a transition state, slowly moving toward capitalism even though the unproductive investments are creating barriers to the pace of its development.

Furthermore, because of the unproductive investment and the lack of industrial development, the laborers are only formally free. For Patnaik, unless the laborers can move to the industrial sector, they should not be considered free. She averred that due to the lack of industrial development, the laborer did not have the freedom to switch from agriculture to industry. Until and unless the center (industry) develops, the wage laborers are going to be tied to the mostly unproductive sectors of the periphery (agriculture), thereby impeding capitalist development and the establishment of a capitalist labor market.

The Dominance of Empiricist and Rationalist Procedure

This exchange between Rudra et al. and Patnaik was followed by a furious debate between the two even though little was added in the debate in terms of substance. The basic underlying theme common to both positions is that of empiricism: the empirical findings will reveal the true reality of the Indian society. The empiricist emphasis at this phase of the debate was followed up by a combination of rationalist and empiricist arguments in the later phase of the debate. In the treatment below, we bring the aspects of empiricism and rationalism into the limelight in order to point out the problems with such epistemological positions. In this context, we want to discuss the ways in which the postmodern Marxist position takes into account most of the problems afflicting different sides in the Indian modes of production debate. Thus our critique of empiricism and rationalism should be seen as a general critique of the epistemological positions taken in the Indian modes of production debate.

Empiricism—an epistemological standpoint—considers reality to be causally prior to theory. Under strict empiricism, reality is considered to be homologous to social totality, and it is assumed that the reality or social totality is singular, that is, there is only one discernible reality or social totality.[4] The social totality is knowable if one can find a correct theory that can reveal the true nature of the social totality. Thus, only one theory is ultimately capable of revealing, and hence knowing, the truth. Truth then is the representation of reality by theory where reality reveals itself through the neutral medium of sensory observation. The theory most successful in approximating reality, through this neutral medium, is the one capable of revealing the real truth. This is often called good, scientific theory where science refers to this problem of understanding and measuring material reality.

The important thing then is to define the theoretical space so that it conforms to the true reality in such a way that the empirical results will tell us whether capitalism exists or not. Many differences between Patnaik and Rudra involved the correct definition of capitalism because in their framework there is only one theory that could conform to the truth given by the empirical reality. This knowledge production in terms of "right" against "wrong" theory leads one from epistemological essentialism to theoretical essentialism in the sense that all other theories are excluded at the expense of one specific theory considered capable of revealing the truth. Keeping in line with historical materialism, these theorists reduce the concrete-real to that of the economic. The noneconomic aspects of society are only reflections of the economic aspects.[5] Therefore, to reveal the omnipotent economic is to reveal the concrete-real. This economic essentialism was the trademark of all those works that used empiricist procedures in the Indian modes of production debate.

Also, there is a major problem of reductionism involved with such empiricist procedures. By looking at what is called the "class character" of a few farms, these theorists announce the existence or nonexistence of capitalism in India. This is an extreme form of reductionism since it effaces all other sites from the social space, thereby reducing their unique existence to that of the few farms they are studying.[6] That is, the complex nature of society is reduced to a specified set of enterprises that are somehow assumed to represent the whole of society. This empiricist procedure was popular in the Indian modes of production debate and all such efforts face the problem we have just outlined for the case of Patnaik and Rudra.

More often, as will be seen later on, Indian Marxists used rationalist arguments and sometimes a combination of rationalist and empiricist arguments to bolster their analysis. *Rationalism*—another epistemological standpoint—inverts the causality of empiricism such that it is the theory that is causally prior and capable of expressing the reality. As in empiricism, reality is singular and taken as given. It is assumed that there exists an essence (core aspect) of reality, sometimes also called human reason or the rational element, that is unobservable and hence can only be captured by the correct theory. The essence forms the core around which social totality is constructed and to which all other aspects of society are reduced. The theory that is able to find the true essence of reality is the one most capable of revealing the truth. Under rationalism then theory determines and validates any facts. Facts contrary to the theory would be considered to be unimportant, misguided, or irrelevant. That is, true reality must mirror the correctly posited theory.

It is now a commonplace lemma that, in classical historical materialism, the forces of production are considered to be the rational element of history. However, in addition to that, the Indian orthodox Marxists also consider class (relations of production) to be an essential core of the reality. Along with the forces of production, class is taken to be the reason or the rational element, the hidden truth of the existing reality (true social totality). While the forces of production give an indication of the historical movement of society, class relations give an immediate explanation of the present configuration of relationships in society. Only a theory driven by class, which is produced in the context of its relationship to the forces of production, can correctly capture the phenomenal reality. In contrast to other theories, Marxist theory that considers class to be ontologically prior is the only universally true and scientific theory.

As in empiricism, under rationalism all other theories are excluded at the expense of one specific theory—the theory most capable of revealing the essence (core truth) in society. In other words, essentialism in epistemology is an essentialism of theory. Also, the rational elements—the forces of production or class or some combination of both—are aspects of economy, and such elements may also serve as causal economic essences whereby the social existence of other aspects of society are reduced (in terms of being causally explained) to the economic aspect. Rationalism is often tied closely to causal essentialism producing economic essentialism. Thus both rationalism and empiricism may produce economic essentialism.[7] The Indian modes of production debate is replete with economic essentialist arguments resulting from its epistemological standpoint of rationalism in addition to its empiricist procedure. Sometimes theorists would start from a rationalist argument but when faced with criticism of their choice of the rational elements would resort to empiricism. Thus both are used to bolster the theory. In this context, the most interesting work is that of Patnaik (1987), who criticizes the empiricist procedures of many Indian theorists (including many Marxists) as unacceptable while giving a privileged status to rationalist arguments. Yet after giving rationalism the privileged status, she goes back to empiricism to bolster the status of the rational element (class) she espouses in her framework. As she writes,

> Without the use of the only available scientific theory (meaning historical materialism) for studying historical transitions, we cannot . . . understand India's history. . . . By contrast, those who deny the applicability of Marxist theory to India, fail to provide themselves anything but empiricist description of existing aspects of reality. Empiricism is no substitute for theory; the minutest descriptions of aspects of reality, useful though they may be as description, tell us nothing about the immanent laws of motion of the economy. Further, even the very categories within which description is carried out, as we shall argue later, often [serve to obfuscate reality] because they enshrine an implicit theory which is [non-realistic]. . . . The scope of our present attempt at formulating and applying an empirical index for aggregating agricultural households into classes, related mainly to the question of the [descriptive depiction of existing class reality] in rural areas. (Patnaik 1987, 5–6)

In this passage, a complex interplay of rationalism and empiricism come to the forefront. Patnaik while criticizing empiricism does not back away from empiricist procedure. Rather, her point is that an empiricist procedure must conform to the true reality given by the class aspect (the rational element) in Marxist theory. Patnaik goes on to define class as an analytical concept and then uses empiricist procedure to describe the true class reality of India. This division between the analytical procedure and empiricist procedure produces an additional problem of reductionism about which we will express our disquiet while analyzing Patnaik's concept of class in the next chapter.

In general, the Indian mode of production debate was totally dominated by such empiricist and rationalist epistemological positions that produced an extreme form of economic essentialism and an ontologically pre-given privileged position to Marxist theory as opposed to other types of theories.

In contrast, the postmodern Marxist school builds on the criticism of essentialist epistemology by the postmodernist and poststructuralist theories. They also accept the position that there does not exist any intertheoretic standard of truth. Truth, and knowledge of reality are discursively produced, that is, produced from a particular standpoint via its complementary theory or discourse. However, they also significantly depart from the postmodernist and poststructuralist theories by refusing to abandon the concept of epistemology. The postmodernist and poststructuralist theorists have made a theoretical blunder by conflating epistemology and essentialism. Their critique of epistemology has failed to account for the fact that epistemology can also be nonessentialist, as the concept of overdetermination shows us. The strength of the postmodern Marxist theory lies in its ability simultaneously to posit closure and openness at the conceptual level: they are able to close the system (through entry point concept of class)—which most of the postmodernist and poststructuralist theories are unable to do—while maintaining the system as an open and contradictory play of differences (through the epistemological concept of overdetermination), which the orthodox Marxists involved in the Indian modes of production debate are unable to do. The nonessentialist epistemological concept of overdetermination and the entry point concept of class theoretically intersect, reinforce, and compensate for one another, thereby integrating closure and openness simultaneously within the framework.

The concept of overdetermination has enormous implications for resolving the problems of epistemological essentialism in Marxist theory. As we have already pointed out, essentialist epistemology produces not only a division of the empirical and theoretical but, given the division between the economic and noneconomic, may also produce economic essentialism. The concept of overdetermination resolves this autonomous and independent existence between the empirical and theoretical and that of the economic and noneconomic at one stroke, thereby undercutting the very basis of economic essentialism or, for that matter, any form of essentialism. The concept of overdetermination implies that the empirical is constituted by the theoretical and vice versa. The concrete-real is as much constituted by thought process as thought process by the concrete-real.[8] The same is true for the relation between the economic and noneconomic. These are distinct concepts but they are not independent or autonomous from one another. Our emphasis on class—a space carved out from the economic field—is a discursive emphasis and not an ontological one. As Resnick and Wolff point out, "The stress of Marxist theory upon economics in general, and upon class in particular, is a matter of its particular conceptual approach to social analysis. That approach should not and cannot be confused with the concrete knowledge it produces. Class has a role of conceptual priority in the former but not in the latter" (Resnick and Wolff 1987, 50). For the latter case, by the logic of overdetermination, class process is constituted (literally brought into existence) by nonclass processes (including noneconomic effects) and, hence, is not the essence of society. This breakdown of economic (class) essentialism along with the division between the empirical and the theoretical marks a complete departure from the methodological basis that guides the Indian modes of production debate.

Paresh Chattopadhyay versus Utsa Patnaik

Paresh Chattopadhyay brought the issue of Indian modes of production into the limelight. In his papers (1990a, 1990b), he concentrated his attack on Patnaik by pointing out the inadequacies of her definition of capitalism.

Chattopadhyay made two major criticisms of Patnaik's work. First, he charged that Patnaik got the definition of capitalism wrong. He defines capitalism or the capitalist mode of production as "the highest stage of commodity production where labor power itself becomes a commodity." The two conditions of capitalism are: (i) commodity production is the general form of production and (ii) production is performed by free wage labor. The generation of surplus value and its reinvestment follows as a logical corollary of this definition.

Patnaik (1978, 1990c) replied that the two conditions of capitalism may correspond to the Western European model but that the Indian reality makes it imperative to add the condition of reinvestment of surplus as a third condition. She observed that productive capital was absent in the sphere of agricultural production. Instead, money capital was being used for unproductive investments in trading, moneylending, and land purchasing. Given the precapitalist relations of production and the absence of alternative avenues of investment (due to the British policies), investment in trading, moneylending, and land purchasing was more profitable than investment in a surplus-value production process. Colonial exploitation through the revenue system and the pervasive presence of circulating capital prevented capitalism from growing in Indian agriculture. The pauperization and (partial) proletarianization via primitive capital accumulation through the British policies of land settlement had the purgatory effect of reinforcing precapitalist relations of production, thereby blocking the passage toward a capitalist revolution even though these policy measures led to the commercialization of Indian agriculture. Unlike in Western Europe, neither commodity production nor incipient capitalism grew organically out of the precapitalist modes. Therefore, since capitalism did not and cannot grow organically out of precapitalism, the criterion of accumulation and reinvestment of surplus value must be added in defining capitalism in

India. In such a scenario, the "destitute peasants-turned-laborers" or generalized commodity production cannot be a sufficient condition for defining capitalism in Indian agriculture.

Chattopadhyay (1990b) in his reply reiterated his earlier position and criticized Patnaik for mixing up definitions with empirical reality. He observed that one cannot have two nonequivalent definitions of capitalism, one for Western Europe and the other for India. Capitalism as a concept has only one specific, precise definition. It cannot be subjected to empirical variations. If one allows that to hold then we will have multiple definitions of capitalism depending upon different empirical realities in different places.

The second criticism directed against Patnaik by Chattopadhyay regarded her point that wage labor is not truly free since it is tied to agriculture and not to industry. This is an untenable Marxist position since the wage laborer could be tied to either agriculture or industry and yet be free in a double sense.[9] Marxist theory does not require wage labor to be tied to industry. It is the content of wage labor that matters and not its particular form of use.

Weaknesses in Chattopadhyay's Framework

While Chattopadhyay's critique of Patnaik was an important development in the debate, it was not without its own problems. The most important deficiency in his argument is the concept of capitalism. His definition of capitalism based on commodity exchange and production by wage labor has nothing to say about the processes related to surplus-labor generation. From a postmodern Marxist perspective, it is not the aspects of commodity production and wage labor but rather the processes of performance, appropriation, distribution, and receipt of surplus labor (the relations of exploitation) that is the focal point of organizing the Marxist concept of society. This difference is crucial as can be exemplified by the different ways, depending on the different focal points, in which the former Soviet Union can be differentiated. By Chattopadhyay's definition of capitalism, the Soviet Union was socialist but by the postmodern Marxist approach it was predominantly (state) capitalist (Resnick and Wolff 1993, 1994, 1995, 2001). By reducing capitalism to the two aspects, Chattopadhyay excludes the surplus labor effects on society (relations of exploitation) from his framework and, subsequently, ends up reducing their effects to that of the above-mentioned aspects.

In the Indian modes of production debate, the concept of social totality is exactly similar to that conceptualized in historical materialism: social totality is a complex whole of the economic, political, cultural, and social consciousness that is ultimately reduced to the economic aspect of modes of production. This centered social totality simplifies the complexities in society to core economic aspects such that the existence of the noneconomic aspects are explained away by the economic aspects of mode of production. As we have already indicated, this causal essentialism was heavily criticized by the postmodernist and poststructuralist theories and, subsequently, abandoned as a mode of explanation by the postmodern Marxist theory. The concept of overdetermination says that no aspect of society is ontologically prior to others and that social totality cannot be reduced to a single aspect. Furthermore, in the Indian modes of production debate, the economy is conceived to be uniformly given by the mode of production. Capitalist society, in its ideal form, entails that all sites of the economy accumulate capital. This aspect of uniformity is virtually impossible to hold at the micro-level sites of enterprises (both state and private) and households where class processes, which are uniquely constituted, differ from site to site.[10] This criticism of capitalism as a centered social totality (or any other such totality) driven by the mode of production on which all other aspects of society are dependent is true for all definitions of capitalism that were espoused in the Indian modes of production debate. The breakdown of economic uniformity means that the concept of mode of production collapses. And so does the orthodox Marxist concept of social totality defined in terms of mode of production. This collapse of the crucial concepts of social totality and mode of production causes unrecoverable damage to the orthodox concept of transition. In fact, without the use of these primitive concepts, the question of transition of Indian society as put forward in the Indian modes of production debate cannot even be posed.

Finally, Chattopadhyay includes free wage labor as a criterion for defining capitalism. This is an open and shut case for him: the capitalist class will employ wage labor while the working class will hire out their labor for a wage. However, the situation can be far more complicated. What if in addition to farming his land a small capitalist agricultural farmer also hires himself out to work in another capitalist farm? Here he may hold two class positions simultaneously—as a capitalist farmer expropriating the surplus labor of his workers and as a worker being exploited by another capitalist farmer. How then to account for the class position of the individual? These issues are not normally addressed in the literature, and when they are addressed the normal procedure, as we will explain in the treatment on class in part II, is to reduce the individual concerned to one class position.

Thus ended the first phase of the debate. The debaters were struggling to define capitalism and feudalism. The second phase of the debate opened with an article by Amit Bhaduri (1973), in which he called India's mode of production semifeudal. This article started a vigorous debate on the question of India's mode of production and divided the participants into three broad camps—the *semifeudalism school*, the *capitalist school*, and the *colonial mode of production school*. Among these three schools of thought, the colonial mode of production school failed to take off; consequently, we will ignore it.[11] Let us now review the debate between the semifeudal and capitalist schools, since that debate was by far the most important and intense.

Semifeudalism versus Capitalism

There is no doubt that the characterization of the Indian mode of production as semifeudal constituted a major position in the debate. The term "semifeudalism" was first coined by Bhaduri (1973), whose position was supported by economists like Prasad (1973, 1979, 1990), Chandra (1974, 1975a, 1975b, 1975c), Sen Gupta (1977) and Sau (1975, 1990). But it was Bhaduri (1973, 1977, 1979, 1981, 1983, 1986) who articulated the category of semifeudalism with sophistication and gave it the necessary theoretical punch. Consequently, we will concentrate on Bhaduri to present the arguments on semifeudalism.

The most severe critique of Bhaduri's position and that of the semifeudal school in general came from the "capitalist school" led by Bardhan (1980, 1982, 1984a, 1984b, 1986, 1989), Bardhan and Rudra (1978, 1980, 1981, 1986), Rudra (1984, 1990c), Griffin (1974), Ghosh and Saith (1976), Newbery (1975), and Srinivasan (1979). The debate that took place between the semifeudal school and the capitalist school around the term "semifeudalism" is arguably the most intense and furious that ever took place in the Indian Marxist academic circle.

Defining Capitalism and Semifeudalism

Bhaduri defines capitalism as the highest stage of commodity production where labor power itself becomes a commodity such that it can be bought and sold freely like any other commodity. Capitalism entails the existence of the free wage laborer who enters into a voluntary, impersonal exchange relationship with the capitalist. Alternatively, semifeudalism signifies a system where the market for labor power has not been fully developed—that is, wage labor, if it exists, is not free to be bought and sold like other commodities. Sau (1990), arguing along this line, asserts that such concepts as the capitalist farmer and capitalism are impossible without free wage laborers. Drawing a distinction between essence and appearance, he argued that even if wage labor in Indian agriculture exists significantly in quantitative terms on the surface or at the level of appearance, it is not free at the level of essence. According to him, Marx qualifies his definition of wage labor by pointing out that the basis for the process of capitalist accumulation lies in the "double freedom" of the wage laborer, since of that is a prerequisite for the creation of a capitalist labor market based on an impersonal, voluntary exchange relationship between the buyers and sellers of labor power. It was pointed out by proponents of semifeudalism that unequal exchange relationships around institutions such as usury and trading, sharecropping, and other precapitalist community relations continue to mediate and determine the ability of laborers to freely sell their labor power and buy commodities. According to the semifeudal school, these precapitalist relations do not allow labor power to be bought and sold freely.

Furthermore, it was pointed out that in precapitalist economic formations like that of India, not only was labor power not exchanged in a voluntary, impersonal manner but, in addition, the labor market was inadequately formed since a majority of agricultural producers who worked as laborers also owned land—that is, means of production. Hence both of Marx's conditions on the labor market (operating as the basis of capitalism) are violated. The capitalist form of wage labor—the appearance—is mediated by the precapitalist content—the essence. Indian agriculture is called semifeudal because of this noncorrespondence between the form and the content. As Bhaduri notes, "Such an agrarian economy (meaning India) is precapitalist in the sense that production is not organized on the basis of a contractual wage payment and a market for the exchange of labor power has not been adequately formed" (Bhaduri 1983, 17). The solution to the problem of creating capitalism in agriculture in India is to overcome all precapitalist elements (usury, sharecropping, and community relationships acting as barriers to capitalist development) that sustain the bondage of wage laborers, inhibit the creation of a capitalistic labor market, and perpetuate the backwardness of Indian agriculture.

A Critique of the Semifeudal Definition of Capitalism

The semifeudal school defines capitalism in terms of an exchange relationship—buying and selling of labor power—thereby reducing its class content to exchange. It then goes on to talk about "free" wage labor versus "unfree" wage labor at the level of exchange as the criterion for identifying capitalism. The criticism we made of Chattopadhyay's treatment of capitalism also applies here. First, the semifeudal school's definition of capitalism is wrong if one takes relations of exploitation as the constitutive factor in the definition of capitalism. In that case, the entire position of the semifeudal school that "capitalism" does not exist in India collapses. Second, as we pointed out, from a postmodern Marxist perspective, the concept of mode of production (society as a closed entity such as capitalism or feudalism) cannot be sustained. And since the concept of mode of production (capitalism, semifeudalism) is flawed, the question of whether India is semifeudal or capitalist is wrong to begin with. That is, the fundamental premise on which the semifeudal school asks and argues the question is faulty.

The Controversy over the Features of Semifeudalism

The main features of semifeudalism in Indian agriculture, according to Bhaduri are: (a) sharecropping, (b) perpetual backwardness of the small tenants, (c) prevalence of modes of exploitation through usury and land ownership by the same economic class, and (d) inability of the small peasants to enter the market as and when desired. These institutions (sharecropping, usury, trading, etc.) signify relations of production that act as a fetter to the development of modern and improved technology, that is, the forces of production. This produces agricultural stagnation and signifies a crisis in the mode of production that can be resolved only through a change in the relations of production. Unless these features of semifeudalism are obliterated, labor power cannot become free and agrarian capitalist development cannot take place.

What is the critical factor in the semifeudal relations of production? The critical factor is the parallel existence of exploitation through forced commerce based on usury and the landowners' traditional property right to land (which they lease out to sharecroppers), allowed for by the existing semifeudal relations of production. However, it is usury, or debt bondage as it is often called, that is driving the system in the semifeudal argument. Also, as we shall indicate later on, this concept of forced commerce driven by usury is critical for Bhaduri's theorization of primitive capital accumulation; forced commercialization becomes the historically specific form of the process of primitive capital accumulation in backward agriculture.

Consider a small peasant class and a moneylender-cum-merchant class.[12] The small peasants suffer from the inability to enter or exit the product market as and when they desire.

Typically, prices go down sharply just after a harvest but rise just before the harvest. The small peasants would gain if they could keep the product in storage and sell it at the end of the season. However, they are unable to do so because of the high storage and transport costs involved and the nature of unequal exchange that binds them to the landlord-cum-moneylender class. The unequal exchange relation is based on the social arrangement whereby immediately after the harvest, in order to meet their debt obligations from past years and other necessary cash requirements, the small peasants are forced to sell the produce at the most inopportune moment (that is, at the beginning of the year) and are unable to meet their consumption needs in the latter part of the year. During the last quarter of the year, when prices are very high, they end up taking consumption and other loans from the moneylender-cum-merchant class. This involuntary involvement in the market exemplified by the selling of products when prices are low and the buying of products when prices are high is what Bhaduri calls a system of forced commerce. This compulsion of forced commerce is based on consumption loans (merchant cum moneylender's capital).

The moneylender-cum-merchant class charges high rates of interest on consumption and other loans. Moreover, the moneylender fixes the time of repayment of debt at the beginning of the next harvest. The loans or debts could be of two types. The loans could be repaid by paying them off in cash, by selling the grain at the beginning of the harvest season, or by working for the landlord. In the former case, the repayment mechanism produces an extraction of surplus product in the market for food grains. As Bhaduri points out, "The distinguishing feature of this commercial exploitation is that 'unequal exchange' of paddy sold and bought under distress takes place directly in the 'product market,' i.e. in the market for food grains rather than in the labor market. In this sense, commercial exploitation stands in contrast to capitalist exploitation" (Bhaduri 1983, 19). This produces interlinkage between the credit and product markets.[13]

If the peasants work as contractual laborers in order to meet their subsistence needs, they will not be free.[14] They become tied to the landlord. This produces an interlinkage between the credit and labor markets. So the small peasantry and the wage laborers lack any free (in the sense of voluntary entry and exit to the market across time and space) access to the commodity market as sellers.

Often, the landlord, on top of advancing consumption loans, also leases out land and advances working capital to the sharecroppers at the beginning of the harvest season. Principally because of their extreme poverty, the sharecroppers as buyers and borrowers lack access to the modern capital market and have to depend on noninstitutional sources for credit. As the sharecropper's survival depends on such advancement, the landlord charges a sum as tribute or rent. The amount is so charged that at the beginning of the season, net income becomes less than zero.

The landlord class charges rates of interest and extorts tribute from sharecroppers not just with an eye for economic gains but to keep the sharecroppers permanently tied in a subordinate, unequal relation vis-à-vis the landlord class. The exchange relations between the sharecropper and the landlord or between the agricultural laborer and the landlord are involuntary and are not principally conditioned by economic criteria. The credit market, which is driving the interlocking nature of different involuntary transactions, does not operate by economic norms. The debt relation signifies extra-economic coercion that is the basis of feudal exploitation. This is also the basis for forced commercialization since sharecroppers no longer have the option to enter and exit the market as and when they like. They are tied to the product market in such a way that surplus could be extracted from it. The growing indebtedness over time only adds to the concretization of such a mode of interactions and relationships.

The attack of the capitalist school against the semifeudal school was led by Ashok Rudra and Pranab Bardhan. Rudra (1990c) points out that feudalism is essentially characterized by (i) extraeconomic coercion that ties together different classes and (ii) ownership of the means of resources by the tenant. According to this school, since (i) and (ii) are absent in Indian agriculture, India's mode of production cannot be termed as feudal or semifeudal. Institutions like usury or sharecropping are not by definition semifeudal and there is no one-to-one correspondence between these institutions and technological backwardness. Sharecropping or usury may very well adapt themselves to the capitalist mode of production, and they could be technologically enhancing. For relations of production derived from usury or sharecropping to be semifeudal, one needs to show that these relations are based on extraeconomic factors. According to the capitalist school, India's relations of production can be described on the basis of the economic. The economic decisions pertaining to the credit, landlease, labor, and product market are not based on extraeconomic characteristics but are a product of the voluntary, strategic behavior of agents.

Bardhan (1980, 1984a, 1989) and Rudra and Bardhan (1978, 1980, 1981) note that sharecropping is not a result of semifeudal relations of production based on some form of extraeconomic class exploitation but is governed by strategic decisions by both employers and employees. Similarly, the labor market is determined by strategic decisions on the part of both employer and employee. The crucial point is that these decisions are not made independently in each market. Rather, decisions in the labor market are tied to decisions in the credit market and decisions in the credit market are tied to decisions in the land-lease market.

Let us first look at the interlocking nature of the labor market and credit market as described by Rudra and Bardhan. A high percentage of laborers take consumption loans, and they are attached to the landlords (personalized relations), but this phenomenon is not characterized by extraeconomic coercion. The laborer, due to uncertainty of credit, employment, and wages, would prefer a long-term contract to ensure against these uncertainties. The landlord, on the other hand, needs a dependable and readily available labor supply. If the landlord personally knows the laborer then it reduces the search cost, monitoring cost, contract enforcement cost, and shirking. Both the landlord and the laborer have an incentive to enter into and abide by the contract since that insures them against the uncertainty of the future. These are strategic decisions that are (implicitly) contractually enforceable. This has nothing to do with extraeconomic coercion. However, there is a relation of economic dependence/domination since the bargaining power of the two sides is unequal. The landlord can always maintain control over the laborer and the labor process by (i) threatening to cut off the contract and (ii) dividing the workers by playing off attached workers against casual workers.

The relation between land-lease, labor, and credit markets (taking the form of sharecropping) is also based on strategic, voluntary decisions. Sharecropping tenancy is a partial response to the inadequacies or imperfections that exist in other markets. The landlord's cost of recruitment, monitoring, and supervision backed by the uncertainty of weather and the tenant's uncertainty regarding employment, wage rates, and consumption loans are all contributing factors to the existence and reproduction of the sharecropping institution. This is a contract that again insures against uncertainties on both sides and has nothing to do with extraeconomic coercion.

Bardhan and Rudra (1978, 1980, 1981) in a series of empirical papers found that though a high proportion of landlords were also moneylenders, moneylending was not the chief profession of the landlords. The landlords were actively involved with tenancy farming and often shared with the tenants the cost of production. They also found that often the landlords would give consumption loans to the tenants and permanent workers at very low rates of interest, sometimes even a zero rate of interest. Hence, usury is not the dominant mode of exploitation in rural India. The credit market, being a market relation, does not involve any extraeconomic coercion and the institution of usury is the site of contractual exchange between borrower (sharecropper or the laborer) and lender (the landlord-cum-moneylender) where each side makes a contractual agreement based on a need to insure oneself against the uncertainties noted above. Each individual makes rational decisions, maximizing his own preferences subject to constraints. There is no extraeconomic coercion involved here. However, economic power relations are embedded in this contractual agreement since the landlord clearly dominates the agricultural laborer or tenant; such economic dominance, however, is not peculiar to semifeudalism. Therefore, in sum, since usury per se does not play a dominant role in Indian agriculture and credit markets do not involve or lead to extraeconomic coercion, there is no reason to call India's mode of production semifeudal.

Bhaduri (1983, 1986) replies by noting that in their empirical findings, Bardhan and Rudra considered only the explicit rate of interest and not the implicit rate of interest. All the risk is transferred to the borrower that cannot be determined by the economic arrangement of demand and supply. The nature and significance of debt relations are crucially linked by their ability to produce forced commerce. The crucial point to understand is the "treatment of collaterals, i.e., securities, against which such loans are advanced" (Bhaduri 1986, 670). Credit markets do not operate via a voluntary exchange relationship between the borrowers and lenders. All the risks of the lenders are transferred to the borrowers, since, given the unavailability of loans from organized credit markets, the lender is in a position to substantially undervalue the collateral of the peasant. That is, the credit arrangement with borrowers taking all the risks is a product of extra-economic factors (unavailability of organized credit market, personal knowledge of the peasant's position, the peasant's previous debt position, etc.).

Forced Commercialization and Primitive Capital Accumulation

For Bhaduri, primitive capital accumulation is intrinsically linked to forced commerce and usury. In fact, as he writes, "forced commercialization in backward agriculture . . . becomes the historically specific form of the process of primitive accumulation, resulting in a process of alienation of land from the small peasantry. . . ." (Bhaduri 1983, 108). Forced commercialization leads to the economic subjugation of the small peasantry such that they become hopelessly tied to the landlord. As we have explained, this economic subjugation operates through the medium of usury. Debt bondage keeps the small peasantry under the control of the landlord. According to Bhaduri, such indebted peasants put up "extreme economic resistance" in their attempt to cling to their traditional methods of livelihood. Their resistance is, as Bhaduri put it, partly due to their deep psychological attachment to land and partly because of the limited alternative economic options available to them. However, after a certain period of time, the compulsion of debt reaches a point where this resistance by the peasant is broken and they have no option but to allow for the transfer their land to the landlord. It is in this sense that forced commerce merges with primitive capital accumulation resulting in the process of alienation of land from the small peasantry to the landlord.

According to Bhaduri, a crucial difference between his theory of primitive capital accumulation and the traditional theory of primitive capital accumulation is with respect to the mechanism that brings about the alienation of land. In the traditional theory, it is state coercion that makes the alienation of land possible, while, in his theory, it is the mechanism of forced commerce driven by usury that brings about the alienation of land. But the primitive capital accumulation is incomplete until its reverse face (as Bhaduri calls it)—normal capital accumulation (accumulation through productive capital investment)—takes place. In backward agriculture, it is not clear whether forced commerce or primitive capital accumulation will lead to normal capital accumulation. It might very well be the case that the new means of production appropriated by the landlord may not be utilized for productive use; in this case, the productive capacity of agriculture remains unchanged. On the other hand, they may be utilized for productive purposes leading to normal capital accumulation. "A continuous *interaction between that normal process of accumulation and forced commercialization remains a central mechanism in shaping the process of change in backward agriculture*" (Bhaduri 1983, 109). Bhaduri deploys a class analysis to reveal the different possibilities of such interaction and their implications in a backward agricultural country like that of India. We shall come back to this in the next chapter on class.

The capitalist school did not have much to say about Bhaduri's analysis of primitive capital accumulation, and one can understand why. Their basic criticism of Bhaduri is that there is no forced commercialization in India and, consequently, the issue of forced commerce as a historically specific case of primitive capital accumulation does not arise.

When it is raised, there are deep theoretical problems associated with the concept of primitive capital accumulation that are not confronted by theorists in the debate but which undermine and undercut many of the major positions about the process of transition that are espoused. Some problems are internally generated while others are related to the viability of the concept itself as seen from the postmodern Marxist perspective.

Critique

(1) In historical materialism, primitive capital accumulation is considered as a single submoment of history. Without primitive capital accumulation, there would be no movement toward capitalism. Describing primitive capital accumulation as a necessary, inevitable historical process within the narrative of historical materialism precludes any alternative route of historical evolution. This universalization of the transition process of society obliterates contexts and contingency from the social space. As we explained in the first chapter, this process of decontextualization and historicism, whereby primitive capital accumulation is assumed to hold under all circumstances, was heavily criticized by Marx (Marx 1983, 97–139) himself.

However, Marx did conceptualize primitive capital accumulation as part of the historical development of West European society. The context for him was to be found in the difference between the Western European development process and the non-Western development process. He did point out the contextual difference between the two but did not question the presence of historicism in the concept of primitive capital accumulation.

(2) This way of conceiving primitive capital accumulation as a submoment within a metanarrative description of the evolution of society cannot

be accommodated within a nonhistoricist and nonessentialist Marxian framework. We have explained why and how, within such a framework, both epistemological and causal essentialism are overthrown by the usage of the nonessentialist concept of overdetermination. Within that framework, a transition process cannot be a constitutive part of a historical process produced within a parable like that of historical materialism. The essentialist and historicist aspects associated with the concept of primitive capital accumulation—which are what gives the concept its bite and importance within the orthodox Marxist framework—makes the concept untenable and, consequently, it needs to be abandoned. Unlike in Marx, who contextualized Western Europe as against non–Western European countries, the level of contextualization in such a Marxist theory is deeper, that is, at the micro-level site of class processes. Any rethinking of the concept of primitive capital accumulation has to be posed in that context.

(3) The idea that primitive capital accumulation is the only condition for the creation of wage labor or labor power as a commodity is fundamentally wrong. By the logic of historical materialism, primitive capital accumulation emerges as a necessary and essentialist concept, because without it, it is supposed that wage labor will not come into being. The problem with such essentialism, which is embedded in the historicism guiding the model of historical materialism, is that other dimensions of the provenance of wage labor are ignored.

Orthodox Marxism has often been characterized by empiricism where one of the many forms in which it was practiced was to look at the data for wage labor and infer from the findings whether or not primitive capital accumulation has succeeded and consequently capitalism has been successfully established in a society. However, the problem is that the creation of wage labor does not necessarily imply a case of primitive capital accumulation. An individual may become a free wage laborer for a number of reasons. Consider a case of a not too rich capitalist farmer in India who produces crops seasonally. In the case of a one-crop production per year, there is, typically, a period of six months during which the farmer would be unemployed. Many such farmers migrate seasonally to work in the cities as wage laborers. The seasonal labor force that migrates to the cities forms a large proportion of the total labor force, especially in the informal sector. Such creation of wage labor involves no primitive capital accumulation and hence the historical origin of wage labor may be due to factors other than primitive capital accumulation. Empirically, it can be misleading simply to look at the increase in the number of wage laborers and infer that primitive capital accumulation has been completed. There is no necessary, one-to-one historical homology between primitive capital accumulation and the origin of wage laborers. This seriously undermines Marx's and the orthodox Marxist idea of primitive capital accumulation as the 'divine' spark of the historical origin of wage labor.

(4) For many Marxists, primitive capital accumulation leads to the destruction of community relationships to which precapitalist direct producers are closely bound. This may very well happen: the state could uproot and dismantle an entire community, including people's property. But to infer a general and necessary relation between destruction of community and primitive capital accumulation is a fundamental error, because these theorists do not make any distinction between community relationships and property relationships. They assume that destroying the precapitalist property relations via primitive capital accumulation automatically leads to the destruction of community relationships. There is a leap in this argument that is unsubstantiated since there is no explanation of the process or mechanism through which the destruction of property relations is supposed to lead to a destruction of community relations in general. Freedom to be a wage laborer and freedom from any ownership or possession of means of production do not imply that an individual is free from community at all levels. Freedom from community, through primitive capital accumulation, is a limited freedom—limited to the aspect of the disappearance of property ownership of a mass of direct producers combined with their newly acquired ability to sell labor power through voluntary exchange. It affects that part of the community that is held together by the aspect of property. It may very well happen that, under certain favorable circumstances and with additional reasons, the expropriation of property may obliterate communities but to reduce the (meaning of) community to simply the aspect of property is an example of a type of economic reductionism that obliterates from the social space all other economic and noneconomic aspects that make up a community. We will discuss this point further in the chapter on the subaltern studies, where this conflation will be shown to be more pronounced, especially in the work of Partha Chatterjee.

The Debate on Agricultural Stagnation

The question that remains to be resolved is why the landlord doesn't adopt modern, productivity-enhancing technology. The answer is to be found by looking at the gain and loss of the landlord class both economically and in terms of the sociopolitical power vis-à-vis the sharecropper. Landlords will be discouraged from adopting new technology if their incomes are reduced or their socioeconomic power declines. The socioeconomic power is assumed to decline if the sharecropper can move out of debt bondage.

The results of the models proposed by Bhaduri crucially hinge on the assumption that interest rates and the sharecropping ratio are exogenously given and the assumption that tenants will reduce borrowing as their income increases. As we shall soon indicate, these assumptions became the object of fierce criticism. According to Bhaduri, given these assumptions, the sharecropper moves out of perpetual indebtedness as a result of the adoption of new technology if his net income increases. This will clearly not be in the interest of the moneylender-cum-landlord class, for it will lead to a weakening of the system of semifeudalism. On the other hand, the landlords will be discouraged from adopting new technology if their net income declines. It is not economically advisable on the landlord's part to increase production if the adoption of new technology simultaneously increases the income of the sharecropper and makes him less dependent on loans from the landlord, leading to a fall in the landlord's income from usury—sometimes so much so that his total net income falls. Thus, usury becomes an obstacle to technological development. Its existence requires that the semifeudal relations of production be torn asunder and new relations of production develop conducive to the growth of the forces of production. Decline of the institution of usury, sharecropping, as well as decline in the power of the moneylender-cum-merchant class, and other socioeconomically powerful classes, must happen. According to the semifeudal school, such a phenomenon—a movement toward capitalist agriculture—did occur in northern Indian states like the Punjab and Haryana but most of the other regions in India could not satisfy those conditions and remain semifeudal.[15]

There are two major critiques of Bhaduri's position on usury perpetuating agricultural stagnation. The first was put forward by Srinivasan. Srinivasan (1979) argued that it is improper to consider borrowing as an inferior good. In Bhaduri, when the tenant's net income increases as a result of adopting a technological innovation, the tenant will reduce borrowing in the next stage. If this holds repeatedly over time, then in the limiting case, borrowing will become zero. Bhaduri's result crucially hinges on this assumption (borrowing as an inferior good). Srinivasan considers a model of a rational peasant maximizing discounted utility over an infinite time horizon and shows that at a constant rate of time preference and a constant interest rate, borrowing cannot be an inferior good. When the rate of time preference exceeds the interest rate, borrowing would in fact increase with increasing output. So technological improvement will not necessarily lead to a fall in the interest component of income of the landlord. The possibility of increased borrowing with increasing output as a result of adopting new technology creates a major problem for Bhaduri's claim that usury is the driving mechanism of agrarian stagnation and, hence, semifeudalism.

In his reply Bhaduri (1979) expressed skepticism over Srinivasan's depiction of reality. He argued that he was right to consider consumption loans an inferior good since "consumption loans obtained by poor peasants at high interest rates against undervalued collateral transfers the risk of capital loss *to the borrower* in case of default" (Bhaduri 1979). So as peasants become better off, they will not take the risk of borrowing. Only the poor peasants borrow for consumption purposes. Bhaduri claims that his assumption better represents the reality of Indian agrarian society.

The second critique was initiated by Keith Griffin (1974) and was reproduced by Newbery (1975), Ghosh and Saith (1976), and Bardhan (1980, 1984a). The basic argument is that the assumptions of the interest rate and the sharecropping ratios as being exogenously given are not consistent with the socioeconomic climate as depicted by Bhaduri. Given the disproportionate amount of power that the landlord is allowed to wield, there is nothing that prevents the ruling coterie from going for technological innovation, thereby increasing their output and income as well as keeping the tenants to their subsistence levels by changing the sharecropping ratio or the interest rate in the landlord's favor. For example, if the landlord's income from interest declines as a result of less borrowing by the tenants, the landlords can manipulate the sharecropping ratio to maintain the old income level of the sharecropper, thus successfully keeping the latter in poverty and dependence. The onus is on Bhaduri and the semifeudal school to explain why, given the socioeconomic environment they envisage, the landlord should not use the instruments (sharecropping ratio, rate of interest) available to keep the subsistence level of the tenants at the old level and innovate with new technology to increase output. That is, they must answer the question of why usury is inconsistent with technological innovation.

Bhaduri (1986) considers the above critique as referring to descriptive inaccuracies and not methodological shortcomings. According to Bhaduri, one needs to look at the effects produced by "convention" on the constitution of the rental share. In other words, the rental share might not be totally economically determined. The point is to realize that the power of the landlord may be conditioned by the noneconomic principles that guide the moral boundary of the villages (meaning traditional culture and custom) and that such variables may lie "outside the control of the exploiting class" (Bhaduri 1986, 270). One can use Rudra's analysis of power in Bhaduri's defense where Rudra argues that there are different types of power in a village society, one of which is the ideological force that is "part and parcel of a culture and tradition which operates at a much higher level than the village" (Rudra 1984, 253). Both the landlord and the laborers are bound by this level of power. Not even the seemingly all-powerful landlord has the moral sanction to completely transcend the norms and customs thus set in place.

According to Bhaduri, much of the debate on semifeudalism produced more heat than light because his critics were using a different methodological framework than he was. Bhaduri's point is that his critics are formulating the Indian scenario from a nonhistorical, neoclassical framework of supply and demand, using a utility maximization model of agents to set up the problems and viewing the efficiency criteria as a means to define "market." This is true even of some of his Marxist critics, such as Bardhan, who explicitly prefers a neoclassical framework to a model based on class in order to answer Marxist questions regarding the historical evolution of society. Bhaduri, on the other hand, claims to be looking at the Indian scenario from a class perspective, and his central objective is to identify the modes of exploitation that condition Indian agrarian society. He avers that in his model price-quantity adjusts without any relation to excess supply or excess demand. It doesn't reflect neoclassical market criteria:

> The function of exchange is not to "clear" the market in some cases, but simply to give advantage to one party at the cost of another. Exchange relations, under these circumstances, are better understood as a mechanism for surplus extraction. Consequently, the "market mechanism" is also better understood not in terms of its allocative efficiency but as the mechanism for extraction of surplus by one class from another. Under such forced commerce, exchange relations may be "efficient" from the point of view of the surplus extracting class, quite irrespective of whether or not they satisfy the neoclassical postulates of allocative efficiency. To understand certain types of economic institutions and arrangements in terms of their [class efficiency] for extracting surplus has been the main purpose of our inquiry into backward agriculture. Not surprisingly, neoclassical economics with its heavy emphasis on considerations of allocative efficiency has been mostly irrelevant and, at times misleading, for analyzing this range of issues. (Bhaduri 1986, 268)

Despite Bhaduri's spirited defense, it seems to us that Bhaduri is on weak ground. This is especially true regarding criticism from Griffin, who uses the specification of Bhaduri's model to show that there is no reason why the sharecropping ratio or the interest rate cannot be manipulated in the landlord's favor. This is an extremely powerful critique, as it completely undercuts the semifeudal position that usury is incompatible with the development of the forces of production. Bhaduri's reply in terms of the moral boundary of the village is not well explained, since such forms of social relationship are not specified in his model. Furthermore, even if Bhaduri's point were true, the landlord could still change the tenurial arrangement, switching from sharecropping either to farming with hired labor or renting out land at a fixed rent, thereby bypassing the boundary of moral sanctions that Bhaduri invoked in his defense.

In addition to the above criticism, Bhaduri's theory of class analysis and modes of exploitation are questionable. As we pointed out earlier, Bhaduri and the semifeudal school do not consider class in terms of processes relating to the performance, appropriation, distribution, and receipt of surplus labor; rather, class and modes of exploitation are explicitly reduced to exchange relationships. For Bhaduri, surplus extraction is an exchange phenomenon that takes place in the product market through the operation of usury, but this clearly conflates the production aspect of surplus labor extraction with the circulation aspect of redistribution of that surplus. This results in a displacement of aspects of class processes from the production sphere to the circulation sphere. We will expand further on this point when we explicitly deal with Bhaduri's analysis of class in the next chapter.

Finally, in general, the Indian modes of production debate crudely differentiated between agriculture and industry by concentrating solely on the former as the determinant of the nature of the mode of production. This emphasis is made since most of the people of India live in villages, and thus it is assumed that it is reasonable to analyze Indian agriculture to determine the character of the Indian modes of production (that is, of Indian society as a whole). This is a very simplifying assumption that has the deleterious effect of totally effacing millions of sites of the capitalist and other noncapitalist class processes in the cities from the social space even when a claim is made on the nature of mode of production of India in its entirety. If such sites of production are taken into account, under what criterion can Bhaduri call the Indian mode of production semifeudal? There is no reason to believe that enterprises in the cities, as in the agricultural sector, cannot be disaggregated to different types of class processes. In that case, the relations of production construed in terms of class processes cannot be uniformly identified with any particular type of class process like the capitalist or feudal class process. If that is true then Indian society may be characterized by a configuration of capitalist and noncapitalist class processes, leaving no basis for even initiating the debate about whether the Indian mode of production is uniformly capitalist or feudal or colonial. In other words, the central question regarding the character of the Indian modes of production becomes, then, a nonquestion.

The exclusion of the household is also striking. It is now a well-established position among many Marxists that households are sites of a surplus generation process and that most of the household enterprises are noncapitalist in character (Fox 1980, Barrett 1988, Fraad, Resnick, and Wolff 1994). To ignore millions of sites of such noncapitalist class processes is bound to weaken any analysis of the social totality. The characterization of the Indian modes of production as "capitalist" immediately collapses with the inclusion of household class processes. The same is true for the "semi-feudal" characterization of the Indian modes of production debate since the household class process could be independent or communal. Since the household economy contains such a diverse group of class processes, making it impossible to consider the economy as uniform, the exclusion of households in this analysis complements and reinforces our concern over the basis for posing the question regarding the character of the Indian modes of production.

Conclusion

Thus ended the first stage of the debate. With the intensity of the debate around "semifeudalism" slowing down by the early 1980s, there was a growing dissatisfaction among many participants over the direction of the debate and whether anything substantial was being achieved by taking this route (Patnaik 1990e). The stage was set for a switch in emphasis—an explicit analysis of class in the context of India—to which we turn in the next chapter.

CHAPTER 3

Class and the Question of Transition

Redrawing the Contour of Marxism in India

Many of the participants in the Indian modes of production debate realized that nothing substantial was being gained in terms of explaining the transition process by simply referring to some broadly defined institutions or social arrangements as "semifeudal" or "capitalist." They felt a need to explain the particular configuration of class relationships that were inhibiting the development of the forces of production and the capitalist mode of production as a whole. The debate consequently shifted to the concepts of class, class formation, and the effects of class differentiation on the Indian economy, especially the class effects produced by the transition of Indian society from one mode of production to another. In our analysis, we will consider three attempts made variously by Patnaik, Bhaduri, and Rudra because (i) they are by far the most important positions on class developed so far by Indian Marxists in the debate and (ii) their concept of class takes into account most of the concerns regarding the theorization of class that was put forward by other traditional Indian Marxists. In short, they represent the most comprehensive attempts to theorize class in India's context.

While the three attempts differ in many aspects, they are united in their emphasis on the concept of class as a homogeneous group of conscious people who are capable of formulating and executing decisions, class as the true causal essence of society, the division between class in itself and class for itself, and the definition of class as based either on power or property relations. Our review of their class analysis will be followed by a detailed critique.

Patnaik's Concept of Class And the Effect of Class Differentiation on the Transition Process

There are three central features of Patnaik's concept of class:

1. For Patnaik, the concept of class is a means to distinguish one individual from another. Criticizing those who adhere to the view that an individual can hold multiple class positions, she points out that, "One cannot get further from the Marxist concept of class, where each individual belongs to one, and only one class (incidentally what would be the point of a 'classification' at all if actual individuals cannot be assigned each to one class?)" (Patnaik 1987, 8). She uses a set of criteria to divide individuals into homogeneous groups of actors that she calls classes.

2. Her object is to show the process of class differentiation for the case of India because, according to her, that will reveal the true essence of society's conflict and the possibility of transition to a capitalist society. The economic relations of production from which class is derived is the true essence of society and all other phenomena must be explained in terms of the economic in order to reveal the actual nature of society. All other explanations of the "reality" of society are spurious. She takes the example of caste and argues that noneconomic explanations of the caste phenomenon in India do not reflect the truth about Indian society. Caste phenomena must be explained in terms of the economic and, more specifically, in terms of the concept of class. This is in line with the orthodox Marxian argument that the cultural and the political are surface phenomena reflecting the essence of the society, which is the economic. This economic essentialism is not only adhered to by Patnaik but, as we will argue, other Marxists such as Bhaduri and Rudra also build their concept of class on such a presumption. For these theorists, the process of class differentiation reveals the true source of conflict in India, bringing into the open the antagonistic relationship of classes.

3. The third characteristic of Patnaik's concept of class concerns the division between the empirical and the theoretical. This requires an understanding of what she means by class. Using Lenin and Mao's analysis of the agrarian society in China and Russia, Patnaik posited five classes:

(i) *Landlords*: The landlords cultivate land by employing labor power without using their own manual labor. They produce largely for the market, that is, they are net sellers of product.

(ii) *Rich peasants*: The rich peasants are similar to the landlord with the difference that they do manual labor in the field.

(iii) *Middle peasants*: self-sufficient (subsistence) farmers who neither hire labor nor hire themselves out for wages.

(iv) *Poor peasants*: those who cultivate their own land but also hire themselves out as wage laborers.

(v) *Agricultural laborers*: those who work solely as wage laborers.

Further, there are *three criteria* that are used to demarcate the agrarian population into the five classes:

(a) exploitation of labor criterion (who is the buyer and seller of labor power).

(b) possession of the means of production, especially cultivated land (those who own or possess significant land will dominate and exploit those who either possess insignificant land or no land at all).

(c) marketable surplus of the product (who are the net sellers of the product and who are net buyers).

According to Patnaik, the analytical content of class is determined by these criteria and it is wrong to reduce the content of class to any one of them (Patnaik 1987, 32).[1] However, in a curious move, after having spelled out the content of the rational element of class, she reduces class to the labor exploitation criterion with the obvious effect that, as summarized in her own words, "to take out one criterion in isolation from the rest undoubtedly represents *reductionism* of a complex concept to a simpler one" (1987, 50). She performs this reductionism "in order to make use of the concept of class in actual *empirical* analysis" (1987, 50) where, "a certain degree of reductionism seems unavoidable, at least in arriving at the first-stage classification . . . we develop an empirical index to capture the class status of individual households, as a first approximation" (1987, 50). Having demarcated between the theoretical and empirical by reducing the analytical content of class to what she calls the "most important single aspect of the concept of social class"—the labor exploitation criterion—where the term "most important" refers to the closest approximation to reality, she captures the labor exploitation criterion by a labor exploitation ratio, E.[2] As she points out, "It must be stressed that the E ratio has been formulated as an empirical, and therefore descriptive, *approximation* to the analytical concept of economic class" (Patnaik 1990d, 200). In Chapter two, we explained our disquiet over the usage of such rationalist and empiricist procedures of analysis.[3] Later on, we will also comment on a troubling contradiction in Patnaik produced by the above bifurcated empirical and theoretical meanings of class.

Patnaik's innovation, complementary to Lenin and Mao's contribution to the study of the peasantry, was to bring in the concept of leasing out and leasing in of land (tenancy) to further differentiate the five classes. Thus landlords were divided into two classes: capitalist landlords ($a > b$, labor hiring greater than rent) and feudal landlords ($a \leq b$, labor hiring at most as high as rent). Similarly, rich peasants were differentiated into a proto-bourgeois and a proto-feudal class depending upon whether labor hiring is greater than or less than rent (that is, $a > b$ or $a \leq b$). Also, the poor peasants were differentiated into agricultural laborers with land whose hiring out is greater than rent ($|a| > |b|$) and petty tenants whose rent is at least as high as hiring out ($|a| \leq |b|$).[4] Patnaik ignored the trader and moneylender class because they represent capital in the circulation process and are considered to be secondary to direct production relations in explaining exploitation. It should be noted that capitalist exploitation is not predicated on processes related to performance, appropriation, distribution, and receipt of surplus labor but to the phenomenon of hiring in and hiring out at the level of exchange. The objective is to identify individuals who hire in (exploiters) and hire out (exploited).

Patnaik's analysis of the Indian class structure revealed that there are high levels of precapitalist ground rent and that is impeding technological innovation and progress of capitalist development in agriculture. The reason for the high levels of absolute ground rent and India's stagnation of capitalist development is the large scale presence of small-scale petty producers creating barriers to output expansion through productive (capitalist) investment. According to her, a comprehensive land reform program that will redistribute land from the landlords (who lease out land to these small-scale peasants) to the small farming peasantry, tenants, and landless laborers is a necessary condition for a successful transition to capitalism.

Bhaduri's Concept of Class and the Effect of Class Differentiation on the Transition Process

Bhaduri (1981, 1983) reduces the definition of class to the ownership of the means of production. Those who own the means of production have more power over those who do not own the means of production. Exploitation, as the expropriation of surplus, is then reduced to power and the ownership structure. Bhaduri insists that,

> For surplus arises from "unequal exchange" of labor power as a commodity, which in turn is made possible by the nature of control

that capitalists exercise over the labor process. Being separated from the means of production, labor power has to be surrendered at a price or wage rate below the productivity of labor. "Unequal exchange" then emerges as the source of profits, only because there is class control over the means of production. . . . It is this question (question of source of profit) which cannot be answered without focusing on the economic power bestowed on the capitalists through their class monopoly in the ownership of the means of production. Herein lies the real significance of the classical view of profit as surplus. (1983, 4)

Capitalist exploitation occurs because of the unequal exchange of labor power that arises due to the contrasting economic power of the buyer and seller of the commodity, which in turn is based on an unequal ownership structure. The ownership structure is the essence of the economic structure and of society in general. However, Bhaduri points out that since the capitalist labor market does not exist—that is, the labor power cannot be exchanged freely—capitalist exploitation (exploitation through hiring in and hiring out of labor power) in the Marxian sense is not applicable to a backward economy. Exploitation is understood not as an appropriation of surplus labor in production but rather as an appropriation of surplus product in exchange. Unequal exchange is displaced from the labor market to the product market. We have already shown how this exploitation takes the form of forced commerce driven by usury. However, the logic of exploitation as described in the quotation still holds: exploitation in a backward economy arises in the sphere of exchange due to contrasting economic power which in turn is based on the underlying ownership structure.[5]

If the ownership structure is the essence of class in Bhaduri, then class relations are the essence of understanding any change in society. "A process of agrarian change is sustainable only when it is compatible with evolution in the underlying relations among the classes. Agrarian change in a historical perspective is therefore essentially a process of formation of new classes and changing class configuration" (1983, 127). Thus, like Patnaik, Bhaduri considers the process of development of class relations as the key to understanding changes in society.

Classes in India and the Process of Class Differentiation on the Transition Process

Bhaduri's concept of class gives rise to four classes: agricultural capitalists, the moneylending and merchant class, small peasantry, and agricultural laborers.[6] The ruling classes in India are the agricultural capitalists, the moneylenders, and merchants, while the exploited and oppressed classes are those of the agricultural laborers and small peasantry. Bhaduri argues that the northwestern region of India is dominated by capitalism. There, agricultural capitalists are the major ruling class and the class of money-lender and merchant is either weak/secondary or extinct. The eastern part of India is dominated by forced commerce where the class of moneylender and merchants is the ruling class while the agricultural capitalist class is weak, of secondary importance or extinct. Such class relations constitute the semifeudal mode of production. In Bhaduri's class analysis, the rela-tion between the two ruling classes—agricultural capitalist and money-lending and merchant capitalist—are antagonistic. He assumes that the class of agricultural capitalists is associated with productive investment that leads to normal accumulation, by which he means increases in the level of output.[7] The class of merchants and moneylenders is associated with unproductive investment that leads to forced commerce, and hence stagnating agricultural growth.[8] The mode of appropriation of surplus is through forced commerce, and its medium is consumption debt (unpro-ductive investment). In backward agriculture, unproductive investment, which takes the form of consumption loans to poor peasants, is inimical to rising agricultural growth and its purpose is to strengthen the grip of forced commerce and intensify the level of semifeudal surplus extraction from the peasants. Thus two types of income relating to productive and unproductive investment accrue to the two types of investors.

The crucial point in Bhaduri's framework is the relationship between the two ruling classes. Their relationship can take three forms:

Case I. The relationship between productive and unproductive investment is that of strict complementarity. That is, investment by a class of agricul-tural capitalists helps to strengthen forced commerce and vice versa. There is a possibility of class alliance in this case.

Case II. The relationship between productive and unproductive invest-ment is that of strict competitiveness. Here, productive investment weakens the grip of forced commerce and vice versa. This signifies a contradictory and antagonistic relation between the two classes with the possibility of ex-tinction of one class. Such relationships hold out possibilities for the quick transition from one mode of production to another.

Case III. The relation between productive and unproductive investment is part complementary and part competitive. There are two subcases:
C.I. Forced commerce helps in the expansion of production and normal accumulation while normal accumulation creates barriers to the develop-ment of forced commerce. Here, forced commerce is an independent en-

tity. It can exist without any help from other entities. However, normal accumulation depends on forced commerce. Thus, its existence is parasitic. Furthermore, this parasitic existence of normal accumulation is harmful for forced commerce tending to create barriers for forced commerce by reducing their accrual of income. Since the economic power of agricultural capitalists is feeble compared to that of moneylenders and merchants, the former makes economic concessions to the latter by keeping its productive investment low vis-à-vis unproductive investment.

C.II. Normal accumulation helps in the development of forced commerce while forced commerce hinders normal accumulation. Here, forced commerce is the harmful parasite gaining from normal accumulation but harming it in return. In order to exist, the class of moneylender and merchants makes an economic concession to the class of agricultural capitalists by keeping its unproductive investment at a low level.

In northern India, either C.II or Case II holds. In the first case, the moneylender/merchant class is the "harmful" parasitic class; in the second case, that class becomes extinct. In both cases, the ratio of productive to unproductive investment is either high (C.II) or rising (Case II). This results in a high growth and dynamic capitalist economy.

Under semifeudalism, as in eastern India, either C.I or Case II holds. In the first case, the agricultural capitalist class is the harmful parasitic class, while in the second case that class becomes extinct. For both cases, the ratio of productive to unproductive investment is either low (C.II) or decreasing (Case II). This results in strengthening the grip of forced commerce and intensifying the stagnation and backwardness of the economy.[9]

Bhaduri points out that agrarian reform should concentrate on transforming the semifeudal class relations such that the contradiction between the two ruling classes is settled at the expense of the moneylender and merchant class. The semifeudal class—merchant and moneylending class—must be made extinct. Also, reforms of rural credit, subsidies, and marketing should be directed to make the initial productive investment substantially high. This maintenance of a high level of productive investment vis-à-vis unproductive investment is critical for setting free the forces of production and producing a capitalist transformation of the stagnant semifeudal society. These two aspects—extinction of the semifeudal class and high productive investment—should be the task of state reform and revolutionary politics of the Left.

There are many problems in Bhaduri's notion of class. Firstly, in his framework, the class of small peasantry and the class of agricultural laborers are only needed so that the scope of the operation of the two ruling classes can remain wide. Especially, he needs a large number of small peasants for forced commerce to operate. However, given these classes, the movement of the economy toward normal accumulation or forced commerce will depend on the economic power (which in turn is given by the ownership structure) that the ruling class wields. The class of small peasants and agricultural laborers are affected by the changing pattern of investment without affecting them at all. Thus the fate of the economy depends on the relation between the two ruling classes while the actions of oppressed classes are taken as given and passive. The implicit presumption is that the ruling classes can form into a class for itself while the ruled classes have no possibility of transforming themselves from a class in itself to a class for itself. Hence, the latter can play no active role in the transition process. The role of the state and the politics of the Left should consequently be geared toward intervening at the nodal points in the antagonistic relations between the two classes to turn the tide of history in favor of capitalism. This image of the hapless small peasant and agricultural laborer at the mercy of the ruling class, unable to act on their own and waiting to be rescued by the Left (Communist) forces reflects the deeply ingrained mistrust and doubt about the "peasant class" among orthodox Marxists.

Also in Bhaduri, the ownership structure drives the dynamics of the economy and society. The crucial point for Bhaduri is that the moneylender-cum-merchant class embodies unproductive investment (based on a semifeudal ownership structure) and is responsible for the stagnation of the Indian economy. The critics of Bhaduri attacked him on this point. Some showed that the moneylender and merchant class might not carry out only unproductive investment (Bardhan and Rudra 1978, 1980, 1981), while others showed that the moneylender and merchant class' power is overemphasized (Griffin 1974). Along this line, some made the argument that there is an alliance between the two classes in India, that is, an objective condition for Case I to hold. The two classes are not necessarily antagonistic. Forced commerce can very well adjust itself to capitalist agriculture (Bardhan and Rudra 1978, 1980, 1981; Rudra 1988).

Rudra's Theory of Class and Its Role in the Transition Period

Rudra (1988) criticized what he called "the received theory of class" by pointing out that it is not applicable for the case of India. According to him, the problem with the Indian modes of production debate is that the theorists took as given what he perceived as a "Eurocentric" definition of class and went on to analyze whether the Indian mode of production is capitalist, feudal or colonial. Class analysis specific to India's context was generally ignored. In contrast, Rudra's goal is to produce a definition of class in the Indian context.

Rudra defines class as a "set of individuals" who have "similar relations with the means of production (owners of means of production and users of means of production, etc.) and who are such that they have no "contradictions" among themselves but who have "contradictions" with members of other classes" (1988, 485). There are three important characteristics of this concept of class:

(i)   Class as an identity is a subject, representing a group of individual members of society with certain homogeneous characteristics. Different classes indicate opposed relations between groups of people and class struggle is a struggle between such groups.

(ii) Class is defined with respect to the criterion of ownership of the means of production. Those who own and possess the means of production belong to one class and those who do not belong to another class. However, there is something more attached to the ownership criterion. That something is power that represents relations of domination and dependence. Those who own or possess means of production must have the power to dominate, not just at the point of production, but at every level of society. Power is predicated on ownership of the means of production. That is, one cannot exercise power without owning means of production, but it is also the case that those who own the means of production cannot always exercise power. If somebody who owns the means of production does not have the power to dominate rural society, then he or she does not belong to the ruling class.

(iii) Class conflict or division between classes is intrinsically related to the concept of contradiction. By class contradiction, Rudra means the conflict of economic interest between members of different classes; conflict that is structural in origin, historical in dimension, and potentially antagonistic.[10] Not every conflict of economic interest implies contradiction. For example, a conflict of economic interest between members of the same class (interclass conflict) may not lead to contradiction or may be insignificant. According to Rudra, even if such interclass conflict is based on contradiction, it is unimportant so far as historical change is concerned. Therefore, (a) not every conflict of economic interest implies contradiction and class conflict, (b) some contradictions are important while others are not, and (c) class contradictions imply that interclass conflict is more important than intraclass conflict of economic interest.

Three results follow from the above analysis. First, not all social groups constitute a class. In order to constitute a class, a social group has to satisfy all aspects of points (i) to (iii). Second, many individuals in society may not belong to any class. Thus, in a society there are class individuals and there are nonclass individuals. Third, the essence of the concept of class is an economic concept based on ownership criteria. The ownership criterion produces the relationship of dominance and dependence, and it is also the structural root of the conflict of interest that produces contradiction. While class conflict refers to conflict permeating the whole of society between groups with contradictory interests, its origin is economic in character. Therefore, economic essentialism grounds the concept of class and class conflict in Rudra. Class, defined in terms of the performance, appropriation, distribution, and receipt of surplus labor, is subsumed in Rudra's definition of class and almost no mention is made of it.

Classes in India and their Role in the Transition of Indian Society

Rudra, applying his theory of class, observes that there are only two classes in India. The ruling class is the class of big landowners while the oppressed class is the class of agricultural laborers. A third class, the middle class, may conceptually exist but is insignificant in numbers in India and is ignored by Rudra.

The class of big landowners includes "all those members of the ruling society who derive a certain economic and social power from the ownership of relatively large quantities of land with the help of which they dominate the rural society" (1988, 492). The important point to note is that no distinction is made between feudal landowners, capitalist landowners, and rich peasants, since no contradictions exist between these groups of people.[11] Together, they form a single class—the class of big landowners.

Individuals of this class can be engaged in many different activities. Their different exploitative occupations include cultivation with the help of hired labor, leasing out land to tenants, usury, trading, and so on. Thus, an individual may be a farmer, moneylender, and trader simultaneously. Another individual may be just a moneylender. These are all noncontradictory occupations and individuals may occupy such different occupations without any (antagonistic) conflict of economic interest. The economic interest that is based on the ownership structure is assumed to be given and flowing from it. Individuals with these different occupations have the same economic interest. Any intraclass conflicts that may exist are insignificant while their relation to other classes (interclass conflict of economic interest) is significantly antagonistic.

The other class, the oppressed class, is that of agricultural laborers, which includes:

(i)   Landless laborers who sell labor power to meet their subsistence requirements.
(ii) Landed laborers, that is, those who might possess small amounts of land that they cultivate without any significant amount of hired labor.

This class encompasses landless laborers, poor peasants, and tenants who do not hire any laborers to any significant degree. They are all united by the fact of being dominated by the ruling class of big landowners.

The rest of the agricultural population are not considered to be members of a class. Either they are too weak to dominate or their power arises from structures other than the ownership structure. Any contradiction within such residual groups or between such groups and the two classes is diffused, blunted, and secondary and does not play any role in bringing about change in society.

The main contradiction is between the two contending classes, which, while founded in the economic structure, percolate through relations of dependence and domination to all aspects of society. The development of the forces of production will intensify the contradiction between the two classes leading finally to a change in agrarian social structure.

In India, the contradiction between the two classes operates in particular settings. Power relations operate in the space where each village unit is an isolated unit. Economic transactions between the two classes are highly personalized, leading to the interlinkage of factor, credit, and product markets. The personalized form of transaction is especially true in the labor market which takes the form of an economic contract satisfying the double coincidence of wants—reducing transaction costs for big landowners and reducing insurance costs for agricultural laborers. Labor markets are restricted to each village. This leads to a uniformity of wages inside the village (reflecting the community consciousness of agricultural laborers) but also to variation in wage from one village to another. This uneven distribution of wages reflects the failure of agricultural laborers to unite across villages. Similarly, any homogeneous structure of consumption loans and production loans is restricted to each village while varying from village to village. Thus, because of the isolated nature of the villages, agricultural laborers have not been able to transform themselves from a class in itself to a class for itself. They lack the consciousness of belonging to a class. Their community consciousness in the village fails to translate into class consciousness across the society.

Big landowners, through their various modes of operation and linkage with the outside world, are able to consciously come together and organize themselves around the common interest (given by the economic structure). They have successfully transformed themselves from a class in itself to a class for itself. They are conscious of their power, interests, and historical role. Thus, because of the contrasting tendency toward class formation, the (potentially) antagonistic contradiction between the two classes in India has failed to take its pure form as yet. Any transition in India can only take place when the class of agricultural laborers has successfully transformed itself from a class in itself to a class for itself.

A Critical Look at the Concept of Class and Its Surroundings

The main criticisms that could be leveled against the class analysis in the Indian modes of production debate are the following:

Class as Subject and Class as Interest: Some Doubts

In chapter 1 we arugued against the concept of the working class as a pre-formed subject, that is, as a homogenous group of conscious social actors, and against the concept of a pre-given class interest. According to Hindess (1987, 1988), classes (such as the working class or capitalist class) cannot be regarded as social actors who struggle against each other. Unlike actors such as human individuals, and social actors such as capitalist enterprises, trade unions, political parties, and state agencies, these classes have no definite means of formulating and executing decisions that can be considered as the minimal condition required for a conceptual existence of an actor.

Furthermore, unlike the orthodox Marxist class analysis, which has treated classes as social forces representing some given common (class) interest originating from the positions they occupy in the relations of production, Hindess has argued that the assumption of real or true interest (class interest) as given or reflecting some social structural location is logically wrong and assumes away explanations of any event.

The above-mentioned twin points related to the conceptual hollowness of class as social actors and that of reflective interests implies that class as a social force representing class interests cannot exists. Thus, we need to abandon the orthodox Marxian concept of class, thereby problematizing the agents of transition (that is, classes) in that framework.[12]

The Invisible Nature of Class "Processes"

In most theories of class, the concept of class as *processes* referring to surplus labor is reduced to (and therefore the analysis pertaining to societal relationships is displaced to) either power or property structures. More often, since power is predicated on property relations, class is ultimately reduced to property relations. However, by reducing class to relations of property structure, the theorists in the Indian modes of production debate interrupt any analysis of class by rendering mechanisms flowing directly from those processes as passive and preformed. Their approaches exhibit a tendency to reduce the class aspects of society to some other chosen entry-point concepts that, in turn, are empowered to operate as the essence of society in the theory. Like all other aspects of society, class comes to be defined in terms of some other entry-point concept (meaning the same as discursive focus point) and it becomes logically secondary in the hierarchy of explanation. Reducing class to power or property, which is given an apriori explanatory privilege, only obscures the complex nature of the social existence of classes and explains away the effects produced on and by the processes related to the social phenomena of performance, appropriation, distribution, and receipt of surplus labor.

Patnaik's definition of class embodies three criteria that, as seen from the quotation from Patnaik in note 1, could be reduced to property relations since there are positive correlations among the three. However, via an empiricist procedure, Patnaik reduces and, thereby, displaces class from its complex dimension to a simplified labor exploitation criterion that is related to aspects of hiring in and hiring out and not to the processes related to surplus labor generation. This reductionism not only leads to the obliteration of processes related to surplus labor generation but also to relations of property. The latter obliteration is particularly interesting since while property relations are considered important at the analytical level, they are displaced by labor exploitation at the empirical or "real" level. Patnaik fails to resolve this contradiction between the "rational element" of class that places property relations at the center stage and the empirical "reality" that effaces property relations from the domain.

The Problem of the Reductionism in Class Analysis

In the postmodern Marxian framework, the concepts of capitalist and worker are disaggregated in terms of the process of performance, appropriation, distribution, and receipt of surplus value. Those who appropriate surplus value are defined as productive or industrial capitalists. Others who receive a part of the surplus value are unproductive capitalists, like "moneylending capitalists," "merchant capitalists," "landlord capitalists," and so on. The adjectives before the term "capitalist" capture the different standpoints in the processes of performance, appropriation, distribution, and receipt of surplus labor. The modifier "industrialist" before the term "capitalist" reveals one standpoint (appropriator of surplus value) distinct from another modifier like "merchant" that posits another standpoint (receiver of surplus value). The worker, in turn, is disaggregated into productive worker and unproductive worker where the modifiers "productive" and "unproductive" are names for the distinct standpoint of the workers for the economic space of the process of performance, appropriation, distribution, and receipt of surplus labor. Similarly, other class processes, such as independent, slave, feudal, or communist class processes, can be disaggregated in terms of performance, appropriation, distribution, and receipt of surplus labor. Society, from a class perspective, is a disaggregated totality based on a configuration of social relationships defined in terms of subsets of class and nonclass processes. From such a perspective where the analytical primitive is the process and not the individual, terms like "landlord" or "moneylender," as used in the Indian modes of production debate can be a source of deep confusion. Let us illustrate.

From a postmodern Marxian perspective, the "landlord" as the owner of land signifies a standpoint that emphasizes the receipt of surplus labor. To be the receiver of rent payment and to be the appropriator of surplus labor are two different social functions (related to the two different class positions), and it is conceptually wrong (as the Indian Marxists often do) to reduce the latter to the former. Similarly, the "moneylender" does not appropriate surplus labor but receives a return (interest) for the loan he or she advances. The social function of moneylender in the class process is as a supplier of money capital and not as an appropriator of surplus product. Bhaduri may object by pointing out that the loan provided to the poor direct producers (assuming that they have no other means of earning income) in the case of the Indian economy is a consumption loan and not a loan for production purposes. But if it is a consumption loan then it is a nonclass loan, meaning that this loan has no direct bearing on the fundamental class process, appropriating surplus labor. Against this loan, the moneylender receives an interest payment out of the surplus product since, as we have assumed, the direct producer has no other means of earning income. Consequently, the moneylender occupies two social positions, one class position as the receiver of surplus product and the other nonclass position of a supplier of consumption loans. The surplus product could then be appropriated by the producer himself (in the case of independent class structure) or the nonproducer (in the case of slave, feudal, or capitalist class structures) or a collective of direct producers (in the case of communist class or nonclass structures), a part of which is then distributed to the moneylender in the form of interest payment as a subsumed class payment even though the loan in this case is a nonclass loan. These different social functions that individuals or collectives perform refer to their occupation of different class and nonclass positions pertaining to specific class and nonclass processes. It should be noted that the primitives here are the class and nonclass *processes* and not human individuals. To reduce the moneylender to the position of an appropriator just because the social (class) position that makes possible the social function to be performed allows the concerned individual to get a portion of the surplus product is a conflation of two distinct social functions (appropriator and receiver of surplus product)—a conflation made possible by reducing one to the other. That is, the statement that the moneylender-cum-merchant class can appropriate surplus labor from the producer because of the role of the usury (thereby reducing appropriation to the level of usury, i.e., to the level of receipt of surplus labor) is untenable from a postmodern Marxian perspective.

Differentiating classes at the level of human agents may also lead to problems of identifying the class nature of the individual. That is where we turn next.

The Differences in the Meaning of Class Differentiation

The traditional Indian Marxists, to their credit, generally do consider the peasantry to be a disaggregated class but their theorization of classes, especially their theory of the social constitution of an individual, has problems of its own. They understand classes in terms of homogeneous groups of people tied together around a common class interest flowing from relations of property (like land ownership) or power. Class relations are understood as relations between such groups of people with shared characteristics. The differentiation of the peasantry necessarily implies showing which individuals fall into what classes and more often than not involves reducing the class identification of individuals to a single class because individuals with two class interests are considered to be theoretically untenable. For example, a landowner cannot also be an agricultural laborer and so on. Thus the population is typically divided into five nonoverlapping classes (landlord, rich farmers, middle farmers, small peasantry, and agricultural laborers) as in Patnaik, or four classes (moneylender-cum-merchant, landlord, small peasantry, and agricultural laborers) in Bhaduri, or two classes (class of big landowners and agricultural laborers) in Rudra where no individual can occupy two class positions simultaneously.[13] And even if individuals do occupy two or more class positions simultaneously, then by using a "net method" approach they are reduced to one class position consistent with their main class interest.[14] Let us illustrate the problems associated with the "net method" approach.

Traditional Marxists like Patnaik have been perturbed by the problem associated with the presence of peasants who hire in labor to cultivate land and also hire themselves out as agricultural labor. This poses a problem since, according to Patnaik, no individual can occupy two class positions simultaneously. If individuals do occupy two or more class positions they then have to be reduced to one class position—the most important one for the individual. Here Patnaik uses the "net method," by which she subtracts hiring out from hiring in such that a positive (negative) value will reveal the social existence of the individual as an exploiter (exploited). There are two problems with this method. First, from a value theoretic standpoint, she should be taking into account the problems related to the heterogeneity of labor. As hiring in and hiring out might take place in two different sites, they need to be reduced to abstract or homogenous labor that Patnaik does not do. Second, by emphasizing the aspect of being either exploiter or exploited, she is virtually obliterating one site of the economic. To reduce the complexity in different sites to that of a single site in order to reduce the individual's social existence to a single class position is indeed a very transparent form of reductionism. Such a problem does not arise in the nonessentialist postmodern Marxian theory. There, an individual can occupy different class positions (both as an exploiter and as exploited) and, in fact, one of the emphases of such a class theory is to reveal the complexity regarding the social constitution of the individual and that of society and not to reduce and thereby simplify one's social existence to a single class position. Let us expand further on this.

Since, for postmodern Marxian theory, process, and not the individual, is the primitive, any social position, and in particular, that of the class position, is constituted by a subset of processes. An individual may occupy many such class and nonclass positions simultaneously, and this determines the social constitution of an individual from a class perspective.[15]

From the standpoint of such a Marxist analysis, Bhaduri's moneylender occupies a class position (as a receiver of surplus product) and a nonclass position (as a distributor of consumption loans that are not used for productive purposes). If he distributes loans for productive use then he occupies another class position (as a distributor of money capital). Thus an individual (like the moneylender) may occupy multiple class and even nonclass positions simultaneously and to reduce such complexities to a simple solution, as Bhaduri does (usury, for Bhaduri, is a guise for appropriation—the real activity of the moneylender), is a fundamental error. This is so because such reductionism washes away all of the different effects that bring their own unique character in the social constitution of an individual and his decision-making process.

The Peasantry as Backward People

Most Marxists in the Indian modes of production debate have treated the peasantry unproblematically as an unconscious object to be integrated by the nationalist or communist movements led by the bourgeoisie or the working class. This treatment reflects a view of the peasantry as a backward group that does not have the consciousness and the knowledge (because of the fragmentary nature of village units and the consequent fragmentary nature of the protests by the villagers) to work toward producing historical change. That privilege is accorded either to the bourgeoisie or the working class. The participants in the debate were united in their depiction of the peasantry as a backward group of people as regards historical change.

Patnaik, for example, linked capitalism's development with industrial development because without industrial development, she argued, the working class would not become numerous enough to launch a movement for transition. Also, there are two roads possible in Patnaik's writing to bring about full-fledged capitalism, state intervention, or left revolution led by the working class to initiate land reform in the countryside. It should be noted that both of these initiators of social change are from outside the agricultural sector. Bhaduri, similarly, never considered the possibility of small peasants or agricultural laborers bringing about a transition of Indian society. Social change depended on the power configuration between the moneylender-cum-merchant class and the landlord class. If, as in the case of India, the power configuration led to a fettering of the forces of production, then one needs intervention of the state and the left forces (led by the working class) in bringing about social change. Rudra is perhaps the only traditional Marxist who seriously contemplated the revolutionary aspect of what he called "the class of agricultural laborers," but he also did not see any hope of social change coming from this class. He pointed to the fragmentary nature of the village units as an important factor in the failure of agricultural laborers to transform themselves from a class in itself to a class for itself. As a result, by default, change in the class relations of production has to come from the direction of the center (industrial base, state, or working class) to the periphery (agricultural base or the villages).

The Problem of Subjectivity, False Consciousness, and the Working Class

Orthodox Marxism's class analytical framework consists of three categories: class position, class formation, and class struggle. *Class positions* are those positions that individuals occupy in the production process in a society, and in the Indian modes of production debate on Marxism, are given by property relations. Class positions are often referred to by the term "class" in itself.

Class formation refers to the transformation of class in itself to class for itself, where class for itself is the consciousness that an individual must have about his social and historical role as a member of a particular class.

To hold a class position does not mean that an individual is aware of his social and historical role as a member of the class. A problem with the transition from capitalism to socialism or from precapitalism to socialism is that workers may not be aware of their exploited class position or that their historical role is to overthrow the system. As seen by theorists in the Indian modes of production debate, this unawareness is one of the major problems in the transition of Indian society. *Class struggle,* in orthodox Marxist theory, refers to two or more classes struggling against each other based on some pre-given conflict of interest. It reflects a struggle between two groups of people.

In the argument below, our first objective is to show that the so-called materialist theory of historical materialism is based on a metaphysical or idealistic foundation of an immanent spark of consciousness embedded in the working class. Second, we shall problematize the process of class formation. The results are important for two reasons. First of all, they raise questions about the viability and purpose of any concept of a centered totality of the subject, false consciousness, and vanguard party. Second, because all the participants in the Indian modes of production debate took class formation as a central point of their class analysis (the transition from class in itself to class for itself), our critique will seriously call into question such types of class analyses.

The Metaphysical Basis of the "Working Class"

In orthodox Marxism, the working class is considered as a totality[16] and the individual subjects only reflect the positivity of this totality. The totality of a subject means that his world—action and thought—are limited within the context in which the totality, here working class, is defined. The subject must reflect the class interests derived from his class position. Any other interests signifying other subject positions are subsumed under the interests derived from the working class. Since his subject position is conceived as a totality, he should both think and act as a working-class person should. The working class is assumed to have some core thought processes that are passed on to individual subjects holding that class position. That is, the relationship that exists between the working class as a whole and the working-class person is that the working class has a pre-given, self-constituted intelligibility and knowledge of itself and the "reality" that potentially can trickle down to the individuals holding that class position.[17] The crucial presumption is that the working class knows itself and its mission in the process of the development of society.[18] However, how it knows itself or its mission is not explained. It is taken as given. This is, in fact, characteristic of a rationalist way of thinking about the world with the concept of totality as working class. It is a burden for the Marxists to explain how a theory supposedly grounded on materialism is based on such a metaphysical idea—that of a working class that is a priori knowledgeable about society and history. The second problem, a logical one, is to explain why the knowledge embedded in the working class, whose origin is assumed away by taking it as given, should automatically pass onto the individuals holding a particular class position.

Class Formation and the Illusion of False Consciousness

It is commonly assumed in orthodox Marxist theory that in the ideal situation working-class consciousness would automatically translate into the consciousness of individuals holding that class position. This imputed consciousness is structured by the knowledge and intelligibility flowing from the totality—the working class. The actual consciousness may be completely different. The individuals holding working-class positions and consequently belonging to the working class may not know the "truth" about their social and historical role. They may not know their true identity—that is, their true interest.

Marxist theorists, like Lenin and Lukacs, were aware of this problem of irreconcilable duality between the imputed and actual consciousness. It was recognized that individuals holding class positions may not be aware of their "true interests" and hence of their historical mission. If the worker does not act as prescribed by his position within the totality—inside and outside the production process—then he does not fully know his identity, the truth about himself. This results in false consciousness. In order to supplant false consciousness, one needs a vanguard party of the working class that educates those individuals holding the working-class position about their historical role. In socialist countries, vanguard parties formed the basis of so-called working-class domination.[19] There are three instances that show that the solution for false consciousness as formulated by the concept of the vanguard party has deep problems.

First, it is assumed that the vanguard party—mirroring the pure form of working-class consciousness—knows the historical interests of its social classes, knows the direction society and history must take. But the question is, how does the vanguard party know what the historical interests of the working class are, and, at a different level, how does the working class know what its historical interests are? In other words, how does this knowing come into being and what is its basis? Orthodox Marxism has conjured away the problem by considering knowledge and interest as autonomous, self-reflective, and pre-given. This assumption of knowing signifies a metaphysical foundation that is contrary to the self-proclaimed materialistic basis of historical materialism.

Second, the new social movements that are springing up all over the world suggest that the actual "totality" of a subject position is not centered around the objective interest emanating from the totality—the working class.[20] In fact, the actual "totality" of a subject is better thought of as decentered. An individual holds many subject positions simultaneously. An individual holding a working-class position also belongs to a gender, race, ethnicity, nationality, caste, etc. Thus, the individual subject—totality of a subject—is a composite of multiple subject positions, thereby overflowing with excess meaning. In our scheme, the totality of the subject is as Laclau called the "kaleidoscopic movement of differences" where the individual's subjectivity cannot be reduced to a simple class interest.

Third, false consciousness or unrecognized (true) interest explains the existence of the vanguard party and provides it with a reason for social action. But false consciousness does not explain the social actions of the individual actors in the working class, because if they do not recognize their true interests then they have no operational means to act on that basis. That is, if we do not perceive our "interest," how can we base our action on something we do not know? So the basis of these individual's actions lies somewhere other than their structural class location, and this is not explained in the orthodox Marxist theory. Thus false consciousness cannot explain the link between the individual actor's structural location and his actions and neither can the concept of the vanguard party solve it. The main problem with class analysis in orthodox Marxism is not so much the totalitarian consequences it sometimes has generated but rather the logical problem that such class analysis is based on a metaphysical foundation.

Rather than explaining the problems it is supposed to answer, false consciousness and vanguard party helps to explain them away. For example, in response to questions such as why the people in the Soviet Union revolted, one typical answer is that the people were suffering from false consciousness. Thus, if the vanguard party had been more careful in disseminating "true" meaning in society, the revolution would have been avoided. In our view, such explanations shy away from the more important causes of the revolt and try to shift the burden of explanation onto the concept of false consciousness. False consciousness creates an illusion of explanation (of actual consciousness) that needs to be dropped as an instrument of explanation of behavior of the individual's action and historical events. The emphasis should be on the causes explaining the formation of actual consciousness: how consciousness is constituted at a particular time and location. More precisely, in the case of class theory, the emphasis should be on explaining how class identity in the political arena is formed and not taken as given. The construction of class identity in terms of class struggle is key. Class struggle and class identity should be conceptualized (and this is still an open problem for Marxists) as a means to explaining concrete actions of social agents in society.

As a result of the above three problems, the concepts of working class, class formation, and class in general as understood by orthodox Marxism (where it is treated as a subject) are thrown into jeopardy. In this framework, it seems almost impossible to close the gap between the economic concept of class that gives an ontological privilege to the working-class and the political concept of working class action signifying human subjectivity without invoking the concept of false consciousness and vanguard party, which, as we have demonstrated, are deeply problematic and cannot be sustained as a means to explain the complexities of human behavior.

Conclusion

Our critique of the issues and concepts surrounding the question of the transition process in Indian society has seriously undermined the concept of transition as conceived in orthodox Indian Marxist theories. The theoretical problems in the Indian modes of production debate, which were common to all descriptions of the transition in that debate, centered around the underlying presence of epistemological essentialism, economic essentialism, centered social totality, mode of production, historicism, ontological privileging of class, monadic conception of subject, etc. This means that the concept of transition as argued in the debate can no longer be theoretically sustained as an explanation of the process of transition, especially from a postmodern Marxian perspective.

The Indian modes of production debate, for whatever its shortcomings from a Marxian perspective, was at least a serious attempt to conceptualize the process of transition in the India context. The decline of the Indian modes of production debate can be traced to the internal and external critique it has received in recent times and the decline and subsequent loss of the symbolic father figure of orthodox Marxism—the Soviet Union. Its demise has created a lacuna in the Marxist critique in the ongoing debate in India about the pros and cons of the liberalization policies. This is especially important in light of the recent attempts by neoclassical economists in India to exorcise Marxism from the academic and social domain. It has to be understood that the main criticism leveled against Marxism is not related to the substantive part of its arguments but the one regarding the legitimacy of the Marxist paradigm and its vision. As we will explain in Chapter seven , the ongoing transition debate is threatening to be reduced to a one-sided neoclassical approach to transition with its rhetoric of efficiency, market, and competition and the underlying theme of antisocialism where it conflates socialism with state involvement.

To defend the feasibility of a Marxist approach (or many approaches, if possible) to transition against the neoclassical attack has to be the most important priority for the program of Marxian political economy, especially in the Indian context. This calls for some soul-searching and hard choices. The emphasis in analyzing the Indian modes of production debate, as should be clear by now, was not simply on the substantive differences (many surveys have done that) but mainly on the methodological underpinnings and primitive concepts guiding the professed mechanisms of transition in the debate. The shortcoming is precisely here, at the methodological level, at the level of the process of construction of the concepts holding up the theory.

There is no escape from this trauma; the methodology (driven by essentialism and historicism) guiding the Indian modes of production debate must be abandoned and its many founding concepts (such as class, social totality, etc.) need to be reformulated.[21] These are the hard choices one must make in order to raise the Marxist paradigm from its presently quiescent state and begin the process of constructing an alternative nonessentialist, nonhistoricist, decentered, class-focused concept of transition that can pose a serious challenge to the neoclassical theory of transition. That is why a confrontation with the past—the Indian modes of production debate—was necessary. The confrontation illuminates the present by warning us of the pitfalls that must be avoided in the process of this work of alternative construction concerning the theory of transition.

By the mid-1980s, the Indian mode of production debate was overtaken by *subaltern studies* as the dominant Marxian discourse. It claimed to have departed from the central methodological underpinnings that have guided the Indian mode of production debate. However, as we will explain in the next two chapters, subaltern studies, despite its protestation to the contrary, was not immune from many of the problems we have described in this chapter. In addition, its juxtaposition of economic essentialism with power essentialism created its own set of problems. Consequently, as we will point out, its analysis of the transition process in India is also living with insurmountable problems of essentialism and historicism. Thus its claim to be unorthodox in its Marxist approach is fraught with tension. The trauma that characterizes the Indian modes of production debate carries over to the subaltern studies theory of transition: a passage from one type of crisis to another for Indian Marxism.

CHAPTER 4

Transition and Development

A Marxian Critique of Subaltern Studies

The *subaltern studies* group (Guha 1982–1990; Chatterjee and Pandey 1992) dominated the Indian academic scene during the 1980s and 1990s, interrogating the elite, the orthodox Marxist, and the West. They have gained currency in the West as an alternative academic movement that implied a break from the past. We will show in this and the following chapters that so far as transition and development are concerned, there is more heat than light in the subaltern studies contribution: it is only a different version of historical materialism. In this context, in the next two chapters, we will deconstruct the basic features of the subaltern studies theory of transition from a postmodern Marxist perspective indicating, as we go along, its major differences from the traditional Marxists who took part in the Indian modes of production debate, its contributions to the theorization of transition of Indian society from a Marxist perspective, and, most important, the problems facing its theorization of transition.[1]

To begin with, one can divide subaltern studies discourse on transition and development into two phases in terms of a historical reformulation of India's tryst with capitalism. The first stage is concerned mainly with the colonial period while the second stage is with the postindependence phase. In terms of theory, the first stage looks at the failure of capitalism to take the classical route while the second stage is more concerned with the route capitalism takes in light of the failure of capitalism to take the classical route to history. The first stage forms the heart of subaltern studies while the second stage, though a constitutively independent discourse in its own right, can also be reconstructed as a derivative from the first one.

We will unravel the basic features of the subaltern studies theory of transition from a postmodern Marxist perspective grounded on class qua performance, appropriation, and distribution of surplus labor, revealing in the process the problems facing its theorization of transition. We will reveal the *methodological structure* that binds together the subaltern studies theory of transition, questioning any assessment of that discourse as being antimodernist and antihistoricist and demonstrating that its claim does not match up with the methodological structure it adopts. So we focus principally on the *logic* of the subaltern studies theory of transition (that is, stage one/this chapter) and then point to the marks of essentialism and historicism emanating from that logic that informs the theory of passive revolution of capital (stage two/the following chapter).

This reading is a difficult exercise because while, as we shall see, subaltern studies announces its central problematics as specially designed to study transition in an underdeveloped, agriculture-based rural society such as India, it is not always explicit on the linkage between the case studies and the problematic in its analysis. So, as in a detective novel, one has to unravel its theory of transition and the underlying principles driving the logic of the theory. In addition to dissecting the intricacies involved in the subaltern studies' theory of transition, our critical reading will help bring to light a particular form of misunderstanding regarding subaltern studies (that has arisen especially in light of its reading in the Western world). The misunderstanding arises because of a perception in some Western academic circles that subaltern studies is a subset of postmodernist and poststructuralist discourse (Callinicos 1995). Because of its influence in the Indian academic circles/press and the connection of its leaders with the West, this misunderstanding has turned subaltern studies into an exotic discourse of the East in the West and, back home, as something very Eastern in its formative character, a belief stamped, of course, by the knowledgeable West and hence incontestable in the intellectual circles. This romanticism is legitimized by the characterization of subaltern studies discourse as arising out of a critique of the Indian modes of production debate and the methodology of classical Marxism inherent in that debate—which, as we demonstrated, is essentialist and historicist. However, a disbelief of the economic essentialism and historicism in the Indian modes of production debate does not automatically translate into a nonessentialist and nonhistoricist discourse in the case of the subaltern studies. This is what we want to show: how the subaltern studies theory of transition is characterized by an essentialist logic along with the damaging consequence of subsuming class under power, carried on with an objective of finding some pre-given truth by revealing the "inner" consciousness of groups of people it calls subaltern and elite within a definitive historical model that is only a variant of the historical model called historical materialism.[2] In other words, if nonessentialism and nonhistoricism are to be criteria for identifying a discourse as postmodernist, then subaltern studies and its theory of transition, in its present dominant form, cannot meet this test. This result is devastating for that school of thought because subaltern studies, among other things, claimed for itself a place within Marxism outside of traditional Marxism by emphasising its disquiet over the logic of historical materialism. And, yet, as we shall demonstrate, its logic of transition despite its effort to be otherwise remains a prisoner of the underlying methodological principles driving the logic of historical materialism: essentialism and historicism.

In order to avoid confusion regarding our purpose and direction of reading we want to make clear at the outset the space in which we are not operating. We do recognize that subaltern studies is a vast (common) space inhabited by multiple st(r)ands. This narration is neither an attempt to provide a critique of the subaltern studies school per se nor an attempt to reform it. Rather the focus is on a critical reading of a specific subspace of subaltern studies—its theory of transition and development—and an extension of that theory in a different space of hegemony. Our discussions on class, consciousness, and so on, are legitimate only insofar as they inform our approach to the subaltern studies theory of transition and development. When we do talk about the tension within subaltern studies it is again made only insofar as it throws light on the differences in the act of theorization over transition and development. We also recognize that further development on subaltern positions are taking place, for example, by Gayatri Chakravorty Spivak or Dipesh Chakraborty (in fact one of the authors has dealt with the position of Spivak elsewhere—Chakrabarti and Chaudhury 1996/97), and we welcome them. However, none of the new positions regarding the subaltern is contextualized as part of a rethought theory of transition and development. Consequently, as our focus is on transition and development, we ignore the new developments unless otherwise applicable to our problematic, just as we ignore the multiple positions regarding other areas within subaltern studies. This explains our concentration on certain works of Ranajit Guha and Partha Chatterjee (and to some extent Dipesh Chakraborty), as these authors have tried to articulate specific concepts of subaltern, consciousness, class, and so on, to address the issues of transition and development. Of course, how much of our critique of the subaltern studies theory of transition and development translates into a critique of subaltern studies per se is for the readers to judge. Thus, as in the Indian mode of production debate, the subaltern studies debate has many components, not all of which are possible or desirable (given our theme) for us to discuss—only the theory of transition and development forms our discursive focus.

As mentioned earlier, there are two stages in the subaltern studies theory of transition. In the first stage (to be studied in this chapter) theorists look at the failure of the classical (Western European) route to transition for the case of India. The proof of the failure lies, according to these theorists, in the presence of the subaltern autonomous domain. Consequently, they carry out a detailed exercise of this domain to flesh out the reasons for the failure of modernism (capitalism) to destroy tradition (precapitalism). Summarizing the objective of subaltern studies, Guha points out:

> It is the study of this *historic failure of the nation to come to its own,* a failure due to the inadequacy of the bourgeoisie as well as of the working class to lead it into a decisive victory over colonialism and a bourgeois-democratic revolution of either the classic nineteenth-century type under the hegemony of the bourgeoisie or a more modern type under the hegemony of workers and peasants, that is, a "new democracy"—*it is the study of this failure which constitutes the central problematic of the historiography of colonial India.* (1982, 7)[3]

Subaltern studies focuses on the (conscious) role of the subaltern at the moment of the historical failure of a Western European–type full-fledged capitalism (with uncontested hegemony of the bourgeoisie) or new democracy to take hold. This emphasis on the subaltern autonomous domain and its consciousness also marks a clear departure from the Indian modes of production debate.

The principal difference between the traditional and subaltern school can be located on the question of the theoretical status of the "residuals" of the precapitalist relations of production. The traditional school believes that as we move from feudalism to capitalism, the residuals (the precapitalist institutions and groups) play a negative role. Feudal institutions or groups like the feudal landlords, artisans, moneylenders, and caste and religious systems need to be eliminated as they act as an impediment to the development of the forces of production. This is in perfect harmony with the argument of orthodox historical materialism that requires the supersession of the precapitalist relations of production by the capitalist relations of production. The subaltern studies group, in contrast, believes in the possibility of the positive role of the residuals. It believes that the residuals may play an important role against oppressive systems and are mostly concerned with studying the consciousness of those groups who constitute the residuals. By abandoning the base-superstructure correspondence model of historical materialism it strives to provide an alternative Marxist way of looking at Indian historiography. This noncorrespondence between base and superstructure also indicates the subaltern studies group's critical response to the domination of economic essentialism in the Indian modes of production debate. However, in their theory, as we will explain in detail, economic essentialism is replaced by power essentialism.

To critically analyze the subaltern autonomous domain is, then, our discursive focus here. The objective is to bring to light the essentialisms ingrained in the subaltern studies discussion of the autonomous domain. This discussion covers features related to the question of elitist historiography versus subaltern historiography, the role of power as the chief explanatory element, and the subsumption of the economic phenomenon of class process under it, the role of subaltern consciousness, especially peasant consciousness, as a repository of truth of the subaltern group or class along with the implications of such a truth-finding mission and the relation between the peasant class and the working class. In contrast to how subaltern studies is often projected in the West, our critique is intended to bring into the open the forms of essentialism and reductionism that afflict the subaltern studies school. Discussions of these features are also important because the concepts (power, class, etc.) analyzed here flow into the concept of the passive revolution of capital that takes up the second stage of the subaltern studies theory of transition (to be studied under the next chapter).

If capitalism in India has not yet been successful in developing in the mirror image of the Western European model, then what form does it take? It is to be noted that the subaltern theorists concerned with this problematic do not question the existence of a capitalist system; instead, they are concerned with the route that capitalism takes especially against the background of the establishment of the planning system and industrialization policies undertaken by the postindependence Indian government. The question posed by the Indian mode of production debate about the existence or nonexistence of capitalism is a superfluous question for the subaltern studies school. The real question is how and in what form capitalism has established its rule in India. Here, subaltern studies bring in aspects related to the consciousness of the elite and analyze the form in which the elite establishes capitalism's hegemony over the working-class and precapitalist elements. More specifically, subaltern studies focuses on the implications for the elite's hegemonic construction process of the "passive revolution of capital" in light of capitalism's inability to transcend the precapitalist elements where the passive revolution of capital roughly signifies a type of bourgeois hegemony given capitalism's failure to overcome precapitalism.

According to subaltern studies theorists, as a result of the transition process from (semi)feudalism to capitalism, capitalism takes the form of a passive revolution of capital in an underdeveloped country like that of India. However, their interest is focused on the path beyond capitalism. As we will explain, the stage from passive revolution of capital (capitalism) to the next stage in an underdeveloped country like India is not that of the Western European model of socialism but the context-specific system of "socialism of communities." In other words, as in historical materialism, one can discern a pattern of historicism in the transition theory of subaltern studies. In sum, by dissecting the theory of passive revolution of capital we will show that the subaltern studies theory of transition is essentialist and historicist in character, thereby undercutting any claim of its discourse to be a fundamental departure from the orthodox Marxist theory of transition.

The Elitist Historiography versus Subaltern Historiography

Subaltern studies primarily represents exercises in historical scholarship. It is an attempt to rethink the relation between history and anthropology from a perspective that displaces the central position of the Western anthropologist or historian as the subject of discourse and Indian society as its object. In short, it puts into doubt colonial and nationalistic historiography. In this context, the subaltern studies school argues that Indian history, particularly during British rule, has been written from the standpoint of the Indian elite as an extension of the nationalist movement in India (led by the elite). Guha and the subaltern studies school question this elitist historiography and the absence of an active, autonomous subaltern space in its discourse. They replace the elitist historiography by a subaltern historiography. Their objective is to show how one can attribute an autonomous domain to the subaltern, independently of the elite. Through various case studies they show how the subaltern acted on its own, created its own organizations and affected historical events.

Economic Essentialism versus Power Essentialism

In this section, we will discuss how subaltern studies replaced the economic essentialism that dominated the Indian modes of production debate with a power essentialism and why this form of essentialism has the deleterious effect of demoting the economic effect of class to a subset of processes based on power.

The subaltern studies group criticizes the traditional school for its undue emphasis on the economic (signifying economic determinism) and failure to appreciate the role of the political and cultural elements in Indian society. It rejects the base-superstructure paradigm of classical Marxism because of its undue emphasis on the economic (the base) as the explanatory element. Subaltern theorists argue that it is problematic to reduce the complexities of Indian society to only the economic. Elements related to the cultural and political domain play a more important and dominant role in constituting not only Indian society but also the economic. The economic is taken to be passive and remains nonproblematized in subaltern studies. The discursive principle now becomes focused on the relations of power, where the economic is reduced to power. While the Indian mode of production debate is characterized by economic essentialism, the subaltern studies approach is characterized by power essentialism.

In subaltern studies, the social space is divided between the elite and the subaltern, organized in terms of the relations of domination and subordination (power relations). The elite definitely (definitionally) commands and oppresses the subaltern, whose role is to obey. And when the subaltern does not obey, there is an inversion of the relations of power. However, this inversion is momentary since the subaltern, for reasons we will outline later on, lacks the consciousness to transcend its traditional characteristics. The elite takes advantage of this weakness and sabotages the subaltern movements into submission. So, in the end, in the subaltern studies literature, the elite always stays dominant and the subaltern subordinate.

In the context of India, why are the relations of power more important than the economic relations of production? Subaltern theorists like Guha agree with the semifeudal argument in the Indian modes of production debate (Bhaduri 1973, 1983; Prasad 1973, 1979) that, from the colonial time, the economic relations pertaining to class exploitation in India have been conditioned and controlled by noneconomic power relations. Guha (1983, 6–8) argues that before 1900, rent constituted the main source of income while the common constitutive aspect of agricultural relations

> ... was the extraction of the peasant's surplus by means determined rather less by the free play of the forces of a market economy than by the extra-economic force of the landlord's standing in local society and in the colonial polity. In other words, it was a relationship of dominance and subordination—a political relationship of the feudal type, or as it has been appropriately described, a semi-feudal relationship which derived its material sustenance from pre-capitalist conditions of production and its legitimacy from a traditional culture still paramount in the superstructure. (Guha 1983, 6)

Though the British changed the land system to permanent settlement in the east, ryotwari in the south, and some combination of the two in the rest of the country, the basic relations of production did not change and remained semifeudal despite the fact that, due to the changes, there was a general trend toward commercialization of agriculture and the rise of usury as an additional (to rent) mode of exploitation.[4] According to Guha, the landlord, the moneylender, and the state formed a triumvirate against the peasant where the essential element that constituted the relation between the triumvirate and the peasant is that of power and not any aspect (like exploitation) related to the economic:

> His (the peasant's) subjection to this triumvirate . . . was primarily political in character, economic exploitation being only one, albeit the most obvious, of its several instances. For the appropriation of his surplus was brought about by the authority wielded over local societies and markets by the landlord-moneylenders and a secondary capitalism working closely with them and by the encapsulation of that authority in the power of the colonial state. Indeed, the element of coercion was so explicit and so ubiquitous in all their dealings with the peasant that he could hardly look upon this relationship with them as anything but political. (Guha 1983, 8)

If power is so overwhelmingly present as the dominant social relation during peacetime, the main target of peasant uprisings would be (a political task of) inverting those relations of power, which in turn would affect the economic relations of production. It is wrong to look for economistic explanations for peasant uprisings, since the primary explanatory factor for them is the political aspect and not an economic aspect. And as the economic is subsumed under the political, the emphasis should be on the consciousness of the peasant and the elite, for it is at that level that power relations (an aspect of the political) can best be understood.[5]

From a Marxist point of view, an important question that needs to be asked is how subaltern studies conceptualizes class in light of the abovementioned concept of power that is given the privilege of being the central explanatory factor. What precisely is the relationship between the two? More specifically, since we understand class as processes related to the performance, appropriation, distribution, and receipt of surplus labor, how is this class concept accounted for, if it is in the subaltern theory of class?

In subaltern studies, class is explained by relations of power and, consequently, reduced to it. To explain this point requires first of all an understanding of its usage of class. In subaltern studies, class is defined as a homogeneous group of people where the source of homogeneity can be derived from a combination of (i) class as an ownership/nonownership of means of production and (ii) class being social actors with some pre-given common social interest. Let us begin by taking the first element of class—class defined in terms of ownership criteria—and then see how it is linked with class as social actors.

Classes as defined in terms of ownership criteria refer to those groups of people who own the means of production (constituting one class) and those who do not own the means of production (constituting another class).[6] Also, those who own the means of production are assumed to exploit those who do not. However, in the subaltern literature, exploitation (extraction of surplus labor of doers by nondoers of labor) embedded in the relations of production (given by ownership criteria) are further subsumed under the political aspect of power since, as Guha pointed out, the economic is only one aspect of the political (the relations of power being the singularly most important aspect of the political in subaltern studies). Thus, the political aspect of power emerges as the crucial explanatory factor in subaltern studies. There is a one-to-one correspondence between exploitation (or property relations) and relations of domination-subordination. Explaining the relations of power will explain the relations of exploitation and via exploitation will reveal the relations of class, that is, the property relations. The class that exploits also dominates while the class that is exploited is also dominated. For the subaltern studies school, it is the relations of power that reveal the relations of class. Power is the ground—the container—of relations of exploitation. Since classes are reduced to groups of people who are dominated by another group of people (subaltern and elite), the social analysis of subaltern studies is displaced to the configuration of power relations among groups of people who now emerge as social (and also class) actors—groups who are assumed to be capable of formulating and executing decisions.

Because class is reduced to power, class defined as a homogeneous group of people is conflated with the concepts of subaltern and elite. Terms like "elite class" and "subaltern class" crop up in the subaltern literature time and time again. The dominated group of agents called subaltern also constitutes the subaltern *class* because the aspect of subordination includes the aspect of exploitation (and nonownership of resources). Subaltern studies will say that exploitation is telescoped in domination, which in turn means that class as surplus labor is a passive, nonproblematized concept described in terms of relations of power. Notice that with the usurpation of (surplus labor) aspects of class by aspects of power, the subaltern studies school can now put forward a power analysis that they can claim, as they do, is simultaneously a (surplus labor) class analysis. This group of agents is treated as social actors who are tied by relations of domination and subordination.[7] Since the relations of domination-subordination are simultaneously a relation of classes, those groups of agents as classes also act as social actors. Thus, for example, in subaltern studies, the peasantry (a subaltern group) is treated as a homogeneous group of people who are called an (oppressed) class. The peasantry as a class is considered to be a collective of homogeneous social actors capable of formulating and executing decisions.[8]

Reducing class to relations of domination-subordination is an essentialist move because explanations of class (relationships) based on processes of surplus labor extraction are now constructed in terms of power relations. Subaltern studies does not produce a class theory but a power theory of class. This produces a very different interpretation of social relationships than what we would have under the postmodern Marxist framework. Let us give an example of how similar power relations can imply different forms of class relations.

Consider a hypothetical relation in an Indian village between an upper-caste landlord-moneylender who advances money capital and land to a lower-caste sharecropper. The sharecropper then might employ other laborers to produce commodities for the market. Given the power structure embedded in the caste system, the former dominates the latter. The subaltern theorists will also say that this aspect of domination-subordination encapsulates the relations of class (exploitation) since the class that dominates owns property (the precondition of being an exploiter) while the class that is dominated does not own property (the precondition of being exploited). The sharecropper is exploited by the landlord-moneylender because of the one-to-one correspondence between exploitation and relations of power. Thus, by reducing the class aspect to the power relations given by its caste aspect, one gets a power theory of class. Now consider the same relations from a postmodern Marxist perspective. There is no doubt that relations of power will shape the social relationship between the upper caste and the lower caste individual. But it does not follow that there is a one-to-one correspondence between this relation of power and mechanisms of appropriation. While the upper caste would dominate the lower caste, the lower-caste individual, the sharecropper, would appropriate the surplus produced in the land, a part of which would then be distributed as subsumed class payments to the landlord-moneylender for the land and capital advancement. Unlike the case for the subaltern power theory of class, the sharecropper may turn out to be an exploiter or a self-exploiter.[9] Whether an individual exploits or not is determined here by the subset of processes related to production and appropriation of surplus labor and not by relations of power. This is not to say that power relations have no impact on the mechanisms of the surplus labor generation process; far from it. Because of the relations of power in our example, the landlord-moneylender could demand a greater amount of surplus product than usual as subsumed class payments. This will affect the retained surplus of the sharecropper and may act as a disincentive, thereby changing the composition of investment in the next period. However, all of these effects do not change the point that the sharecropper is either an exploiter of others' labor if he employs labor power or a self-exploiter if he does not. Consequently, in our example, the relation between the sharecropper and land-lord-moneylender could turn out to be different for the two cases. In sub-altern studies, it signifies the relation of exploitation predicated on relations of power between the two, while in the case of the postmodern Marxist theory it embodies a relation between the appropriator, distribu-tor, and receiver of surplus product—that is, relations between fundamen-tal class exploiters and subsumed class receivers of surplus product. In other words, the social relations around the concept of class as a distinct set of processes are explained away by the usage of the subaltern school's power theory of class leading to a different explanation of social relation-ships than what one would get under the postmodern Marxist theory, even when they are claiming to be explaining the relations of exploitation per-taining to the mechanisms of surplus generation.

There was a debate in the 1980s that took place in the journal *Social Scien-tist* (a journal of classical Marxists) and the *Subaltern Studies* volumes be-tween traditional Marxists and the subaltern theorists over the treatment of class in the subaltern literature. For the traditional Marxists, the abandon-ment of the discursive privilege of class in favour of power was tantamount to abandoning Marxism. They also criticized the subaltern move to reduce class relations to a simplistic binary division of society into elite and subal-tern. The subaltern studies group thought otherwise. Chakraborty (1985), replying to the above criticism, argued that class was still given an ontologi-cal privilege but the discursive focus point has shifted from class to power since class relations are subsumed under the relations of domination-subordination. Subaltern studies refers to ". . . the specific nature of class relationships in India, where the relationships, at almost all levels, are sub-sumed in the relations of domination and subordination between members of the elite and subaltern" (Chakraborty 1985, 375–376). That is the reason subaltern studies use the terms "elite class" and "subaltern class." Class is not openly referred to because it is assumed that the discourse on power en-capsulates the discourse on class following the collapse of the latter into the former. Revealing the power relations will automatically reveal the class rela-tions. Thus, Chakraborty ended up reaffirming the reductionism involved in the power theory of class.

Let us sum up. The power discourse of subaltern studies produces a no-tion of class that totally subsumes those processes that relate to the pro-duction, appropriation, distribution, and receipt of surplus labor under the rubric of the relations of power. That is, the subaltern studies concept of power involves a reductionism of class processes to that of the relations of power. However, we have been emphasizing the point that power and class are distinct (though not independent and autonomous) concepts; de-finitionally, the latter is produced in the realm of the economic while the former is produced in the realm of the political. Conceptually one cannot be reduced to the other. A power theory of class will reveal the intricacies of relations of domination-subordination and not those related to the mechanisms of appropriation, distribution, and receipt of surplus labor, even though it claims to be explaining the mechanisms of surplus labor. Its explanation of class processes is, however, a spurious explanation where its spurious nature stems from its act of explaining away the relationships related to class processes in terms of relations of power.

Subaltern Consciousness as Pure Consciousness

The following discussion on consciousness pertains to the question of agency and its role in determining the path of transition and development. Subaltern studies theorists are unified with the orthodox Marxists in their belief in a repository of (inner) consciousness as playing a major role in the transition logic. However, as we saw earlier, subaltern studies displaces and subsumes the category of class—which constituted the inner consciousness in orthodox Marxism—to that of power where the category subaltern and elite forms an analytical binary. In this regard, the subaltern studies group criticizes the traditional Marxist school for demoting the importance of subaltern groups as conscious agents of history. In contrast, the focus of subaltern studies is on the consciousness of the subaltern, particularly that of the peasant and its role in effecting transition and development. This is in sharp opposition to the orthodox Marxist or non-Marxist historiography in India, which represents the subaltern, and particularly the peasantry, as mere (unconscious or unaware) objects to be integrated either by the elite nationalist or communist movement of India. This is because such historiography identifies politics with organization. Because the peasant movements were so spontaneous, fragmentary, and lacking in planned (which they identify with consciousness) exercises of leadership, they were dismissed as politically unimportant. As Guha points out,

> What both of these assimilative interpretations share is a "scholastic and academic historico-political outlook which sees as real and worthwhile only such movements of revolt as hundred percent conscious, i.e. movements that are governed by plans worked out in advance to the last detail or in line with abstract theory (which comes to the same thing)". . . . To those who prefer this device it offers the special advantage of identifying consciousness with their own political ideals and norms so that the activity of the masses found wanting in these terms may then be characterized as unconscious, hence pre-political. (Guha 1983, 4–5)

According to Guha, these peasant uprisings may have been fragmentary or lacking leadership because of some predetermined political outlook, but that does not imply that these movements were empty of any consciousness or political content. Only their consciousness and political content were different enough to be missed or dismissed by the "scholastic and academic historico-political outlook." The major project of the subaltern studies school is to rehabilitate the peasantry and, more generally, the subaltern, as the (discursive) conscious subject of history. That is why revealing the "inner" consciousness of the subaltern becomes a critical exercise in divulging the logic underlying its theory of transition and development. But this requires a meticulous and careful disclosure of disparate executions undertaken on the concept of consciousness in order to weave them together to display the logic of agency driving the subaltern studies theory of transition and development.

The basic position of the subaltern studies school is that there is an independent and autonomous domain of the subaltern, which can be recovered by studying the consciousness of the subaltern. Here, the subaltern studies school uses Gramsci's concept of contradictory consciousness to articulate their central claim of the autonomous domain of the subaltern. According to them, one fragment of the consciousness of the subaltern is the practical activities (uncontaminated by elite ideology) through which the subaltern transforms the world. If this series of activities can be recovered, then one can construct the autonomous part of the subaltern's consciousness and, via that, the autonomous domain of the subaltern.[10] Let us explain this very important point by illustrating two cases of subaltern consciousness that have been subject to detailed study in the subaltern literature—peasant consciousness and caste consciousness. After having laid out the two forms of consciousness, which because of its complicated discursive existence requires some elaboration, we will discuss some of the major problems related to the study of consciousness in subaltern studies. More specifically, we will discuss problems associated with a concept of "peasant class," ideal social totality, and consciousness as a repository of truth. We will begin our discussion by interpreting the subaltern theorist's interpretation of peasant consciousness.

ant Consciousness as a Subaltern Consciousness

er place to start is with Gramsci's concept of common sense be-
where the subaltern's consciousness is theoretically situated in
'iterature. By common sense (of the subaltern), Gramsci
'ictory unity of two opposed elements where the contra-
he level of consciousness. Contradictory conscious-
.ists of two opposed types of consciousness—the

implicit and the explicit consciousness of the subaltern. The implicit consciousness is the consciousness derived from the autonomous domain of the subaltern. For the subaltern studies group, the presence of such consciousness is an indicator of subalternity. This consciousness can be discovered by looking at the practical activity of the subaltern groups who through their own labor transform the world. The explicit consciousness, on the other hand, expresses the ideas of the dominant class filtered down to the subaltern groups, leading to their ideological submission to the rule of the dominant class. This is not the subaltern's own consciousness but is a derived consciousness expressing the relations of domination-subordination. The common sense of the subaltern is the site of this contradictory consciousness. One of the most important objectives of subaltern studies is to recover the subaltern's pure consciousness (the implicit consciousness)—the marks of subalternity—that will reveal the autonomous domain of the subaltern. It is the task of recovering this zone of implicit consciousness that becomes the focus of the subaltern studies analysis of peasant consciousness.

As Chatterjee points out, "Following Guha, the argument of the subaltern studies group . . . has been that by studying the history of peasant rebellions from the point of view of the peasant as an active and conscious subject of history, one obtains an access into that aspect of his consciousness where he is autonomous, undominated" (Chatterjee 1993, 167). Here, the subaltern studies group is using Gramsci's concept of the common sense of the subaltern as a site of contradictory consciousness. If the explicit consciousness reflects the relations of domination-subordination, then the implicit part of the peasant's consciousness reflects the undominated part of his consciousness where the ideology of the dominator fails to grip the peasant consciousness. It is in this zone of (implicit) consciousness that the peasant denies his condition of subordination and asserts his autonomy. But where does this contradictory unity of peasant consciousness appear? The answer to this for the subaltern studies group is the space of community. For subaltern theorists like Chatterjee, the community is "the *site* of peasant struggle, where the respective rights and duties are established and contested" (Chatterjee 1993, 167).

The notion of community is a crucial concept that needs to be explained. There are two questions related to it: (i) Why is community important in studying peasant consciousness? and (ii) What is the concrete form of community consciousness in the subaltern studies?

According to Chatterjee, the notion of community is the fundamental constitutive character of collective consciousness of the peasant. It is the characteristic unifying feature of peasant consciousness. The collective aspect of peasant consciousness is critical, for without it the content of peasant insurgencies (an expression of collective consciousness) would be rendered meaningless. This peasant consciousness as community consciousness is different from bourgeois consciousness:

> The latter operates from the premise of the individual and a notion of his interests (or, in more fashionable vocabulary, his preferences). Solidarities in bourgeois politics are built up through an aggregative process by which individuals come together into alliances on the basis of their common individual interests (or shared preferences). The process is quite the opposite in the consciousness of a rebellious peasantry. There ... individuals are enjoined to act within a collectivity because, it is believed, bonds of solidarity that tie them together already exist. Collective action does not flow from the contract among individuals; rather, individual identities themselves are derived from membership in a community. (Chatterjee 1993, 163)[11]

This notion of peasant consciousness as community consciousness indicates a paradigmatic shift as and when compared with the bourgeois notion of consciousness. The bourgeois notion of consciousness, in line with its methodological emphasis on individualism, conceives of the peasant as rational where rationality is identified with some form of optimizing behaviour. The methodological setup of an agrarian economy as the aggregation of an outcome deriving from the optimizing behaviour of the "rational" peasant is in stark contrarst to the position held by the subaltern studies group. In subaltern studies, the action (reflecting their level of consciousness) of peasants must not be deduced from some notion of rationality but rather from the notion of community. That is why the notion of community in analyzing the space of the peasantry constitutes a paradigmatic shift (in comparison to the "bourgeois" method of analyzing the peasantry) in the subaltern studies methodology.

Guha's analysis of the peasantry did not give any concrete content to the notion of community. He treated it at a more abstract level, using terms like "clan," "tribe," "caste," and so on, unproblematically to fill in the content of communities. For Guha, the peasant (or subaltern) consciousness refers to the first (rudimentary) glimmers of consciousness. The peasant does not have the vision of an ideal(ized) social totality that can only be conceived by (other) groups with more mature consciousness (for example, the working class). Chatterjee, in contrast, believes in the possibility of the peasant or other subaltern group having an ideal(ized) social totality, which basically means a projected system or community as in the subaltern case that is in positive conformity with the interests or consciousness as reflected by the autonomous domain of the elite or the subaltern. He sees the need to give concrete content to the notion of community such that, by analyzing the concrete nature of the community, one can construct the alternative (to the elite) ideal social totality for the subaltern.

Chatterjee (1993) points out that the time has now come to give concrete determinate content to the notion of community: "what is necessary now is to formulate the concept of community within a set of systematic relationships signifying the mutual identity and difference of social groups" (Chatterjee 1993, 165). Community signifies a unity of identity and difference and one can seek out social structures that would capture this unity. In the Indian context, the one paradigmatic form that community takes, according to Chatterjee, is the system of castes, which signifies a unity of identity and difference. However, the community cannot be reduced only to caste. There are other determinate values (meaning elements like class, race, religion, etc.) that condition the notion of community. According to Chatterjee, community is not static in the sense that it has only one determinate value, like caste or religion. It varies from context to context. Within one peasant uprising, the boundaries of solidarities can shift from caste to religion to class in a few days.[12] As a result, peasant uprisings cannot be reduced to any one of these determinate values. As contexts keep changing, so do the determinate values (and the meaning of community). Consequently, the language and meaning of peasant uprisings undergo a series of transformations and with them the meaning of subordination and resistance. As with the notion of community from which peasant consciousness is derived, the peasant consciousness is not static but is subject to an endless play of self-transformation. And by recovering the "history of this consciousness as a movement of self-transformation," one can reveal the positive (hidden) project of the subaltern groups, like the peasantry or caste. This takes us to the question of caste as a paradigmatic form of community that not only reveals to us how caste systems can operate as a determinate value of the community but also how the activities associated with the working of the caste system produce a subversion of the very idealization of its present existence, which is based on relations of power. This, according to Chatterjee (1993), points to a new form of idealization of the caste system where the content of the new ideal carries with it a different meaning of power (an ideal based on a notion of equality totally different from the western (bourgeois) notion of equality).

Caste Consciousness and the Subaltern Consciousness

The discourse on caste in India has been dominated by two positions until now—the Marxist position and the non-Marxist position. Marxists have looked at caste in two ways. Firstly, the traditional Marxists have treated

caste as an element of the superstructure consistent with a feudal base. That is, caste can only be explained in terms of its economic, more specifically, class foundations. Class relations are ontologically privileged and caste relations are explained in terms of the class relations. As the feudal relations of production are overtaken by capitalist ones, caste as a relic institution of the past will simply wither away. Their point is that caste, an unequal institution by definition, is fundamentally different from the modern (Western) notions of equality and freedom that are the basis of the superstructure consistent with capitalism. Hence caste relations cannot be sustained by capitalism. The other Marxist position (Omvedt 1982) has been that class appears as caste in the context of India, and, hence, caste constitutes the material form of the base in Indian society.

The non-Marxist viewpoint on caste reverses the order.[13] For them, caste is the central (ontological) category of Indian society and class is relatively unimportant. The history of Indian society is the history of caste. The building of modern India is not contradictory to the existence of caste since for them, as Chatterjee points out, "the caste system seeks to harmonize within the whole of a social system the mutual distinctiveness of its parts. This is a requirement for any stable and harmonious social order; the caste system is the way this is achieved in India" (Chatterjee 1993, 174). The caste system is not contradictory to the individualistic aspirations of a modern society. For these proponents of the caste system, the abuses related to caste, which are so transparent, do not flow from its ideal social form, but are its aberrations.[14]

The most famous work of the non-Marxist school is that of Dumont (1970). Chatterjee produces a critique of Dumont to articulate his arguments against what he calls the "synthetic theories of caste." Chatterjee uses the Hegelian distinction between the immediate reality (roughly the practical aspects) and the mediated reality (roughly the reality at the level of ideas) to articulate his analysis of Dumont's work. According to Dumont, the caste system is a *whole* that includes the different castes as *parts.* The parts (different castes in hierarchical order) are a contradictory *unity* of *identity* and *difference,* where the unity is grounded on the system of purity and pollution. This system produces hierarchy within the caste system (difference) but also brings the castes together by making via a clear division of labor each dependent on the other's economic labor (identity). According to Chatterjee, this immediate reality is mediated at the level of idea by the *force* that is also the universal. This force is the universal—*dharma:*[15] As Chatterjee points out,

> In Dumont's treatment, the force that holds together the different castes within the whole of the caste system is the ideological force of

dharma.[16] The construct of dharma assigns to each jatis (the communities of castes) its place within the system and defines the relations between each jatis as the simultaneous unity of mutual separateness and mutual dependence. The movement of force must make apparent the process of uniting the essence of a system with its existence. Here, Dumont's claim is categorical. The central argument of his work is that the ideological force of dharma does in fact unite the mediated being of caste with its ideality. Thus the ideal construct of dharma is actualized in the immediacy of social institutions and practices. (Chatterjee 1993, 172–173)

The universal is also the force because the universal involves a relation of power (domination-subordination) without which the inequality (produced by the hierarchy amongst castes) would not be produced.

For Chatterjee, both the Marxist and non-Marxist arguments are part of the nationalist discourse that sought to face the question of caste from a modernist premise:

> Of the two strategies, one contains a critique of the other. Both, however, accept the premise of modernity, the former espousing it to condemn caste as an oppressive and antiquated institution inconsistent with a modern society, the latter asserting that caste in its ideal form is not oppressive and not inconsistent with the aspirations of individuality within the harmony of a unified social order. The former could be said to represent the pure theory of universal modernity; the latter . . . upholds a theory of oriental exceptionalism. As nationalist arguments, both adopt the externally given standpoint of bourgeois equality to criticize the empirical reality of caste practices and to advocate modernist reform. (Chatterjee 1993, 174–175)

Chatterjee (1989, 1993) and subaltern studies in general do not accept the arguments on caste of either the traditional Marxist or the non-Marxist. Chatterjee abandons the traditional Marxist structure of base-superstructure as a framework for explaining the phenomenon of caste relations in India by pointing out that (i) caste does not necessarily follow from the economic, the base and (ii) the linear stage view of history associated with the mode of production narrative is problematic in the background of the recent critiques of such an understanding of history (Chatterjee 1989, 174–178). As for the argument that class takes the form of caste at the material base, Chatterjee argues that caste and class are dual structures, one internal (caste) and the other external (class)—external because it was first implanted in Indian soil via colonial rule. Since the present production struc-

a notion of "peasant class." First, it is difficult to imagine how the peasant class can be treated as a social actor since class as a collective has no definite (operational) means to formulate and execute decisions. A social actor is a locus of decision and action, where the action is in part a consequence of the decision made by the social actor (Hindess 1987). As with actors such as human individuals and social actors such as capitalist enterprises, trade unions, political parties, and state agencies, concrete peasant organizations too can perform as social actors, but not the peasant class itself. No classes as such, peasant or otherwise, have the means to articulate and execute decisions that can be considered as the minimal condition required for the conceptual existence of any actor. Second, from a postmodern Marxist perspective, the peasantry does not exist as an identity with a total closure but, rather, it exists in a disaggregated form where different sections of the population occupy different class positions depending on the particular type of class process in operation. The primitive in formulating the concept of class are processes and not human individuals, which is also a disaggregated concept in a Marxist theory.

We have already seen from our discussion in the previous chapter that in the postmodern Marxist framework, the capitalist enterprise can be splintered into the concepts of capitalist and worker that are disaggregated in terms of the process of performance, appropriation, distribution, and receipt of surplus value. Those who appropriate surplus value are defined as productive or industrial capitalists. Others who receive a part of the surplus value are unproductive capitalists, such as "moneylending capitalists," "merchant capitalists," "landlord capitalists," and so on. The adjectives before the term "capitalist" capture the different standpoints in the processes of production, appropriation, distribution, and receipt of surplus labor. The modifier "industrialist" before the term "capitalist" reveals one standpoint (appropriator of surplus value) distinct from another modifier like "merchant" that posits another standpoint (receiver of surplus value). The worker, in turn, is disaggregated into productive worker (the "doers" of surplus value producing labor) and unproductive worker (the "doers" of non-surplus-value-producing labor such as those engaged in the reproduction of the subsumed class process), where the modifiers "productive" and "unproductive" are names for the distinct standpoint of the workers for the economic space of the process of performance, appropriation, distribution, and receipt of surplus labor. Similarly, other class processes, such as independent, slave, feudal, or communist class processes, can be disaggregated in terms of performance, appropriation, distribution, and receipt of surplus labor. In this context, the unifying concept of "peasant" exists in one coherent and divided manner: "peasant" as a class is meaningless unless it is disaggregated into the multifaceted processes relating to performance, appropriation, distribution, and receipt of surplus labor.

We see then that the group of persons that subaltern studies calls peasantry or "peasant" class as a homogeneous entity does not give us any insight into the intricacies of class structures of Indian society, unless the notion of peasant class itself can be disaggregated and broken up into the multiple class processes and, subsequently, class positions where individuals may occupy different class and nonclass positions simultaneously. Thus, in the case of the capitalist fundamental class process, a "peasant" who appropriates the surplus labor of performers of labor (where surplus labor takes the form of surplus value) and also hires himself out to produce surplus value elsewhere would simultaneously occupy the positions of a productive capitalist and a productive worker. Similarly, a "peasant" could be involved in both the feudal class process and the capitalist class process. The concept of "peasant class" must be disaggregated into the multiple class processes elaborating many class positions that the individual peasant may occupy. The subaltern studies analysis of the peasantry begs the question of the decomposition of the "peasant class."[20]

Also, in case of subaltern studies, it is not clear at all who is to be included and excluded from the category of peasant class. On one side, the subaltern theorists say that the moneylender-cum-merchant class and the landlord class are not to be included in the subaltern groups because they dominate the others. So groups other than the ruling village coterie are to be included in the category of peasantry. But they also say that these dominant groups (the moneylenders, merchants, and landlords) may be dominated by the state, the industrial and mercantile capitalists, or the biggest feudal magnates and hence, as Guha (1982, 1–8) points out, are to be "ideally" included in the category of subaltern that is their "true social being." So they are both dominant and dominated. By the dominated criterion that defines the subaltern it is not clear at all why this group of people should be excluded from the category of subaltern that after all, as acknowledged by Guha, is their true social being. However, if they are included in the category of the subaltern, then the whole study of peasant consciousness in terms of relations of domination-subordination between the elite and the subaltern will fall apart since the category of elite at the level of what in the subaltern studies are called "the regional and local levels" becomes vacuous.

Even after assuming away the problem of classes as social actors and the composition of classes (like that of the peasant class), the above portrait of the peasantry as a homogeneous entity has two immediate implications. First, any ontological privilege to a particular class (specific group of person), like the working class, will be an essentialist move since it will attach an a priori superior consciousness and explanatory power to this group of persons as compared to other "subaltern classes." We will return to this point below. Second, since these groups that we call classes are derived from relations of power, the discursive space of the economic vanishes or remains nonproblematized in subaltern studies. Groups of people are derived from and engaged in struggles only within the political and cultural space. The economic dimensions of society are absent or taken as given (passive) in subaltern studies. As we have already explained, this "absence" or "passivity" is not a deliberate occlusion but a consequence of their theoretical concept of class as a homogeneous group of conscious people derived from relations of domination-subordination.

2. *The Problem of Ideal Social Totality*

For many years Indian Marxists have treated the peasantry unproblematically as an unconscious object to be integrated by the nationalist or communist movements led by the bourgeoisie or the working class respectively. This treatment had to do with the portrait of the peasantry as a backward group that does not have the consciousness or the knowledge (because of the fragmentary nature of village units and their protest movements) to work toward producing conscious historical change. Instead, that privilege is accorded either to the bourgeoisie or the working class. In the Indian modes of production debate, the participants, despite their effort to theorize the differentiation of the peasantry into multiple classes, were united in their depiction of the peasantry as a backward group of people when it comes to historical change. Guha and others make a scathing criticism of traditional Marxism for having demoted the importance of peasant consciousness in such a manner. Through various case studies, they make the point that the peasants are conscious subjects of history and one can derive an autonomous zone of that consciousness, a zone uncontaminated by any ideological meaning being disseminated from the elite autonomous domain. The proof of their political consciousness is the subaltern's inversion of power relations that is epitomized by the elite's domination of the subaltern. However, peasant consciousness is of a rudimentary nature, the first glimmers of consciousness. Guha bemoans the lack of an ideal social totality on the part of the peasants as an indicator of a lack of mature consciousness. Chatterjee, taking Guha's argument further, argues that the decoding of peasant consciousness and the subaltern consciousness in general reveals the existence of ideal social totalities. While the peasant cannot see it, the social scientist should be able to discern the existence of such totalities. For example, one can derive an ideal social totality of either the lower-ranked caste groups or the peasantry from an analysis of their respective struggles. However, the peasantry cannot achieve this ideal social totality on its own because of the fragmentary nature of the peasant uprisings. It needs another group like the working class to intervene and fulfil its projected ideal social totality. The working class has an ideal social totality of its own, a socialism that will subsume all other moments of the ideal social totalities that Chatterjee talks about.[21]

There is a similarity of Chatterjee's position with that of the theorists in the Indian modes of production debate on the question of the incapability of the peasantry to initiate social change on its own and the subsequent requirement of the working class to provide leadership to initiate that change. However, the difference is also crucial. Chatterjee does give a place to ideal social totalities other than that of the working class, which is not acknowledged by the traditional Marxists. Traditional Marxists talk about social change primarily in terms of the transition from one mode of production to another, where the only relevant subject of social change is the working class. Chatterjee and the subaltern studies group in general do not deny the importance of the working class as a revolutionary subject capable of pursuing changes of momentous dimension, but they also point out the importance of social transitions that lead to changes in superstructural elements (like the caste system) without greatly affecting the basic structure of the economic at all. Their position that such changes cannot be produced by the peasant and lower caste groups on their own is a different question.

But one can certainly also question the usefulness of positing the notion of an ideal social totality. Why should the peasant or the subaltern be interested in the notion of the ideal social totality at all? This is a question that is not even posed in the literature. Guha is critical of the subaltern's lack of mature consciousness in not having the vision of the ideal social totality, while Chatterjee is critical of the inability of the subaltern in fulfilling the ideal social totality it possesses. They record the failures of the various movements as a lack of certain (i.e., mature) consciousness on the part of these groups. But what if the subaltern groups were not interested in the ideal social totality at all? What if they wanted their movements to remain localized and were not interested in the macro-political implications of their struggle? Our point is that this presumption of an ideal social totality is not that of the peasantry but of the social scientists. An interesting exercise would be to read all the "failures" of peasant uprisings in subaltern studies not in terms of lack of certain qualities (in terms of the vision or ability) but in terms of an absence of an ideal social totality at the conceptual level. The rereading of the Barasat peasant uprisings, the Birsa Munda–led peasant uprising or the Kol uprising as pictured by Guha, and the analysis of the Hadis as a social movement by Chatterjee, in light of the theoretical concept of the absence of the ideal social totality may reveal a better and more fruitful understanding of why such movements were consigned to micro politics. Then the "failures" as perceived by subaltern studies may not be failures at all but rather struggles that were produced and whose results were determined contextually. This will also avoid the dangerous implications related to the (dual) division of consciousness (mature and rudimentary, pure and impure, or real and unreal) to which we turn next.[22]

3. Consciousness and the Search for the Truth

The concept of subaltern *consciousness* poses a deep problem for the sub altern studies school. Using Gramsci's notion of contradictory consciousness, they divide subaltern consciousness into pure and impure consciousness. The pure consciousness epitomizing the autonomous dimension of the subaltern consciousness reflects the true consciousness of the subaltern. To recover this autonomous dimension is to bring into the open the truth about the subaltern—its culture, politics, and dreams. The impure consciousness of the subaltern reflects that part of the consciousness that is contaminated by the dissemination of meaning pouring in from the autonomous domain of the elite. This part of subaltern consciousness is its false consciousness. The task of the social scientist is to flush out the false consciousness and recover the true consciousness of the subaltern.

In subaltern studies, the concept of the subaltern is understood as a group of conscious people whose true consciousness is derived from this autonomous and independent domain uncontaminated by any outside influence. This group of people has a pure subjectivity whose origin can be traced to the existence of a pure unmaligned domain. If the pure subjectivity is brought into the open, then it is possible to establish the truth about the subaltern. Also, subaltern studies is a universalistic discourse. The entire population is divided into the two universals—subaltern and elite. Whoever can be shown to be dominated is a subaltern. Similarly, those who dominate constitute the elite group. To establish the truism about the universal subaltern becomes the hidden subtext (the text being the consciousness of the subaltern) of subaltern studies. This is what Spivak calls ". . . the dangerous hook of claiming to establish the truth/knowledge of the subaltern and his consciousness" (1985, 356), though she does not explain precisely how such a danger is produced in subaltern studies.

The search for the roots and subjectivehood (subjectivity) brings a series of essentialist reasonings into the heart of subaltern analysis that have come under sharp attack from postmodernist and Marxist quarters as well. These criticisms are now part of postmodernist commonplaces: (subaltern) consciousness is not something to be disclosed (Laclau and Mouffe 1985; Hindess 1987; Amariglio and Callari 1989); the subject is decentered (Laclau and Mouffe 1985; Laclau 1990; Amariglio, Callari, and Cullenberg 1989; Resnick and Wolff 1987; Amariglio and Callari 1989; Amariglio and Ruccio 1994); false consciousness is a metaphysical concept (Laclau and

Mouffe 1985); there is no universal, no source, no origin (Foucault 1972b; Lyotard 1984; Laclau and Mouffe 1985; Laclau 1990, 1994; Resnick and Wolff 1987). Let us give one illustration of the dangers involved with the subaltern studies search for the true roots of the subaltern. This illustration follows directly from an argument made in subaltern studies that we have already uncovered.

We have explained that subaltern consciousness is composed of two elements, a pure consciousness and an impure consciousness. Recovering the pure consciousness will reveal the truth about the subaltern and, if one goes further, as Chatterjee does, help establish the possibility of the ideal social totality (universal). Thus peasant studies will reveal the ideal social totality of the peasants while caste studies will reveal the ideal social totality of the oppressed castes. However, these ideal social totalities cannot be practically achieved since impure consciousness acts as a barrier; the elite intervenes in these subaltern struggles and appropriates the subaltern collectivities under its rule. The subaltern can only see the micro world and is unaware (unconscious) of the macro world. He does not have the consciousness to intervene and fulfill his dream in the macro world. He does not see the possibility of the ideal social totality. He has to wait for his Godot to arrive, so to speak, to rescue him from his narrowness and to fight and unmask the elite's hegemonic power on his behalf and show him the dreams of which he is made. This Godot is of course the working class, for it is only the working class that has the ability to transform itself from class in itself to class for itself and whose ontological social position gives it the knowledge about society and history (elements of macro politics). It is the class, as G. A. Cohen once put it, that is most able and well disposed to carry out historical change. The working class as the possessor of world knowledge (mature consciousness) brings a notion of ideal social totality of its own that will subsume the ideal social totalities of the other subaltern groups as lower moments. This produces a hierarchy in subaltern consciousness; the working class has a more mature (developed form of) consciousness than other subaltern groups. Hence the discursive existence of a dualistic consciousness produces this dichotomy at the level of subaltern groups and posits as a truism the inferior nature of the consciousness of the non-working-class subaltern groups of people. Also, in terms of social struggle, class struggle conducted by the working class is given a privilege over other forms of struggle.[23] This takes us to the next point—the peasantry as a negative element and its relationship to the working class.

The Peasantry versus the Working Class

One of the subaltern school's main concerns was to shift the idea of the subaltern from its colonial and enlightenment connotation of being a negative residual to something constructive (positive). Their discursive focus point on the peasantry (or subaltern) is an indicator of that shift and was designed to produce a positive image of the subaltern as a conscious group that could organize and act on its own. Yet the conflation of the discursive and the ontological ended up producing a negative image of the subaltern. Propositions like "subaltern politics is consigned to localism" or the "working class has a mission" or the "subaltern awaits in vain for leadership (working-class-led) to raise them above localism" are reflections of this production of the subaltern as inferior and negative.

Subaltern studies considers the subaltern and its further subclassification into different groups (peasantry, lower castes, tribal, religious minority, etc.) as an autonomous and independent category. Thus, the subaltern is independent and autonomous from the elite while the different groups within the subaltern are independent and autonomous from each other. They exist in pure unadulterated form, uncontaminated by any outside effects. Not only is the subaltern independent from the elite but the peasantry is independent and autonomous from the working class. As Guha points out, "This (the politics of the people or subaltern) was an autonomous domain, for it neither originated from elite politics nor did its existence depend on the latter" (1982, 4). Or, as Chatterjee argues, in subaltern studies, "There was . . . an opposed pair: on the one side, the dominators (the state or the landlords or moneylenders) and on the other, the peasants. A relational opposition of power necessarily meant that the dominated had to be granted their own domain of subjectivity, where they were autonomous, undominated. If it were not so, the dominators would, in the exercise of their domination, wholly consume and obliterate the dominated" (1993, 161). The subaltern consciousness and language are the reflection of the independent and autonomous domain of the subaltern (Guha 1982, 1983, 1989; Chatterjee 1983, 1986, 1989, 1993; Chakraborty 1985, 1995).

Guha (1982, 1983, 1989), Chatterjee (1982, 1983, 1993), Amin (1982), Pandey (1982), Mukherjee (1988), and other subaltern theorists made the peasantry and its consciousness their object of study. However, despite giving a discursive privilege to peasant consciousness, Guha assumes that the peasant consciousness is backward vis-à-vis working-class consciousness. According to Guha, the working class, if it achieves its class for itself form, possesses a mature consciousness that the peasants do not. He writes,

> . . . the initiatives which originated from the domain of subaltern politics were not, on their part, powerful enough to develop the nationalist movement into full-fledged struggle for national liberation. The working class was still not sufficiently mature in the objective

conditions of its social being and in its consciousness as a class-for-itself, nor was it firmly allied yet with the peasantry. As a result it could do nothing to take over and complete the mission which the bourgeoisie had failed to realise. The outcome of it all was that the numerous peasant uprisings of the period, some of them massive in scope and rich in anti-colonialist consciousness, *waited in vain for a leadership to raise them above localism* and generalise them into a nation-wide anti-imperialist campaign. (1982, 6)

This translates into a special social privilege accorded to the working class, meaning that the working class is the most important social group and that other forms of consciousness, such as peasant consciousness, are inferior to working-class consciousness. The working class is given this privileged status in terms of being a bearer of social consciousness that will re-create history. The peasantry is stuck in a narrow localism while the working class has a broad vision and knowledge of history. The idea of the backwardness of peasant consciousness is theoretically pre-given in the subaltern studies.

Subaltern historiography would consider the classical road to history (transition from feudalism to capitalism or from feudalism to "new democracy") virtually impossible to achieve for the case of India since the bourgeoisie is not interested in the classical transition route through primitive capital accumulation and the working class has not transformed itself from the class in itself to the class for itself. No other group of people, including the peasantry, has the capability to lead a socialist revolution and to transform Indian society. Revolt by these groups will only promote a symbolic inversion of the elite order without the possibility of transforming society. The subaltern has only a subversive project. Subaltern consciousness is not positively structured in the sense that it would be in a position to re-create and transform society. That privilege is accorded only to the working class. The working class constitutes the vanguard section of the people and its mission is to capture state power. This translation of the discursive privilege accorded to peasant consciousness to the ontological social privilege given to the working-class consciousness is a difficult point for the subaltern studies group that is particularly evident in the tension produced between Guha and Chatterjee.

Guha is clearly not considering the peasant uprisings from a positive angle, implying instead that such uprisings do not have the possibility to lead to radical social changes. The only ideal in Guha is that created by the elite; the subaltern does not have any alternative projected ideals. This absence, for Guha, is a sign of weakness of the subaltern movement. As Chatterjee points out, "because of his (i.e. Guha's) objective of isolating an invariant structural form, in line with the structuralism inherent in his method, he has not attempted to give us a *history* of this consciousness as a movement of self-transformation" (Chatterjee 1993, 164). Implicitly criticizing this dominant trend in the subaltern studies, he writes,

> Perhaps we have allowed ourselves to be taken in too easily by the general presence of an abstract negativity in the *autonomous domain* of subaltern beliefs and practices and have missed those marks, faint as they are, of an immanent process of criticism and learning, of selective appropriation, of making sense of and using one's own terms the elements of a more powerful cultural order. . . . Surely it would be wholly contrary to our project to go about as though only the dominant culture has a life in history and subaltern consciousness is eternally frozen in its structure of negation. (1993, 197)

As we have already explained, Chatterjee is firmly committed to giving a positive content to subaltern consciousness. For him, the subaltern not only protests the condition of his subordination but also leaves behind (fragmentary) imprints of the possible alternative ideal (universal). In recovering the autonomous domain of the subaltern consciousness, the task of social theorists is also to format the traces of the ideal into a theoretical model such that one can begin to address the question of the transition of society.[24] But there is also a tension in Chatterjee's position. While he considers peasant struggles and caste struggles to be capable of revealing marks of a positive ideal that can be discursively constructed, he seems to discount the (practical) possibility that such struggles can lead to major social changes. Such struggles do not have the capability, on their own, to bring about major social change. That is, via this distinction between the discursive and the social practice, he seems to be discounting the role of peasants and castes as an initiator of social change. Thus, the task of building the alternative ideal at the social level requires some other group of people (like the working class), who, armed with the knowledge of the alternative ideal, are capable of leading the subaltern groups to social changes resembling the ideal. One can implicitly read the presence of this tension in Chatterjee's treatise. The construction of the ideal (derived from the autonomous peasant and caste consciousness) in the discursive domain resides with the failure of the caste or peasant groups to construct it at the social domain. For example, studying the genealogy of insubordination and the alternative idealization of the caste system of the Hadis, a lower caste group residing in West Bengal, Chatterjee despairingly points to the hopeless nature of such protests because "it was their (the Hadi's) very marginality that may have taken the sting out of their revolt against subordination, and by asserting the unrelenting negativity and exclusiveness of their rebellious faith, they condemned themselves to eternal marginality" (Chatterjee 1993, 191).

Thus, in the end Chatterjee reasserts the division between the discursive and the ontological. The only difference is that, unlike Guha, he provides a theory of the universal (ideal social totality) for the subaltern at the discursive level without challenging in any fundamental way Guha's ontological claim of the peasant's or the caste's incapability vis-à-vis the working class of realizing that ideal. They have another thing in common, the idea of an ideal social totality (universal). Guha despairs about the lack of the ideal social totality on the part of the peasants, while Chatterjee celebrates the possibility of the peasantry possessing such an ideal social totality.

This contradictory and tension-ridden moment in the subaltern studies school of thought has not been lost on the theorists involved. This school is now at a crossroads between classical Marxism and postmodern-type Marxism. In fact, the school has recently split with eminent classical Marxist theorists, such as Sumit Sarkar, who criticize its agenda. Sarkar blamed the group for its recent friendly postures toward postmodernism and post-structuralism and for its glorification of the negativity of the subaltern (which includes religious sentiments and beliefs), thereby playing right into the hands of the Hindu fundamentalists (Sarkar 1993, 1995). Others are beginning to visualize alternative routes to break away from the image of the negative subaltern. This introspective stage of the subaltern school movement is best characterized in the recent work of Chatterjee (1993) and Chakraborty (1993, 1995).

Chakraborty (1995, 751–759), perhaps the one most influenced by postmodernism, asks the subaltern theorist to be concerned not only with the negativity of the subaltern with the intent "to teach the oppressed of today how to be democratic subjects tomorrow" but also to go to the subaltern and "learn" its positive characteristics. He writes,

> In other words, to allow the subaltern position to challenge our own conceptions of what is universal, to be open to the possibility of a particular thought-world however concerned it might be with the task of grasping a totality, being rendered finite by the presence of the Other: such are the utopic horizons to which this *other moment* (other than the negative one) of *subaltern studies* calls us. . . . The subaltern here is *the ideal figure* of he who survives actively, even joyously, on the assumption that the effective instruments of domination will always belong to somebody else and never aspires to them. (1995, 757)

The problem is that both Chatterjee and Chakraborty end up reaffirming the dichotomies (of elite and subaltern, of pure and impure consciousness, and of the hierarchical ranking of ideal social totalities). The ideal figure of the subaltern or, what is the same, the autonomous domain of the subaltern are marks of this reaffirmation. In the 1980s, subaltern studies was criticized by traditional Marxists for giving a binary status to the subaltern/elite. Replying to this criticism of the subaltern studies school on the question of the binary relationship, Chakraborty (1985), who was at that time a more traditional Marxist, did not find anything wrong with such a dualistic classification and called the move a necessary one for theorization. Ten years later Chakraborty (1995) comes back full circle to criticize the aspect of binary division as essentialist and, in his view, theoretically unacceptable. He criticizes traditional Indian Marxists for holding on to binaries, such as "tradition/modernity," "rational/nonrational," "intellectual/emotion," that are independent and autonomous and, hence, self-referential. Yet he ends up by reaffirming a similar binary status to the "subaltern/elite." He cannot have it both ways. A nonessentialist and nonhistoricist version of subaltern studies, which Chakraborty is now professing, must abandon the binary division between elite and subaltern as constituting an independent and autonomous domain. There is simply no other way.[25]

Conclusion

Subaltern studies posed the question of why the Western form of transition and development anchored on the logic of "industrialization through capital accumulation" failed to take hold in India. It looked for an answer in the autonomous domain of the subaltern, recording the historical events that signaled the failure of modernism to install its order over the Indian society. But it also signaled the failure of the subaltern to overcome modernity and establish its own rule. Given the failure of the subaltern to defeat the elite and that of the elite to overcome and destroy the subaltern, how does the elite establish its dominance, to break the apparent gridlock in the path of transition and development? That is, if the elite cannot subdue the subaltern groups entirely, how does it establish its rule to further capital accumulation? Even though the question is a logical extension from our present discussion, unlike the literature accompanying the arguments dealt with respect to the first stage of subaltern studies theory of transition and development, this problematic was not part of the set of volumes that came to constitute subaltern studies. The literature—also called the neo-Gramscian approach—trying to grapple with this question rose parallel to subaltern studies[26] but some theorists, principally Chatterjee (1993), recast the problematic in elite-subaltern terms that can be viewed as an extension of the theory of transition and development of the subaltern studies as already discussed. In short, in trying to answer to the possibility of a development path in light of the failure of elite to establish its rule without being replaced by the subaltern, theorists such as Partha Chatterjee took to a reconstruction of the Gramscian approach of hegemony giving way to the concept of passive revolution of capital. In this regard we see the literature on passive revolution of capital as an extension of subaltern studies theory of transition and development, if we are to take the latter's problematic as already discussed to its logical conclusion. Our focus here is to see how the methodological problems of essentialism and marks of historicism already discussed in the first stage of transition and development of subaltern studies now unfolds into this theory of transition and development. In elaborating passive revolution of capital, especially as in the influential work of Chatterjee (1993, 1994), we illustrate that the purported antimodernism of the subaltern studies theory of transition—which, as we have described, is construed around the essentialist logic anyway—gives way to explicit historicism in the new concept of development.

CHAPTER **5**

A Marxian Critique of the Passive Revolution of Capital

The second round of the transition theory leading from subaltern studies as discussed in the previous chapter began with the following question: In the case of the historic failure of the classical road to history (capitalism failing to overcome precapitalism), how do the elite establish their hegemony over other (potentially antagonistic) elements? More specifically, the question that is asked is the following: *How do the elite establish their hegemonic rule at this historic juncture of capitalism's failure to overcome precapitalism?* This question became a focal point of debate among Indian Marxists in the late 1980s and continues to be a major impetus of research in the Indian academic scene. The emphasis here is on the consciousness of the elite; how the elite react to the subaltern's political moves to establish their hegemony. This construction of the hegemonic rule of the elite is intrinsically linked with the subaltern studies depiction of India's social reality as a case of the historic failure of capitalism to supersede precapitalism. The concept used to theoretically articulate the central arguments related to the question are through what Gramsci called the passive revolution of capital that may be defined as capitalism's appropriation of precapitalism to create a surrogate or false synthesis (universal).[1] The domain of the passive revolution of capital is to be located at the historical juncture of capitalism's (antithesis) contradiction with precapitalism (thesis), which, as Kalyan Sanyal (1988, 1991–92) pointed out, is a case of blocked dialect representing the failure of society to move to its projected telos as per the logic of classical historical materialism. This implies that the system cannot move from one structure (feudalism) to another (capitalism) as part of a big-bang change but rather, by virtue of the blocked dialectic, capitalism's dominance must be accounted for in the context of a complex social formation consisting of capital and noncapital. Capital has to give space to the precapitalist elements, including the dominant precapitalist groups as their subordinate partners and what Partha Chatterjee calls the aspirations of the popular masses. The creation of this space (that is, the surrogate universal) conducive to conditions of capital accumulation involves a process of hegemonic construction of capital's rule. That is, the production of the surrogate synthesis involves a process of construction of capital's hegemonic rule. But we will of course reveal in the course of our discussion that the case of the blocked dialectic is not a permanent scenario and will give way to an alternative progressive evolution of society toward a higher moment. Passive revolution of capital (a stage in capitalism's triumph) is then only a glint waiting to be transgressed and passed on as a trace (a lower moment—a leftover) of history. What then is never questioned in the literature is the idea of progress—in the Hegelian sense of supersession—understood as part of a historicist logic. The *idea* of progress in its rational, teleological form is not questioned. Rather, the inability to achieve that progress is posed as a problem and, consequently, a search ensues for an alternative path to fulfill that idea of progress. That is why we say that the neo-Gramscian approach is another variant of historical materialism.

Using the concept of the passive revolution of capital to analyze the case of India, we aim to conceptualize the complexities of India's "nationhood" and how via this projection of nationhood (surrogate synthesis), modernism (capitalism) aspires to establish its hegemony by appropriating the traditional (precapitalism). We shall show how the concept of the passive revolution of capital as theorized by these Indian Marxists helps to articulate these aspects at the theoretical level.

The passive revolution of capital becomes an important mode of explaining the pattern of India's economic development in a situation where capitalism cannot proceed via its classical path of annihilating precapitalism.[2] This concept, theorized as part of the route taken from Hegel to Gramsci, is developed by theorists such as Arnold (1984), Chatterjee (1986, 1988, 1993, 1994), Chaudhury (1988, 1991–92, 1994), Patnaik (1988), Sen (1987, 1988), and Sanyal (1988, 1991–92, 1993).[3] Theorists have countered the essentialist inclinations (especially those related to economic essentialism) of the Indian modes of production debate by invoking the Gramscian concept of the passive revolution of capital to explain the complex reality of India's capitalist development.

First, we present the concept of the passive revolution of capital as theorized by the Indian Marxists. Here, we will follow the arguments made principally by Ajit Chaudhury, since he articulated in the greatest detail the theoretical framework of passive revolution associated with the development of the Hegelian route to Gramsci. Second, we will discuss the application of the passive revolution of capital in the context of India. Here we will concentrate on the treatments by Chatterjee and Sanyal, since these have gained the most prominence. We will also explain why this way of looking at India's capitalist development can be counterpoised as a critique of the Indian modes of production debate. After having discussed these theoretical foundations, we will provide a detailed critique of this way of looking at transition. The critique, both from an internal and external perspective (that is, the postmodern Marxist perspective), will range from the essentialist and historicist dimensions involved in this theory to the problems of incorporating class in this framework and the absence of household economy from the discursive domain, to the conceptual existence of a closed social totality such as capitalism, and, finally, to the so-called antithetical relationship between community and capital. As will be seen, these criticisms will seriously undermine the subaltern studies theory of transition and development.

Passive Revolution of Capital : A Tryst with Capitalism

Let us begin, as in Chaudhury (1991–92), with the route from Hegel to Gramsci in constructing the concept of passive revolution of capital. Chaudhury claims to read Hegel's *Philosophy of Right* in the light of Hegel's logic in order to derive the concept of the surrogate or false synthesis (universal) that is critical for conceptualizing the passive revolution of capital.

A crucial phrase in Chaudhury's rendition of the Hegelian logic is that of the unity and struggle of opposites. Particulars or parts, as independent and autonomous, oppose one another while their contradiction is resolved in the domain of the universal (bond of unity).[4] At the domain of particulars, these particulars cannot reconcile their differences and they need another domain—called the universal—that will reconcile the differences and bring order to the system. That is, the unity of particulars is mediated through the universal. The universal is the higher form, the source, from which the particulars flow. According to Chaudhury, in Hegel the state is the universal that holds the particulars (members of civil society) together. As Chaudhury points out,

> The Hegelian state has this property: that it can hold different individuals together, as particulars . . . each viewing his concept of general welfare as flowing from it. In short, the state is the universal (the source, the origin) from which these particulars (members of

civil society) flow. Needless to say, there will be contradictions between the universal and particulars (as also among particulars): the
state is a unity and struggle of opposites. . . . And since the state is
the universal, an expression of a self-determined principle (i.e.
right) internal to the members of civil society, the opposition between the state and civil society . . . disappears. Freedom is realized
in civil society, through the state. (Chaudhury 1991–92, 40–41)

In orthodox Marxism, while the basic structure of Hegel is kept intact,
the positions of the components in the structure are reversed. The economic (capital) becomes the source of the universal from which the meaning of politics and culture flows. According to Chaudhury, in orthodox
Marxism, the state, as a particular, belongs to the superstructure while capital emerges as the universal at the base. The state represents capital and,
since capital is oppressive, the state, unlike in Hegel, is necessarily oppressive.[5]

Chaudhury further points out that Gramsci refused to acknowledge the
validity of the dual division between the base (capital) and the superstructure (state) and the presupposition of the orthodox Marxist position that
the latter flows from the former. In his analysis, Gramsci replaced the base
by civil society and the universal by the state, and he argued that the elements of civil society are not particulars flowing from the universal, the
state. If particulars do not flow from the universal, the totality (unity of
particulars) falls apart and chaos prevails. Chaudhury reinterprets Gramsci to point out that civil society is constituted by many particulars, including that of capital, and since there are many particulars overlapping with
one another, the state as the universal cannot represent capital immediately. So the task is, as Chaudhury points out, to "provide a universal that
can hold its particulars—such will be the central task for a Hegelian reformulation of the state theory" (Chaudhury 1991–92, 42–43).

The universal cannot be the pure universal of the Hegelian type but
rather a displaced, false, or surrogate universal that is able to artificially
hold the particulars together in some form of unity. And yet, the unity
must be such that capital should be able to establish its rule and the process
of capital accumulation. For Chaudhury and other Marxists like Chatterjee (as we shall see in his treatment of passive revolution of capital with respect to India), this is a dilemma for capital. Capital is unable to establish
itself as the universal and yet it must somehow be able to rule. "In short,
capital has its own limit, and since *it is conscious*, it knows its limit. Therefore, capital sees to it that the state character does not represent capital immediately; capital chooses to be ruled by an outsider. This universal,
standing above the particular, i.e. capital, represents the truth of capital's

hegemony, which appears in reality through displacement. The truth of hegemony, also projected by capital, is not a false one: it is *capital's recognition of reason*" (Chaudhury 1991–92, 44). Hence, capital is only a particular—a dominant particular—where its dominance is derived from an ontological social privilege accorded to it. This ontological social privilege for capital is rooted and produced out of the historicism of the Hegelian logic that rules out the possibility of any other options given the stage of history.

The crucial concepts in Hegel's historical analysis, as seen and used by Chaudhury, are those of thesis, antithesis, and synthesis. Thesis and antithesis are different historical moments of the universal and their resolution in the form of supersession of antithesis by a new thesis is called the synthesis (another historical moment of the universal). This captures the idea of historicism embedded in the Hegelian logical structure, as interpreted by Chaudhury. Thesis and antithesis are lower moments of history while their unity (resolution) as synthesis is a higher moment of history. In a standard Hegelian interpretation of Marx, the antithesis supersedes the thesis to create a new synthesis. In the next historical stage, the synthesis becomes the new thesis with the arrival of its corresponding antithesis. The resolution at this historical stage will produce another synthesis and so on. In the present juncture, when capitalism is the antithesis and precapitalism is the thesis, capitalism must emerge as the next universal. That is, at this transition stage of capitalism's ascendancy, it must establish its rule including in the arena of the state. In orthodox Marxism, this poses no problem since capital is the universal that will mirror its own image through the state. However, in the event of capitalism's failure to annihilate precapitalism, how does capital establish its hegemony? In this context, Chaudhury reinterprets Gramsci to call into question the orthodox Marxist proposition of capital's uncontested rule flowing from its universalistic standing by pointing out that (i) capital is not the universal from which the state flows and (ii) capital can only be a particular, albeit a dominant one. There are other particulars, other precapitalist elements that stand alongside capital. If capital is only one among many particulars, and if the antithesis (capitalism) fails to overcome its thesis (precapitalism), then the other particulars must be accommodated. But accommodated by whom? Here, as we mentioned earlier, Chaudhury calls for a production of a surrogate universal (synthesis), which, in this literature, is something beyond state and yet deeply connected to the state (not a pure Hegelian state but a different type of state about which we will say more in the next section).[6] And yet (given the stage of history), capital must establish its dominance— that is, its hegemonic rule—since it is the dominant particular. It must establish its hegemonic rule in the state (the surrogate universal) via an accommodation of other precapitalist elements such that they do not fundamentally contest its rule. However, via this mechanism, the process of accommodation undergoes a transformation into a process of appropriation—appropriation of precapitalist elements by capital. The creation of a surrogate universal to artificially unite the particulars around the dominance of the particular of capital in the event of the failure of the antithesis to annihilate the thesis constitutes an alternative route of legitimizing capital's rule or hegemony. In the next section, we will demonstrate how a surrogate synthesis is created for the case of India.

The domain of the passive revolution of capital is at the historical juncture of capitalism's (antithesis) contradiction with precapitalism (thesis).[7] In this context, Gramsci's concept of the passive revolution of capital can be formulated as the case where the antithesis does not annihilate or supersede the thesis; it appropriates part of the thesis to create a *surrogate or false synthesis (universal)* (Chaudhury, 1991–92, 37–59).[8] Pointing out the major difference between the surrogate universal and the Hegelian universal, Chaudhury writes,

> There remains a fundamental difference—between the Hegelian universal and the surrogate universal. The *Hegelian universal* is real but essentially contradictory: contradictory because the idea is ever changing—it is always implicitly what it is not, its other- in its development, unfolding itself. The *surrogate universal*, on the other hand, creates an illusion, is unreal; but an illusion, rooted in the real—it is not any society that can create this illusion, the illusion is embedded in this society, therefore is not pure imaginary. The surrogate universal resides in a non-imaginary unreal space. . . . The surrogate universal is only a symptom: it is a symptom of the false unity that it represents. . . . To repeat: the unity exists in fact, in real space and time. Therefore, there must be a unity in truth, at least as a possibility. The elite converts the possibility into an actuality, projects a universal which in turn strengthens the unity, makes it relatively permanent, stable. (Chaudhury 1991–92, 46–47)

An example of this surrogate universal (synthesis), in the context of India, is the idea of the "nation," which, according to this group of theorists, is deeply ingrained in the body of the state. We shall come back to this point in the next section. Writing on the role of this surrogate synthesis resulting from the historic failure of capital to supersede precapital, Chaudhury points out that

> The capital/precapital relation, therefore, is a unity and struggle of opposites. The thesis does not negate the anti-thesis; it appropriates

the anti-thesis. In other words, the thesis transforms the antithesis. Capital, as a particular, is conscious of its limit: that it is finite. Therefore, it does not project itself as the universal. It projects a surrogate universal that makes capital the dominant particular. (Chaudhury 1991–92, 58)

Arguing along the same vein, Sanyal (1991–92, 1993) points out that many interpreters of Gramsci have read the inability of capital to establish the uncontested bourgeois hegemony as a failure of capital's rule. Disagreeing on this point, he writes,

> The surrogate synthesis is hardly a "case of failure" on the part of the bourgeoisie to rule by thesis, as suggested by the orthodox Marxist interpretation of Gramsci. On the contrary, the strength of the bourgeoisie lies precisely in its ability to produce the surrogate synthesis and to elicit collaboration from the subaltern classes in favour of the apparently non-bourgeois universal that is associated with it. The hegemonic power of capital essentially rests on its ability to create illusions, weave our truths, make victory look like defeat and defeat, victory. The world of capital is a world of half-truths—but of far more complex ones than what the traditional Marxist interpretation of Gramsci would suggest. (Sanyal 1991–92, 29)

It is worth noting that surrogate synthesis is not the ideal synthesis but, rather, a deformed case arising from the failure or incompleteness of primitive capital accumulation. Primitive capital accumulation, as argued in this literature on passive revolution, is the process through which capitalism (the antithesis) annihilates or supersedes precapitalism (thesis). It does this by destroying the precapitalist subject positions creating in turn the conditions for a mass of new subject positions (the wage laborers or proletariat) to be inscribed within the capitalist economy. The failure of primitive capital accumulation to play its historical role in creating a mass of propertyless laborers and inscribing them in the capitalist production process as wage labor (replacing the subject position in precapitalist economy with capital and labor as the dominant subject positions) leaves behind precapitalist structures that capitalism cannot supersede. In other words, the historical failure or incompleteness of primitive capital accumulation and, consequently, the inability of capitalism to supersede precapitalism is the historical basis for the passive revolution of capital.[9]

It is also worth repeating that capital is only a particular in this framework and not a universal. Chaudhury criticizes the traditional Indian Marxists (those associated with the Indian modes of production debate) by pointing out that they treated capital as a universal at the base. Thus, when they found no capital at the base, they pronounced that capitalism did not exist in India. Chaudhury points out that in the Indian modes of production debate, "The implicit presupposition is that capital is the universal. Therefore, when we argue (meaning the theorists associated with the Indian modes of production debate) that the wage labor is not the dominant mode of labor in Indian agriculture and even when wage labor is not free—we only establish that capital is not the universal" (Chaudhury 1991–92, 59). According to Chaudhury, this is a false way of posing the problem and is highly misleading. Under the passive revolution of capital, capital is no longer the universal but only the dominant particular. Other particulars, such as precapitalist elements, will also be present, but that does not preclude capital from establishing its rule via the passive revolution of capital. That is, the presence of precapitalist elements does not imply the absence of capitalism. The right question for Chaudhury is, "How does capital establish itself as the dominant factor in the specific situation of India?"

Passive Revolution of Capital in India: An Explanation of Capitalism's Triumph

In this section, we will follow Chatterjee's (1986, 1988, 1993, 1994) and Sanyal's (1988, 1991–92, 1993) highly influential analyses of India's capitalist development as a case of the passive revolution of capital. According to Chatterjee, in the context of India, capital is only one among many particulars existing within society though it is assumed to be *the dominant* particular. Its dominance is revealed in the very construction of the project of nationhood. The unity of India as a nation is captured through its projection of a "postcolonial development state" (a term we will explain below) coalesced around the teleology of domination and the expansion of the modern sector, by which we mean the sector that accumulates capital. The continuing process of capital accumulation is the uncontested premise of creating a modern nation, and any challenge to this premise is a challenge to the content of this vision of nationhood. As Chatterjee points out,

> The overall constraint here is to maintain the unity of the modern sector as a whole, for that, as we have seen before, stands forth within the body of the state as the *overwhelmingly dominant element of the nation*. . . . The identification of this sector cannot be made in any specific regional terms, nor does it coincide with a simple rural/urban dichotomy. But because of its *unique standing as a particular interest that can claim to represent the dynamic aspect of the nation itself,* the entire political process conducted by the state, including the political parties that stake their claims to run the cen-

tral organs of the state, must work toward producing a consensus on protecting the unity of the modern sector. Any appearance of a fundamental lack of consensus here will resonate as a *crisis of national unity itself.* (Chatterjee 1993, 217)

The teleology of capital accumulation, as a strategy for India's development, was grounded on the idea of historical progress. Nehru, the first Indian prime minister, was firmly committed to that idea, as can be gauged by the following comment he made: "We are trying to catch up, as far as we can, with the industrial revolution that occurred long ago in Western countries" (Nehru 1954, vol. I, pp. 96). If capital accumulation was the uncontested teleology of India's development state and the essence of India's nationhood, then the welfarist dimension that Chatterjee points out as a political dimension is also an integral part of the postcolonial development state. And this produces an almost unsolvable contradiction that constitutes the basis of the passive revolution of capital in India.

According to Chatterjee, in the classical cases of industrial development, for example, in the case of England, the rigors of industrialization associated with capital accumulation proceeded first through the process of primitive capital accumulation propelled by the coercive machinery of the state. This coercive aspect of the state was legitimized in the political and cultural domain "by the equal right of property and the universal freedom of contract on the basis of property rights over commodities" (Chatterjee 1993, 209). The coercive character of the state was later challenged, leading to laws and legislation that mitigated to a great extent the rigors of industrialization (minimum wage, maximum hours of work, etc.). Over time, the coercive state was replaced by what Chatterjee called the welfare state and, consequently, the concept of welfare was substituted for the liberal concept of freedom.

However, in the case of India, the political leadership that came to power was already committed to the welfarist aspect of state ideology. In fact, it was through its claim to be the protector of the welfare of the nation and its constituent communities that the Congress party built its almost uncontested legitimacy as the voice for the nation against colonial rule.[10] According to Chatterjee, this crucial point is often ignored in both the mainstream and the left discourse on India. The Congress party's opposition to colonial rule was not just grounded on the negative features of the colonial rulers (related to race, ethnicity, and religion) that were present but it also had a positive political agenda that was grounded on the economic (colonial rule responsible for the creation of a backward economy, the transfer of national wealth to England, etc.). Colonial rule was deemed to be oppressive and illegitimate not just because of its negative aspects but also because the rulers economically exploited the nation of India as a whole and failed to protect its communities in times of need (from poverty, natural calamities such as famines, droughts, etc.).[11] This attack on the British had the strong political effect of legitimizing Congress's opposition to British rule and its claim for self-government as the only way in which mother India (the universal) and all its community groups (constituting particulars within the universal) could be protected. The postcolonial state (as conceived by the Congress party) as an embodiment of nationhood took upon itself the role of the protector of these different communities.[12]

The idea of the state as a development state carried (in addition to the teleological goal of capital accumulation) this welfarist aspect within itself that is rooted in the economic critique of colonial rule. This welfarist aspect, broadly captured by the envisaged role of the state as a protector of its community groups, provided the legitimacy for Congress's claim of self-government. As Chatterjee writes,

> Self-government consequently was legitimate because it represented the historically necessary form of national development. The economic critique of colonialism then was the foundation from which the positive content was supplied for the independent nation state: the new state represented the only legitimate form of exercise of power because it was a necessary condition for the development of the nation. (Chatterjee 1993, 203)

The irony, as Chatterjee points out, is that, along with its welfarist role, the Congress party was also fully committed to a modern industrial development strategy directed toward capital accumulation. So the crucial question is how the "rigors" of capital accumulation could be balanced against the welfarist aspect of the state, which is basically the protection of precapitalist communities that are, Chatterjee argues, antimodernist, antiindividualist, and even anticapitalist.[13] The two dimensions of Indian nationalism are fundamentally opposed to one another. How could capital accumulation be legitimized as the dominant economic process? Historical progress, which the modernization project demands, requires capital accumulation and its associated rigors, but the welfarist aspect requires protection of all precapitalist communities and institutions. This immediately aborts the state-sponsored classical road to capital accumulation via primitive capital accumulation since the latter path will involve an assault on precapitalist property relations. Therefore, a tension between capital accumulation and the legitimization of capital accumulation as the dominant aspect of society arises that seems almost unsolvable. How can this tension be kept under control so that the unity of the nation (organized around the dominance of the process of capital accumulation) is not threatened? The resolution of this seemingly unsolvable tension between capital accumulation and the legitimization of capital accumulation is produced through the passive revolution of capital by invoking the concept of the surrogate synthesis.

Capital's inability to annihilate precapital forms the basis of the passive revolution of capital in India. The passive revolution of capital, as we mentioned earlier, is the creation of a surrogate synthesis or universal via capitalism's appropriation of precapitalism. In the context of the passive revolution of capital in India, "the object of the strategy of passive revolution of capital was to contain class conflict within manageable dimensions, to control and manipulate the many dispersed power relations [Chatterjee also calls these the pre-modern or traditional forms of relation] in society to further best as possible the thrust towards accumulation" (Chatterjee 1993, 214). Capital has to give space to the precapitalist elements, including the dominant precapitalist groups as their subordinate partners (subordinate because of the ontological social privilege accorded to capital), and what Chatterjee calls the aspirations of the popular masses. The creation of this space (that is, the surrogate universal) conducive to conditions of capital accumulation involves a process of hegemonic construction of capital's rule. That is, the production of the surrogate synthesis involves a process of construction of capital's hegemonic rule. Alternatively, in this framework, the passive revolution of capital can be understood as the process of creating a hegemonic rule (involving capital's appropriation of precapital) that enables capital accumulation to proceed without any substantive barriers. As Sanyal writes,

> . . . we can discern a complex and subtle form of capital's power exercised in relation to precapital. The frontal assault that characterizes primitive accumulation is now being replaced by an attempt to incorporate precapital as a separate entity within capital's own program. It is appropriation, rather than annihilation, of the former by giving it a place in the latter's world. And since accumulation can no longer be the sole content of development and the universal goal, capital's agenda is revised so that it can now address the needs of precapital as well. In other words, capital's projected ideology now recognizes the existence of precapital, and its particular goals and aspirations. (1993, 124)

To repeat, capital cannot rule directly (as in the case of uncontested bourgeois hegemony) but only by mixing some ideas from the autonomous domain of precapitalism (the traditional) with its own ideology to create a surrogate synthesis with the intention of legitimizing the process of capital accumulation.

What is the surrogate synthesis for the case of India? The answer, as should be obvious by now, is the notion of nationhood that reifies itself in the body of the state. The state, representing all of the different parts of society, embodies the spirit and site of the surrogate synthesis (nationhood), and capital legitimizes its rule via the body of the state.[14] As Chatterjee writes,

> To talk about the state as an "actor" is to endow it with *a will*; to say that it acts according to coherent and rational principles of choice is further to endow it with a *consciousness*. . . . (1993, 51)

> The *reification of the "nation" in the body of the state* becomes the means for construction of this hegemonic structure, and the extent of control over the new state apparatus becomes a precondition for further capitalist development. It is by means of an interventionist state, directly entering the domain of production as mobiliser and manager of investible "national" resources that the foundations are laid for industrialisation and the expansion of capital. (1993, 64–65)

Or as Sanyal puts it,

> . . . capital has to project the nation as a united whole, with precapital as one of its constituents, in terms of one single set of goals: its national identity does not permit it to allow a part of the nation to exist as its outside. The non capitalist goals for the periphery, however, cannot be pursued by capital on its own; the mediation of the state is essential in this regard. (1993, 126)

The state legitimizes the dominant position of capital (accumulation) not just through coercive mechanisms but also through the mechanism of persuasion.[15] The mechanism of persuasion is affected through its welfarist role as the protector of the many disparate precapitalist communities and institutions.[16] According to the theorists of the passive revolution of capital, this political aspect in the making of economic decisions (economic protection for culturally underprivileged and backward groups based on caste, tribe, and religion; subsidies, taxation, pricing, licensing, etc. related to noncapitalist organizations of production) is completely missed by both the proponents of the recent free-market policies and the traditional Indian Marxists. Both of these groups of theorists, in different ways, question the existence of the ambiguities (related to the dynamic productive potential of the process of capital accumulation versus the unproductive legitimization strategy of welfare donations) that can be found in the policies of the state. Chatterjee points out that such viewpoints completely gloss over the complex reality of Indian society. According to him,

First, that these ambiguities are *necessary* consequences of the specific relation of the post colonial development state with the people-nation; second, that it is these ambiguities that create room for maneuver through which passive revolution of capital can proceed; and third, that these ambiguities cannot be removed or resolved within the present constitution of the state. (Chatterjee 1993, 217)

It is important to understand this third point. The state embodying the spirit of nationhood emerges as the virtual representative universal that holds together a unity of particulars. Capital is not the universal but only a particular, albeit a dominant particular. There are other particulars, such as the landlord, the peasantry, caste groups, religious groups, and so on.[17] The unity of the particulars takes the form of "nationhood" (surrogate synthesis) that then reifies itself within the body of the state. The unity of the particulars in the body of the state must reflect the dominance of the particular, capital, as representative of the nation as a whole. Otherwise, the unity will fall apart. The unity of particulars as a construction of "nationhood" is produced in the political domain as a construction of the hegemonic rule of capital. However, we no longer have an uncontested hegemony of capital. Since other particulars are included in the unity, capital's dominance will be contested within the body of the state. The state, as an allocator of resources, takes upon itself (since there are no other universals acceptable to the particulars) the (welfarist) task of distributing resources to each particular's subject to the overall constraint of the whole (given by the universal, which must protect the dominance of capital). As Chatterjee points out, "a development state operating within the framework of representative politics would necessarily require the state to assume the role of the central allocator if it has to legitimize its authority in the political domain" (Chatterjee 1993, 216). Capital establishes its hegemonic rule by hiding behind this state so that, through the legitimizing process of capital accumulation processed through the state, it can proceed with accumulation without facing any fundamental challenge from other precapitalist communities. The ambiguities, seen by the free market proponents or the traditional Marxists, are of course present but it is through the very ambiguities itself that capital establishes its hegemonic rule. Without these ambiguities, the Indian "nationhood" and the state will cease to exist in its present form. Without seeing Indian reality as an instance of the passive revolution of capital, these intricacies cannot be understood. The proponents of the free markets and traditional Marxism read India's capitalist development only in terms of a narrative of capital accumulation when, in fact, the situation is far more nuanced.

In the Indian modes of production debate, the historical process of primitive capital accumulation is considered to be incomplete and not a failure. The development of the country is assumed to progress in the classical way, from the center to the periphery via the mechanism of antithesis superseding the thesis. The basic idea of historical materialism (in the classical sense) is never questioned; capitalism progresses by annihilating precapitalism and the two cannot coexist in the long run. At the present juncture, India is projected to be a transitional economy where the process of primitive capital accumulation has not yet fulfilled its historical role. However, it is also an inevitable, foregone conclusion that capitalism will overcome precapitalism at some point in the future. But why can't capitalism annihilate precapitalism at the present juncture? In response, theorists in the Indian modes of production debate have produced various economic models to demonstrate that precapitalist (economic) relations of production reflected by elements like usury (Bhaduri 1973, 1977, 1983; Pradhan 1990), ground rent (Patnaik 1976), high return from unproductive investment (Bhaduri 1981, 1983), etc., place an absolute limit on the production of surplus value, accumulation of capital and, consequently, on the economic development of Indian society. However, these obstacles are temporary and over time will give way to capitalist relations of production and to full-fledged capitalism.

The role of the state in these circumstances is to undertake economic policies that will lead the country to capitalism. These Marxists consider the Indian state in a very unproblematic manner. For them, the state represents the interest of capital (the economic) at all times and places. Under capitalism, the state immediately represents the interest of capital as an uncontested truth. Any possibility of other (other than economic) aspects of society influencing the policies of the state are ruled out by the very theoretical framework. Policies that do take into account such noneconomic and non-capitalist aspects, as Indian policies have, are considered to be regressive since they will create barriers to the transition of Indian society to a full-fledged capitalist society. That capital cannot establish its dominance within the body of the state is yet another proof that capitalism has not been successful in establishing itself as the dominant mode of production.

The above way of theorizing Indian economic development is found to be unacceptable by those Indian Marxists who went on to theorize the Indian complex reality in terms of the passive revolution of capital. Rejecting the economism of the Indian modes of production debate, they point out that the traditional polity, traditional culture, and the noncapitalist economy play an important role in India's economic development and are not entirely inimical to capital accumulation. They argue that the so-called obstacles are not real obstacles in the path of capitalism; capitalism can rediscover for itself alternative paths of development subject to these limits (Chaudhury 1991–92, 37–60). According to Chaudhury, one alternative path is through the passive revolution of capital whereby capitalism appropriates precapitalism, placing it in a subordinate position in a greater alliance. Capital goes into alliance with the landlords, the small peasantry, and other elements of precapitalism to establish its hegemonic rule (via the creation of a surrogate synthesis) that enables it to accumulate freely. This case of blocked dialectic (antithesis failing to supersede the thesis) implies the historical failure of primitive capital accumulation and not its incompleteness as in the Indian modes of production debate. In other words, the classical route fails to realize its projected prophecy for the case of India but that does not stop or hinder the development of capitalism in India.

Theorists of the Indian mode of production debate have criticized the role of the Indian state in the building of capitalism. For example, some, like Patnaik and Bhaduri, have criticized the state for not advocating a comprehensive land reform, which they consider a necessary condition for the creation of capitalism in the agricultural sector and for India as a whole. However, for Chaudhury, Chatterjee, and Sanyal, they are addressing the wrong question. The right question would be, Given the nature of the Indian state, does it makes sense to support land reform? The answer for both Chaudhury and Chatterjee is a clear no. In fact, the very basis of the Indian state (that is, as a site of capital's appropriation and accommodation of precapital) rules out the question of land reform that will involve a full-scale war against the precapitalist elements. The absence of land reform does not stand in the way of capital accumulation. In fact, the very absence of land reform defines the alternative path of capitalism's success in establishing its hegemonic rule and the process of capital accumulation. As Chaudhury writes, "third world capitalism (meaning India) gets the best of both the worlds: a capitalist base (with modern technology and culture) and a precapitalist periphery which hands over its surplus to the center and absorbs the surplus of the latter. Capital does not desire to have capitalism in agriculture. Capitalism in agriculture is only a sign of weakness of capital" (Chaudhury 1991–92, 54).

Looking at Passive Revolution of Capital Critically: A Marxian Perspective

It is important to point out the essentialisms and historicism embedded in the conceptualization of the passive revolution of capital, because some theorists like Sanyal (1993) and Chatterjee (1993) seem to imply that they are analyzing the passive revolution of capital from a nontraditional, that is, nonessentialist and nonhistoricist point of view. In the West it is often conjectured, wrongly so far as we are concerned, that subaltern studies are part of the postmodernist and poststructuralist discourse. In this section, let us strive to dispel some of these misconceptions by bringing to light the historicism and essentialism embedded in the literature on the passive revolution of capital, aspects that are inconsistent with the postmodernist and poststructuralist literature, and are problematic from a Marxian perspective as well. In pointing out our criticisms, we will be taking recourse to both internal criticisms (arguing from within the framework of subaltern studies) and external criticisms (arguing from outside the framework of subaltern studies).

To begin with, the subaltern theorists do not claim to be following historical materialism and yet their conceptualization takes an explicitly Hegelian approach and incorporates the essentialisms and historicism inscribed in it as its integral components. The basic framework remains the same as in orthodox Marxism except for the displacement of a (true) Hegelian synthesis by a surrogate or false synthesis. The concept of thesis, antithesis, and universal (albeit a surrogate one) remains the basis for theorizing the passive revolution of capital. Consequently, the essentialism and historicism embedded in the Hegelian framework overflow into the theorization of the passive revolution of capital. Let us start by emphasizing the essentialist role of capital accumulation.

The Essentialism of Capital Accumulation and Power

In the theory of the passive revolution of capital, thesis (precapitalism) and antithesis (capitalism) are considered to be independent and autonomous parts of society where both capitalism and precapitalism are explained by the essence—the economic—from which the political and cultural flow as a derivative. In other words, the moments of the universal (thesis and antithesis) are self-referential and are driven by a simple source, the economic. The political and cultural adjust according to the demand of the economic. Thus while political and cultural aspects of society are included in the description of the passive revolution of capital, the fundamental dynamics of the society are controlled by capital or the economic. In this literature, capital accumulation is the essence or driving force of society. For example, capitalism (or its defining concept, capital accumulation) in India demands that its reproduction be legitimized in the fields of the political and cultural (Chatterjee 1993, Sanyal 1993, Chaudhury 1991–92). Political and cultural aspects have to adjust in such a way that capital can establish its rule by which it can accumulate freely. It is ironic that while Chatterjee, Chaudhury, and Sanyal criticize economic essentialism in the Indian modes of production debate, they themselves are not immune from that criticism. Their major contribution is to bring the political and cultural aspects of society under the scrutiny of Marxian theory, but then they also essentialize capital accumulation as the source of change in society. Fundamentally, the passive revolution of capital is an essentialist description of society and history. Driven by the economic (ontological privilege of capital as a driving force of history, the teleology of capital accumulation), which is taken as given, capitalism must move toward either of its pre-fixed historical destinies.

It is important to realize that in this literature, while capital accumulation is given an ontological social privilege, power remains the primary explanatory variable of the discourse. Thus the problem posed is whether capital can establish its rule in the context of the inability of capital to proceed with primitive capital accumulation in a systematic manner. If capital can establish its rule in such a situation, then capitalism exists in India. Thus, whether capitalism exists in India is determined by its rate of success in establishing its dominating role in society. Capital and its associated class discourse are made passive at the level of theoretical exposition. As we have already explained, in subaltern studies, classes are often reduced to power and this reductionism is a feature of the literature on the passive revolution of capital. Thus the popular rhetoric that is often used in the literature on passive revolution is "capital's power" versus the "power of the communities" or the "power of precapital" (communities and precapital are terms that are interchangeably used in the literature).

Primitive Capital Accumulation versus Community

The second criticism refers to our discomfort with Chatterjee's division of Indian society into two independent and autonomous universals—capital and community—as antithetical universals. Capital has an independent narrative that creates a host of complementary institutions around it while community has a similar narrative. As Chatterjee points out,

> For this narrative (that is, the narrative of capital) to take shape, the destruction of community is fundamental. Marx saw this clearly when he identified as the necessary condition for capitalist production the separation of the mass of laborers from their means of labor. This so called primitive accumulation is nothing else but the destruction of precapitalist community, which, in various forms, had regulated the social unity of laborers with their means of production. Thus community, in the narrative of capital, becomes relegated to the latter's pre-history, a natural, pre political, primordial stage in social evolution that must be superseded for the journey of freedom and progress to begin. And since the story of capital is universal, community too becomes a universal prehistory of progress, identified with medievalism in Europe and the stagnant, backward, undeveloped present in the rest of the world. (1993, 235)

Chatterjee then argues that, notwithstanding its universalistic scope, capital remains dependent on its antinomy, community, because it could not proceed with primitive capital accumulation in a systematic manner with respect to it. Thus the universal scope of capital is now tempered by its inability to universalize its rule and therefore it looks for another universal (the nation reified in the state) through which it can rule as a dominant particular. That is, it has to establish its rule via the surrogate synthesis of nation by becoming a dominant particular and consequently,

> The modern state embedded as it is within the universal narrative of capital, cannot recognize within its jurisdiction any form of community except the single, determinate, demographically enumerable form of the nation. It must therefore subjugate, if necessary by the use of state violence, all such aspirations of community identity. These other aspirations, in turn, can give to themselves a historically valid justification only by claiming an alternative nationhood with rights to an alternative state. . . . What, then, are the true categories of universal history? State and civil society? Public and private? Social regulation and individual rights?—all made significant within the grand narrative of capital as the history of freedom, modernity and progress? Or the narrative of community—untheorized, relegated to the primordial zone of the natural, denied any subjectivity that is not domesticated to the requirements of the modern state, and yet persistent in its invocation of the rhetoric of love and kinship against the homogenizing sway of the normalized individual? (1993, 238–239)

So we are asked to choose between the two courses of history. But before questioning the aspect of historicism, let us deal with the antithetical relationship between capital and community and ask whether such an antinomy can be sustained. Chatterjee deploys the concept of primitive capital accumulation to make his claim about the antithetical relationship. Our position is that the traditional definition of primitive capital accumulation does not support Chatterjee's claim about the antithetical relationship as a universal form of relationship. That is, his position is internally inconsistent. This is important since Chatterjee's analysis of Indian nationhood is based on such a relationship between capital and community.

Revisiting the Definition of Primitive Capital Accumulation

Let us first state what we mean by primitive capital accumulation. Marx defined primitive accumulation as ". . . the *historical* process of divorcing the producer from the means of production. It appears as *primitive* because it forms the *prehistory* of capital and of the mode of production cor-

responding to capital" (Marx 1990, 875). This process produces two transformations. First, it transforms the social means of subsistence and production into capital and, second, it transforms the immediate producers
into wage-laborers (Marx 1990, 874).[18] The end result of the two transformations is the creation of a labor market where labor power can be freely
exchanged for money, thereby acquiring the status of a commodity. These
two transformations supposedly constitute the process of primitive capital
accumulation. Primitive accumulation is supposed to accomplish the task
of transforming direct producers to *free* wage laborers where the meaning
of "free" will soon be made explicit. That is, primitive capital accumulation
is the process by which labor from a noncapitalist site is transferred to a
capitalist site such that capitalist production can take place.

Primitive Capital Accumulation and the Conditions of Existence of Capitalism

The two transformations—of social means of subsistence and production
into capital and of immediate producers into wage laborers—are related to
the two conditions of existence of the direct producer, namely its subjective and objective conditions. According to orthodox historical materialism, the first transformation requires that the direct producers be detached
from their objective conditions. This means the direct producers need to
be estranged from their means of subsistence and production (the objective conditions of production). For example, as feudal society is principally
agricultural, this requires the expropriation of land from the peasantry.

The second transformation requires that the direct producers be separated from their subjective conditions of existence. An individual's attachment to the community is what we call the subjective condition of the
direct producer's existence. The direct producer's objective condition cannot be reproduced without this subjective condition. They are intrinsically
linked to one another. Thus primitive capital accumulation requires breaking the community apart by somehow separating the individuals from the
community. In fact, the mechanism of the second separation is related to
the first transformation. It is assumed in orthodox (Hegelian) Marxism
that the whole is fixed a priori. The whole is fixed in meaning and the parts
too are fixed in meaning since they flow from the whole. In Hegelian
Marxism, the community (whole) contains parts (individuals owning or
possessing property). The whole is prior and the parts flow from the
whole. The direct producers own or possess land because they are members of a community, the whole. In a sense, all private property belongs
originally to the community, that is, it is in principle communal property.
Community is the presupposition and individuals own or possess property because they belong to the community. The social existence of the individual's property flows from the community. One should note the point

that the community is driven by its content, property. Individuals exist as either owners or possessors of property.

Thus, if the existence of parts is destroyed, the community (whole) would not have any basis of existence. By getting rid of the content, the concept of community will fall apart. That is why the two transformations, describing the process of primitive accumulation, proceed simultaneously in orthodox historical materialism.

Community versus Capital

The freedom brought about by the process of primitive capital accumulation as emphasized by Chatterjee is freedom from the objective and subjective conditions of existence of the individual. For a worker to be free under capitalism means that he must not own or possess any means of subsistence and production, and he must not be related to the old precapitalist community.

However, this notion of freedom has a limited connotation here. Freedom to be a wage laborer and freedom from any ownership or possession of means of production do not imply that an individual is free from community at all levels. Freedom from community, through primitive capital accumulation, is a limited freedom, limited to the aspect of the disappearance of property ownership of a mass of direct producers combined with their newly acquired ability to sell labor power through voluntary exchange. It affects that part of the community that is held together by the aspect of property. But to reduce the entire community to simply the aspect of property is an example of economic reductionism that obliterates from the social space all other economic and noneconomic aspects that make up a community.[19] Primitive accumulation, through the two transformations, does affect the content of community but it does not necessarily destroy it. There are other elements in community, such as caste, religion, trade unions, clubs, and so on, that survive by adapting to the new conditions or are newly created. Aspects like those of caste, which in Chatterjee fall under the universal category of community, may not be antithetical to capitalist relations of production but may in fact help in the reproduction of capital.[20] Capital may not be supportive of some particular types or forms of communities but it is fundamentally wrong to make the statement that capital is necessarily against community in principle. The mistake that Chatterjee makes is to assume that primitive accumulation gets rid of any linkage of individual with community. Thus, *free* wage labor is confused with complete freedom from community as such.

It is critical for a Marxian analysis of this type to keep in mind the difference between the limited notions of the freedom of an individual from that of the community so that he can sell his labor power from complete freedom or separation of the individual from community. Chatterjee clearly conflates the two. The problem arises because he takes the categories, capital and community, to be independent and autonomous from one another and as such each is accorded an independent logic that is antithetical to one another.[21] In his scheme, capital accumulation proceeds by destroying community via the process of primitive capital accumulation. We have shown that such an antithetical relationship does not follow from the process of primitive capital accumulation. Primitive capital accumulation points to a very specific case of antithetical relationship between community and capital that cannot be generalized as a universal relationship.

Furthermore, there is nothing that prevents an individual from holding the class positions of being property owner and wage laborer simultaneously. An obvious example is that of the shareholder worker, such as the worker in the Infosys company. Such an individual occupies the class position of a worker (doer of labor) while receiving a return on his part of the money capital expended in the process of production of commodities. Thus, he is both a worker and a property-owning capitalist. Another example is that of a wage laborer (say, working in the city) who could also the owner of a farm. Interestingly, he occupies three class positions simultaneously: that of an appropriator of surplus value (fundamental class process), distributor of surplus value (subsumed class process), and as a wage laborer or performer of surplus labor (fundamental class process). There is no necessary antithetical relationship between property owning individual and wage laborer; being a wage laborer does not necessarily mean being propertyless.

The Historicism of the Passive Revolution of Capital

In subaltern studies, capital cannot develop easily through the process of accumulation as theorized by the classical mode of historical change. Hence, it must and does change the course of history by defining an alternative (through surrogate synthesis) path of its development called the passive revolution of capital, which only carries out capital accumulation in a different guise. Let us now extend our argument that the intricate relationship produced between the methodological underpinnings of subaltern studies theory of transition as discussed in stage one and passive revolution of capital as discussed above procreates into a full-fledged historicism.

It is important to realize that the passive revolution of capital, as understood by Indian Marxists, is a historical model that claims history follows a certain trajectory. Its basis is the recognition of the failure of primitive capital accumulation to fulfill its projected historical role, which is to inscribe labor power into the capitalist production process across the space of the economy. Capital cannot develop easily through the process of accumulation as theorized by the classical mode of historical change. Hence, it must and does change the course of history by defining an alternative (through surrogate synthesis) path of its development that is called the passive revolution of capital.

Capital has only two alternatives. It must either follow the classical way—capital annihilating precapital (and the communities through which precapital is produced)—or appropriate precapital to create a surrogate synthesis. The classical way was taken by most of the Western countries while the passive revolution of capital is taken to be the general path of development of Third World societies. That is, the passive revolution of capital is taken to be the general framework of a historical model for Third World countries. As Chatterjee points out,

> It now seems more helpful to argue, however, that as a *historical model*, passive revolution is in fact the general framework of capitalist transition in societies where bourgeois hegemony has not yet been accomplished in the classical way. (1993, 212)

Sanyal (1993) also makes a similar point rather forcefully:

> The total destruction of precapital and the establishment of capital as the universal is what the bourgeois discourse calls a "case of success." But what if the expansion of the domain of capital reaches a limit before the entire periphery is transformed and brought within its ambit, that is, if the dualism becomes a permanent rather than a transitory phenomenon? The bourgeois discourse would immediately label it as a "case of failure"; it does not have a choice in this regard since it identifies development with the annihilation of precapital. Judging by this criterion, most of the third world countries today appear to be cases of failure. The periphery is increasingly turning out to be a permanent existence surrounding the pockets of developed capitalism in these countries and the impossibility of bringing the entire economy under the sway of capital. . . . (1993, 124–125)

The historical alternative to the passive revolution of capital has already been laid out in the previous chapter. Let us repeat and reformulate our point briefly, as it will bring into light the marks of historicism conditioning this literature. Among many forms of communities, one community, other than those produced by the narrative of communities, is the working class.[22] The working class is the only community that is created by the narrative of capital. The working class may be called the internal community (internal to the logic of capital) while the other precapitalist communities are called the external communities (external to the logic of capital).[23] We have already explained in the earlier chapter how ideal social totalities can be produced from the narrative of communities and that these ideal social totalities cannot be achieved by the subaltern groups on their own. The ideal social totality of the working class is socialism or communism. We have also explained that, given the inability of the other communities to achieve social change and the ontological privilege accorded to the working class, one can infer that the next stage of history or society would be one in which the social ideal of the working class subsumes the ideals of the other communities in a higher universal. We call this the socialism of communities. And, as in Chatterjee, if capital accumulation is the central axis of change and subsequently, "industrialisation through capital accumulation" is the process through which to achieve the telos of society, then logically who else other than the working class can be in charge of the next stage of development? We witness a clear flow between the ontological privilege of working class with its so-called ability to assimilate the ideals of other communities—the subalterns—and the privileged logic of capital accumulation via the passive revolution of capital. This is what Chatterjee is asking us to choose between, the universal of capital or the universal of communities (to be led by the working class). This is also Sanyal's objective: "The understanding of the antithetical relationship between capital and its outside—the former's power and the latter's resistance, is a strategical requirement for counterhegemony" (1993, 129). Capitals' hegemony (via the passive revolution of capital) versus the counterhegemony of communities: that is the great division in Third World countries like India.

Let us summarize the historical trajectory as could be discerned from the text of these subaltern theorists. There are two types of sequences, one for the developed country and the other for the Third World or underdeveloped countries. The sequence of development of society in the former is guided by historical materialism, and no substantial objection is raised against it by the proponents of the passive revolution of capital. For the latter case, however, the sequence is the following: (a) the failure of capitalism to accomplish primitive capital accumulation to (b) the passive revolution of capital to (c) the socialism of communities. If capital is the conscious subject of history that makes the first transition possible, the working class as another conscious subject of history will lead the community groups to make the second transition possible. Both of these sequences are a historicist way of looking at the evolution of society, that of a progressive, rationally ordered movement of society from a preordained origin to a teleological ending. The subaltern studies concept of transition then has a common ground with that in traditional Marxism: historicism.

Sanyal tries to accommodate this historicism within a nonessentialist reading of society from a class perspective but his analysis runs into its

154 • Transition and Development in India

own set of problems. However, before we address that issue, let us provide two internal criticisms of this historicism produced in the literature on the passive revolution of capital. First, the point on "failure" as a permanent affair is an assertion and it is not clear at all why it should be the case. For example, what prevents capitalism from achieving its true synthesis at some future point in time, to overcome the presumed blocked dialectic? Capitalism may, over time, become so powerful that it could annihilate precapitalism. In the spectrum of historical possibilities, what prevents us from posing this particular historical possibility? That is, it is not clear at all as to why the passive revolution of capital should necessarily be a stage of history in a Third World country.

Second, both Chatterjee and Sanyal seem to be making the point that in developed countries there are no (or few) pockets of precapital and that developed countries are a case of "success" in that regard.[24] This is a deeply contentious issue and there are now enough extensive studies to question his proposition (McIntyre 1992, 1996; Gibson-Graham 1993; Gibson-Graham 1996; Callari and Ruccio, ed. 1996; Gibson-Graham, Resnick, and Wolff, ed. 2000; Gibson-Graham, Resnick, and Wolff, ed. 2001). These studies show that in the so-called developed capitalist societies, elements of precapital coexist with capital and that there too capital has to deal with its outside, both internal (working class) and external (precapital). It seems that, for the moment at least, developed capitalism is similarly a "failure" (in a qualitative sense) as underdeveloped countries are.

Class, Subjectivity, and Power

Until now, we have argued from within the terrain of the given discourse of the literature on the passive revolution of capital. Let us now step outside it and confront some of its propositions and conceptual tools from an overdeterminist class perspective. The first point to note is the different concept of class.

The subaltern theorists write as if capital has a life of its own; it is the subject who is capable of taking a decision about the best road to development. Capital, somehow, realizes that it cannot annihilate precapitalist communities, and, in this context, the historical role of capital is "to control and manipulate the many dispersed power relations in society to further as best as possible the thrust towards accumulation" (Chatterjee 1993, 214). It must control and manipulate the traditional economy, traditional culture, and traditional polity to legitimize its rule by which it can accumulate freely. The idea seems to be that the narrative or logic of capital is embodying the subjectivity of the capitalist class and capitalism *tout court.* That is, since capital is located in the production process, it has an inherent interest that could be passed on to the individuals who own capital (the capitalist class). We have already argued that the capitalist class (or capital here) as such cannot act. We have also argued that the conceptualization of interest as a priori given, which is passed on unproblematically to the capitalist class, cannot be logically sustained (Hindess 1987, 1988; Laclau and Mouffe 1985; Laclau 1990; Resnick and Wolff 1987; Amariglio, Callari, and Cullenberg 1989). Class is not a homogeneous group of conscious people, rather, class is a subset of processes that have nothing to do with subjectivity or interest per se. The same criticism holds for the way in which terms like "working class" or "subaltern class" are used in the literature.

At heart, the literature on the passive revolution of capital is a power discourse. The economic is assumed to be given and then the focus of debate is the relations of power between capital and its "others," both its internal other and its external other. That is, class insofar as it is being reflected by terms like "capital(ist)" and "working class" (capital's internal other) is subsumed under relations of domination-subordination. The same is true for the relation between the capital(ist) class and the precapitalist classless communities (capital's external other).[25] Class as the performance, appropriation, distribution, and receipt of surplus labor is rendered redundant in such an analysis. These processes are appropriated under a power theory of class. We have already explained in detail our discomfort with this appropriation: the effects produced by class processes on society are not the same as the effects produced by relations of power, and the latter cannot be reduced to the former. That is, a theoretical claim on some untheorized effects in terms of theoretical findings of some other theorized effects involves an argumentative leap that cannot be substantiated, and which has the effect of displacing the level of analysis. This power reductionist move is clearly brought out by Sanyal (1993) when he attempts to reconceptualize the primitive capital accumulation and the passive revolution of capital. His is a very interesting argument because (i) it defines classes in terms of the production and appropriation of surplus labor and then (ii) it reduces class to power in a very explicit way.

Sanyal describes the relation between class and power in the following manner:

> The advantage of power reading is that it also allows us to address capital's relation to subjects that cannot be posited in terms of the traditional, Marxian definition of "class" defined in relation to the production and appropriation of surplus labor. For example, those who remain at the margins of the capital-wage labor relation do not belong to the *dominant* classes (in the sense of being either producers or appropriators of surplus labor), nor are they members of the subsumed classes (in the sense of being in a position to create the

conditions for the production and appropriation of surplus labor). . . . It is only by dislocating "class power" from its privileged position of being the sole domain of power that one is able to understand the complexities and diverse forms of power exercised on those "*classless* subjects," . . . (1993, 118)

And in a footnote in the same paragraph, he writes, "For the concepts of *dominant* and subsumed classes, see Resnick and Wolff (1986)."

This, in our view, is a classic example of the appropriation of class by power. Firstly, Sanyal is using Resnick and Wolff's notion of fundamental and subsumed classes but he substitutes the term "dominant" for "fundamental." This is not simply an innocent mistake but a deliberate strategic move that is made to allow him to appropriate Resnick and Wolff's economic concept of class into his analysis of power. By calling classes dominant, he is able to immediately switch over to what he calls "capital's power." He then analyzes how "class power" reflected by capital's power is able to confront and appropriate the precapitalist communities by producing a system of relations of domination and subordination. Secondly, it should be noted that classes even when defined in terms of the production and appropriation of surplus labor are immediately reduced to homogeneous groups of people who are conscious of their interests and consequently their power. The term "dominant" helps to secure this move, since he can attach the sign of the dominant to the occupiers of these class positions (capital) and thereby reduce social conflict to a relationship of domination and subordination between groups of people: between capital and labor and between capital and precapital. Class as a subset of processes is not what is being discussed here, even though he claims to be following Resnick and Wolff in defining class. Thirdly, once he has reduced society to relations of power, he is able to analyze society in terms of capitalism versus precapitalism as a closed entity. Capitalism is derived from capital (defined in terms of the production and appropriation of surplus labor), which in turn is unproblematically relegated to the domain of power. The logic of capital is the logic of capital's power. Capital's power is exercised not only over its internal other—the worker—but also over the "classless subjects." Capital's dominating stance produces precapital as its negatively defined "other," its meaning closed by its subordinate position vis-à-vis capital. That is, the "classlessness" of the precapitalist communities is an indicator of its subordinate position in society, produced discursively as the negative, or other, of capital's "dominance" as a class.

There are two final points we would like to add as a matter of clarification. Resnick and Wolff do not use the term "dominant class" as a "class power." The term they use for describing the process of performance and appropriation of surplus labor is *fundamental* class process where the term "fundamental" refers to a subset of processes that have no necessary relation to power. Resnick and Wolff (1986, 1987, 1992, 1993, 1994, 1995) have gone out of their way to emphasize this aspect of separation of class from power in their definition of class. Secondly, we do not quite understand why Sanyal argues that precapitalist communities cannot be broken down into classes. After all, class is not specific to "capitalist" fundamental class process and subsumed class process. Social relations of appropriation and distribution of surplus labor are as much a part of the so-called precapitalist societies as capitalist societies. To ignore such class relations by categorizing them as "classless" subjects is in our view a wrong move that has the damaging consequence of obliterating class analyses of such noncapitalist class structures from the social domain.

The Aporia of the Household

As with the theorists involved in the Indian modes of production debate, the subaltern theorists also fail to include the household as a site of the economy in their analyses. This omission has damaging consequences for their analysis of class and transition. The discursive absence of a household class process means that the social relationships relating to processes of surplus labor in millions of economic sites in India are ignored. This has far-reaching consequences for the way in which the transition process is debated in this literature. Consider, for example, Sanyal's position that primitive capital accumulation is not applicable for the case of the developed countries because noncapitalist class processes are absent in their economies. This position can easily be challenged by pointing to the absence of a household class process in Sanyal's framework. Studies now show that noncapitalist household class process, especially the feudal, ancient, and communist class processes, overwhelmingly dominate the household economy for countries in North America and Europe (Fraad, Resnick, and Wolff 1994, Fox 1980, Barrett 1988). The omission of this site of the economy makes the analysis of class and transition palpably incomplete.

The Impossibility of Capitalism and Precapitalism

Until now we have not questioned the usage of the terms "capitalism" and "precapitalism," which are conceived as two distinct complex wholes. These two concepts are also problematic from a postmodern Marxian perspective since the role of class in the specification of these concepts is either absent or, at best, passively present. A discussion of capitalism or precapitalism without class is like fighting a modern war with primitive swords, a highly risky venture for a project that claims to be of a Marxist orientation.

Postscript
Dipesh Chakraborty and the Renewal of Transition and Development

A postmortem over subaltern studies' theory of transition and development by its participants was long overdue. Though it has not dealt with subaltern studies per se or its problems related to historicism that we have highlighted, Dipesh Chakraborty (2000) has stressed the predicament with the concept of historicism implicated in the idea of progress as visualized by the logic of historical materialism or some variation of such theories. He posits a proposition by marking out the logic of capital and that of historical differences conditioning the Indian society (as claimed by Indian experts) as two apparently contradictory instances and yet historicist in their enunciation with the former flowing from a positive angle and the latter from a negative one (as differences being the problem, to be erased by society in order to develop). Then only to reject that (historicist) proposition through a reading of Marx where Chakraborty points out that the relation between the two culminates with capital (analytically) containing its other or its universal form punctured by differences. The question of erasure of lower moments or differences or supersession thus becomes a problem. Subsequently, historicism as the suppression or sublimation of differences cannot be attributed to Marx. As we pointed out in Chapter one, and like Chakraborty, we expressed grave doubts about the representation of Marx as presenting a full-blown historicist model even though, as we also made explicit, a streak of historicism is similarly present in Marx. That is why there are "readings" of Marx and not a single reading even though the unifying theme in Marx's work seems to be on the endeavor (one can almost discern a journey of that in Marx) to understand the political economy in order to produce a critique of it. Furthermore, the category of "capital" in our reading of Marx is an expression following principally from class (the process of performance, appropriation, distribution, and receipt of *surplus labor*), which is clearly demoted in Chakraborty. The purpose of Marx's *Capital* is not simply to show the other of capital but that is incidental to the disaggregated conception of a social totality from a class standpoint with exploitation as the category through which the ethics of Marxian politics proceed and a critique of political economy is fashioned. What is Marx's *Capital* without exploitation? Why write it? And without class, what becomes of exploitation? In other words, the category of *difference* in Marx resides precisely in the conception of class, and noncapital is an expression of the different types of performance and appropriation of surplus labor. Thus in our scheme, via a decentering of the economy from the gravity of capital, *difference* is traced not simply to capital and noncapital but in the further disaggregation of noncapital and even subsequently within each such categories. In Chapter six, we shall show how a multilayered landscape of differences—capitalist and noncapitalist—is produced from the category of class. And, with the logic of overdetermination encapsulating a notion of difference that is mobile, we produce that landscape of differences which, unlike in Chakraborty, can change or be in a state of transition. Thus the moment of nonhistoricity emerges as a theoretical category in our scheme rather than a given category as in Chakraborty.

Being capital-centric even in the context of producing the "other," Chakraborty's conception of social totality—the universal albeit in a punctured manner—is also capital-centric (reducing the economic to capital) and he asks us to struggle within that universal—capitalism—in order to seek a zone of comfort. Thus we are stuck in a static world that has no place for any notion of transition, which Chakraborty understands only in its historicist sense. Thus there are no dynamics of the differences or of their politics in so far as seeking new zones of comfort—with new value systems—are concerned. This can indeed be interpreted as a position of reaction where one may even contemplate the comfort zone in terms of what some call the conservative ethics and value system. The obliteration of class and class differences and the centering of the economy around capital leave Chakraborty's framework without historicism but with no history or the possibility of making one. Clearly, we find such an existence theoretically problematic and politically counterproductive.[26] Despite these shortcomings and omissions, we hail Chakraborty's attempt to read Marx in a new light on the question of historicism because in the Indian context and especially regarding subaltern studies we believe that it marks a significant break on the aspect of re-presenting the *question of theorizations* of transition and development. Those theoretical questions are currently haunting Marxists: if transition is not to be associated with historicism (and essentialism) then what is it, a question that, as we pointed out, is bypassed by Chakraborty with detrimental consequences. Since in classical Marxism transition in certain teleological direction represents development, the same question applies to development. If we are not to adhere to essentialism or historicism as Chakraborty apparently (and correctly) expects us to do, then what type of economy and social totality whose transition and development we are seeking are we talking about in a (postmodern) Marxian scheme? The "differences" Chakravorty raises for India (which are mostly cultural) need to be encountered in the very construction of that economic (to shape the meaning of economic) that is to be employed to subsequently formulate the trope of transition and development. These are the inquiries we attempt in the subsequent chapters: theory of transition, theory of development, the play of differences and "other" characterizing the Indian social totality no matter how much the government—via its new economic policy—tries to overcome those by suturing the being, that is India, into a path of historicism.

Conclusion

Subaltern studies should be applauded for bringing the various noneconomic factors into the heart of Marxist theory. The problem with subaltern studies is that it takes the economic to be passively given and concentrates only on the noneconomic. Also, its rendition of class is problematic and involves a displacement of the surplus-labor definition of class to that of power. This is unsatisfactory for the reasons we have argued, and makes it very difficult to conceptualize appropriately the relation between the economic and the noneconomic from a Marxian (class) perspective. This is in addition to the many internal problems (such as the antithetical relationship between community and capital, the problem of including the peasant into the subaltern category, etc.) that we have pointed out. In the end, the subaltern studies theory of transition and development ends up in the same plane as traditional Marxism, with similar problems of essentialism and historicism. A move toward a more postmodern and poststructural approach to subaltern studies, as is evidently the goal of many of its proponents now, must involve coming to terms with these two elements from a specific, that is, *class standpoint* if this school is to simultaneously retain its Marxian moorings.

CHAPTER 6

A Marxian Reformulation of the Concept of Transition

An Anti-Essentialist Approach

We will develop a nonessentialist, nonhistoricist, class-based concept of transition—a concept of transition that, unlike those concepts of transition as discussed in the Indian modes of production debate and the subaltern studies debate, is micro-focused. This micro-focused concept of transition is built around the concept of class as processes relating to surplus labor and a social totality that is decentered.

The Indian mode of production debate was characterized by its emphasis on class and the idea that the Indian agricultural economy could be broken up into many classes. We consider this emphasis on class and disaggregation to be important. Our analysis of class and social totality helps to break open the apparent unity of society into multiple, uniquely constituted parts. However, in our framework, class as a subset of processes is a name for the economic space of performance, appropriation, distribution, and receipt of surplus labor. This idea of class as process is in direct contrast to the orthodox Marxist concept of class as homogeneous groups of conscious social actors united by a common interest flowing from each individual's occupation of specific class positions in the property relations or the relations of power (or any other structural location in the economy).

The influence of subaltern studies on our rendition of Marxism rests on their effort to bring various noneconomic factors into the heart of Marxist theory. A nonessentialist Marxist theory, such as the one we are laying out, cannot reduce the social space to the economy. It must also account for the noneconomic factors. The problem with subaltern studies is that they go to the other extreme by taking the economic to be passively given and concentrate only on the noneconomic. Also, their rendition of class is problematic and involves a displacement of the surplus-labor definition of class to that of power. This is unsatisfactory for the reasons that have been already discussed and makes it very difficult to conceptualize appropriately the relation between the economic and the noneconomic.

The above-mentioned aspects of the Indian modes of production debate and the subaltern studies debate are reconceptualized and integrated in our approach to Marxist theory. Class and the integrated existence of the economic with the noneconomic are critical for our approach to a nonessentialist and nonhistoricist theory of transition.

The concept of class as process is closely allied to a decentered concept of social totality. In fact, the concept of social totality is produced around the concept of class process. We shall demonstrate that, unlike social totality as conceived in orthodox Marxian theory, this decentered concept of social totality—which is a complex configuration of social relationships where each social relationship is uniquely constituted by a subset of class and nonclass processes—cannot be grounded in any particular social effect. This implies that there cannot be a concept of capitalism as a closed social totality where the aspect of closure is given by a specific element such as the capitalist *mode of production*.[1] No such reductionism is consistent with our concept of social totality.

If social totality is a decentered concept that cannot be grounded on any particular subset of class processes, then how do we conceptualize transition? Transition can no longer be a transition of one unified or closed social totality (feudalism) to another (capitalism) driven by big-bang, macro shifts of modes of production or any other such entities, since such a concept of social totality and mode of production is untenable in our framework. We shall argue that, in our kind of postmodern Marxist framework, transition itself becomes a decentered process signifying a complex flow of effects (relating to mechanisms of surplus labor) from the micro to the macro and vice versa. We shall particularly concentrate, due to the historically unfair demotion, on the case of micro-level change within class structures or between class structures that lead to an uneven and combined development of society.[2] The new concept of transition is not the diachronic, big-bang concept of transition such as is found in classical historical materialist arguments; rather, we are concerned with the synchronic shifts of the disaggregated class structures of a society. The result would be an abandonment of the aspect of historicism and progress as is embedded in the orthodox theory of transition.

Decentering Totality: A Marxist Approach

Let us begin by defining society or social totality from a postmodern Marxist perspective. We can reformulate Resnick and Wolff (1987) to define social totality or society as the totality of all the processes that comprise it. A process for them is the basic element of analysis, the fundamental discursive primitive, which are grouped for convenience into economic, political, cultural, and natural categories. Processes, however, cannot exist alone. They always occur in particular configurations with other processes. We call such configured sets of processes relationships.

A social totality consists of innumerable social relationships and processes, not all of which can be accounted for by a particular theory. Theories use entry points to fix their discursive focus point around which to organize the concept of social totality. For a Marxist theory class is the discursive focus point around which social totality is conceptualized. We will show below that, from a class perspective, the macro existence of society or social totality is broken down into and constituted by multiple subtotalities where each such subtotality is a site of specific social relationships.[3] Because every subtotality is uniquely constituted, society, or social totality as a configuration of subtotalities, is decentered, disaggregated, and uneven. Our pictorial of social totality crucially hinges on the relation between a class structure and that of site: class structures vary from one site to another site.

A site in Marxian theory specifies the context of the analysis. One can think of site as a laboratory with its uniquely defined boundary and interior content. One laboratory is not the same as another because for each their boundary and constitutive interior content are not the same. From a Marxian perspective, each site reflects a unique constitution of the fundamental class process by other processes. The fundamental class process (specified in part by the production process) is here the defining boundary or the locational specificity of the site. The uniqueness is brought about by the specific subsumed class and other nonclass processes (the interior contents) that constitute the fundamental class process.

Each of these processes brings its specific element of distinctness to bear on the fundamental class process, making the latter's constitution unique from site to site. The above-mentioned subset of (class) processes produces a special type of social relationship, a class relationship; social relationship takes the form of class relationship signified by class structure (cluster of class and nonclass processes at a specific site) in Marxian theory. In general, though, clusters of processes can form any relationship at a site in society. So we can define site as literally a conceptually defined space where groups of relationships occur and whose effects constitute the site. In Marxian theory, since these groups of social relationships, and consequently processes (remember social relationships are comprised of a subset of processes), vary from site to site, each class structure is uniquely constituted. For instance, the class structure of one capitalist enterprise is not the same as the class structure of another capitalist enterprise. Consequently, the specification of a capitalist class structure changes from site to site.

Class structures occur typically at three sites: the site of private enterprises, the site of state enterprises, and the site of household enterprises. At a lower level of abstraction, these private, state, and household specific sites can in turn be broken down to numerous subsites where at each such subsite the relevant fundamental class process is uniquely constituted by other processes. Thus, in India, for example, there are a multitude of enterprises where the social existence of each enterprise is unique. Since the social constitution of each fundamental class process is unique and specific to a particular site, class structures can only exist as multiform, uneven, and disaggregated sites. That is, class structures such as the capitalist class structures are not uniform or homogeneous but rather can be disarticulated into multiple uniquely constituted class structures. Each such site of class processes that are constituted by other class and nonclass processes reflects both the whole and a part of the whole.

A process is a whole (subtotality) and a part (a part of the subtotality) at the same time and the strict distinction between part and whole becomes blurred here. A process reflects in itself the totality of society's contradictions, and therefore in that sense is itself a subtotality. Yet each process is constituted differently from all of the other processes and, therefore, also can be conceived as a part.

One can see this relationship between parts and whole by considering the simple class analytic equation of a capitalist enterprise:

$$SV = \sum_i SC_i$$

where $SV =$ Surplus Value and $SC =$ Subsumed Class payments.

The productive capitalists appropriate the surplus value in order to distribute it (in addition to keeping their own profit) as subsumed class payments for the reproduction of the subsumed class processes. Then, the left-hand side represents the appropriation or exploitative aspect of the class structure while the right-hand side represents the distributional aspect of class structure. At each site, the subsumed class processes uniquely constitute the capitalist fundamental class process so that surplus value can be performed and appropriated in a specific manner. But the momentary fixation of the presence of surplus value within the production process is immediately broken up and splintered into multiple parts—parts that are distributed to the agents who are responsible for the reproduction of the subsumed class processes. Thus, a particular site of fundamental class process can only reproduce its existence by distributing the surplus product to its complementary relations that reproduce the processes in other sites—processes that make up those complementary relations. As such, a site such as that of the fundamental class process overflows with excess meaning. Any statement about exploitation at a site of the capitalist fundamental class process, without addressing the issue of distribution of subsumed class payments, is an incomplete statement. Class analysis of a subtotality must account for both the exploitative and the distributional aspects simultaneously, both of which are present (one directly and the other through its constitutive effects) at the site of a fundamental class process. The subtotality, then, is comprised of part (a capitalist fundamental class process) as well as a whole (the entirety of the fundamental class process and its constitutive processes). And since each subtotality is uniquely determined, no one totality can be reduced to another totality.

A social totality is then a complex configuration of social (class) relationships with a dispersed and fragmentary existence since each class relationship (a subset of processes that make up the class structure) develops in its own specific ways, disseminating its own set of meanings and social effects. Furthermore, along with the class processes, class relationships contain all the nonclass processes that constitute the class structure and some such relationships. Thus the concrete knowledge it produces is class-focused but not class-specific.

What exists in society, among other things, at a particular time are class structures where the content and form of the class structures vary from site to site. Capitalist class structures could coexist with feudal class structures or independent/ancient class structures or even communist class structures. Social totality, from a class standpoint, is a decentered totality that cannot be defined solely in terms of a particular type or form of class structure. At a particular time, each part (a process) is uniquely constituted and hence reflects a meaning specific only to its unique manner of constitution by other parts (processes). Each fundamental class process is a part, but at the moment of their overdetermined constitution by other parts, they become a whole—a subtotality. Thus each process is both a part and a whole (subtotality) in a coherent and divided manner. A subtotality, then, is as much a ground for the collective, harmonious existence of the parts as it is for their fragmentation, a decentered existence indeed. Since each such part can be conceived as a subtotality in itself (each unique in character), the social totality as the configuration of social relationships derived in turn from an overdetermined subset of all these parts (or sub totalities) overflows with excess meaning. These subtotalities include not only all of the different forms of capitalist class structures but also all of the other forms of noncapitalist class structures (feudal, slave, independent, and communistic). In other words, the concept of social totality cannot be closed and fixed by any specific class effect. To talk about capitalism or communism as a centered social totality requires positing some form of uniformity and pre-given dominance of a specific class structure that cannot be sustained under a decentered concept of social totality or society that is conceived as an ever-changing, overdetermined configuration of unique, multiform, and uneven class structures.

The idea of transition must then pose itself in a space in which class processes are the cause and the effect of each other and other social processes and where changes, resulting from such cause and effect, are produced within a society leading to change in the dynamics of society itself.

The Economy and Social Totality

Under the decentered concept of social totality, the economy is uneven and dispersed (i.e., it cannot be held together by a particular gravitational force operating at a "deeper" level like capital accumulation), where each site of the economy is uniquely constituted and hence is different from the other sites. Also because of the assumed overdetermined logic, the economy (specified by class processes) cannot be conceived of as independent of and autonomous from the noneconomic aspects of society. Rather, the economy is constituted by noneconomic processes in such a way that the failure to reproduce various noneconomic processes will create a serious crisis for the reproductive process of the economy. As a result, the idea that there is an economy in which the capitalist enterprise exists and which has determinate effects on the capitalist enterprise independent from other "noneconomic" aspects of society is now certainly a problematic one. Not only is the economy not a homogenous space, the very concept of an economy as such, existing somehow independently from the rest of the society, with its own independent "economic" logic, cannot be sustained in the context of the decentered totality.

In sum, then, the decentered concept of social totality, which is critically based on the concept of class as subset of processes and the epistemological concept of overdetermination, produces a different reading of social relationships, the meaning of society (like capitalist society), and finally of the economy. What does such a reading of totality do to the concept of transition that tries to capture the complex nature of society from a class perspective?

Toward a Marxian Reformulation of the Concept of Transition

In postmodern Marxist theory, each process is a site of multiple contradictions. This is because each process is constituted by other processes with contradictory qualities, influences, etc., which push and pull the original process in various and distinct directions. Contradiction signifies the differences in terms of effects of processes that inject and, hence, constitute a particular class process. Each of these other processes brings some distinguishing qualities that determine the uniqueness of the conditions of existence of the original process. A change in any one process imparts a new contradictory effect on the original process, thereby reconstituting its social existence. The change in the original process will, in turn, lead to a change in the other processes that it constitutes. This produces a condition of ceaseless change, with cause and effect flowing back and forth. In this framework, transition means a change in the existing class structure—a transformation that is taking place not just diachronically between class structures but also synchronically within class structures.

The concept of overdetermination and contradiction not only leads to unique changes in class processes but, almost simultaneously, in a chain reaction, also leads to changes in other processes thereby transforming the meaning of the subtotality itself. Thus, the transition of any class process will reverberate across those class and nonclass processes that make up its conditions of existence, changes that will come back to rearticulate the original class process.[4] This micro-level transition of class processes producing unique change in each class structure leads to a transformation of the social totality, which is a configuration of the social relationships derived from these class structures or subtotalities. Society is then a complex configuration of class-focused social relationships where each class relationship (a subset of processes) develops in its own specific ways and the concept of transition records this uneven change.

The decentering of the social totality into subtotalities, which, in turn, are further decentered by their constitutive parts means that the transition process of social totality becomes micro-focused even when we are analyzing the concrete existence of the macro level of the social totality. Similarly, the changes in a social totality brought about by the mutation in the micro-level class structures will react back to produce changes in those micro-class structures. Therefore, the micro and the macro become fused together, undercutting any possibility of a hierarchical structure: micro (part) is simultaneously the macro (whole).

However, along with the uneven development of class processes in society, overdetermination and contradiction simultaneously produce a combined process of development as well. At any moment in time, any fundamental class process' existence vis-à-vis other fundamental class processes is not only uniquely constituted (the basis of unevenness in society), but it is also constituted in some combination by other class and nonclass processes (the basis of combined development in society). Each such combined development is unique because the internal condition (the exploitative aspect) and external condition (the distributive aspect), which articulate together, are specific for each class structure.

As an example, consider a government reduction in its agricultural subsidy (an external condition of existence for agricultural farms) that will produce a change in the articulatory constitution of internal and external conditions of existence, thereby producing a unique change in class structures of the affected agricultural farms vis-à-vis other class structures. Due to the reduction in revenue, a farm may intensify supervision of laborers employed thereby changing the internal conditions of existence (the rate of exploitation). Here a change in the distributive aspect propels a chain reaction that, by changing the exploitative aspects, leads to a *new combination* of internal and external conditions of existence of the farm leading to a change in the nature of its class structure. For every such farm where the effect of agricultural subsidy is felt, the combination of its internal and external conditions will be unique to its own existence. Consider another example of a capitalist enterprise taken over by the workers who, say, have also succeeded in changing the fundamental class process of the firm to a communist one. This transformation of the internal conditions of existence of the firm will reverberate across the subsumed class and other nonclass processes that make up its class structure. The firm's relationships with the banks, government, and financial institutions have to be redrawn. In other words, here a change in the exploitative aspect of the firm produces profound changes in the distributive aspect, and thereby transforms the class structure by creating a new combined existence of internal and external conditions of the firm.[5]

Features of the Decentered Concept of Transition

There are six features surrounding this new concept of transition that require discussion, features that mark out its uniqueness and usefulness and also our fundamental differences from the Marxian concepts of transition as reviewed in the Indian mode of production debate and the subaltern studies debate.

(i) The Class Dimension of Transition

In the traditional Indian Marxist literature as well as in the subaltern studies literature, transition implies either a change in the property structure or in the power relations of society. For example, in the Indian modes of production debate, the transition of Indian society from precapitalism to capitalism requires a change in property structure, and, consequently, the measure of land reform is often invoked to break open the precapitalist relations of production. Similarly, in the traditional Marxian literature, the change in the property structure in the former Soviet Union was considered as the case of transition to socialism because erasing private property relations signified the creation of a classless and, in line with the reductionism involved (of surplus labor to property), a nonexploitative society.

In the postmodern Marxist case, however, transition refers not to a change in property structure per se but to the change in class structures. Thus a change in the feudal class structure to a capitalist class structure is a case of transition that requires a transformation of the mode of performance and appropriation of surplus labor. By this logic of transition, the change in the property structure did not imply in and of itself a change in the content of fundamental class processes in the former Soviet Union. Property relations are a condition of existence of the fundamental class process and a change in the property structure, by the contradictory effects it produces, may change the form of the capitalist class structure without changing the content of its fundamental class process. According to Resnick and Wolff (1993, 1994, 1995), this is exactly what happened in the former Soviet Union, which witnessed a change in the form of capitalist class structure—from private capitalist class structure to a state capitalist class structure. This is clearly one type of a transition process (from, for example, private capitalist enterprises to state capitalist enterprises) but it does not resemble the transition process popularized in the debates on class in the former Soviet Union. The change in class structure brought about by a change in the subsumed class or nonclass process (the conditions of existence of fundamental class process) must not be conflated with direct changes pertaining to the mode of performance and appropriation in the fundamental class processes itself. On the other hand, a change in the mode of appropriation—that is, the fundamental class process—does not mean that its complementary subsumed and nonclass processes will remain intact. As we will discuss below, this important point of cause and effect flowing back and forth, which is often overlooked in Marxist literature, can have far-reaching consequences for the way Marxists visualize politics and class struggle, and finally transition.

(ii) Transition as an Articulation of the Revisionist and Revolutionary Dimensions of Change

Orthodox Marxists, especially of the Second International variant, have long espoused the now famous view that Marxian politics is revolutionary because it calls for change in the type of the fundamental class process, a radical rupture in the way the mode of performance and appropriation of surplus labor or to the element to which it is reduced—property or power—is reproduced. This is in direct contrast to the so-called "revisionist" or social democratic approach of bringing about change by not attacking the type of fundamental class process per se but rather changing the distribution of income or what we are calling subsumed class and nonclass payments. For decades, this distinction between fundamental change versus distributional change—the two different visions of the mechanisms leading to transition—has been one of the most contentious issues that has fractured radical movements the world over.

Using the new concept of transition, it is important to take into account not just one but both dimensions of change simultaneously. We pointed out in the last section that surplus-labor production and its distribution together overdetermine the exact specification of a class structure. Any direct change in the fundamental class process will lead to repercussions between and among its complementary subsumed and nonclass effects and consequently affect the distributional composition of subsumed class payments. This change might lead either to the demise or rise or a qualitative change of many subsumed and nonclass processes that previously constituted the fundamental class process. Similarly, a change in subsumed class or nonclass processes will alter the conditions of existence of the fundamental class process it constitutes, thereby leading to its strengthening, weakening, or even demise. Each such change will force a transformation in the meaning of the class structure. Thus, changes in the subsumed class process or in the fundamental class process overdetermine one another, and their indissoluble existence in the form of the decentered totality cannot be ignored.

Class struggle *over* processes related to class should take into account the multiple repercussions of any change, in particular processes that constitute class. It would be one-sided to reduce the complexity of transition to a simple aspect, such as the change in either the fundamental class process or subsumed class process. Any approach toward transition in the form of class struggle should address the multiplicity of effects of a change in class process.

At times, governmental policies and the opposition's response to them are based on the premise of a uniform effectiveness of those policies. This premise is problematic since any policy will likely produce multidimensional effects on the economy resulting from the different effects that policy has on each of the uniquely constituted class structures. Thus, one can think of the effect of a policy as having not a scalar but a vector dimension. Class struggles, such as the one presently being carried out in the Indian political arena over liberalization policies, are often conducted over government policies where both sides assert the scalar (that is, the uniform) effect of those policies as against the vector (that is, the series of different) effects. This belief in the uniformity of aspect usually dominates over the aspect of differences that are normally rendered passive. Subsequently, development policy measures come down to the simple fact that either the common mass of the population will unambiguously enjoy the benefit of the policies or will unambiguously lose out. This form of class struggle simplifies the complex nature of effects of development policies and carries dangerous implications due to the social importance of such struggles in society. The micro-focused concept of transition concentrates instead on aspects of differences within the "unity" of the social totality. It looks at the disaggregated existence of class structures and assesses the specific effects of such policies on each class structure, emphasizing the unique (i.e., different) character of transformation, if any, within and between such class structures.

(iii) The Micro- or Disaggregated Focus of the Transition Process
In the Indian modes of production debate, transition is attributed to a once-and-for-all macro shift in the mode of production (the economy) and the subsequent change in the "complex social totality." In the subaltern studies literature, transition implies a move from the passive revolution of capital (the form capitalism takes in underdeveloped societies) to a socialism of communities. These macro concepts of change are in direct contrast to the disaggregated, micro-focused concept of transition, which explicitly theorizes changes in distinct types of class process (say, from capitalist to feudal) as well as changes in the forms of class processes themselves.

In order to see the potential multifaceted class nature of society, we use the idea of class sets to define specific types of class processes (Cullenberg [1992], Chakrabarti and Cullenberg [2001]). This framework of class sets is a useful way to see the disaggregated class nature of society and the complexity involved in the process of transition. We identify sets in terms of the appropriation of surplus labor and its relation to the mechanism of (a) remuneration to workers as either wage (w) or nonwage (nw), and (b) distribution of output as either commodity (c) or noncommodity (nc). The combination of the different possibilities among the three gives us the twelve different class sets seen in the accompanying table:[6]

Class Sets

	Surplus Labor Appropriation	Worker Remuneration	Output Distribution
1	A	W	C
2	A	W	Nc
3	A	Nw	C
4	A	Nw	Nc
5	N	W	C
6	N	W	Nc
7	N	Nw	C
8	N	Nw	Nc
9	S	W	C
10	S	W	Nc
11	S	Nw	C
12	S	Nw	Nc

$A = all$,[7] N = none,[8] S = shared,[9] W = wage, Nw = nonwage, C = commodity, Nc = noncommodity

The first four class sets refer to individual appropriation, sets 5–8 to exploitative appropriation, and sets 9–12 to shared appropriation.[10] At any point in time, all of these distinct class sets could coexist within a society. Each of these class sets in turn depends on other economic (including other class sets) and noneconomic conditions of existence, whose articulated existence is what we have called the class structure. As we pointed out earlier, the distinct conditions of existence and the contradictions involved with these class sets could further differentiate them into a more variegated set of class structures, each distinct from the other.[11] In that case, transition, resulting from changes in the conditions of existence of the class sets, not only refers to the changes in class structures of the firms from one class set to another (for example, from set 4 to set 5), but it must also address itself to changes *within* class structures (that is, for example, while remaining as set 4, the class structures could undergo a change in their form). That is, contrary to orthodox Marxism, transition in a postmodern Marxist theory has to consider the distinctive micro changes taking place on a plateau of ever-changing, uneven and disaggregated class structures.

As an illustration of the multifaceted class nature of a social totality, consider the class configuration of the Indian society, and how it might be divided into the various class sets listed above. By focusing on these class sets, a picture of the class differentiation within Indian society can be gleaned. Take the class sets 5 and 6. Clearly, private capitalist firms and state capitalist firms can take the form of either class set 5 or 6. While 5 represents the typical situation of a private capitalist firm, private capitalist firms can take the form of class set 6 in case of a vertically integrated system of production where the lower-tier firm hands over the output (as means of production) to the higher-tier firm such that the higher-tier firm sells the produce, appropriates the surplus value, and distributes part of its surplus value to the lower-tier firm as subsumed class payments. In such a setup, the lower-tier firm would represent class set 6. The same argument goes for those state capitalist firms where, for example, some of the defense firms in India fit this class set. This is because the output they produce is simply handed over to the army without any monetary exchange while their financial existence is funded through government consumption expenditure. However, recently, Indian defense firms have also started to sell their produce in the market, especially the international market. In that case, those defense firms would resemble class set 5. In fact, such a firm could be a site of both sets 5 and 6 simultaneously—a very complex existence indeed. Similarly, other government firms could fall into either class set 5 or 6 or both.[12]

There are also numerous independent class structures in India that range from class sets 3 to 4. Sets 1 or 2 are rarely likely to happen since it is improbable that the worker should pay himself in money form. In many independent firms like handloom, leather, coir, and pottery, one would expect to find numerous class structures resembling class sets 3 or 4. Also, many agricultural farms may be operated by a single worker who produces and appropriates the surplus himself. Depending on whether the surplus is exchanged for money, such class structures could end up in either 3 or 4.

The communist firms, resembling class sets 9–12, are also not uncommon. In India, they are sometimes referred to as the cooperative sector. Some of the Khadi and Village firms could also resemble any of such class sets. Again, because of the depth of commercialization, we would expect the communist class structures to be closer to class set 9.[13] Also, many family farms could resemble class sets 11 or 12, where the family workers who produce surplus labor also appropriate it collectively. On the other hand, family farms could also be of a more feudal type, resembling 7 or 8, where the surplus produced by the family in the farm could be appropriated by the head of the household while the production procedure would involve employing family labor paid in kind even when the produce can be either sold in commodity form or exchanged for goods or simply consumed.

The feudal class structures could resemble either 7 or 8. It will not be very off the mark to assume that a bulk of such class structures would be farms in the agricultural sector. The sharecropping system could be characterized in terms of either the feudal class structures or the capitalist class structures. Depending on the tenurial arrangements, the sharecropping system could take the form of class set 5. Under this capitalist class structure, the sharecropper could employ wage labor, sell the produce as commodity and appropriate the surplus value himself, paying off a certain ground rent (subsumed class payments) for the land leased from the landlord. The sharecropping arrangement could also be constituted by a feudal class structure resembling class set 7 or 8 where the landlord leasing out land to the sharecropper to work as direct producers directly appropriates the surplus product himself and then distributes part of it in kind to the sharecroppers. The classical sharecropping arrangement resembles class set 7 or 8 but, as we have been discussing, the sharecropping arrangement is not identical to only this variant of class set. Interestingly, under the sharecropping system, there can even be independent class structures resembling class set 3 or 4 where the direct producer, who is also the only producer, appropriates his own surplus labor, part of which is then distributed as ground rent to the landlord. Thus, the sharecropping system has a complex existence, its complexity constituted by multitude of nonuniform class structures ranging anywhere from independent class structure to capitalist structure, depending on whether the class structure resembles a class set with "a," "n," or "s" forms of appropriation.

Finally, Indian families are typically characterized by feudal household class structures that would resemble class set 8 where the surplus labor of the housewife is appropriated by the husband or the husband's family. Independent household class structures (single family household), while rare in the case of India, would be characterized by class set 4 while the communist household class structure (where surplus labor jointly produced inside household is appropriated jointly) would represent class set 12. In other words, the Indian household class structure is complex even though, arguably, the feudal (patriarchal) class structure is the dominating class structure. But there is also no doubt that in the present era of globalization and changing values, the Indian household class structure is changing rapidly with communist class processes becoming numerous in numbers. The drive toward a relative surplus value production process is paradoxically creating the conditions (and hence possibility) for many household class structures to take communist forms.

The overall point we are making is that Indian society, disaggregated in terms of class sets, is heterogeneous in its structure, and the deployment of this class set framework helps us see the complex configuration of class structures and that of Indian society. That is, the definition of these class sets implies a multitude of class structures that could fit either of these twelve forms of appropriation. Evidently, class description of Indian society, never mind a theory of its transition, becomes an extremely complex process since, due to its overdetermined and contradictory effects, the exact specification of class structures can shift from any one of these class sets to another. In other words, because of this complex nature of Indian class society, the contemporary transition process in Indian society resulting from the liberalization policies enacted by the Indian government, say, should be theorized in terms of an uneven, disaggregated, and complex series of changes in the types and forms of class structures. This line of the analysis—transition of the Indian economy following the adoption of the new economic policies— will be taken up in considerable details in chapters 8 and 9.

(iv) Transition and Historicism

Unlike the case for orthodox Marxism, the new concept of transition is in opposition to historicism, that is, a historicist description of the evolution of society predicated on a preordained point of origin and a teleological point of ending. In such historicist descriptions a number of elements are present: the movement of society is grounded in some preordained totality (also called essence or reason), which develops periodically in a certain manner over time until it reaches its telos, where more complex social unities or totalities are reduced to the simple totality or essence; where order, certainty, and continuity are the principles of arranging events and time; where commonality (of description) is worshipped against the chaos of the uncommon, the unpredictable, and the unknown; where changes are no more than the reflections of the journey of the essence; and where revolutions are simple manifestations of the historical consciousness emanating from the essence. This group of characteristics is what Foucault (1972b) called "total history"—the arrangement of time and events by a holistic totality which is driven by a philosophy of history (like historical materialism), possessing the features mentioned above. In line with Foucault's idea of total history, in the traditional Indian Marxian literature, society is understood to evolve in a rational ordered manner moving in a series of macro shifts from one mode of production to another. The order of the history is pre-given and moving in a progressive manner, each stage reflecting the developed state of the forces of production. In different ways, a similar total history is developed by the subaltern studies school, where history is guided by certainty, order, and progressive movement of society from precapitalism to passive revolution of capital to finally arrive at socialism of communities.

The postmodern Marxian framework is inconsistent with any form of historicism. Also, the disaggregated, micro-class structure outlined earlier precludes any notion of preconceived and necessary order, certainty, and continuity in the transition between and within class structures. Thus, contrary to orthodox Marxism, where the progressive order of the evolution of society has to be maintained, in the new micro approach to transition, capitalist class structures can be transformed ("reverse back") into feudal or independent class structures. Nothing in the postmodern Marxist theory precludes such a transition. In fact, by the logic of overdetermination one should expect such cases of transition going on in society all the time. History has no inner logic, no way in which it can be arranged into a series of periods driven either by the teleology of reason, as with

Hegel, or the succession of the modes of production or the progress of some historical consciousness. History in this framework is not a progression of some universal truth that could be deciphered by a theory (such as historical materialism). Rather it is always and everywhere contingently produced. History signifies the moment of irruption of change or transition of class structures. The transition of class structures, due to its process of uneven and combined development, results in (i) the discontinuity of social order, (ii) differences produced in terms of social effects, (iii) the failure of social totality to close itself via any particular class effect, (iv) the unpredictability of the movement of class processes and its associated social processes, and (v) the mutations and transformations produced in other areas of society as a result of the change in class structure. All these are effects of transition in class structure, and history is the discursive disclosure of these effects at the context governing the very moment of the arrival of change. The ceaseless process of transition due to overdetermination and contradiction of social processes, creates and re-creates history all the time, in many different ways and looks. This is not a chaotic theory of history, as is often mistakenly understood, but rather a synchronically ordered and systematic theory of history (the order and system being given by the discursive focus point of class) that is able to describe the reproduction of society in all its chaotic dimensions. What is lost, however, in this approach to transition, is the eschatological, diachronic, and systematic ordering of societies according to some notion of "progress."

(v) Transition and the Meaning of Progress

The approach to transition found in orthodox Marxism and the subaltern studies school depends intimately on the concept(s) of progress linked to the driving forces underlying linear evolution of society. This idea of progress acts at the same time as both the essence of societal development and the telos of the transition process. The idea of progress is used as a benchmark to define and describe the direction in which society develops.

Our decentered Marxian approach to transition is not agnostic or indifferent to the direction of societal change it favors. It advocates a change in society that replaces exploitative class processes with nonexploitative class processes so that those who produce surplus labor also appropriate it. Such profound changes in society's fundamental class processes are also bound to affect subsumed class processes since the two are linked. Therefore, the distribution of surplus labor/product is intimately linked with the production of that surplus, even in a society dominated by communist class structures. In our scheme, the surplus or proceeds of labor that are produced are immediately distributed as subsumed class payments to different members of society so that they can fulfill their various social functions. The surplus has to be distributed to reproduce production's technical conditions of existence, to reproduce other subsumed class processes that include distributing money for health and education, to provide funds for expanding production, and so on. The rest, whatever remains, is then distributed among the workers if it is a communist enterprise, kept by the exploiter if it is an exploitative class structure, or kept by the individual if it is an independent class structure. The important thing to understand is that both the production of surplus product and its distribution have to be taken into account in order to conceptualize progress or development in the postmodern Marxist theory.[14]

There are two points to note about a society dominated by nonexploitative class processes. First, in such a society the nonexploitative class processes would be comprised of both independent and communist class processes. Postmodern Marxists like Resnick and Wolff (1987, 1988) and Fraad, Resnick, and Wolff (1994) have tended to identify nonexploitative class processes with communist class processes only. It is unclear why the independent class processes should be left by the wayside since its form of appropriation is nonexploitative too. If one wants to identify nonexploitative class processes exclusively with communist class processes, then one needs to admit additional reasons for doing so. Such additional reasons are not spelt out in the postmodern Marxist theory. Second, since subsumed class processes are going to change with the establishment of nonexploitative class processes, there is a need to rethink the social aspects related to the distribution of income. As Marx pointed out in his critique of the Gotha Programme, every society including those dominated by capitalist class structures has a dominant concept of "fair" (or just) distribution that is overdetermined by political, cultural, and economical aspects. Marxists, too, will have to construct a concept of "fair" distribution. Very little research has been done on this area even though this is an important field of research.[15] Marx, in his comment on the Gotha program, did argue for an increased investment of surplus in education, health, and for the amelioration of poverty and unemployment. However, there is no one-to-one correspondence between nonexploitative class processes and a "fair" distribution that takes into account some of Marx's concerns. The relation between the two will be contextually determined.One can imagine a nonexploitative class-dominated society with an extremely "unfair" distribution of surplus. For example, the workers who appropriate the surplus may not want to give away any portion of the surplus to the unemployed and the poor. One can also imagine a situation where most of the surplus appropriated by the workers is paid as subsumed class payments to government bureaucracies who do not spend money in the ways that are considered part of the "fair" distribution. Because of the possibility of such a hideous society dominated by nonexploitative class processes, there is a need to articulate a concept or concepts of "fairness" to go along with the nonexploitative class processes. It is not that such a "fair" society will definitely be reached (it will depend on the contextual situation); rather, that one can then open up a range of possibilities in conceiving of a society dominated by nonexploitative class process.[16]

In the postmodern Marxist theory then, progress and development are concerned with the specific form of transition of class processes, and Marxists should support struggle (that is, conduct class struggle) in favor of those specific forms of class processes. Transition of class processes toward nonexploitative class structures and the transition of class and nonclass processes leading toward a "fair" redistribution of wealth (whose different possibilities need to be developed) is what we mean by progress and development.[17] Consequently, from a Marxist standpoint, one needs to differentiate between policies that address those concerns from ones that do not.

In the case of a society dominated by exploitative class processes, Marxists might also desire a redistribution of income from the "nondoers" of labor (that is, exploitative fundamental and subsumed classes) to the "doers" of labor (exploited fundamental and subsumed classes). One might want to ameliorate the unequal distribution of income in favor of the doers of labor. Thus, issues of poverty, the minimum wage, gender discrimination, and so on, are issues of concern for Marxists, qua Marxists, because decisions taken over these issues affect the class processes (fundamental and subsumed) in important ways.[18] Many of the decisions taken in these areas concern the issue of the distribution of wealth (or subsumed class payments), and Marxists will take various sides depending on whether or not redistribution will travel from the nondoers to the doers. The objective is to increase the influence of the "doers" of labor in the economic and political sphere of society so that political groups and social agencies supporting the cause of the "doers" will undertake or influence the direction of policies in favor of a transition of class processes in society toward a dominating presence and influence of the nonexploitative class processes. Thus, the political or ethical emphasis is on a change in both fundamental and subsumed class processes in specific directions.[19]

The important point to recognize is that the above meaning of progress and development has no originary, teleological, or evolutionary bias. Nothing in postmodern Marxist theory says that evolution of society follows some pre-given pattern such that it will move inexorably toward a nonexploitative and relatively "fair" society. What it says, in contrast, is that it is a desirable solution and one should advocate and fight for it. But struggling for it, of course, does not guarantee that it is going to happen. Furthermore, even if we assume that such a social state of affairs is achieved, the concept of overdetermination and contradiction prevents that state from likely being a permanent state. By the logic of cause and effect moving back and forth with its resultant emission of contradictory effects, some class structures might move back to exploitative forms and the social distribution of wealth may again become extremely "unfair." In other words, to imagine a permanent state of a society without exploitation and with a relatively "fair" distribution of income as the end of history is a utopia that is problematic in our rendition of social totality and transition. In this context, class struggle to maintain domination of nonexploitative class structures is part of a "permanent revolution."

This loss of a paradise (communism) as a permanent society, or an end of history, in the postmodern Marxist framework is compensated by other possibilities that were not accommodated in the orthodox rendition of Marxism. Since the complex, micro-focused concept of transition implies a continuous process of micro changes within and between class structures where the direction of change is not pre-given, there is ample space to work for changing class and nonclass processes that may have the possibilities to produce the above-mentioned desired progress and development in society. That is, since capitalist class structures cannot close society on their own, there remain possibilities for other class structures to make their presence felt. Marxists should situate their politics of class struggle within that range of possibilities.[20] This, of course, displaces the concept of progress and development and that of the associated politics of class struggle to a more micro level (as compared to orthodox Marxism), but given the failure of attempts at macro transitions to socialism, this should be a desirable displacement.[21]

Our approach to transition supports a radically different idea of progress and development. By progress and development, we mean the transformation of the class structures toward a nonexploitative form and a tendency toward a more "fair" distribution of the total value of products produced in the economy. It is crucial for Marxists to begin to theorize concepts of fairness to go along with the nonexploitative class structures so that Marxists could have real alternatives to put forward in the political arena as substitutes to the dominant neoclassical approaches. We suggest that our concept of progress and development—the dual sword of nonexploitative class structures and "fair" distribution—will help produce the new conceptions of society that are both decentered yet radically progressive. This is a vision that Marxists need to put forward as a countervision to the more mainstream approaches to transition and development. What we have sketched as progress and development or, what is the same, developmental progress, needs to be further elaborated in light of the transformation that the concept of social totality and transition has undergone in our hands. This will be the topic of the next chapter.

Primitive Capital Accumulation, Hegemony, and Transition

Our critique of the orthodox concept of transition as visualized in the parable of historical materialism has displaced many received concepts in

Marxist theory—one of which is the historically celebrated concept of primitive capital accumulation. In the traditional Marxist literature, primitive capital accumulation is used to describe the process of transition from precapitalism to capitalism. The attack on and rejection of the concepts of closed social totality along with that of mode of production as visualized in classical Marxism and its methodological underpinning of essentialism and historicism associated with the transitional schema of historical materialism means that primitive capital accumulation conceptualized as a preconceived historical moment of transition can no longer be conceived as a viable concept. We discussed some of the problems related to primitive capital accumulation in chapter 2 and chapter 5. Additionally, we can infer from our current analysis on transition that without the mark of historicist logic reflecting a rational ordered progressive movement of society from a preordained origin to a teleological ending the received concept of primitive capital accumulation loses its bite and relevance.

But notwithstanding its historicist undertone, the idea of primitive capital accumulation is powerful and extremely relevant, especially for our decentered concept of transition. That idea captures the process of expropriation of conditions of existence—private and common—and not only will make extinct some of current processes of performance, appropriation, distribution, and receipt of surplus labor but at times may even obliterate communities in certain areas. We will continue to use the name "primitive accumulation" ("capital" is no longer in the middle, for now the historicist moment of the process as necessarily forming the origin of labor power drops out) as a process of expropriation of the conditions of existence of the direct producers without the additional criteria of this being supported by the absorption of those dispossessed people as wage laborers. There is thus no historicity attached to primitive accumulation: if the dispossessed become or are made to become wage laborers, then it is only contextual and contingent—one form that this process could have taken on. It is in this regard that we read Marx's description of the process of industrialization of England in light of what he called the transition from feudalism to capitalism as being facilitated by primitive accumulation, pioneered to a large extent by the state (facilitating the conversion of the dispossessed into wage laborers). But primitive accumulation, as we shall soon indicate, may not always be so elaborate but something that happens intermittently in dispersed time and space. Thereby deepening the process of decentering, unevenness, and heterogeneity of transition of a social totality such as that of India's. In the current scenario, this is more pervasive and hence relevant than an elaborate form of primitive accumulation as illustrated by Marx.

It is to be noted that the above definition of primitive accumulation contains the possibility of dismembering community. However, as our discussion in the previous chapter showed, community is not unilaterally derived from an essential core such as property, but is an existence constituted by an overdetermined network of relationships that we will later define as shared environment. If community is to be destroyed then it would involve the appropriation of the entire network—not just property—that makes up the community. Now, under certain circumstances, such appropriations may very well happen. It, however, could be for the process of capital accumulation or for any other reason and not necessarily done with the purpose of creating a body of wage laborers. That is, primitive accumulation could very well dismember a community but such an event cannot be derived from any naturalized or "rational" inner logic of history.

Primitive accumulation, as has been theorized by orthodox Marxists, has currently taken a back seat in the toolbox of relevant concepts because of its essentialist and historicist moorings. It has, to a large extent, been replaced by the concept of hegemony, which is constitutive of the "other" of primitive accumulation—nonviolence.[22] While there is no doubt that hegemony is particularly useful in explaining the existence of certain regimes, orders, or institutions, especially where actors operate within a democratic system, the theoretical demotion of primitive accumulation, with its feature of dispossession through coercion (that may take a violent form), has been unfortunate and misplaced. In an underdeveloped country such as India, an analysis of social totality and its transition without the complexity of hegemony and primitive accumulation could only be a half-baked one—hegemony is complemented by primitive accumulation and vice versa. While this is too important an issue to be given such a short shrift, we do offer certain insights that of course can only serve to indicate an opening for carrying out a full-fledged study of that complexity.

We begin with the example of the Narmada Valley project, which is a design to create thousands of dams—big, medium, and small—along the river Narmada stretching across the states of Maharashtra, Gujarat, and Madhya Pradesh. The objective of these dams is to provide water to people in drought-prone areas in the states mentioned. The Indian government, along with the respective state governments and big industrialists, has backed to the hilt the project, which unfortunately also calls for the dispossession of tens of millions of people from their conditions of existence—from the only environment these people have known, living as part of communities that have graced the terrain of history for thousands of years. What is glaringly portentous in this particular process of (redefined) primitive accumulation is the "loss" of environment—more specifically the truncation or, in many instances, as in our current example, extinction of the space of "shared" environment.[23] The cost of building the series of dams in the Narmada Valley project is simply not the displacement of the people from those well-known conditions (such as land or property) that enabled them to reproduce their class activities but also the loss of the (shared) "environment" in which people have undertaken their various class reproduction processes. The content of this shared environment is bigger than but includes natural factors like rivers and forests or property relations, all—that goes into creating the possibility of sharing in economic/non-economic reproduction that required centuries to build and integrate into the knowledge/information structure within the operating system, are lost forever.[24] Other than the professed objective of providing drinking water, Arundhuti Roy (1999) describes in detail how, through a vast network of intertwined institutions including the organizations of the state, the ruling regime in India is effectively redistributing in its favor the wealth/productive capacity/surplus labor of the affected people via the construction of the Narmada Valley project. In her scheme, the Dam is a further medium—a different context—through which the process of redistribution of the above-mentioned from the poor to the rich is unveiled. And in the end, when the process of dispossession from conditions of existence obliterates the shared environment, it is not the surplus but the entire shared environment that is appropriated. This process is not reflective of any process of hegemonic formation in which attempts are made to create faith in an idea but instead signifies a process of primitive accumulation with the state being directly complicit in it.

Primitive accumulation is taking place in India in the twenty-first century in every nook and corner of the country due to, among other things, pressure from the entry of multinational capital. Primitive accumulation is not simply a First World historic relic of the eighteenth and nineteenth century or a primitive submoment of history to be transgressed and left as a relic of the past. Furthermore, its form is changing, even intensifying. Let us touch on one such change in form.

It is not that the process of primitive accumulation is always undertaken by multinational capital or government directly for all of its projects. Some of them clearly have only symbolic connotation attached to the procedure. For example, in order to attract multinational capital, the government may undertake "faceliftment" measures such as removing hawkers from the city pavements, removing slum dwellers who are eyesores to investors and foreign visitors, removing villagers from their land to build up cities that could be paraded as infrastructural development, and so on. In case of hawkers, land/pavement—common space—that condition of existence without which hawkers cannot perform their economic (including class— mostly subsumed) activities have become a bone of contention. The entire objective of the measures aimed at dispossession of such conditions of existence is to create a "signal" that will function to reveal the "business-mindedness" of the government, thereby creating a symbolic show of support/friendship for the potential (big—global as well as domestic) capital. There is now clearly cutthroat competition between state governments in India to send as many "signals" as possible (especially to foreign multinationals for foreign direct investment), since the image of investor friendliness of the respective state governments will be judged accordingly.

The massive disjointment in economic space resulting from the above process of primitive accumulation is re-creating the meaning of what is right and wrong (the moral economic values) and hence the meaning of politics/cultural as well (via the overdetermined process). For example, one position that has become popular in India only recently is that hawkers are a nuisance to modern society and an eyesore for investors of domestic and foreign capital. Getting rid of the hawkers (by dispossessing their current but contested "rights" over common space that enables them to take part in class processes) will of course rob them of their livelihood in the short run but, via the signal creation process, will be compensated in the long run with jobs to be created with the entry of domestic and foreign capital. The language of politics has accordingly undergone a transformation. Hawkers were nowhere conceived as a problem in the 1980s in a place such as Kolkata but liberalization and the advent of globalization with their implanted rhetoric of competition have changed all that. Suddenly the hawker has become a problem—an object of inquiry and politics—and an object of inquiry from the concern of big capital. The metonyms of capital—efficiency, competition, market, capitalist progress, and so on—constitute the communities (the body of hawkers, agricultural people holding land, slum dwellers, etc.) developing and distributing reasons as to why their destruction (via the process of primitive accumulation) is necessary and then, having performed primitive accumulation, through a network of media and political interventions backed up by a set of compensations further legitimizes the exclusion of the lost community from its rule. The communities may, at times, simply disappear into oblivion and yet the people will remain. It may so happen that instead of breaking the faith in the hegemonic rule, the primitively accumulated people—the excluded bunch now—become grateful to the regime for receiving the benefits (compensation) in return or are simply awed by the growth of the cities so much so as to respect and even sing the praise of the state/"capitalism" that in turn further legitimize the process of its rule. And at other times, when communities remain in place but the primitive accumulated people get out of the surplus economy and manage a living in a different space—of subsistence/need economy—the government that has ruined them as well the international agencies will send their agents (government bodies or NGOs) to "help" these people not to integrate into the surplus economy but to enable them in reproducing their life in the need economy.[25] In the process of discharging this role, these agencies emerge as the metonyms of the capitalist regime. In fact, this is one possible medium through which the regime of capital could create its hegemony, which has been called synthetic hegemony (Chaudhury 1988, 1994; Chakrabarti and Roy Chaudhury 1999/2000; Chaudhury, Das, and Chakrabarti 2000, Chakrabarti, Chaudhury, and Cullenberg 2002). This system of inculcating faith via the process of ruling by exclusion (from the surplus economy) does not pose any threat to the capitalist regime. Quite the reverse: it not only reduces the cost of the capitalist regime but also enables capital to emerge as the benevolent outsider. Here is a possible case where primitive accumulation and (synthetic) hegemony implodes into one in a series of unfolding events.

Coercion—sanctioned by the state, the media, the judiciary—through primitive accumulation is then an additional part of any rule, sometimes performed pervasively and sometimes selectively. Hegemony, on the other hand, is not exactly violence/coercion. Hegemony thrives on producing a system of adherence/legitimacy/trap for/by the rule by inculcating faith/ belief/respect in the system/regime/order among concerned agents. However, hegemony and coercion complement one another in any rule. Often coercive mechanisms are followed or simultaneously backed by faith or respect building measures. Hegemonic rule is not fortified by simply taking but also has to be supplemented by the act of giving that will produce the belief/faith/respect in that rule. The state may take away the land and "shared environment" of people (through primitive accumulation), but by measures of compensation, selling of rosy pictures (future job/wealth prospects for those losing land), which even may come true, reinforces the faith/belief/respect in the rule:

> Power is fortified not just by what it destroys, but also by what it creates. Not just by what it takes, but also by what it gives. And powerlessness reaffirmed not just by the helplessness of those who have lost, but also by the gratitude of those who have (or *think* they have) gained. (Arundhuti Roy 1999, 72)

Primitive accumulation and hegemony, violence and dialogue, taking and giving, fascism and democracy are all present working side by side and inside one another overflowing from one to the next and back and are important phenomena with monumental effects on the transition of the social totality (such as India's). And yet we find this moment of overdetermination generally missing from the literature which, hopefully, our newly developed concept of primitive accumulation has brought to the forefront.

Household Classes and Illustration
of the Meaning of Transition

Here we will give an initial illustration of our concept of transition in the context of household (we will deal in details with transition taking place in the other sectors of India in the event of the adoption of the new economic policies in a later chapter) and bring to light possible overdetermined relations between the household sector and the firms, specifically capitalist firms in our case. While many Marxists (Seccombe 1974, 1980; Hartmann 1981; Delphy 1984; Barrett 1988; to name a few) increasingly accept the endeavor to conceptualize the household as a site of class relations where class is understood in a nonsurplus sense, it has only been very recently that the panoptic gaze of the academic world has fallen on the household sector as part of a surplus-labor-defined, class-focused analysis (Resnick, Wolff and Fraad 1994, Chaudhury and Chakrabarti 2000, Fraad 2000). And since the meaning of transition from such a class angle is newly formulated through our presentation here, hardly any analysis worth the name exists depicting the overdetermined relations between household class process and other class processes as well as their transition dynamics within and across the different classes. Our focus here will be on how the transition of household process takes place and how this transition in one sector may initiate a transition process in another sector through its constitutive relationships and thereby produce a broader transition of the social totality.

The household sector is constituted by many dimensions, among which one is the performance, appropriation, distribution, and receipt of surplus labor.[26] Studying the processes related to surplus labor throws up the important point that this is a sector almost totally dominated by noncapitalist classes, since whatever is being produced (cooked meat, for example) inside the site of household is crucially constituted by personalized elements such as love, emotion, fear, etc. (see Fraad 2000), and consequently it would be practically impossible to find relationships within the household sector that are simply governed by wage labor and commodity exchange of products created therein (since these are to a great extent based on impersonal relationships). The existence of class processes in the noncapitalist household sector has been extensively analyzed by Fraad, Resnick, and Wolff [hereafter FRW] (1994). Spivak (1994), in an incisive introduction to FRW, points out that FRW's analysis of the household has created a new opening for class analysis through their theoretical move to produce Marxian analytical concepts loosened from historicism and thereby making it possible to inscribe the household at the site of the economic and capable of being subclassified into different fundamental class processes. FRW argue that the household is a site of noncapitalist class processes and produces a portrait of the house-wife as a noncapitalist laborer (feudal, independent, or communal) within the very heartland of the so-called "capitalist society" of the United States. This novel intervention also marks out the opening for our theoretical inter-vention, which additionally builds on the "domestic labor" debate that took place in the 1970s and 1980s (Seccombe 1974, 1980; Humphries 1977; Himmelweit and Mohun 1977; Hartmann 1981; Fox 1980; Delphy 1984; Barrett 1988 to name a few).[27] Many of the propositions developed in this literature influence our treatment below, especially the one related to the constitution of the commodity labor power by the household labor process.

We begin by arguing that orthodox Marxists (including Indian Marxists) have commonly overlooked the production process of the commodity labor power and, consequently, the housewife and household's role in that production process. Since household labor is a condition of existence of the commodity labor power and the commodity labor power, in turn, is a condition of existence of the capitalist class process, household labor working to reproduce the commodity labor power emerges as a condition of existence of the capitalist class process. Similarly, capitalist class pro-cesses will have great effects on the way surplus labor is performed, appro-priated, and distributed inside the household sector.

The Household's Overdetermination of the Commodity Labor Power

We are interested in the origin of the commodity labor power, and we pro-pose that, among other things, the commodity labor power in its prevail-ing form cannot be (re)produced without household labor. Consequently, our interest is confined not to the household class process per se but, rather, to the overdetermining moment at which the household class pro-cess through the performance of household labor constitutes the com-modity labor power and, consequently, the capitalist class process.[28]

Let us begin by reconsidering the simplest value equations of Wolff, Roberts, and Callari (1982, 1984) abstracted from the heterogeneity of labor:[29]

$$V_j = \sum_{i=1}^{n} p_i a_{ij} + a_{oj}, j = 1, 2, \ldots n.$$

$$V_L = \sum_{i=1}^{n} p_i b_i$$

where, V_j = unit value of the jth commodity.

a_{ij} = i^{th} commodity required to produce one unit of the jth commodity.

a_{oj} = (direct) labor time required to produce one unit of the jth commodity.

$\sum_{i=1}^{n} p_i b_i$ = the reproduction cost of a unit of variable capital in labor hours or price of one unit of labor power.

V_L = unit value of the labor power.

$\{b_i\}$ = consumption set or subsistence basket of the laborer for the reproduction of one unit of the labor power.

This equation for the value of the labor power (the form the commodity labor power takes in value terms)—defined as the reproduction costs of the labor power for the family of the laborer—does not include household labor as part of this reproduction cost.[30] The reproduction cost of the labor power means the cost of the socially determined subsistence basket bought from the market in labor-hour terms. It does not include, for example, the labor hours necessary to bring the raw meat bought from the market to home, or to transfer it into cooked meat and deliver it to the table. It is often forgotten that there are many labor hours between the cup and the lip, the kitchen and the table, the cradle and adulthood.

There are two major implications of this forgetfulness. The first, as we have already mentioned, is that related to occlusion. While orthodox Marxism openly banishes the housewife (and the household) in the typical patriarchal family from the realm of the economic and makes her invisible, the postmodern Marxist approach in recent years has made important progress by trying to incorporate the household class process within its framework. However, the inclusion of household remains incomplete in the postmodern Marxist theory since it has not yet attempted to face the consequence of including household labor within the value theoretic framework. This takes us to our second point.

Inherent in the exclusion of household labor from the value of labor power is another forgetfulness: that of consumption as a process and how it is overdetermined by the production process. This is an important point and needs to be explained. Marx in his now-famous introduction to the *Grundrisse* (1973, 83–111) pointed out that production and consumption are each other's condition of existence; one cannot logically pose the social existence of (consumption) production without (production) consumption (1973, 90–94). Capitalist production processes involve the consumption of the means of production and labor that must presuppose the production of the means of production and the commodity labor power. Both require the labor process and labor time for capitalist production to take place. Since the household class processes in part constitute the site of the production process of the commodity labor power, the production (labor) process of the commodity labor power should include the site of

the household class process. The site of the household class process is constituted by, among other elements, a household production process that
involves (like class processes at other sites) household labor to reproduce
the social existence of the members of the household. It will be difficult for
the capitalist enterprise to reproduce itself in its present form without the
production process of the commodity labor power and, subsequently, that
of (household) labor involved in the household production process. However, Marxists (especially Indian Marxists, who irrespective of their other
differences must take collective blame for the failure to see this point) have
ignored the production process involved in the capitalist's consumption of
the commodity labor power.[31] They focus on the capitalist labor process
(or for that matter, any noncapitalist, nonhousehold labor process) as their
exclusive site of production by keeping the household out of their sight
and therefore out of their discursive domain.

All commodities require direct labor in order to be produced, except the
unique commodity—labor power—whose value representation does not
include any kind of direct labor. In other words, the capitalist's consumption of the means of production includes the production process involved
in producing the means of production while the capitalist's consumption
of the commodity labor power involves an element of forgetfulness of the
production process of labor power.[32]

The above discussion implies that there is a close linkage between the
dynamics of capitalist firms and noncapitalist households. In the case of
our noncapitalist household model, a transfer of labor time takes place
through household labor's constitution of the commodity labor power
where the expenditure of labor time occurs, since the household production process constitutes one tier of the vertically integrated production
process for producing the commodity labor power.

Household labor contributes to surplus labor in capitalist enterprises
through its role in constituting the commodity labor power. Household
labor constitutes the commodity labor power, which in turn is an indispensable condition of existence of producing surplus labor in the capitalist
class process. Thus, household labor provides one of the necessary conditions of the existence of surplus labor creation and its appropriation in
capitalist enterprises.

The form of labor transfer will vary according to the type and form of
noncapitalist and capitalist class processes in question. The nature of this
transfer from an independent household class process to a capitalist class
process is not the same as the nature of a transfer from a feudal household
class process to a capitalist class process. The differences in class processes
will have a profound effect on how the second tier of the production pro-

cess of the commodity labor power will take place. For example, the household labor that produces a single member inside the household without expending surplus labor for others (independent class process) will be qualitatively different from the household labor that involves reproducing other members of the family by exerting surplus labor for them (feudal class process). The nature of the labor transfer to the capitalist class process is consequently different for the two cases. Thus, while one of the overdetermined moments involves the common phenomenon of the transfer of noncapitalist household labor to the capitalist class process, the form of transfer is dispersed and differentiated.

An important point to understand is that the transfer of household labor time epitomizes only one but critical condition of existence of the reproduction of the commodity labor power. There are many other social aspects that overdetermine the commodity labor power. Without such conditions of existence, the reproduction of the commodity labor power in its prevailing form will not materialize. For whether all the entitlements (as Amartya Sen would put it)—such as school and college, health care system, and so on—needed for a child to become employable in the future are available in the area is an important consideration for the making of the labor power. Additionally, a capitalist enterprise's internal and external conditions of existence related to elements like supervision and control of the labor process, the power of its union, trade (both international and domestic), competition, financial positions, and relationships with financial institutions, and so on, will determine the prevailing form of existence of the commodity labor power. The production of the commodity labor power requires all of these conditions of existence to fulfill its social function. What we are saying is that a transfer of labor from a noncapitalist household sector enterprise to the capitalist enterprise is another crucial condition of existence of labor power, a condition without which, as is the case with all the other constitutive elements, the commodity labor power in its present form will cease to exist.

The above analysis solidifies many of the characteristics presented earlier in portraying the postmodern Marxist approach to social totality and transition. First, it demonstrates that class analysis cannot accommodate concepts of closed social totality like them of capitalism or feudalism; there are instead a multitude of uniquely constituted class processes in any society. Social totality consists of a configuration of social relationships derived from the subtotalities of class processes, each of which are unique and distinct. Thus social totality encompasses capitalist and noncapitalist class processes, thereby undercutting the theoretical proposition of a closed social totality like that of capitalist society. This means that a social totality determined by a mode of production, which requires the uniform presence of class processes, cannot exist. This collapse of a uniform society and mode of production follows from our displacement of the primitive of Marxian analysis to the micro level space of class process. If transition can no longer be conceived as a macro-level change from one mode of production to another, the question then is how to reconceptualize it from the micro-level perspective of class process. This is done by conceptualizing transition in the presence of a multiplicity of uniquely constituted, distinct class processes such as that taking place in the household sector. It is argued that transition, as in the case of orthodox Marxist development theory, involves a change in social totality. But the crucial difference is that the movement has been displaced from onetime big-bang change to a continuous transformation of class processes that involves no reference to any centripetal force or historicity. As one class process (which is constituted by other processes) changes, the social totality undergoes a change via a chain reaction of effects that follows from and results in disturbances percolating throughout the fundamental class process and the other processes embedded to it in a relation of constitution. Subsequently, changes in society are unevenly distributed, and yet the unevenness is produced out of a combined existence of different class processes, each affecting the others in unique ways. Transition, consequently, captures this uneven and combined development of society.

Second, while any two sites of class processes are conceptually distinct (that is, they can be defined distinctly), they are not independent of or autonomous from one another. The sites of capitalist and noncapitalist class processes coexist as overdetermined by one another.

We now intend to explain the overdetermined relation between the household and capitalist class processes with the help of illustrations from the dynamics in two countries—the United States and India. The analysis of the United States is adapted from Fraad, Resnick, and Wolff (1994), and the other looks at the effect on the overdetermined relation between the noncapitalist household class process and the capitalist class process in light of the ongoing liberalisation policies in India. This will bring into light the complex relationship between constitutivity of classes and transition of the social totality.

Transition of the Household Class Process in United States

The specific overdetermined juncture of the capitalist class process and the noncapitalist patriarchal household process is constituted by its contradictions. In our scheme, the contradictions may be so constituted that the housewife may decide to become a wage laborer in the capitalist economy. FRW pointed out that the United States household has been undergoing a class revolution since the late 1960s, such that the traditional feudal households are giving way to independent or communal forms of households. This transformation was driven to a large extent by the constitutive effects of changing gender perception following the feminist movement. Such household classes are more conducive to allowing the housewife to enter the workforce in the nonhousehold sector. The entry of women in the workforce was also a response to falling real wages occurring since the 1970s, which had a lot to do with the internal and external conditions of change taking place within corporate America. As Richard Wolff argues,

> Real wages over the 1980s and 1990s trended downwards. Indeed, the falling wages combined with the labor-saving technical changes—the "computer revolution" phase of the classic automation process—to produce many of the boom levels of corporate profits. . . .
>
> US families responded to falling real wages by sending more family members out to work for more time. According to the Economic Policy Institute's annual statistical analysis (The State of Working America, 2000–2001), the average US married-couple family with children saw its income rise by 21.3 percent from 1979 to 1988, but if the wife's contributions to that income were excluded, the rise would have been only 5.9 per cent. (2001, 47–48)

The above-mentioned factors caused a migration of housewives into the capitalist firms as wage laborers. One result the entry of women into the workforce was that the capitalist labor process would have to be reorganized to take into account the gender differences in workplace; new laws might have to be brought in to take into account sexual harassment and unequal payment schemes for the same job; affirmative action or some variant of it would have to be evented to push women up the promotion ladder; new institutional processes (such as day care) might have to be created to support the children of working women; and so on. Again, there is no need to emphasize that such changes in the internal and external conditions of the capitalist enterprise led to a transformation of the capitalist class process, in the manner in which surplus was performed, appropriated, and distributed and received. As one can imagine, the reverse effect on household class process ensuing from this migration of women could only have been seismic, and it was (see FRW 1994 for details).

Transition of the Household Class Process in India

Let us now look at the dynamics of the overdetermined existence of the capitalist economy and the noncapitalist household economy in light of India's liberalization policies formally adopted in 1991. This will explain some of the mechanics through which the noncapitalist household in constituting the capitalist economy may get constituted by the latter at the very moment of their interaction with one another.

The socially necessary amount (both in a qualitative and quantitative sense) of the means of subsistence acceptable to the laborer is determined by "historical and moral elements" in Marxist theory.[33] There are no hard and fast rules or formulae as to what constitutes the means of subsistence. They vary from time to time and by region. The socially necessary acceptable means of subsistence for a United States laborer is both vastly different from and greater than that of an Indian laborer as the historical and moral elements that constitute what is socially necessary for the reproduction of the family of the laborer is different for the respective countries. A change in the historical and moral elements would produce a change in the society's perception of what the socially necessary means of subsistence are, and such a change may be overdetermined by the subsequent supply of a new set of wage goods produced by capitalist production process.[34] This new set of wage goods would in turn bring about a change in the second tier of production of the commodity labor power, the household production process. This may produce a transformation of the ratio of surplus labor to necessary labor inside the household by changing the necessary labor time required to reproduce the social existence of the housewife. For example, in India, during the 1980s and especially after the liberalization of the economy began in 1991, there has been a definite change in the meaning of what is socially necessary for the reproduction of the laborer (the subject) and his family. The effects have been felt on two fronts.

First, a new set of wage goods has replaced old ones on the list of necessary items. Televisions, refrigerators, gadgets, personal vehicles, fashion clothes, and so on, are now increasingly becoming common goods in an Indian family.[35] It is not the case that all Indian families have such a set of wage goods; rather, the point is that this set of wage goods is being projected as socially necessary. The socially necessary basket of commodities requires the presence of this new set of wage goods. The liberalization of the economy makes available such variegated goods in plenty and through (global) competition, as well as supply-side reforms, such goods to be produced at cheaper costs and sold at lower prices. Second, and especially with the advent of the liberalization era, a revolution is taking place in the production process inside the household. A new set of time-saving technologies like dishwashers, washing machines, microwaves, and other cooking gadgets produced by capitalist enterprises are being projected as socially necessary for the reproduction of the household production process.[36] This set of wage goods is advertised and sold as household-friendly since they reduce the time required in performing the old set of household activities. With more and more women joining the workforce outside the household (sometimes due to the higher cost of living brought about by the socially necessary commodity index defining the new standard of living), this technological upheaval is being projected as a necessity since now time inside the household becomes more valuable and so does the opportunity cost of time.

The economic effect is overdetermined by the cultural aspect that can be attributed to a change in the social perception of what are the socially necessary baskets of commodities for a household unit. In the sociology literature, this cultural aspect is also called cultural capital, since the change in culture is attributable to a change in the penetration of commercial commodities inside the household. The changes in the cultural aspects in turn react back on the economy, helping to reproduce the new social conditions of existence of fundamental class processes that produce such consumer goods. If, as a result of the economic and cultural changes, the household decides to (i) increase productive expenditures in order to change the production process of the household economy and (ii) increase its expenditure on nonproductive items (such as fashionable clothing), then there are three possible consequences. First, the socially necessary labor time required to reproduce the housewife can decline sharply such that the housewife now has the option to spend her excess time either on herself or on her husband and children. Second, the socially necessary labor time required to reproduce the housewife and possibly the surplus labor time she exerts increases due to a revision in the standards of "cleanliness" inside the household. Third, there could be an increasing tendency toward outward mobility of the housewife to the capitalist class process due to an increase in the cost of living. Here, we will discuss the first and the third case for they are comprehensive enough to capture the complexity of any process of societal transition.

Take the first case. Consider where out of an average eight hours of working time of the housewife, three hours of labor time was socially necessary for her social reproduction as a housewife. The rest of five hours surplus labor time was spent on the creation of the commodity labor power of her husband.[37] Now suppose that technological improvement inside the household causes a reduction in the socially necessary labor time of the housewife by one hour. It might very well happen that the housewife decides to spend this extra hour gained on her husband or children. In fact, this is happening in a lot of Indian families, where the mothers are paying more attention and exerting more labor time on the activities of their children. In the case of India, one can witness a mass of educated mothers who, through the activities of childbearing and child rearing, are playing a critical role in changing the quality of the labor force entering the labor market and the capitalist production process.[38] This new mass of a more healthy and productive labor force in turn is and will be playing an important role in changing the process of the production process in Indian capitalist enterprises and, consequently, the rate of exploitation (SV/V_L) deriving from it. Without the changing process of household production and the mass of educated mothers, the rhetoric of efficiency and competitiveness of Indian enterprises and the Indian economy as a whole would be a difficult proposition to realize.

The above scheme emphasizes the point that the commodity labor power is constituted by household labor and that household labor constitutes the capitalist class process. Simultaneously, the value of the means of subsistence produced through the capitalist class process enters the site of the household economy by constituting its production process. The capitalist class process is shaped by the household class process while the household class process is constituted by the principles of the capitalist class process. Evidently, the commodity labor power, by suturing the two distinct sites of class processes, helps to produce a very complex existence of the process of transition.

Let us now go over to the third case. One effect of the liberalization policies could be an increase in the household expenditures on the means of subsistence required to reproduce the commodity labor power. This happens due to a change in an upward direction of the meaning of what is socially necessary for the reproduction of the commodity labor power. This increase in the total expenditure of the subsistence basket of commodities means that many of the average Indian families are unable to afford the subsistence set of goods given their present wage level, thereby throwing the mode of reproduction of the existing household class process into jeopardy. This creates one condition for the outward mobility of the women to the capitalist labor market. Instead of spending more time on household affairs, a housewife may now decide to go to the labor market to work in a capitalist enterprise.[39] In fact, along with the first phenomenon, this one can also be detected in the Indian labor market.[40] We are witnessing a mass of female workers entering the capitalist labor market. As in the case of U.S. women, this is also going to produce profound changes in the capitalist enterprises and the noncapitalist household class enterprises, since for both groups the internal (changes in labor process, supervision, etc.) and external (entry of new commodities, change in credit process, change in cultural perception, etc.) conditions of the respective enterprises will undergo a transformation. It is again worth remembering that this creation of a new body of (female) proletariat requires a continuous transfer of household labor from the household production process to the capitalist production process, though the qualitative nature of the transfer will of course have changed due to the transition within the household class process. It is an underestimation to say that the overdetermined relation between the household and capitalist class process is fundamentally changing the makeup of the social totality that is India.

The above analysis brings up an interesting point. The separation of individuals from their previous standing in a noncapitalist site into a capitalist site does not imply that the noncapitalist site disappears along with its noncapitalist class positions, though it points to the complex nature of the transition process as capturing the uneven, decentered, and heterogeneous change in class structures. This is in stark contrast to the orthodox Marxian rendition of transition as ultimately a onetime historic shock capturing an irreversible transformation from one mode of production to another.

Conclusion

We have constructed a concept of transition that does not share the diachronic, big-bang approach to transition that is found in classical historical materialist arguments, but we have advocated one concerned with the synchronic and diachronic shifts of the disaggregated class structures of a society. In this context, we have discussed in turn the micro or disaggregated class approach to transition, the nonhistoricist developmental structure of our approach, and the alternative idea of progress implicit in our approach.

The new concept of transition, which tries to capture the complexity of society in terms of the micro-focused configuration of class structures is qualitatively different from the concepts of transition as developed in the Indian modes of production debate and subaltern studies, which are characterized by an attempt to simplify the complex existence of society in terms of a big-bang, macro theory of change. The major difference between the two approaches is based on the methodological schisms imposed by our adherence to a nonessentialist, nonhistoricist approach as against the essentialist and historicist approach in the Indian debates on Marxism. As we tried to show, the construction of this new concept of transition makes it possible to reconceptualize social totality, capitalist society, economy, progress and development, history, and primitive accumulation without relapsing into the twin problems of essentialism and historicism.

The next question is, in what direction should Marxists want the development of society to go? We have pointed out that desirable society from a Marxian point of view constitutes transition to a nonexploitative fundamental class process with a fair distribution of surplus. But because we have not elaborated on both, the desirable society stands undertheorized and hence incomplete. Consequently, development as signifying a notion of "progress" in a postmodern sense remains undertheorized. Addressing this issue is additionally important since the ethics underlying the desirable society would critically constitute the possibilities of Marxian politics on development. In the next chapter, we systematically build a Marxian theorization of development (as progress) in a postmodern economic space that we have so constructed in which the transition of society is uneven, disaggregated, and heterogeneous and without any projected telos inherent in the rethought idea of progress.

CHAPTER 7

Class and Need

An Alternative Political Economy
of Development

Since its official inscription in the Erfurt program of 1891, radical development theories have had a long and rich tradition. We traced some of their theoretical renditions in chapter 1 and then analyzed in detail its Indian counterparts in the form of the debate on the Indian modes of production and subaltern studies debates. Despite the differences and debates on the stages of history that underlined all such variegated radical theories, there was a general consensus among radical thinkers regarding the trajectory of development and transition. Development proceeds from the *center* to the *periphery*. The center is *advanced* in the sense that it possesses a more developed form of the forces of production while the periphery is *backward* because it lacks it. There are different levels at which the center-periphery or the advanced-backward criteria could operate. The center might be the West while the periphery the backward non-Western countries. Within the Western and the non-Western countries, the center might be the industrial sector while agriculture is the periphery.

The privileged status accorded to the center at some level is never questioned in these radical theories. The transition debates in Russia also never questioned this dualism and, in fact, theories of transition were consciously devised (war communism or primitive socialist accumulation) to make the center powerful. In the context of transition to capitalism or socialism, all such debates had a clearcut end in mind—the development of forces of production epitomized by technological advancement. Industrialization through capital accumulation was the strategy identified to achieve that and subsequently became the key term in the debates. For society to progress, the center must be strengthened and once that is done, development would percolate to the periphery. So development came to be associated with the rate of development of capital accumulation. Even the world system theorists, like Frank and Wallerstein, who identified the developed countries—the center—as the cause of underdevelopment in the peripheral countries, considered the growth of industrial center in the peripheral countries to be crucial for the development of the periphery. For them, it was the fettering of the industrial center in the periphery by the center countries/developed world that led to the underdevelopment of the domestic center in the peripheral countries and of the peripheral society as a whole. More broadly, this emphasis on industrialization through capital accumulation was not exclusively held by Marxists. The mainstream, too, emphasized the role of industrialization through capital accumulation (see, for example, Lewis 1954 and Harris and Todaro 1970). Generally, the literature on "industrialization through capital accumulation" gave a naturalized, ontological emphasis on technological change (for example, the forces of production in historical materialism) and its development and, in that context, took capital accumulation as being the harbinger of progress of society. While industrialization through capital accumulation was considered a commonly held virtue by both camps, the radicals generally believed in the inability of capital accumulation to industrialize the periphery. Thus, in almost all debates on transition and development (such as that on the modes of production in India or the subaltern studies theory of transition and development), theorists understood underdevelopment as a blocked development of capitalism or its higher form, socialism. As a result, the debate over the possibility or impossibility of "industrialization through capital accumulation" became the key to the twentieth-century development discourse.

Despite the fissures and fractures conditioning the road map of development, radical developmentalism—as epitomized by the Indian modes of production debates and the subaltern studies debates—was consistent in upholding the presence of a societal essence: the economic centered on capital, and defined its own dynamics around the logic of capital accumulation acting as a ground to the conception of a social totality and its evolution. Subsequently, the social totality in the development literature was divided into hierarchies constitutive of independent and autonomous spaces that are self-reflective—mode of production and superstructure, forces of production and relations of production, industry and agriculture, capital accumulation and need. This hierarchical division that was generally telescoped under the terms "center" and "periphery" or couched

in a similar nomenclature with similar connotation became the most po-
tent form of constructing debates of development. These economic categories produced a series of binary divisions often charged with ethical and
moral undertones—good and evil, forward and backward, modern and
primitive, West and East.

Critiquing the received radical approaches to economic development
as being guided by the methodological principles of essentialism and historicism, Ruccio and Simon (1986a, 1986b), Ruccio (1991), Chakrabarti
(1996, 98), Chakrabarti and Cullenberg (2001a, 2001b), Gibson-Graham
(1996), and Gibson-Graham and Ruccio (2001) argue for adopting a contrasting notion of a discursively created, disaggregated class-based social
totality for debating the issue of development. Our critique of the Indian
debates on transition and development along these lines assimilates com-
prehensively and develops in new directions this anti-essentialist and antihistoricist approach to transition and development. This critique of the
orthodox approach to transition and development along with the alternative idea of social totality is consistent with those that point to the generally overwhelming emphasis on capital accumulation–based approach as
being essentialist (Resnick and Wolff 1987, Gibson-Graham, Resnick and
Wolff 2001a, Norton 1986, 1988, 2001).

Alongside this critique of radical developmentalism, a parallel critique
was developed that came to be known as the antidevelopmentalism/post-
development school of thought. Arturo Escobar's (1995) attempt to critique "industrialization through capital accumulation" based development
is typical of such reactions (also see Nandy 1987, Shiva 1989, and essays in
Marglin and Apffel-Marglin 1990).[1] We generally agree with Escobar and
the anti-postdevelopmental school of thought regarding their critique of
the essentialism of the received theory of development. However, in the
same spirit as Gibson-Graham (1996) and Gibson-Graham and Ruccio
(2001), we are critical of the unproblematic way in which a capital-centric
notion of the economy is accepted by Escobar and others. The focus of the
postdevelopmental discourse is on the cultural and political aspects and a
critique of the pre-given, naturalized, capital-centered economy. Having
criticized the received notion of the economy without having problematized it to begin with, Escobar and the postdevelopment theorists abandon
the concept/field of development as economic development. Thus, both
the economy and development as contested spaces are effectively abandoned in that discourse.

Postmodern Marxist theory displaces the economy from the locus of
capital accumulation to a decentered, disaggregated notion of class defined
as processes of performance, appropriation, distribution and receipt of
surplus labor. The renewed problematization of the economy opens up a

new class-based language that rejects any allusion to a totalizing frame-work, naturalized ontology, atemporal fixity, certainty, uniformity, and es-chatological meta-narrative. Given such a postmodern discursive space, the focus is to provide a critique of a monolithic conception of capitalism as centering the discourses on development and on the discovery of diverse noncapitalist possibilities (existing alongside capitalist class process) that have hitherto been suppressed. The complexity of such class processes that comprises variegated ways in which surplus labor (or as its physical coun-terpart, surplus product) is performed and appropriated is what Gibson-Graham and Ruccio (2001) called a class mapping of development or what we named a class set of development (also see Chakrabarti and Cullenberg (2001a). Thus, from development we are back to class analysis and in fix-ing attention on the transition of class processes the moment of develop-ment disappears from the postmodern scope, a disappearance that we want to interrogate in this chapter. But a lingering doubt remains: If not capital accumulation, what moment of development are we talking about, about whose disappearance we are so concerned?

It is worth remembering that development is not simply about "indus-trialization through capital accumulation" but consists also of the dual/other of capital accumulation—*need*. The above-mentioned critiques of orthodoxy, including that of Escobar and the postmodern Marxists, prob-lematized the logic of capital accumulation but not need. And unlike the postdevelopment theories, even though the economy is problematized in the postmodern Marxist frame, development as need remains unaccounted for. While post- or anti-developmentalists like Escobar (quite paradoxi-cally) *fetishized capital*, postmodern Marxists have ended up *fetishizing surplus labor* for no matter what noncapitalist class space one generates, it is still part of the nodal point of surplus labor (albeit a provisional one). The dimension of need and hence of development in that imaginary is suppressed.

How then do we account for development as need in a postmodern economic/class/surplus space? Answering this question is the primary objective of this chapter. We develop an articulation of the notion of class with development (as need) with the goal of constructing a mutu-ally constitutive relation between the two. That is, we build a nonessen-tialist and nonhistoricist theory of development as need from a Marxist standpoint, a new radical alternative to the received theories of develop-ment economics.

The class mapping/set of development proposed by postmodern Marx-ists is a relatively new approach that understands the economy and its transition in terms of an overdetermined relation between production (epitomized by fundamental class process or FCP as performance and appropriation of surplus labor/product) and distribution (typified by sub-sumed class process or SCP as the distribution and receipt of surplus labor/product). The fundamental class process may be exploitative (if the appropriator appropriates the surplus labor of others who themselves do not appropriate), self-exploitative (if a single performer appropriates his surplus labor), and nonexploitative (if those who perform surplus labor also appropriate it). The concept of transition we have developed as a de-centered, uneven, and heterogeneous change of society also makes the no-tion of development in our scheme anti-essentialist and antihistorical However, transition and development are not the same (Chakrabarti 1996, Chakrabarti and Cullenberg 2001a, Sanyal 2001). We need to ask further whether postmodern Marxist theory is consistent with the dual conditions of development—ending exploitation and providing a "fair" distribution. While much progress has been made in identifying the space for a dis-course of development in a postmodern Marxian context, serious lacunae remain when it comes to confronting some fundamental questions in that context and exploring those. Given the unsettled status of self-exploitative class processes that has been discussed in chapter 6, and the repression of the communitic (to which we will come to the next section), which funda-mental class processes are desirable/progressive from a Marxian stand-point is not clear. Also, while the discussion in chapter 6 brought the importance of fairness in distribution to light, it is again unclear what ex-actly we mean by fairness and how a linkage of subsumed class processes with fairness could be established. Moreover, how are both questions con-nected to class related to the issue of development as need? Is there a con-nection between classes and development, and if so can we contemplate a commonly held desirable social arrangement that restricts exploitation and expands the sphere of need?

Section I concentrates on the first dimension of progress—the transfor-mation of fundamental class process from exploitative to nonexploitative. We discuss a new form of the class process—the communitic—and the principle of sharing that goes with it (Chaudhury and Chakrabarti 2000 and Chakrabarti and Roy Chaudhury 1999/2000), as well as the principle of exclusion (Cullenberg 1992). Specifically, the self-exploitative classes may qualify as desirable from the principle of exclusion but may fail the same test from the principle of sharing that the concept of communitic brings with it.[2] The convex combination of the principle of exclusion and that of sharing may in fact be claimed as a theoretical defense of the posi-tion that communist and not self-exploitative class moments be consid-ered as a desirable target. Bringing back the hitherto-repressed economy of the community gives a new meaning to the class mapping/set of develop-ment and catapults the complex of communist and a type of communitic class process into an ethically desirable social arrangement at the level of fundamental class process.

Notwithstanding the above differences regarding the desirability of specific nonexploitative class moments among postmodern Marxists, development as progress involves invoking some idea of distribution as fairness (Chakrabarti 1996, Gibson-Graham 1996, Chakrabarti and Cullenberg 2001a). We take up this dimension of progress—distribution in the context of subsumed class process—and come up with the point that there is no necessary linkage between development and class. The linkage has to be constructed. Development with its emphasis on need is conceptually different from class, with its moorings in exploitation. But simply identifying nonexploitative class processes is no longer sufficient for achieving development as progress. Cases for and against certain types of distribution of surpluses must also be made. Furthermore, the point is not to look at distribution as simply a facilitator of production but also to consider the process of distribution (and as a corollary, production) from a consumption perspective—that is, we must take into account the criteria of need when considering desirable (re)distributions of surplus.[3] This means that the surplus distributed due to production requirements may not necessarily be the same as surplus distributed for the purpose of need, and, consequently, this makes it imperative to problematize the received concept of surplus distribution. We must therefore present the conception of need that includes the need-based economy as distinct (but not independent or autonomous) from surplus-based economy. The general conception of need entails its fulfillment from the surplus economy while need-based economy functions in a distinctly nonsurplus production space in order to achieve the same.

The challenge, then, is to develop a connection between class and need, and identify the set of the class and nonclass processes that are most likely to fulfill the aspirations of the different needs in an economy, in order to have a notion of development as progress from a Marxian point of view. In order to address this issue we develop a new idea of surplus called social surplus (as distinct from production surplus) in the context of achieving distribution that binds class and need together. After incorporating the idea of repressed communitic, we arrive at the important conclusion that expanded communism—as a complex of communist and communitic class processes and/or classless economic arrangements—is the desirable goal of development from a Marxist point of view even though this social arrangement is neither inevitable as an outcome nor fixed in meaning if achieved. Such a progressive communitic class process is particularly shown to have the characteristics of individuality (in addition to sharing) that was so absent in the strict definition of communism. In contrast, the self-exploitative class is shown to be undesirable as a progressive class process. An expansion of the developmental space of need is likely under expanded communism and in this sense expanded communism (the desirable goal of Marxists) is also a desirable/progressive social arrangement from a development perspective. Since social surplus creates a necessary connection between class and need-focused struggles, the similar desirable goal of expanded communism creates a political space based on a powerful ethical thematic involving a much wider band of processes and populace than either strict communism or exclusive developmentalism could ever offer. Another powerful feature of expanded communism is that it exhibits a new internationalism based on sharing of social surplus across national boundaries. Since much of what constitutes need is determined in an international context, struggling for such a new internationalism, which de facto also entails advocating for expanded communism (since the former flows from the latter).

Development as Transition of the Fundamental Class Process

Let us begin by briefly recapping the idea of fundamental class process and its transitional dynamics as advanced in the received postmodern Marxian theory of transition and development laid out in the previous chapter. Class analysis structures society in terms of the category of exploitation and then maps a disaggregated existence of a social totality in terms of fundamental class processes (FCP) that are exploitative, self-exploitative, and nonexploitative class processes. Further classification of fundamental class processes by including nonclass but closely related elements of different ways of distributing the goods and remunerating the direct performers of surplus labor maps the social totality into capitalist, communist, self-exploitative, slave, feudal, and maybe other configurations which we have called class sets. Further constitution of class sets by other processes produces the class structure. However, as demonstrated earlier, even though class sets are extremely useful as analytical categories, the ethics of transition of class set is located in the manner of appropriation of surplus labor, that is, in the fundamental class process. In this section we shall focus on the fundamental class process even when it should be obvious by now that any change in fundamental classes will produce changes in the class set (as well as the class structure) of any society. In that context, the transition of fundamental class process in a specific direction—the transition of class set towards nonexploitative forms—is what postmodern Marxists call development as progress.

While a lot of transitional dynamics can be captured and illustrated in terms of the received milieu of fundamental classes, we argue that the class mapping/set of development as put forward by us in chapter 6, and elsewhere by other postmodern Marxists, is incomplete. Specifically, postmodern Marxism suppresses the *communitic* from its scheme. Recently, Chaudhury and Chakrabarti (2000) brought this issue to the fore by revealing the repression of the class dimension of the communitic. Since this is a relatively new concept we will take some care in re-presenting its class dimension, specifically its fundamental one. Our economic reading of the communitic in class terms will not only reveal newer existences of the noncapitalist class processes as Gibson-Graham (1996) and Gibson-Graham and Ruccio (2001) exhort us to do, but also change the terms of reference for looking at a meaning of development as progress from a postmodern Marxist standpoint. Specifically, we will bring into the body of the text the principle of *sharing* as a criterion for judging development as progress which, as we shall argue, opens a whole range of issues hitherto left untouched.

Reconstructing the Fundamental Class Process in the Context of Community

The idea in this section is to extend the meaning the fundamental class process by incorporating the principle of sharing as a basis to justify the nonexploitative class processes. But bringing sharing into the forefront reveals the contradictory existence of the self-exploitative class process from a justice point of view. Under certain conditions (to be specified later on), self-exploitation may become an unjust class process and subsequently nonprogressive from a developmental perspective.

Let us start with the economic of the community. Community like all other entities has its own economic, political, and cultural conditions of existence, each overdetermined by the others. The usual conceptualization of community designates it by the political and cultural only: community is a space structured by shared myths, totems, and taboos. Ruccio describes this well:

> Instead of thinking community in the terms of a "common being," it is now possible to reinscribe community as a "being in common". . . . One of the conditions for the emergence of such "decentered communities" is a form of social agency radically different from the individuality that is constituted in a society characterized by commodity exchange. Such a "collectivity" represents a new subject position—a "collective subjectivity," a consciousness of being in common. (1992, 19)

Ruccio's idea of collectivity implies some sense of sharing involving the simultaneous process of giving and taking at one moment. This is radically different from the individual-based social agency that subscribes to the view of taking without any intention of giving. As in other renditions of community, Ruccio also continues to ground community at the level of consciousness. This is what produces community in its most powerful form at the political and cultural level. However, we would argue that aspects of sharing may also punctuate social spaces that are not quite captured in terms of a collective subjectivity, and as result we delete the notion of consciousness from the general definition of community. Community is then defined simply as the "being in common" as adjudicated by the different practices telescoping the process of sharing. Sharing can take place at different axes, ranging from the political and cultural to the economic. For example, there may be instances of sharing in the economic space at the level of performance or appropriation of surplus labor where community as "being in common" needs therefore to be supplemented by an articulation of its economic.

Following Chaudhury and Chakrabarti (2000), we conceptualize the economic in terms of class process, more correctly, in terms of fundamental class process (FCP). A set of class processes can be represented in terms of a matrix along the axes of agencies of production and appropriation as shown below:

Production of Surplus labor	Direct Labor (A)	Appropriation of Surplus Labor	
		Nonlabor (B)	Collective Labor (C)
	AA	AB	AC
	Fractured Community–CA[1]	CB	CC
	Fractured Exploitation—CA[2]		

In this matrix, the rows indicate production (of surplus labor) performed by direct labor (A), nonlabor (B) and collective (C), while the columns capture the appropriation (of surplus labor) by A, B, and C. The six types of fundamental class processes in terms of which society can be organized are:

A A => Self-exploitative or ancient
A B => Class exploitative
A C => Community
C B => Class exploitative
C C => Communistic

CA ⟨ Fractured Exploitative
      Fractured Community

In the above matrix, AA and CC designate self-exploitative class process and communistic class process, AC and CA represent community class process, and the rest map out different kinds of exploitative class processes to be further classified as capitalist class process, feudal class process, and slave-based class process.[4]

What this matrix includes are certain class processes that are not covered by the conventional rendition of class in postmodern Marxism, specifically the CA and AC class processes. These class processes have a common feature: sharing is fractured, holding at one level (say, appropriation) while failing at another level (say, performance). In other words, the class process moves from sharing in one axis to nonsharing in the other axes. We name such class process as *communitic* class process.

It is to be noted that there is a fine distinction between the communitic class process and communistic class process. Resnick and Wolff (1987) evoked the communistic class process to distinguish clearly between exploitative and nonexploitative class process. Communistic unlike communitic is a category that has conceptually nothing to do with exploitation.[5] Sharing must hold at every instance; there is to be no dichotomy between the performers and appropriators of surplus labor with respect to the instance of sharing. Communitic, on the other hand, embodies the aspect of a fractured class process with sharing taking place in one instance but failing in the other.

Let us now focus on the meaning of the two types of community class process—AC and CA. AC emphasizes one of the forms related to the process of the performance of labor that can go along with collective appropriation, but is not exactly similar to the collective performance of labor in the sense of being shared. This is the reason why AC is a noncommunist class process (in contrast to CC) even though it shares the latter's feature of collective appropriation. Definitionally, an ideal community class process (AC) symbolizes a situation where the "community" appropriates the "fruit" collectively while jobs at the other (lower) levels of the production are done jointly by individual laborers on the basis of a clear division of labor. Division of labor requires that each individual perform multiple different but clearly distinct tasks such that within that structure of work no individual has the option to do any other kind of work. This exclusion may be culturally given. Agricultural production might provide a typical example of the community production where individuals sow the seed (and do other kinds of related jobs including household work) and the community reaps and appropriates the harvest collectively. In the context of the household, cooking is an example of a community class process if the household members collectively appropriate (and perhaps distribute) the cooked food with the male partner doing the related "outside" jobs (such as shopping and gathering fuel), the female partner doing the "inside" jobs (such as the act of cooking).[6] The aspect of sharing is then getting fractured, presenting itself in one place but disappearing in others.

The two specific forms of class process that are associated with CA are fractured exploitative and fractured communitic. We are adding the adjective "fractured" before CA in order to capture the nonuniformity of its exploitative character. The aspect of sharing that constitutes the community, as "being in common" is present in the two forms of CA even though one of the forms is geared toward an exploitative class process. In other words, the economic meaning of community may very well be exploitative.

The specificity of a fractured CA class process resides in the shared environment of a space as input at the level of production. The environment of any space is constituted by many elements. The river supplying water, the air it breathes, the land it tills, the birds it watches, the men and women its members talk to, the forest nearby, the kinship relationship it sustains, the knowledge/information of the terrain its members have—all of these together constitute that space's environment.[7] This environment is shared because members of the "space" can draw upon this configuration of natural and social network without excluding other members in order to reproduce their life(style), including their economic reproduction. In fact, this network may very well become one of the sites of performance of labor that constitute class. If that happens, then the performance of surplus labor and its appropriation may take place at two different but vertically integrated sites. Generally, under a CA-type class process, one of the components of fundamental class process (performance of surplus labor) is based on sharing while the other is not (appropriation of surplus labor). Appropriation may be based on individual/self-exploitative or exploitative appropriation. Let us briefly discuss these two forms of CA class process— CA class process that is exploitative and then CA class process that is individual/self-exploitative.

Exploitative CA class process

One part of CA signifies a situation where work is done collectively in the sense of being shared with none of the members excluded but one member (or a group) of the collective appropriates the total surplus labor performed including his own. CA can then be exploitative since others' labor is appropriated. The critical feature that distinguishes this form of exploitation from other forms (such as capitalist) is that here the appropriator is also a performer of labor and appropriates all surplus labor including that of his own while for the other cases (such as capitalist) the appropriator is not a performer of direct labor and thereby only appropriates others' surplus labor. An example would be a family farm where the entire family (head of the family, brothers, sisters, children, wife, cousin, etc.) takes part in the production process jointly without any remuneration at that level but only one person, such as the "head of the family," appropriates the surplus labor of all including that of his own, which he then distributes according to some norms. CA can then be exploitative since others' labor is appropriated by the head of the family.

Self-Exploitative CA Class Process

There is another possibility that CA can be community-based but fractured in a different direction. There is a crucial difference between community-based CA and exploitative-based CA where individuals appropriate their own surplus labor but not the labor of others. An example could be the production of drawing milk from a goat/cow. This is common in Indian villages where goats/cows are bunched together to be taken for grazing/taking fresh air/bathing (set of critical labor activities for the final act of appropriation of drawing milk). People in the village join together collectively to take the goats/cows out. The economic value of goats/cows depends critically on the state of the goat/cow in terms of its capacity to give milk, which in turn crucially depends on the performance of labor (shared here) in generating that state. Then at home, individually, the milkman draws the milk from the goat/cow. The performance of labor is joint/shared while the appropriation is at the individual level. The grazing ground/forest/river—the shared environment or a part of it—and the house are two vertically integrated production sites where two different constituents of fundamental class process—performance and appropriation of surplus labor unravel.

In the light of the above discussion, our class mapping/set is no longer composed of the self, communist, and exploitative (slave, feudal, and capitalist) class processes but also includes an array of hitherto unrecognized class processes—AC and CA. If we use sharing as the principle of looking at the categories of exploitation then what are the possible types of desirable FCP that may be considered as progressive from a postmodern Marxist perspective? That will reveal a new meaning of desirable class processes.

However, before we use sharing as the principle of eliminating the unjust class processes, let us look at another principle—of exclusion—that has also been used at times in this literature (Cullenberg 1992, Chakrabarti and Cullenberg 2001a). Using the principle of exclusion, again certain types of exploitative class processes may be eliminated. Interestingly, we will see that a comparison of the principle of exclusion and the principle of sharing does not give us a common set of just class processes. This throws open altogether the Marxian development question of progressive class processes.

The Principle of Exclusion and Just Class Processes

We consider here the issue of development as progress as a movement from an exploitative fundamental class process to a non-exploitative fundamental class process. Specifically, we are interested in the desirability of self-exploitative and communistic class process. Even though we pointed out that it is not clear why the communist class process alone should qualify as the desirable FCP, we have not explained either why the self-exploitation should qualify as a desirable FCP. Nowhere is the justification clearly spelt out in the literature. It is to be noted that the communist and self-exploitation are conceptually two very different class processes with fundamentally different mechanisms of appropriation. The question remains as to what binds them together. We believe the answers that the principle of exclusion creates commonality in the process of appropriation.

Cullenberg (1992) states the principle of exclusion in the following manner:

> To appropriate surplus labor . . . implies that a certain well-defined set of rights or rules of exclusion are in place. . . . appropriation refers to one of the following three types of exclusion: either (a) the performer of surplus labor can exclude all others from appropriation and therefore appropriates the surplus labor completely and individually; (b) the performers of surplus labor are excluded themselves from any appropriation; or (c) all performers of surplus labor share in its appropriation, and therefore no one is either completely excluded from appropriation or can exclude others. (Cullenberg 1992, 71)

By the exclusion principle, what qualifies as progressive FCPs are AA, CC, and AC. In the case of AA and CC, the performer of surplus labor is not excluded from the process of appropriation. For AC the direct laborer is not excluded from the process of appropriation. Hence AC qualifies as progressive. CA does not qualify as progressive since others are excluded in the process of appropriation in favor of one performer of surplus labor. So by the exclusion principle, not all self-exploitation is desirable; only the AA types are.

The Principle of Sharing and Just Class Processes

By the sharing principle only the CC and AC qualify as progressive. While sharing may take place at the level of performance, our exclusive focus on exploitation as the criteria to differentiate just class process from unjust ones makes sharing at the level of appropriation the proper criteria in this case. By this principle, AC is progressive because appropriation is collective even though labor is individual. CA fails because appropriation is individual or exploitative and hence not shared.

Thus we see that by sharing principle, all forms of self-exploitation are to be rejected as not being progressive. This brings forth clearly the point that there is no one-to-one correspondence between sharing and nonexclusion. In case of AA there is nonexclusion but no sharing.

Which principle should be chosen? This is a moral/justice question to be answered on the level of ethics. Postmodern Marxian development economists have focused on the transition from exploitative class processes to nonexploitative ones. Furthermore, we have argued that self-exploitation and communist class processes are distinct from exploitative ones based on the principle of exclusion. This principle implicitly underlies the existence of the self-exploitation as a putative, progressive class process.

On the other hand, in an almost contradictory manner, postmodern Marxist theorists also celebrate the aspect of sharing (as opposed to individuality) that underlies any notion of collectivity.

> Is it possible, therefore, to pose the notion of the working class as a different form of community—a "real" community, one that has an identity of *being in common*? Presumably, such an identity would be formed within a variety of social sites, including the political arena, an identity that is the result rather than the condition of class politics. Such a working class would then occupy a different space, one in which it can (as, de facto, it has done so many times in the past) negotiate with other communities, can make explicit the differences implied by and form coalitions with other identities and agents, can recognize the contradictory (changing, heterogeneous) constitution of its own identity. *(Callari and Ruccio 1996b, 44)*

> It is this complex collective subjectivity that, until now, has been repressed in existing societies—both capitalist and socialist—and ignored by economic determinist Marxism. In this lies one of the key failures of socialism. Therefore, the theoretical and political issues concerned with community and collective subjectivity are as relevant after the collapse of 1989 as they were before, in the East as in the West. Exploring these issues, and not the traditional debate of markets versus planning, represents the challenge to critical Marxism and the future of socialism. (Ruccio 1992, 20)

As we have pointed out, if we take the principle of sharing/being in common as the guiding theme of differentiating desirable from undesirable class processes, then self-exploitation cannot be accommodated. The contradictory existence of self-exploitation underlies the entire thematic of Marxian transformative politics. And subsequently that of development as progress.

What happens if we create a convex combination of the two? We take only class processes that satisfy both the principles simultaneously. Then only CC and AC emerge as the desirable FCP. This can be conceived as justification of the other position (Resnick and Wolff 1987; Resnick and Wolff 1988) that considered only communist class process to be progressive.

Even an initial look into the progressive content of fundamental class processes reveals the problem with including self-exploitation in the desirable Marxist armory of classes. The new class mapping/set of development with sharing integrated in its body awaits the justification of the self in its rank of desirable class processes. Until now we have identified development with class mapping/set and identified development as progress is identified with certain nonexploitative classes—types CC and AC. The postmodern Marxist development literature does make some remarks about distribution but they are not made in connection to a specific meaning of development. What we will investigate in the next section is the problem of posing the *development* question into the heart of the *class*-based Marxian mapping/set.

From the Subsumed to the Need: Development Revisited

Class analysis structures society in terms of the category of exploitation and then reveals a disaggregated existence of a social totality in terms of fundamental class processes (FCP) that are exploitative, self-exploitative, and nonexploitative class processes. Transition involves changes within a specific fundamental class process or it may involve change in class process from one fundamental entity to another. The transition of class processes in a specific direction is what postmodern Marxists call development as progress. But although transition of class process and certain changes in the direction of society as a result of it are a necessary condition of development from a Marxian perspective, they are not a sufficient condition, since development arises in the different milieu of need and from a consumption standpoint. There is no necessary linkage between development and class. Class analysis is about exploitation and development is associated with some idea of progress in terms of fulfillment of need—both individual and public—of social agents. In order to account for this notion of development, postmodern Marxists add the aspect of distribution to that of exploitation. This aspect of distribution comes from the processes related to the distribution and receipt of surplus labor or subsumed class processes (SCP). In this context the postmodern development theories conceptualize development as progress in terms of a transition from exploitative class process to nonexploitative class process and that as one simultaneously fulfilling some notion of "fair" distribution.

Let us explore what Marxists mean by fair distribution and its linkage with the question of the fulfillment of need. This is a basic question of development (and not of class), and we find little substance about it in postmodern Marxist theory. Postmodern Marxists correctly point out that producers are not simply engaged in the act of sharing in but that they also share out. After all, the appropriators are also the distributors of surplus labor. So the principle through which the appropriators distribute the surplus labor is also to be considered from the point of view of justice. However, the principles guiding appropriation are not necessarily the same principles guiding decisions about distribution.

How is the issue of fairness and need to be addressed in a Marxist context? To begin with, let us see how fairness has been traditionally dealt with in economics. What constitutes fair distribution in a society? Differences on this notion abound. There are those who say that distribution should be done on the basis of (Pareto) efficiency conditioned by equality (fairness) at the level of opportunities. This means that rules and procedures regarding private properties and institutions need to be properly defined and made legally binding, and that every citizen's behavior irrespective of race, gender, caste, income, and so on, should be held accountable in terms of those rules and procedures. Then there have been those who say that income should be distributed equally among the citizens of a society. During War Communism and the Stalinist phase in the former Soviet Union, this notion of fairness was common. Finally, there are those who talk of "fairness" in terms of some sort of safety net. This means that while some of the income will be distributed according to the Pareto norm of efficiency, the rest should be taken away to create a safety net for the vulnerable section of the population in order to protect them from unsavory contingencies and invest to avoid the same in the future. Others such as Amartya Sen point out that the criteria that underlie the definition of development must be particular ends and not necessarily the means, and as such distribution itself is fundamental. The ethical or political connotation of distribution lies in the perceived connection of the virtues of distribution to the needs of society. In Sen, the above ethical standpoint finds expression in terms of a capability approach that culminates in a notion of freedom. Differences exist regarding what to distribute, how to distribute it, and, more fundamentally, to whom to distribute. For example, Sen's capability approach is not the same as that of the neoclassical welfare-based approach, Rawls's primary goods approach, Dworkin and Roemer's resource-based approach, or Van Parjis's Basic Income approach. However, notwithstanding the differences between them, these theorists have been unified in their allegiance to the idea of distribution grounded on the ethics of need.

The debate on "fair distribution" addresses issues around the problem of need. In presenting our conception of need and its operational/functional space, two contexts of need are posed. First, consider a no-production economy other than a surplus-producing one, that is, one in which the onus of the satisfaction of need is always on the surplus economy. Second, consider a surplus production economy that has as its "other" a non-surplus producing economy operating in tandem and through which certain needs could also be accounted along with the rest via the surplus economy.

Need I

We refer to this realm of need as being constituted by that human beings regard as the required/subsistence/necessary conditions for reproducing their life(style). Necessity refers to conditions without which human beings' material existence will be threatened. Thus, issues on destitution, famines, hunger, or education and health (quantitative and qualitative) and even something as diverse as aesthetics are part of this realm of need. The objects of need may be material or symbolic goods whose gratification we call consumption.

Need as argued here possesses certain distinct characteristics: (i) need is not about satisfaction or happiness founded on *homo economicus* but refers to certain processes constitutive of a specific state of being human, (ii) need is contingently produced as what is considered subsistence/necessary is socially constructed and hence is in a ceaseless state of change across space and time. The notion of need is produced as part of a configuration of flight, renewal, and creation of material and sign goods. Thus, as in Baudrillard (Poster 1988, 1–56), need is a fluid, dynamic concept, and there is no one definition of need, (iii) need does not arise from labor alone, but is also constituted by many other aspects, (iv) need is spatially dispersed, unfolding differently at different sites of society, and (v) even though need is conceptually different from surplus/class, agents may live a contradictory existence between class and need consumption. An individual may be simultaneously producing surplus at one space and performing/seeing what is voluntary/free theater (fulfillment of his aesthetic need) at another space. There is no one-to-one correlation between the spaces of surplus production and need consumption.

What has the realm of need got to do with "fair" distribution? By the adjective "fair" we mean production or distribution of surplus that guarantees those necessities that satisfy the material existence of humans. Since economic fairness is described in the context of need, that too is always in a continual state of change and annulment. But what necessities are we talking about? Many debates have gone into this question but we now know two things. First, as pointed out above, necessities will be contingently produced and hence cannot be pinned down to a precise and unchanging set of objects (material or symbolic). Second, fulfilling human necessities does not mean equality in terms of the same per capita income. Chaudhury (2001) observes:

> Recall that we have built our argument on one key premise: that the differences in activities lead to differences in (subsistence) needs. . . . Different activities might require different consumption of goods to produce one hour's capability of working. For example, consumption (nutrition) requirements of women living in the shelter and of those leaving the shelter to gather food might never be the same. (195)

Or as Marx would suggest

> But one man can excel over another physically or intellectually and so contributes in the same way more labor, or can labor for a longer time; and labor, to serve as a measure, must be defined by its duration or intensity, otherwise it ceases to be a standard measure. This equal right is an unequal right for unequal work. It recognizes no class differences because every worker ranks as a worker like his fellows, but it tacitly recognizes unequal individual endowment, and thus capacities for production, as natural privileges. It is therefore a right of inequality in its content, as in general is every right. (1875, 30)

Given this, the question of need is contextually posed appearing in variegated forms, diversely at both the individual level and in different societies (such as the United States and India). Just as the economy in terms of class is disaggregated, so is the development space in terms of need. When we talk of local development such as village development, we mean distribution of surplus such that no person in the village suffers from the absence of certain agreed-upon—collective—necessities of life. In the context of a nation, we would consider the economywide national distribution that accounts for another set of agreed-upon necessities. We may also consider fair distribution in terms of need and its contested expression in a global context. Recently, Oxfram criticized the multinational pharmaceutical companies for waging a price war on the poor of the world by making life-saving drugs (especially HIV/AIDS-related ones) at a cost beyond their affordable limits. Oxfam subsequently demanded that either these companies reduce the price charged for the drugs (thereby reducing the surplus appropriated) or that part of the amount appropriated be distributed for fundamental research in medicine. In this case, Oxfam is participating in the need or development (as well as class) struggle on a global scale.

Class processes consist of the distribution of surplus as one of its moments while class struggle deals with conflict over the distribution of surplus. Marxists do not deal simply with the transformative politics involving favorable change in the fundamental class process but also with that of subsumed class processes as well in particular directions. This entails not simply the distribution of surplus for reproducing the surplus-based production process but for its additional distribution to satisfy the needs in an economy as and when they are articulated.

In this context it is important to realize the contradiction here. Both exploitation-free classes and fair distribution are not means to achieve some ends but are ends on their own, and hence valuable. The focus on ending exploitation requires a movement toward a particular set of FCPs depending on the acceptable underlying nonexploitative criterion chosen, while the focus on "fair" distribution requires a specific direction of distributional change depending on the relevant criteria of need. Development from a Marxian point of view requires the simultaneous movement toward the two goals, which necessarily may not be compatible with one another. We have already discussed in chapter 6 the case of a hideous communist system. In that system the class processes may be communist but distribution is highly unfair. In contrast, we may have a benevolent capitalist system where most of the FCPs are capitalist but the distribution is "fair" (witness the welfare states of the Nordic countries). If development is to be our goal, then neither of the above-mentioned cases are acceptable. The former celebrates the end of exploitation but lives with the blight of a very unfair society. It takes care of the ethic of sharing in but not that of sharing out; hardly an attractive or an in the long run feasible option. The latter, on the other hand, celebrates the ethic of fairness but is governed by rules and rights that generate an exploitative society. This takes care of sharing out but not that of sharing in.

This presents Marxists with a very tough choice. Not all nonexploitative class-based societies are acceptable. The emphasis until now has been on explaining the unsavory image of an exploitative-based class society but if our goal is to address the issue of development, we must shift our attention in explaining various images of nonexploitative based societies. We now know that our society is replete with nonexploitative class structures (Resnick and Wolff 1987; Fraad, Resnick and Wolff 1994; Chakrabarti 1996; Gibson-Graham 1996; Callari and Ruccio 1996a; Gibson-Graham, Resnick, and Wolff, ed. 2000; Gibson-Graham, Resnick, and Wolff ed. 2001; Gibson-Graham and Ruccio 2001; Chakrabarti and Cullenberg

2001a, 2001b). Marxism's goal is to make them dominant. However, this alone is no longer sufficient to generate development. Marxists have emphasized the ethics of production (fundamental classes) via the category of exploitation but ignored the ethics of distribution (subsumed classes).

Need II

There is another way of addressing need that we wish to consider. Marx and Marxists have long talked about the idea of primitive communist social arrangements. A distinctive feature of this space is the absence of class. Such a system functions on the criteria of need. This is what Chaudhury (2001) calls a need-based economy or socially determined subsistence economy to distinguish it from the surplus-based economy. And we use the term *need-based economy* to distinguish it as well from the general phenomenon of need that we have already discussed. Our focus is on the operational/function space of need production that is distinguishable (but not independent) from surplus production.

We define *need-based economy* as a different space of production and distribution defined from a consumption standpoint where production and distribution of surplus (that fulfills its production conditions of existence), that is, class-based economic activities are ruled out. Surplus always contains its implicit other—a need-based economy. The need-based economy, in the Lacanian sense, is the small "other" that talks in the language (production, distribution and consumption of goods and services) of the "big other." Consequently, the need-based economy is simultaneously the "other" of surplus/class economy as well as its difference, while gender, caste, etc., are only differences and not others (as is often mistakenly referred to), because they are not expressed in the same language as the surplus-based discourse. One can also theorize the "otherness" of a surplus economy that is a need-based economy in terms of the Derridean concept of *differance* (1982, 3–27 and 1981). Postmodern Marxists have considered the importance of economic difference but not the simultaneous moments of deferral and difference as encapsulated in *differance*. Chaudhury (1992, 133–146) accounts for this absence in a Derridean analysis of Althusser's structure, and here we can address the same with respect to the postmodern surplus economy. Postmodern Marxism considers the surplus economy but misses the "other" economy that forms its outside, and without whose presence a surplus economy cannot be conceived. This "forgetfulness" is, in our context, the need-based economy. The need-based economy is not only the difference but, as Derrida would say, this difference is produced—deferred—by *differance*. As such, it also becomes the other of surplus economy. The text here is the economy, and Derrida reminds and warns us repeatedly to read *differance* in the context of a text: everything that forms the outside as differences of a text/economy cannot be part of the absence/other in the constitution of *differance* (the system). That is why, as with a Lacanian reading, the other (and difference) of surplus economy is the need-based economy and not just any other elements/differences as postmodern Marxists would have suggested.[8]

It is interesting to note that need-based space characterizes the consumption aspiration of economic agents, unlike the surplus space that looks at the economy from a production standpoint. We have already discussed some of the dimensions of need that would constitute the need-based economy and those that any society would have to account for. The consumption desire of the agents may be individual-based or collective-based in the form of public goods. The idea that a need-based economy considers the economy from a consumption standpoint does not imply the exclusion of production in such an economy. Quite the reverse. A need-based economy must also consist of the *production* of the subsistence basket of goods and services when that is not based on any surplus criteria. For example, a group of doctors could be running a health center in a village in a commercial way (that is, by employing wage laborers and charging fees for their services) and extracting surplus out of the production (of service) activity. On the other hand, the same group of doctors could form a health community in the village and with the cooperation of the villagers could be running a health club that takes care of the required necessities of the villagers.[9] Such experiments presently going on in distant parts of India in large numbers are changing the lifestyles of millions of villagers. While the same service is given in both the cases, the focal point of that activity is different. The surplus-based activity is production-directed while the need-based activity even in its production performance is consumption-focused. That is, production and consumption are overdetermined in both cases but the standpoints of the two are different. What then critically distinguishes the need-based economy is the distinct functional space that generates the developmental question of required/subsistence basket of goods and services to fulfill the necessary criteria of agents.

To see why we are saying something fundamentally different from what has been proposed until now in the class-focused development literature, consider the following:

> Noncapitalist practices are also often portrayed as being the *opposite* of capitalism as, for example, when they are seen to be "primitive" or traditional, stagnant, marginal, residual, about to be extinguished, weak. Communal or tribal practices of hunting and gathering, craft activities, or indigenous agricultural production involving the production of use values that are not commodified

and/or of commodities that are not designed to garner profits in the market are viewed as incapable of growth and development in their own right (de Janvry 1981, Sender and Smith 1986). Despite their resilience and viability over centuries of practice, these non-capitalist activities become the negative image of capitalism which is characterized as dynamic, powerful, and endowed with the capacity for infinite expansion. Modernizers attribute to traditional activities the condition of "backwardness" (they must be eliminated or transformed so that development can take place) while left critics and the advocates of postdevelopment may see them as signs of underdevelopment or of ineffectual "resistance" to development (since the development of global capitalism more or less inevitably constrains, undermines and, eventually, eliminates them). Here, a hierarchy is established between a vigorous, effective capitalism and its passive and insubstantial noncapitalist other. (Gibson-Graham and Ruccio, 167, 2001)

We agree with the above critique of the attempts to compartmentalize activities into backward and forward. Where we do differ is again in the repression of the communitic class process and the implicit fetishization of surplus when the authors tend to describe the noncapitalist other as being noncapitalist classes sans communitic ones. Many of the noncapitalist activities that are pointed out may belong either to a communitic class process that is repressed in the present postmodern frame, or they are part of economic activities that have nothing to do with class—that is, they belong to an outside space, our constructed need-based economy. The latter activities, as we pointed out, are not guided by "industrialization through capital accumulation," or growth, or surplus, but rather by consumption-focused needs. These activities posited in Gibson-Graham and Ruccio (2001) as belonging to noncapitalist class practices are not really so—they in fact belong to nonclass activities. Not only are these not capitalist class practices, they are not even class practices. Our construction of the development framework is in a sense a paradigmatic break for, even in the context of class analysis, it allows one to defetishize surplus and further disaggregate and disperse the meaning of economy as well its numerous dimensions. Postmodern Marxism makes us aware of the exigencies of noncapitalist economic processes as well as systematically dealing with the problem of naming (defining, describing, locating) them.

Our focus is on the inflexion of the need-based and surplus economy. But the problem is not to be underestimated: the aspect of necessities, as we shall see in the next section, may present a serious challenge to any class-based social formation. A need-based economy as a different economy is something that even the seemingly all-powerful surplus economy can neither discount nor dispel. Surplus must face up to need.

We have understood need as those ever-changing necessities that constitute the life(style) or material and symbolic existence of people. Discussions of the Need I version pointed to the importance of further distinguishing nonexploitative classes in order to locate social arrangements that will fulfill the need criteria. The Need II version directs us to analyze the overdetermined moments of the need-based economy and surplus economy.

The Panoptic Gaze of Need: From Class to Classlessness

We begin with a relatively neglected paper by Resnick and Wolff (1988), which we will unpack and then develop in order to derive a new notion of desirable society. Specifically, we draw on their distinction between the communist class process and classless society, and their conception of communism. We contend that communism as a desirable objective needs to be supplemented by the hitherto repressed communitic in order to create an *expanded communism* with far-reaching consequences for the status of self-exploitation and the viability of a desirable society from a Marxian perspective. Also taking Resnick and Wolff (1988, 1993, 1994,1995, 2001) as our point of departure, we develop a new idea: "surplus" can be of different forms—production surplus and social surplus. Postmodern Marxist development economists have only operated in the realm of production surplus and hence within class boundaries. Our newly constructed social surplus, as a leakage from production surplus, in the context of the social formation of expanded communism allows us to see the class mapping/set of development in a new light, helping us to theoretically capture and animate the space of need from a postmodern Marxist standpoint.

Let us begin by constructing the new concept of social surplus. The focus of Resnick and Wolff (1988) is on the distinction between necessary and surplus labor. It is a commonplace that the direct producers are paid according to their—historically defined—minimum subsistence level and that that is the necessary labor equivalent of payment. Anything above that is the surplus equivalent of surplus labor, which then is distributed to account for all those processes that help in its reproduction. We name this surplus *production surplus*. We use the adjective "production" to capture the sum of subsumed class payments arising from the surplus generated in the production process, payments that reproduce those conditions of existence that ensure the procreation of the performance and appropriation of surplus labor. In this sense, there is no leakage of this surplus to nonclass processes or other agents outside the point of appropriation:

The last intervention we would like to review is one focused upon the internal operations of the capitalist enterprise as a site of generative possibilities for noncapitalist class practices. Our anti-essentialist class analysis highlights the importance of the distributive as well as the exploitative class process. The distributive class process involves the allocation of appropriated surplus labor (in whatever form) to a range of claimants who all in turn provide the conditions of existence for continued class appropriation. Within the capitalist enterprise surplus value is distributed, for example, to a wide variety of destinations both inside and outside the enterprise, including investment in capital expansion (accumulation), the payment of supervisory labor, accounting, merchanting, the servicing of debt, state taxes, bribes, etc. Each constellation of such distributions is the result of competitive tensions and struggles, negotiations and agreements that take place in and around the firm. Diverse economic and social practices are currently enabled by flows of surplus value that percolate around and through capitalist enterprises. We are interested in exploring the possibilities of changing the quantitative and qualitative dimensions of those flows and exploring their potential for creating new class practices. (Gibson-Graham and Ruccio, 176–177, 2001)

The almost exclusive focus of postmodern Marxist economists has been on what we are calling production surplus, even when dealing with distribution. However, such distributions do not suffice to address the development question, linked to the question of need. What about the agents who are not involved in the surplus-generating production process but who must be accounted for as economic agents from the point of view of consumption? We are talking here about the destitute, the unemployed poor, the elderly and children, the displaced, the disabled and otherwise defenseless, as well as other people living within the realm of need. Such populations fulfill no conditions of existence of production of any surplus and yet their state of being must be reproduced. To account for the reproduction of these populations there must be a surplus over and above the production surplus. Surplus over and above the production surplus is what we name as *social surplus.*

Surplus in an economy is then redefined as being equal to *production surplus* plus the newly created category *social surplus.*

There are two ways to account for this social surplus. One way to create more surplus than is required to meet the different conditions of production processes existence is to reduce the necessary labor equivalent of wages. Resnick and Wolff discuss this possibility in the context of the Soviet Union:

In claiming that the state had created a successful "socialism", Soviet spokespersons pointed to the extensive provision of "free" collective consumption: education, medical care, and so on. It was "free," of course, only because the state distributed a share of the surplus for such purposes. This distribution supplemented the relatively low real wages received by these workers; it expanded their collective ("public") consumption at the same time that their individual ("private") consumption was being constrained. (1995, 226)

It is to be noted that the collective or public goods and services deriving from social surplus are not to be exclusively enjoyed by the worker but also by other members of society not connected with class process. However, the Soviet Union case study as revealed by Resnick and Wolff (1993, 1995) also tells us that the continuous generation of such social surplus on an expanded scale—one that is based on reducing the real wage of the worker—may not be sustainable in the long run.

The other path of generating social surplus does not involve reducing in any way the necessary labor equivalent of wages. This could be done by massive productivity increases or by devoting more surplus labor. Either way, extra surpluses exist—which we call social surpluses—to meet the social needs of human society. In our scheme, development from a Marxist standpoint calls for addressing questions regarding how this social surplus is to be generated, under what conditions, and who will get what portion of the surplus. These questions are fundamentally dissimilar to those class questions regarding the performance, appropriation, distribution, and receipt of surplus labor even though the two are intrinsically connected, for it is in class process that surplus of either type, social and production, is procreated.[10]

Social surplus binds the element of class and need together. The distribution of subsumed class payments has direct bearings on the amount to be distributed as social surplus for need purposes and, conversely, demand over social surplus affects the retained amount of appropriated surplus to be distributed as subsumed class payments. And, since typically those who appropriate also distribute surplus, the developmental questions regarding social surplus may end up affecting the fundamental class processes as well. Thus, the resolution of the developmental, need-focused struggles is the direct outcome of class struggles and vice versa. Social surplus makes the connection between the two necessary and unavoidable. This also gives a new meaning to the class conception of the economy that has until now been a prisoner of the distributive flows connecting the variegated moments of class-based production and appropriation but which now must also explicitly account for a leakage of those distributive flows in the form of social surplus. As an example, recall Oxfam's directive to the pharmaceutical companies to pay a portion of surplus for fundamental research or cut down prices, thereby transferring a portion of the appropriated surplus to those who need the drugs. This move by Oxfam constitutes a class struggle as well as a developmental struggle that tries to restructure the distribution between production and social surplus in favor of social surplus—a developmental struggle since it is a struggle over social surplus and a class struggle as the redistribution toward need would also involve struggles over subsumed class processes of the pharmaceutical companies such as paying lesser dividends to its shareholders. In contrast, consider the Narmada Bachao Andolan (NBA), which has traditionally focused on the (environmental) struggle to stop the construction of dams along the Narmada River and which has recently suffered a series of defeats at the hand of the government and the courts. Subsequently, they (the activists) have presently turned their attention to the inadequacy of compensation for people displaced from their style of living as a result of construction of those dams. But that begs the question, Where are the resources to be used for such an endeavor going to come from? While compensation and putting together a new life are need or developmental struggles, these cannot be accomplished unless a social surplus is forthcoming either through budgetary allocations to be achieved through class struggle at a macro level, or as part of the manifestation of local struggles over production, appropriation, and distribution and receipt of surplus. The NBA's present focus on need struggle is, it seems, without an understanding that it has to be complemented by a class struggle for the former to have any possibility of success. If it could have created the articulation between the two struggles, the movement would have expanded beyond an environmental one in which it remained stuck. The apparent (in terms of result) failure of the NBA—which is also common among many new social movements—lies in the inability to see the connection between development and class, and in the present fashion among these movements to demote and avoid economy/class.[11] It is not clear how these new social movements will ever succeed by disconnecting their struggles from one of the major networks of society—the economy. Our present framework, using both the nonessentialist language of class and the concept of social surplus that we have developed here, gives back to these movements the possibility of economy, albeit as a decentered, disaggregated, contingent, and heterogeneous space. Whether they will rub their eyes and wake up is of course a different matter. As a final point, let us reconsider Oxfam's conflict with the pharmaceutical multinationals. Because Oxfam raised the connection between appropriation and need—that companies were retaining higher production surplus by making the life-saving drugs unaffordable to the people who needed it—it was able to give the HIV/AIDS issue a new moral dimension. Without the articulation of class and developmental struggles, this could not have materialized. Resulting from the success of conjoining the two struggles, the governments and other world bodies were forced to take notice and the pharmaceutical companies were squarely defeated in this conflict with some companies like Cipla announcing that it would supply some drugs for free.

Until now we have undertaken Marxist theory with class as the focus. However, what happens if class qua surplus labor as a concept disappears from history, where the difference between necessary and surplus labor no longer exists. This signifies the era of classless society as Resnick and Wolff (1988) put it:

> The very phrase, "classless society," defines a social arrangement in terms of what is not. What is missing is such a society is the distinction between necessary and surplus labor, that is, the fundamental class process.... The production, appropriation and distribution of surplus labor disappear from the social scene. They pass from history in the same sense that political forms such as absolute monarchy or cultural forms such as religious rituals of human sacrifice have faded from the twentieth century. Indeed, the absence of class processes is the only possible meaning of a "classless" society, given Marx's theory of class and the various forms of class societies. (1988, 33–34)

As broached in the quote, the distinction between necessary and surplus labor arises because one of the major economic goals of society remains the process of surplus appropriation. However, what if the goal of surplus appropriation and therefore class disappears from history? The distinction between the necessary and surplus, and that of social surplus would then not make any sense. Everything that is produced in society is related to human necessity. The realm of necessity pervades the space of production and its outside. The economy becomes functionally different. Need—expressed in this case through our need-based economy—displaces class/surplus as the focal point of addressing the issues of economy. To give the subsistence wage to the worker is no more different from giving the subsistence wage to the pensioner. The moral contract between citizens takes a different form: every citizen has the right to their need, whether it is in individual or public form. It should be noted that we are not talking about equal income or equal resources as fair distribution. The criteria of need pertain to the necessary baskets of commodities of the respective citizens, which may differ from individual to individual. The contract between citizens must be on a moral plane because it involves accepting the possibility that somebody is going to get a bigger basket than you. It also involves accepting the viewpoint that there is nothing called fairness as indicating in some form the fulfillment of material existence of agents:

> Let us invoke India: The Big One—Mahabharat here to drive our point.[12]
> The mother of the Pandava: Kunti, when distributing the gathered food among her five sons, Yudhishthir, Bhim, Arjun, Nakul and Sahadeb, would keep aside half of the whole booty for Bhim alone, and divide the rest among the others. It is the commonsense of the primitive—who knows that the consumption of a big-bodied warrior like Bhim can never be equal to the intake of semi-ascetic and intellectual Yudhishthir. (Chaudhury and Das 1999–2000, 3)

The notion of fairness in distribution arises because there is a "surplus" to be distributed. With the disappearance of the concept of surplus, fairness (from this economic perspective) becomes moot.

It is in this sense that being in common bears its fruition in the economic (and hence societal) plane. By discarding exclusion and nonsharing from the economic field, people learn to live only by sharing. This is a totally different way of conceiving an economy. A new way of learning to live (but as is mentioned in the quote not at all utopian in its glimpses—we will give more concrete examples of classlessness later on). The classless society, unlike class-based expanded communism, guarantees the developmental idea of progress since in this system the concept of class qua surplus labor is absent.

Communism, then, is much bigger than the different forms of communist class process. As Resnick and Wolff point out,

> Communism denotes a social formation in which communist fundamental class processes and classless production arrangements predominate (in varying proportions) in the production of goods and services. (1988, 38).

In light of the discussion above regarding the communitic class process and on the desirable classes as consisting of CC and AC type, we make the following important point: *a desirable society is bigger than communism.* Since it is closely connected to strict communism, we name it "expanded communism." Specifically,

Expanded communism = communist class process (CC) and a communitic class process (AC) + classless productive arrangement.

If expanded communism is to be the desired objective for Marxian and development politics then a Marxian notion of development as progress needs to be posed.

Expanded communism as class process: Development as progress refers to a social arrangement pertaining to those types of nonexploitative class processes (AC and CC) producing social surpluses that are capable and likely to satisfy or meet the need of society in whatever form and at whatever level (that is, in private or public form).

Expanded communism as classless society: Development as progress refers to a social arrangement pertaining to those types of economic activities requiring the obliteration of the distinction between necessary and surplus labor with the sole objective of satisfying the need of society in whatever form and at whatever level. In this context, the economy becomes differently organized and is akin to our need-based economy.

Let us discuss each of the forms of expanded communism and their relations to need.

Class-Based Expanded Communism and Need

If class-based expanded communism is to be the desired objective and if it is achieved, then the AA—self-exploitative—class process will disappear from history. Self-exploitation is based on an individualistic logic and has nothing in common with the aspect of sharing that underlies the process in arriving at the two forms of expanded communism—the class and classless one. We have read the self-exploitation only in light of exploitation and found it appropriate because it is nonexploitative. However, if we read self as part of expanded communism or as helping in the creation of expanded communism, then it is certainly not progressive. Given the ethics of sharing, not all nonexploitative classes are desirable. In contrast, the CC and AC class processes, being part of expanded communism, are also most conducive in effecting a transition toward classless production arrangements. Of special importance is the AC class process, since it combines the individuality in the performance with the sharing/social in the appropriation and distribution. Communistic (of whatever type) because of its overwhelming emphasis on the collectivity has often been criticized as repressing the individual performance and hence being inimical to creativity. It has also been said that, by repressing individuality, communistic systems distort the incentive structure and hence produce an inferior solution. AC class process provide a way out because it delivers an economic arrangement in which the creativity of the individual is combined with sharing the fruits of that creativity with others. This also helps enormously in preparing for the transition to a classless society. We have already discussed that even under a classless society the scientist working in a pharmaceutical firm would not be paid the same amount as a porter. One of the criteria that govern the necessity condition is the work atmosphere. The work pressure, creativity, and tension of a scientist are not the same as that of the porter, and this is going to affect their respective needs. For example, the scientist may very well need an air conditioner, which may not be true for the porter. Given that everything else is the same between the two, the scientist will require a bigger basket of goods vis-à-vis the porter by the singular criteria of work atmosphere. In other words, for the individuality of work to remain, the scientist and porter must accept conceptually the differences in parameters that determine the material necessary needs of the two. AC class process is useful in moving the system forward toward such a possibility because it seems to be the most acceptable class process that combines the process of sharing and individuality in one coherent and divided manner.

The consequence of the repression of the communitic and its usefulness can be seen in our critique of the following quote of Resnick and Wolff:

> Another condition of existence of classlessness might be the systematic rotation of all work tasks among individuals to prevent any technical division of labor from hardening and possibly becoming class divisions . . . there would be education of all in the multiplicity of tasks to be accomplished if rotation were to be possible. There would need to be education for all in the coordinating and designing of tasks as well as their performance. (1988, 35)

Given the complexity of an already existing world, this would require the creation of a mass of superheroes. Also, even if they were somehow produced in society, the cost of doing so might make the effort nonviable. All in all, this is an example of communism that has been asked to do so many things, something that Cullenberg (1992) asked us to be wary of, especially in light of what happened in the former Soviet Union. However, despite its unreality, Resnick and Wolff pose this condition of existence of communism in order to avoid the collapse of spirit of sharing. Here is where the AC class process makes an important contribution. Individuality, at the level of labor performance, may be inimical to the social formation of strict communism but that still does not make it an undesirable objective to follow from an expanded communism standpoint. The lack of sharing and the presence of individuality at the level of performance in the production process does not necessarily imply a fall into noncommunist class process if we understand communism in an expanded form. Individuality in conjunction with sharing the proceeds of labor—the AC class process—may very well hold together the progressive content of society in the form of expanded communism. This makes the condition of de-skilling and the task of educating people in achieving that de-skilling redundant and removes, in our opinion, one of the major burdens of achieving the desirable condition of expanded communism. Marxists can then advocate a just society of expanded communism in terms of both types of performance of labor—individual and sharing—even when sharing the surplus proceeds of labor becomes a binding constraint in such society.

But why should someone concerned with extending the milieu of development as need be bothered about class-based expanded communism? First, as has already been explained, need cannot avoid class because of the generation of the social surplus. Struggles over social surpluses are intrinsically connected to class struggles. Thus from a need perspective it is imperative to explore which class processes are conducive for facilitating the process of need fulfillment. Since need is a dynamic concept, its fulfillment requires an institutional configuration in terms of a set of class processes (and additional factors) that must be so constructed as to internalize the changing pattern of need. Second, in exploring the above point, social surplus implies a leakage from the immediate requirement of the surplus-based production process and hence reflects a demand on it of a social (macro) nature. This means that there must be a *commitment* on the part of the producer, appropriator, and distributor to part with a portion of surplus depending on the social requirement. In this context, the question is, which set of class processes is most likely to support such a social commitment? While there is nothing that prevents an exploiter from sharing his wealth with others, we can reasonably conjecture that an economic system will never be sustained simply by gifts. Of course, governments can appear as an outsider with social mandate to (forcibly) tax heavily the surplus of these exploitative firms, as in the Nordic countries, but this might create a divergence between the interest of such companies (who do not want to share out) and the government (who force the companies to share out), thereby creating a crisis in the system—exactly what has transpired in the Nordic countries. And, in the underdeveloped countries, such an option is very limited anyway: the government has little freedom or desire (in light of the liberalization policy) to suitably tax the appropriators of surplus. In other words, need-focused development is best suited to an environment in which its fulfillment is a result of a social commitment and achieved without force among members of producers, appropriators, and distributors of surplus. The institutional configuration of classes that is tailor-made to generate such an environment of social commitment is likely to be our desired set of classes from a need/development perspective. We recognize that further studies on expanded communism and its institutional mechanism are necessary but we also perceive it as arguably the best-equipped class arrangement to address such social questions. Those who share out in the production process are the ones most likely to listen to and address the problems of need and to share out their produce of wealth at the societal level. Because of the characteristic of sharing and the complementarity of actors' positions, class-based expanded communism seems the most appropriate social arrangement from the perspective of need. However, this is not to say that achieving expanded communism will inevitably arrest (developmental) struggles over social surpluses. Rather, what is being emphasized is that since the developmental struggle is connected to the class struggle, a desirable resolution of the conflict over social surplus as that which extends the milieu of need is most likely to happen under a social arrangement of expanded communism.

Development and the New International

Historically, communism had always been associated with some form of internationalism. That internationalism, though, had collapsed long before the demise of the Soviet Union. One major reason for the collapse of internationalism was the absence of any linkage between it and the functional operation of the economy. As such, despite the best efforts of theorists like Lenin and Trotsky, the concept of internationalism remained fully utopian. In contrast, we would argue that one important characteristic of expanded communism is that it embodies a new form of internationalism that is particularly relevant in the current politics over the creation of a new global (economic) architecture. This internationalism arises in the context of social surplus as an articulation/convergence of class and developmental struggles beyond the nation state. This internationalism is an articulation of both ethical desires and economic functions.

What should happen to the extra social surplus that remains within a country after accounting for the needs of its citizens? Expanded communism entails the moral/ethical position of sharing out, and it should proceed from enterprise to society or nation state, to the international domain. Consequently, this aspect of sharing, once achieved, carries an inbuilt sense of *obligation* for countries with excess social surplus to look for other countries where social surpluses may not be forthcoming to fulfill the respective needs there. The possibility of transfers of social surplus from the surplus to the deficit countries as part of this obligation (and not as debt) is today a real possibility. A new *moral* contract between countries/social actors will have to be created along with appropriate institutions that automatically guarantee such transfers. Creation of this moral obligation rooted in the articulation of class and need is what we mean by a *new international*. We recognize that sharing out may stop at the doorstep of the nation and that there is no inherent mechanism that guarantees its overflow outside its boundary. But that is precisely the reason for striving for a new international—a creation of a moral obligation between countries/actors that will guarantee the transfer of social surplus across borders. This new international is politically attractive and viable because it is also rooted in the functional operation of the economy. Since much of what constitutes need is determined in an international context (take our Oxfam case or the debt repayment issue), struggling for such a new international becomes a requirement for the expansion of developmental need at the domestic level. This possibility is another reason why those who seek developmental justice should simultaneously strive for expanded communism as an appropriate social arrangement. Since the social surplus is initially located in the class process, struggles over need issues cannot avoid class struggle or the struggle to seek out social arrangements that are best equipped to generate the new moral contract capable of producing the new international.

This new internationalism could also be interpreted as the Marxian response to GATT, TRIPS, and other transnational agreements that today constitute an attempt by the leaders of the G-8 countries to create an internationalism of a different order. Postmodernists, and especially Marxists among them, have found it difficult to interpret the recent counterstruggles against such a vision. This new idea of internationalism produces a definite space for Marxian struggles amid these differing positions. Issues raised in the international demonstrations like that of the debt problem in the "Third World" countries are as much a problem of class as of development if we understand surplus partly as social surplus. The problem of debt is substantially a struggle over the distribution of social surplus and the claims over it. Debt, from a Marxian perspective, is not something to be reclaimed in the future but is a part of social surplus over and above the domestic requirement that then is distributed to the citizens of other countries. That is why it was given as "debt" in the first place. However, in our context, the "debt" is not a debt but a transfer of surplus over the required social surplus from one country to another, and the new international makes it morally obligatory for countries to part with that surplus. That is what should make the debt repayment issue contentious from a Marxian perspective. Class struggle then becomes a struggle over issues of development as well, and thus the articulation of the two struggles in this context takes on an international dimension. Such struggles based on the moral obligation of sharing at the international level linked to the developmental needs give a powerful ethical punch to the desirable goal of Marxists—expanded communism. Postmodern Marxists should not shy away from such struggles and in fact take a lead in those that are part of its scope, such as the one over the debt issue. Struggling for the new international thus creates a space where the politics of Marxists and developmentalists could mutually constitute one another to forge a political counterhegemony against the global architecture being propounded by the leaders of the G-8 nations and other world institutions.

Classless Society and Need-Based Economy

We have focused on exploring the linkage between development and class and delineating the social arrangement—that of expanded communism—as being the desirable goal of both development and class politics. Expanded communism signals a goal beyond simply the *transition* of classes—the goal now becomes the *developmental transition* of classes.

There is also a different way to think about classless society in terms of the developmental question and a need-based economy. A need-based economy is dynamic because such an economy is not simply satisfied with the present level of subsistence but also in creating greater levels of subsistence over time. This requires a rethinking of what constitutes necessary labor. The necessary product equivalent of necessary labor has traditionally been understood in terms of some historically determined subsistence basket. But this avoids the question of how future subsistence is formed. We distinguish between present and future subsistence baskets in order to conceptualize the expansion of the future need economy as the future subsistence basket increases. One example of this expansive need economy could be a cooperative that decides to create a water pool in the village in order to avoid future drinking-water problems. Another example could be the creation of dredges in rivers by villagers to avoid future flooding. A different example could be individuals deciding to plant trees on their property; with everybody doing the same, the result is reduced pollution in the future, which was the initial purpose of planting trees. None of these nonsurplus productive activities necessarily requires tapping into the class-produced social surplus, and in many concrete instances they do not. We recognize, however, that some of such expansions might require tapping into the social surplus (via, for example, loans or grants from the World Bank) that arise from class processes, but in other cases this might not be necessary.

The expansion of such a need-based economy while offering benefits at a public level involves labor performed at an individual level (in case of planting trees) or with sharing (the other two cases). Thus if we are to look at the transition of class-based economic activities that produce the above-mentioned future goods to nonclass need-based economic arrangements, then again CC and AC class arrangements provide the most appropriate way of bringing about such transition. This again is another way of justifying CC and AC–type class process from a developmental perspective.

It is also interesting to note that the need-based economy in its nonexploitative form generates its own corresponding form in the surplus economy. The production of flood-control dredges by private contractors may be supplanted by a people's cooperative, thereby making flood-control dredges with a surplus arrangement noncompetitive. Such activities done from class standpoint are replaced by need-based production arrangement.

Resnick and Wolff's (1988) idea of communism as classlessness considered communism as a fundamentally separate system that could function on its own. We differ sharply on this point. If we treat the need-based economy as simultaneously the difference and other of the surplus economy, then the *differance*—the articulation of the two—can never be overcome. That is, classless society (just like class-based society) on its own is an impossibility. That being so, the contradiction between the need-based, classless economy and the surplus economy is a permanent feature of society. This, on the other hand, is not inconsistent with the postmodern Marxist logic, which would agree that the evolution of an expansive need-based economy as a nonexploitative social arrangement should be overdetermined by the surplus-based system. And, unlike in the previous examples, this mutual constitution may not be necessarily in conflict, but it could generate an expansion of both the surplus- and need-based economy. An example would be the case of agents in the need-based economy sometimes simultaneously serving in the surplus economy often as, say, a wage laborer. In this instance, it is existence of the need-based economy in its expanded form that takes care of many of necessities that may serve to reduce the offered subsistence basket in the surplus economy. Then, even with a reduced real wage, the surplus-based economy could remain viable in the long run. In fact, interventions by international agencies such as the World Bank as well as various governments committed to liberalization programs directed at expanding the need-based economy in the Third World could be read in this light. Such interventions are designed to reduce the burden on the surplus-based economy in order to make the liberalization process successful. Here social surpluses may be transferred via the metonyms of government and international agencies (such as the NGOs) for the production of consumption goods and services for collective use in the need-based economy.[13] In other words, above and/or outside the production surplus, a portion of social surplus could also be created to be directed to help in non-surplus-based economic activities to reproduce and expand the material existence of the above mentioned economic agents. Such an expansion of the need-based economy, unlike in the case of the previous instances of expansion, is not incompatible with the growth of a surplus-based (exploitative) economy. Here, the surplus-based exploitative economy in one space breeds nonexploitation in another space. In fact, one can say that the nonexploitative need economy provides a condition of existence for the reproduction and growth of the surplus-based economy.[14]

An expansion of need-based economy may be accompanied by a contraction of the surplus-based economy if the former replaces the production activity of the latter. In that moment of contradiction and when the surplus-based class processes are exploitative Marxists should support the expansive need-based economy, for such a developmental move produces an expansion of the nonexploitative social arrangements. Expanded communism on a class basis or a classless basis: the contradictions between the class-based way of living and the classless one are bound to be severe.

The Question of Development Practice

We have advocated supporting an expanded communism that encapsulates the dual ethics flowing from the eradication of exploitation (production from a surplus standpoint) and need (distribution from a consumption standpoint). In particular, we have advocated an expanded communism that in class space would lead to a social formation with nonexploitative classes and fair distribution or, alternatively, for expansion of need-based economy at the expense of a class-based one. However, while expanded communism of whatever form is the political goal of Marxists, there is nothing in the social dynamics in our overdeterminist frame that would invariably lead to such a social formation, nothing that says that such a social formation if achieved will be a permanent state. Instead, the social totality will be a configuration of complex classes (exploitative and nonexploitative) and distributions (fair and unfair). While class provides the entry point of forming a Marxian discourse, along with need of a Marxian discourse on development, the ethics flowing from that discourse constitute its political counterpart. In this regard, an accounting for the different possibilities of development politics within a class framework is especially significant.

The matrix below indicates that the social totality will oscillate across time and space, and hence it is critical that Marxists formulate strategies dealing with the different possibilities both at the micro (for example, politics at the level of firm) and macro level (for example, politics at the level of state). There are thus development stages, not given diachronically but synchronically pulling and pushing development in different directions. In this regard, our analysis does provide some guidance to the political role of Marxists.

Marxian Politics in a Class Frame		
	Fair Distribution—Accounting for Need	Unfair Distribution—Does Not Account for Need
Exploitative Classes	Strategically Situated	Unacceptable
Nonexploitative Classes	Political goal of expanded communism —Class-Based	Strategically Situated

The matrix indicates that the pair {exploitative classes, unfair distribution} is unacceptable and that Marxists should reject a system dominated by such a pair. In this regard, movement to any of the other pairs will be acceptable even though {nonexploitative, fair distribution} will be most preferred. There is no hard and fast rule as to where one should move. Given a specific context, it may be strategically feasible to be moving to a state of {exploitative, fair distribution (indicating the expansion of the need space)} or {nonexploitative (indicating constriction of the exploitative space), unfair distribution}. One may make further distinctions about exploitative classes, preferring one set against another. For example, as we will discuss in chapter nine, given India's transition process following the New Economic Policies it might be sensible to formulate a political strategy against big capital including multinationals by forming a coalition supportive not only of nonexploitative classes but also noncapitalist self and capitalist classes in small sector segments where production may be more from a *concern* of need than (accumulating) surplus, even though we can and do distinguish the production space in terms of surplus (that is why many of these small-scale producers are named capitalist).[15] Every such strategy, of course, is one among multiple possibilities, as our matrix suggests.

Further strategies would entail a transition from the pairs of {nonexploitative classes, unfair distribution} and {exploitative classes, fair distribution} to the goal of expanded communism or {nonexploitative classes, fair distribution}. Again, there is no hard and fast rule regarding the path to be taken or the mode of action to achieve it. The matrix and the possible further subclassifications point to the fact that the Marxian politics on development could involve a complexity of strategies over time.

Conclusion

Our analysis has laid down the theoretical groundwork for an alternative approach for studying transition and development in India, especially the historic changes resulting from the recent enactment of the New Economic Policies. This is the task we undertake in the following chapters. We will argue that economic policies emanating from the NEP seeking developmental progress are having a profound effect on the class processes leading to an ongoing process of transition of the Indian economy, transition that unlike the projections of the Indian policy makers is uneven, decentered, and heterogeneous. We will bring to bear many of the complexities related to transition that we have developed in the previous chapter with the intention of showing the efficacy of applying such a concept of transition to a study of the concretely evolving scenario of India amid the competing notions of development as progress.

CHAPTER **8**

The Political Economy of the New Economic Policies

In this chapter we will illustrate the newly produced concept of transition by sketching an analysis of the changes that are taking place in the class structures of India as a result of the ongoing liberalization/reform policies (also called the New Economic Policies, or NEP) adopted by the Indian government. We will simultaneously inquire as to the outcome of the competing notions of developmental progress resulting from the transition process, focusing especially on that proposed by the NEP proponents since it is their set of policy which is the object of analysis here.

A class analysis of the transition process is in sharp contrast to the more popular neoclassical approach (Jalan 1991; Bhagwati and Srinivasan 1993; Bhagwati 1993; Parikh, Narayana, Panda, and Kumar 1995; Joshi and Little, ed. 1995, World Bank Country Study 1995; Joshi and Little 1996; Ahluwalia and Little, ed. 1998; Sachs, Varshney, and Bajpai, ed. 1999) that projects India's transition in terms of the criteria of efficiency and market-based pricing mechanisms purported to deepen and expand the process of growth. The transition process that is let loose by the NEP is supposed to take India toward a path of a certain preconceived unifying developmental progress. For these authors and proponents of the New Economic Policies (NEP) generally, the transition process implies a transformation from the government control of the economy to a "free" (meaning free from government influence) market capitalist economy that should also couple a switch from an import substitution regime to an export promotion one. This systemic change—focused at the micro level—is supposed to be led

235

by and conversely leading to the reinvigoration of the growth parable—the logic of industrialization through capital accumulation. In defense of that logic in the initial period of India's independence and the need to pursue it more purposefully now, one of the leading proponents of India's liberalization policies suggests

> Accelerated growth was thus regarded as an instrumental variable; a policy outcome that would in turn reduce poverty . . . I have often reminded the critics of Indian strategy, who attack it from the perspective of poverty which is juxtaposed against growth, that it is incorrect to think that the Indian planners got it wrong by going for growth rather than attacking poverty: they confuse means with ends . . . the populist notion that pushing growth to kill poverty is a passive and conservative "trickle-down" strategy is wholly obtuse. In the Indian context, it was an active and radical, what I have called "pull up" strategy. (Bhagwati 1998, 25)

Bhagwati and others point out that the growth logic as encapsulated in "industrialisation through capital accumulation" is the key to the development of India, that this logic was derailed in the middle and that the purpose of the current reform, including the micro-level adjustments, should be designed to enhance the function of that developmental logic. What is important is to realize that at no point in India's postindependence history was the logic of development as "industrialisation through capital accumulation" abandoned, but, rather, the mainstream critique of the previous system and defense of current reform is based on the point that the intermittent years were constitutive of policies that created and weakened the pace of the very logic that drove the train of India's development.

In contrast, our way of conceiving of development, as we have built up in chapters 6 and 7, is in terms of the transformation of the class structures in the economy in an uneven, decentered, and heterogeneous manner and not of the above developmental logic that we have already criticized as being essentialist and historicist. Such a class analysis of transition will give a profoundly different perspective on the changes taking place in Indian society following NEP and of whatever happened to its developmental progress. This different perspective—a Marxist perspective—is what we want to propose and describe in this chapter, in order to show how a class analysis of transition can be counterposed against the more mainstream analysis of India's transition where this transition telescopes simultaneously the road to development as progress and is read as a movement from a government-controlled system (some call it socialism) to capitalism.

Our analysis is especially important in the current context of an absence of any concerted analysis of the liberalization policies by Indian Marxists, who are clearly at a loss to explain their opposition to government policies from a Marxist qua class perspective. This quandary arises from their previous well-established opposition to the system of mixed economy that India had. Broadly speaking, the left had considered the Indian economy to be nonsocialist despite the substantial presence of state enterprises, for two reasons: (i) state enterprises are only socialist in appearance while in essence their relations of production are based on bureaucratic power relations favoring capitalist classes defined in terms of power relations, and (ii) the state enterprises, even if they are public property, are geared to help the private sector gain a foothold and, eventually, dominance in the economic and social sphere; that is, here too the appearance of state enterprises as socialist hides their role in reproducing and strengthening the capitalist system. But if, by their own account, the state enterprises are in essence capitalist or serving the capitalist system, how could the left parties oppose their disintegration, brought about by the New Economic Policies? At the present juncture of the New Economic Policies, the left parties have placed themselves in an awkward position by defending the state enterprises in the name of self-sufficiency and freedom from foreign interference, and sometimes even describing them now as reflective of the socialist imaginary. The reformers and the pro-reform media have time and again ridiculed the left by pointing out that the New Economic Policies are going to liberate the forces of production, ushering in a dynamic capitalist economy, and, consequently, that the left parties should be supporting the economic reforms instead of opposing them. It is indeed interesting that some non-Marxist parties and exponents are now criticizing the Marxist parties and intellectuals by using the rhetoric of historical materialism, and that Marxists are unable to provide any concerted response to those criticisms. And, in the context of the methodology of historical materialism, with its developmental logic of "industrialization through capital accumulation," nothing more can be expected. Since both orthodox Marxists and mainstream economists commonly share the developmental logic of industrialization within a big-bang, macro theory of transition of the economy, albeit with different telos but a telos nevertheless, the set of policies that inhibit the logic clearly lose out.

We, on the other hand, find it a fruitless exercise to defend the indefensible—the prereform Indian economy—a production of a system that created and sustained high poverty, displaced people from their livelihood on a massive scale, perpetuated illiteracy and ill-health, furnished a perverse licensing system that choked investment and led to widespread corruption benefiting the rich, increased the inequality of assets as well as the concentration of capital, and augmented the extent and depth of exploitative class processes. Furthermore, the radicals' obsession with state enterprises as the political space of effecting change to "socialism" or any other competing social order has made it easier for its detractors to lump together state and socialism in a critique of the radicals' agenda. Again, we distance ourselves totally from such a notion of a desirable society, which, as we explained in the previous chapter, is something very different in our case—that based either on the creation of nonexploitative classes with the aspect of fair distribution to be integrated institutionally. This effectively means defending and struggling for either classes comprising expanded communism or, alternatively, the replacement of the classes by the need-based economic activities. All in all, we are unable to agree with the radical position that finds virtue in many of the characteristics of the pre-reform system or oppose the NEP for the sake of opposition. Our reservations regarding pre-reform India, on the other hand, stem not only from the substantive fall out of that system, but our disquiet multiplies to the very logic of a big-bang, macro development, telescoped in the dynamics of industrialization through capital accumulation that produces those bad outcomes. Such a system demands reforms, not to choose between two competing forms of "industrialization through capital accumulation" as we are being effectively asked to do so presently. Reforms are needed not simply at the substantive level but at the level of vision that underlies the functional or operative axis of the economy. It is clear that conceptions of transition and development that mark out a paradigmatically distinct anti-essentialist and antihistoricist vision, that highlight the organization of society from the standpoint of class (with a concern about need) with its moorings on the mechanics and forms of exploitation (as well as forms of distribution) would require a methodological space and focus that is uniquely different from that which is commonly offered by both the mainstream and the hitherto-radical schools. In this context, we want to situate our class-focused approach to development with its disaggregated theory of transition as servicing an altogether unique vision of the economy and of its development that can be seen as a response to end the paralysis of Marxist discourse with regard to the New Economic Policies.

We will try to illustrate the usefulness of the new decentered concept of transition by demonstrating that the transition of Indian society is not moving in a unidirectional path. Rather, the seemingly uniform liberalization policies are producing complex changes in society by producing a chain of differentiated and uneven effects on class structures. This produces a new, class-focused understanding of the transition process in India that has no parallel in any variants of the neoclassical theories of transition or radical ones. This, we hope, helps to put the agenda of Marxian exploitation right in the heart of the discursive map as far as discussing India's transition process is concerned.

Finally, a word of caution: we are not going to focus on laying down an alternative left political role or program, because that would be practically and theoretically inconsequential in this context.[2] We will, on the other hand, be referring to the left's present position on the New Economic Policies while discussing the struggle over class processes in India. The argument we want to emphasize is that of our alternative class analysis of transition and development as a counteranalysis to the more mainstream approaches of the same as well as an alternative Marxist approach to conceptualizing the transition and development process in India. To defend the feasibility of a Marxist approach to transition and development against the neoclassical attack on those is the (political) program of this chapter and the next one. This is especially important in light of the recent attempts by neoclassical economists in India to exorcise Marxism from the academic and social domain. This attack on Marxism in the discursive plane is having a profound effect on the political domain, since Marxists are now being challenged to defend the relevance of their approach, which according to its opponents is indefensible in the present post–Cold War globalization period. We want to take up the challenge here and, in opposition to the neoclassical skeptics, demonstrate the vibrant nature and relevance of a Marxist discourse on transition and development—a (postmodern) Marxist discourse on transition and development that attempts to liberate the Indian intellectual psyche from the totalizing vision of Indian social totality drawn up by the orthodoxy, Marxist and neoclassical.

The Government Rationale of Economic Reforms and Class Analysis

The government rationale for the New Economic Policies, as espoused in the early 1990s, is a combination of what has been referred to as a response to a macroeconomic and microeconomic crisis situation. The macroeconomic crisis is seen in turn as being both internally (the fiscal deficit) and externally (the balance of payments crunch) produced while the microeconomic crisis signifies serious efficiency and incentive failures. This set of crises created serious barriers to the growth path of the Indian economy, impeding the development logic of industrialization through capital accumulation. According to the government, the two sets of problems are linked, since the microeconomic problems of inefficiency and incentive failure have played a role in intensifying the macroeconomic crisis. As Bhagwati and Srinivasan, the two main exponents of the government's economic reform, put it, "The macroeconomic problems . . . had been accentuated by, if not largely been a result of, the microeconomic inefficiencies" (Bhagwati and Srinivasan 1993, ii). The New Economic Policies are directed toward redressing these sets of macroeconomic and microeconomic or structural problems even though clearly the essence of the macroeconomic problems is traced to microeconomic distortions. That is why the thrust of the reform has been on transforming the micro-level sites of production and distribution of goods and services. And because the micro problems are mainly identified in terms of efficiency and incentive failures, the reforms at that level can be dubbed as supply-side reform designed to affect the way in which production and distribution of goods and services happen. Our theory of transition because of its class-focused conceptualization of social totality as disaggregated and heterogeneous is tailor-made to address the dynamics following the New Economic Policies.

From the perspective of India's policymakers, the NEP can thus be understood as a set of policies that are designed to change the fundamental and subsumed class processes and thus the meaning of social totality in a certain manner and direction. But our claim is that, unlike what the policy makers think, since the social totality is disaggregated the class changes that will be brought about will be uneven, pulling and pushing the social totality that is the Indian economy in different directions. This undercuts the possibility of any predication of a change of Indian economy to a telos of capitalism resulting from the NEP, as its proponents would have us believe, while at the same time revealing and generating the possibilities of multiple class practices that are currently being shaped by the NEP. While we do not intend to provide a political program for the left here, we contend that this range of variegated class practices being advocated by the NEP could serve as a moment of opportunity rather than hurl us to the depths of despondency as the current left seem to be suggesting. The opportunity is reflective of the possibilities of taking the moments of transition into a totally different direction (to sets of class processes that are nonexploitative while simultaneously serving the societal demand of fair distribution) than where our NEP proponents would want us to go. In this respect, we have already discussed in the last chapter the range of political practices that Marxists can conceive over development from the standpoint of the dual ethics of exploitation and need. This recognition of numerous developmental practices—epitomizing a displacement and reversal of the meaning of transition following NEP—could be the axis in which the new radical agenda in this new age relocates itself.

Let us start our exegesis by explaining the vast influence of the state on the economy, and thereafter in the following chapter we will discuss the ways in which a change in policies can affect the economy in a fundamental way by changing not only the forms of class structures but, in some cases, also their type.

The Prelude to the New Economic Policies

In India until the end of the 1980s, the state owned a large number of industries and had a virtual monopoly in many important service sectors such as life insurance and banking. Appendix Table 4 reveals the extent of the state's involvement in the Indian economy.[3] The table shows the large percentage share of the public sector in gross domestic product (GDP), saving, capital formation, and consumption expenditure before the liberalization policies began. Appendix Table 5 shows employment in the government sector, which in 1990 when the NEP was first introduced, is almost two and a half times greater than that in the organized private sector.[4]

Furthermore, the state enterprises were concentrated in the capital goods sector, and their virtual monopoly over these sectors gave the state control over what might be called the commanding heights of the economy. The private enterprises depended on the state enterprises for survival because most of their indispensable inputs come from the state sector. The quantitative involvement of the state in the Indian economy was backed up by qualitative involvement, which was critical for the reproduction of the private fundamental class processes. This qualitative involvement came about through a complicated licensing system that made it mandatory for private enterprises to seek licenses for establishing new units and for expanding the capacity of the existing units, control over imports through licensing, restrictions on exports, administrative control over exchange rates, a large sum of transfers to the agricultural sector and other sectors like health and education, high income and corporate taxes as well as control over the banking and the insurance system.

By the 1980s, the government's reach had spread across the length and breadth of the economy, covering directly or indirectly almost every aspect of the economy. Other than its own state capitalist enterprises, in the agricultural sector the state has subsidized fertilizers, seeds, water, electricity, input prices, and interest rates; fixed administrative prices for food grains; and protected the agricultural products from foreign competition, making the conditions of existence of the agricultural fundamental class processes crucially dependent on the state. By controlling banking services and through complicated licensing policies, the state provided many indispensable conditions of existence for the private capitalist enterprises. The same is true for its protection of the small-scale traditional industries like the handicraft, sericulture, coir, leather, and handloom production.

With such an economic background, the target of the liberalization program is to decrease the state's influence in the overall economy including its overthrow by the market as the principal allocation of resources. The effect of reducing or cutting off many such indispensable conditions of existence across the broad spectrum of economic activity is bound to have important, often unintended, effects on the economy and the society as a whole.

The central government traditionally incurred expenditures mainly in three areas. First, there is consumption expenditure that consists of defense and other government administration expenditures. Second, there are transfer payments that, among other things, include interest payments, subsidies, and grants to state governments and union territories. The final form of expenditure is the gross capital formation out of budgetary resources, which includes both physical and financial assets.

Due to the fact that revenues became less than expenditures, the state, over the years, borrowed a large sum of money, both from internal and external sources.[5] This created a rising fiscal deficit problem that, according to the government, had the following purgatory effects:

> They had led to high levels of borrowing by the Government from the Reserve Bank, with an expansionary impact on money supply leading directly to high rates of inflation. High fiscal deficits contributed directly to the large current account deficits in the balance of payments and thus aggravated the problem of external indebtedness. Large fiscal deficits also pre-empted a significant proportion of the savings of society to support the budget, with a consequent scarcity of funds for productive investment. This was reflected in very high interest rates facing the commercial sector, which discouraged new investment and also reduced our international competitiveness. (Government of India Discussion Paper 1993, 6)

The growing fiscal crisis was compounded by a crisis in the balance of payments in 1990–91, when the foreign exchange reserves plummeted. This was followed by intense pressure put on India by global institutions like the International Monetary Fund, the Asian Development Bank, and the World Bank, who have been asking India to reduce its fiscal deficits by downsizing the state sector enterprises, reducing the involvement of the state in the economy, and abandoning its import substitution policies. In response to all of these pressures, the government has, in the long run, taken the road to reduce the fiscal deficit by cutting down its expenditures, especially its transfer payments, by dramatically reducing subsidies, selling part of the state industries to private sectors, and closing or cutting down many service operations; a shift toward a more market-determined exchange rates and open-door trade policies; a new set of industrial, agricultural, and banking policies that pay more attention to principles of competition, profitability, efficiency, and outward (export) oriented growth, and calls for less involvement of the government in economic decisions, especially those related to output and pricing. Policies designed to effect these changes are still unfolding, both at the planning and functional level, but there is no doubt as to the direction of the changes mentioned above. This uniformity of government policies seems interesting if we remember that between 1991 (when the NEP was officially announced) and 2001, five different governments (constituting different political formations) were in place. The Indian government is also devising policies to complement these actions by in effect creating an environment conducive to the rise of dynamic, relative surplus value producing capitalist fundamental class processes such that Indian enterprises can be at the cutting edge of global competition.[6] As the Government of India report unveiled,

> Investment in people and capital is necessary, but not enough for rapid productivity growth. We must foster an environment that encourages full utilization of our material and human resources and ensures that they are deployed in the most productive manner. What kind of economic environment will achieve this? Decades of development experience in dozens of countries show that a good economic environment combines the discipline of competitive markets with efficient provision of key public services, such as, primary education, primary health care, transport and communication and, of course, law and order. Government should foster the maximum flowering of personal initiative and effort, but it must also step in where markets fail or are abused by powerful sectional interests. . . . We should ask ourselves why do millions of our countrymen and women who migrate abroad prosper? Because the environments they go to reward hard work, efficiency, discipline and social responsibility. (Government of India Discussion Paper 1993, 1)

To promote an environment that fosters growth with efficiency became the new development slogan of the government. As explained earlier, the government has been involved in almost all aspects of economic life, thereby making its presence felt in important decisions of the private economic units. In class terms, the state provided many critical subsumed and nonclass conditions of existence of the private fundamental class structures. In addition it also occupied, along with the private sector, a site of the fundamental class processes producing output which, because it was concentrated in the commanding heights of the economy, provided critical conditions of existence (as a supplier of raw materials and machines) for private class (fundamental, subsumed, or both) processes. The New Economic Policies, which by changing the meaning of development are, among other things, geared toward challenging the prevailing meaning of government by radically altering its role from active and all-encompassing involvement in the economic sphere to the promotion of a particular economic environment. In our discussion of the passive revolution of capital, we explained how the Indian state was conceived of as a developmental state whose role is not simply restricted to the promotion of a particular economic environment but extends to cover almost every aspect of economic life. The developmental state was projected as a protector of different groups of communities defined in terms of caste, religion, or income. Such a role for the government complements the development strategy of growth (or capital accumulation) with equity (which involves the welfare-guaranteeing role of the state). The data we presented earlier capturing the scenario of pre-reform India is an indicator of the state's deep involvement in the economy. In contrast, the new meaning of development—growth and efficiency—is complemented by the new role of the government not as an active player in the economy but as a promoter of a particular environment, interfering selectively only when the market mechanism fails. This signifies a transformation of the government from being an active player in growth creation along with its protective or welfare-guaranteeing role to that of a promoter of an environment that in the first instance would foster growth with efficiency. As the government discussion paper put it, "The emphasis in the future must be on promotion rather than excessive regulation and protection" (Government of India Discussion Paper 1993, 34).

The set of government policies indicated above has directly or indirectly affected the class processes (both fundamental and subsumed) in the state enterprises, private agricultural farms, private capitalist industrial enterprises, private noncapitalist enterprises, the household sector, and such service sector units as banking and insurance that provide critical conditions of existence for these enterprises and farms. They have set in motion a process of transition that is still in the making. Our purpose here is to see whether and in what ways the government policies have affected and can affect the class structures of the Indian economy. Where are the possibilities in the path of transition of the Indian economy and what are its effects on politics—class and developmental? We will concentrate on the effect of the New Economic Policies on agriculture, private industry, and the state industry.[7] Since the effect of the New Economic Policies on households has been dealt with in chapter Six, we will ignore it here.

CHAPTER **9**

Transition and
the Class Structure
in the Indian Economy

The set of government policies indicated in the previous chapter has directly or indirectly affected the class processes (both fundamental and subsumed) in the state enterprises, private agricultural farms, private capitalist industrial enterprises, private noncapitalist enterprises, the household sector, and such service sector units as banking and insurance that provide critical conditions of existence for these enterprises and farms. They have set in motion a process of transition that is still in the making. Our purpose in this chapter is to see whether and in what ways the government policies can affect the class structures of the Indian economy. Where are the possibilities in the path of transition of the Indian economy and what are their effects on class politics?

Class and Transition in the Agricultural Sector

Among other things, the government's "agricultural policy" was initially directed to (i) to raise the ratio of agricultural gross capital formation to current government expenditure on agriculture and (ii) to decrease the government's involvement and increase the role of the private sector in agriculture (Economic Survey 1994–95, 130–132). The government has targeted current expenditures like fertilizer subsidies, input subsidies, and interest subsidies, and is bent on increasing investment in irrigation and rural communication, which is supposed to lead to an increase in capital formation. Also, to encourage private investment, it is opening up previously closed sectors (for example, in the power sector and irrigation sector) for private investment, increasingly freeing the internal agrarian market from government control, and thereby enabling the farmers to reap gains from favorable terms of trade in the domestic market and using open-door trade policies (which is supposed to turn the terms of trade in favor of agriculture) to encourage the private sector to invest on agriculture to garner additional gains from trade through exports.

Since fertilizer subsidies, input subsidies (especially for water and electricity), interest subsidies, administrative price supports, easy loan guarantees, and many other services by the government provided the conditions of existence of the agricultural production sector, the reduction in these subsumed and nonclass revenues may be perceived as an attack on the very process of the reproduction of the existing fundamental class processes if it so happens that the reduction in revenue from these effects outweighs the increase in revenue coming from increasing output prices or output quantities. The reduction of subsumed class payments or expenditures of the state sector overdetermines the class analysis of the agricultural farmers by reducing the corresponding revenue that would go to the farmers, assuming again that the resulting increase in output and/or output prices does not outweigh this effect. Also, for the services rendered previously by government agencies, these farms may now have to pay a higher amount of subsumed class payment to agents carrying out processes that secure those particular conditions of existence of the fundamental class process. Thus, an attempt by the government to overcome the crisis in the state sector may end up producing a crisis in many agricultural farms where, due to the reduction in the subsumed class revenue and nonclass revenue and probably a higher subsumed and nonclass payment, the class equation of such farms might become:

$$SV + \Sigma SCR + \Sigma NCR < \Sigma SC + \Sigma X + \Sigma Y \qquad (a)$$

where, SV = Surplus Value produced and appropriated by agricultural farm;

ΣSCR = Subsumed Class Revenue;
ΣNCR = Nonclass Revenue;
ΣSC = Sum of Subsumed Class Payments;
ΣX = Sum of Payments Made to Secure SCR;
ΣY = Sum of Payments Made to Secure NCR.[1]

Under the new conditions, $\{\Sigma SCR + \Sigma NCR\} < \{\Sigma SCR + \Sigma NCR\}_1$, where, $\{\sum SCR + NCR\}_1$ are the subsumed class and nonclass revenue prior to the government intervention.

Also, $\Sigma SC > \{\Sigma SC\}_1$, where $\{\sum SC\}_1$ are the subsumed class payments such farms made prior to the government intervention.

In class terms, any agricultural unit is defined to be in a crisis situation if its revenue side becomes less than its expenditure side, as in (a).[2] Many agricultural farms would likely have to deal with such a crisis situation resulting from the government's policies to severely curtail subsumed and nonclass transfers to such farms.[3]

The government's response to the above criticism has been to defend its action as pro-agricultural by pointing out that its policies of steady withdrawal from the decision-making process of the agrarian enterprises should not be interpreted as a case of removing the protective shield but one of ridding the shackles that have enslaved the agricultural sector (to the industrial sector among other things). Its policies will in fact turn the terms of trade in favor of agricultural products and will benefit the farmers in the long run (Gulati 1998, 130). According to the pro-reform group, a major consideration of projected reform in agriculture is this sector's linkage with the process of globalization and the benefits it can garner from that linkage. This entails taking certain measures, principally:

- Removing export controls that depress domestic prices below export prices. Particularly important are the controls on the export of cotton, wheat, and common rice.
- Removing import controls and setting zero or low tariffs on highly protected commodities. Particularly important are edible oils and oilseeds, sugar, and rubber.
- Removing regulatory and other domestic controls that would otherwise impede the transmission of world price signals to farmers. (Pursell and Gulati, 1995)

Over time, in line with the above-mentioned policy prescriptions, the government has slowly removed restrictions (on input, output, and pricing decisions) for certain agricultural products with the motive of increasing the trend toward a more favorable terms of trade for agriculture. The process of removing some of the above-mentioned controls has hastened in recent times in tune with the projected removal of a set of controls—domestic and international—as per the GATT/WTO agreements, which is supposed to unfold in the immediate future. The ability to now freely export commodities like grapes, onions, and so on, has further enhanced the benefits of liberalization policies for such farmers. Furthermore, it is argued that the removal of agricultural subsidies in developed countries as required by GATT/WTO will drive up the international prices for agricultural products, thereby benefiting the farmers and the agro-industry from India who enjoy a comparative advantage in these products. Also, due to international competition, Indian agricultural farms will be forced to upgrade their technological capability, thereby moving the labor process to a stage of relative surplus-value production. Because of higher agricultural prices with its impact on the terms of trade between agriculture and industry and better economic environment, private investments would flood in, thereby further facilitating growth in agriculture that in turn will produce a demand-driven growth in industry and so a virtuous cycle would materialize (Gulati 1998, 130). Thus, we are told that the Indian agrarian class structures, by undergoing this transformation of the existing fundamental class processes to a new form or type, will enter a new era of growth and prosperity. However, in line with our experience of more than ten years since the beginning of the reform process, we need to be cautious regarding the effects of government policies.

First, it is to be noted that higher agricultural prices will benefit only those farms whose majority of output is marketed and whose marketable return outweighs the loss from an increase of subsumed class payments and other nonclass expenditures. For other farms, which are likely to be run by the most vulnerable section of the population, this policy of detachment by the government can create severe problems concerning the reproduction of the conditions of existence of the farm's fundamental class processes. For some of these farms, because of the increase in the input cost and other expenditures, the expenditure side epitomized by the subsumed class payment of the farmers will increase substantially and some of the components of the revenue side might come down so much that decrease in income would outweigh any increase in revenue from increase in output prices. This situation implies a crisis for such farms because the amount required to maintain the conditions of existence of the fundamental class process may not be available. The increase in payment for processes providing the conditions of existence for the reproduction of the fundamental class process can lead to a process, in the case of some farms (especially small ones), whereby the farmers involved would be compelled to transfer the right of appropriating surplus product in their farm to their richer counterparts because of the condition given by (a). For example, the decline in subsidies for inputs, like water or electricity, may force many farmers to increase the subsumed class payments to money capital for loans to finance the deficit in the production process. Often the private moneylender may charge an amount in interest payment that could ultimately lead to a transfer to those moneylenders of the rights of appropriation over the produce. This transfer definitely would lead to a transition of the class structures of such farms. In that case, typically, the farmers either go back to a family business, become agricultural laborers or some combination of both, or become unemployed. This surrender of the rights over appropriation may lead to a concentration of capital in agriculture and to greater intensity of exploitation and incidence of inequality, unemployment, and, if the trickle down effect is not properly channeled, to poverty.

Second, while it is true that the terms of trade may turn in favor of certain agricultural commodities (and it did happen in the last few years), this will benefit disproportionately the rich farmers of those commodities. A large proportion of the agricultural population in India is composed of agricultural laborers and small farmers who buy agricultural products in the market to reproduce their families. Some of these small farmers either do not produce for the market or have little access to the market. Whatever little marketable surplus these small farmers have is normally taken away by the traders or middlemen who (rather than the farmers) would in this case gain most from any increase in prices. On the other hand, with higher prices of food grains, the expenditure side of the family budget will increase, leading to a crisis in the process of the reproduction of such families. This crisis of such farmers' household class process could in turn create a crisis situation for the class processes of the agricultural farms. The situation may be further aggravated by the process of surrender of the rights of appropriation over the surplus product that will increase the number of such crisis families.In the case of India, the high inflation rate in the early part of 1990s and in 1998 (and altogether averaging over 8 percent in the years associated with the liberalization policies—see Appendix Table 9) has added to the misery of families living around the poverty level since, unlike the bouts of inflation in previous periods, this inflationary pressure has been driven by a sharp rise in food-grain prices, which constitute the means of subsistence of such families in India. Furthermore, this higher food-grain price is also bound to intensify urban poverty.[4] In this regard, a former governor of RBI and an ardent leader of the NEP confesses,

> Apart from these economic costs, inflation has much wider social implications in developing economies, like India on account of its adverse impact on the real income of the poor, who are largely unprotected from price rise. The adverse distributional implications of even a moderate inflation is significantly high in India in comparison to the output gains of inflation. This underscores the importance of the social dividends of a low and stable price environment, which have a far greater ramification than the perceived growth benefits of inflation. (Rangarajan 1998, 58–59)

Apart from agreeing on the deleterious effects of inflation on the poor, this quote is interesting for separating out the effects of inflation on the real income of the poor from that of "economic costs" due to costs originating from uncertainty especially in the credit market and the fiscal cost of inflation. It is as if what happens to the real income of the poor and their economic space is not a component of true economic costs and hence not to be included as part of the usual economic discourse. Moreover, Rangarajan (1998, 68–70) suggests that the appropriate inflation rate in India must never cross 6 percent and should preferably be much below than that. If we consider India's inflation rate in the last ten years (over 8 percent) and as being driven principally by an increase in agricultural prices, the inflation impact of the NEP on the poor simply cannot be underestimated.

The third problem refers to the need of inducing private sector investment in agrarian infrastructure. By the government's own account, private sector investment in agriculture has not been a success and its policies do not seem to be working. The Ministry of Finance's Economic Survey and the Reserve Bank of India has the following to say on the issue:

> Private sector real investment in agriculture has increased in absolute terms from Rs. 2840 crore in 1980–81 to 3552 in 1992–93, though its share in total gross domestic capital formation has declined significantly during the period. This decreasing share of private investment in the total gross capital formation seems to suggest that the agriculture sector is relatively less attractive for private investment as compared to the other sectors of the economy. (Economic Survey 1994–95, 130)

> The share of capital formation in agriculture as a proportion to gross capital formation has declined from 9.9 per cent in 1990–91 to 8.0 per cent in 1999–2000. The decline in capital formation has been more pronounced in the public sector, reflecting the persistent and large revenue deficits. The share of agriculture and allied activities in total Plan outlay declined from 6.1 per cent in the Sixth Plan Period to an estimated 4.9 per cent in the Ninth Plan Period. The share of irrigation and flood control in total outlay also shrunk from 10.0 per cent to an estimated 6.5 per cent over the Plan periods. (RBI, 2001)

The long gestation period of many such capital formation projects, uncertainty over returns, fear of political stability of government policies in the context of rural areas and lack of "insider" knowledge of working in rural areas are all factors that may be dissuading private parties from undertaking big time investments in the rural areas. This is especially true for investment in rural infrastructure.

In a curious juxtaposition to its earlier position, the economic survey of 1996–97 and the above RBI quote blames the poor state of gross capital formation or investment in agriculture on the tardy pace of public investment whose share of investment in total gross capital formation in agriculture has decelerated since 1980–81. If the present trend continues, then the government may have to interfere and initiate projects on its own which, as will be argued below, the government itself confesses is not forthcoming.

Some of the reasons attributable to the unacceptable state of public investment in agriculture are the diversion of resources from investment to current expenditure (in the form of increased subsidies for food, fertilizers, electricity, irrigation, credit, and other agricultural inputs rather than on the creation of assets), inadequate rural infrastructure and research, lack of effective credit institutions in the villages, relatively lower allocation of resources for irrigation, relatively more emphasis on food security, larger (inefficiently high) expenditure on maintaining the existing projects. As already pointed out, the situation has also been compounded by the policy of replacing public investment with private investment which government is currently trying to rethink. However, it is also true that contradictions are inherent within this specific distributional mechanics. As the RBI report tells us,

> While public investment in agriculture is declining, subsidies for agriculture are increasing. The increase is concentrated on input subsidies, though food subsidies are also being incurred to maintain high levels of food stocks. In this context, a conscious choice needs to be made, given the overall resource constraint, between subsidies and investment. The question that has to be raised in the context of the overall balance is whether it would be worthwhile shifting spending on subsidies to investment, especially in terms of contribution to agricultural employment and poverty alleviation as well as to spread the benefits to backward and dry land tracts. This leads to the issue of the ideal instruments for agricultural credit delivery and the appropriate institutional changes that are required to ensure necessary credit flow to agriculture. (Reserve Bank of India, 2001)

The contradictory themes on public investment point to a confusion at the level of government as to who should bear the main burden of investment in agriculture—government or private sector.[5] The second related contradiction arises from the resource trade-off between agricultural investment and subsidies. Pro-reform schools point out that cutting subsidies may have short-term bad repercussions by negatively affecting the FCP, as we pointed out earlier, while increasing investment will have long-term benefit. The latter to be achieved by cutting subsidies, however, may also have repercussions, as already pointed out, in terms of an increasing concentration of capital in agriculture and to greater intensity of exploitation and incidence of inequality, unemployment, and, if the trickling down effect is not properly channeled, to poverty. Moreover, the government and policy makers are wary of the immediate impact on FCP resulting from a sizeable extinction of subsidies and subsequently, that is, politically, are demonstrating their reluctance in cutting agricultural subsidies even if they perceive it to be the correct economic policy to follow. All in all, the above-mentioned set of contradictions points to the absence of a separate clear-cut agricultural policy as well as the need for one so far as the government is concerned. Given the importance of capital formation in sustaining and expanding the agricultural sector, this confusion and paralysis in policy making may turn out to be costly in the long run.

Again, it is crucial to understand that the class structures in agriculture are not qualitatively the same as in the industrial sector. Free market plays will not affect the two sectors in the same manner, because the conditions of existence governing the fundamental class processes in the two sectors are different. If one takes class differentiation within the agricultural sector, the situation becomes more complex. Recognition of such complexities present at different levels involved with the differentiated nature of class structures constitutes one of the rationales (a class-based one) for a separate agricultural policy that will try to internalize many of the complexities in the framing of any policies. This is not important simply for devising a policy for raising public investment or taking into account other crucial agricultural aspects but also for recognizing that the agricultural sector overdetermines the other sectors of society in important and contradictory ways. Such "spillovers" must also be taken into account within the agricultural policy framework, for as we will indicate below the spillovers have the capacity to undercut the purpose of the reform, the potential gains from these as per NEP logic, and much more.

This brings us to the fourth problem that a complete emphasis on market forces (reflecting the terms of trade) determining the output decisions of the agricultural class enterprises could have a dangerous macroeconomic implication. It may lead to a shift in cultivation from food-grain crops to cash crops, thereby altering the class structures of these farms in important ways (Pattnaik, 1996).[6] The effort of the government to reduce its role in the agricultural sector can compound the problem, since its gradual withdrawal (removal of fertilizer subsidies, for example) may force many small and middle-class enterprises into a crisislike situation arising out of their inability to meet the input expenditures or from the removal of price protections. Given that food-grain production may not be profitable, farmers (especially the financially vulnerable ones) could change the form of production to cash crops. From a macroeconomic perspective such decision making based on profit calculation could be viable in a developed country but may not be so for an underdeveloped country like India especially under the given parameter that government has the responsibility to feed the vulnerable section of the population.

Such a transition in output decision may, in the long run, produce a situation of excess demand for food grains, which may force India to import food grains, thereby creating an additional burden on the exchequer and undercutting the original goal of the government's liberalization program. Additionally, if the Indian demand for food grains is sufficiently high, then the international prices may shoot up, at least in the short run. This will be disastrous (with certain segment of the population not being fed) even though the international food-grain market will clear. Both possibilities present a daunting scenario for a country like India. It can also be safely assumed that the transaction costs involved in transferring goods to the vulnerable section would also be quite high. Such a (potential) macroeconomic crisis cannot be resolved at the level of market since market forces reflect the situation as it is and not what it may be in the future. That is, the farm enterprises will only be concerned with the immediate situation as reflected by market forces, and they will formulate and execute decisions accordingly. The crisis at the aggregate level in the long run cannot be the concern of these enterprises. This is a potential case of coordination failure that may put the Indian economy under severe strain in the future. This presents an urgent need for a coordination of investment plans—to be drawn up by the government or any third party—to internalize the potential crisis within India's economic system that may arise as a result of the changes in the economic dynamics emanating from the withdrawal of government from the decision-making process of agricultural farms. What is needed, then, is paradoxically a government intervention (of course, of a different kind given the present scenario) on the basis of a clear-cut agricultural policy in the era of globalized market. Unfortunately, as we are repeating, such a clear-cut agricultural policy (which recognizes the difference of class structures between and across sectors as well as the spillovers of agricultural class structures on industries and other sectors and vice versa) is absent in the present juncture.[7]

There is another type of coordination failure connected to the agriculture sector that demands attention. Among many roles of government, one important role that is still effective is the enforcement of minimum support prices (MSP) applicable on certain food grains such as wheat and rice and products such as oil seeds. MSP is designed to protect the farmers, and it has been increasing over the last decade. MSP changes the incentive structure of production in favor of food grains accounted for by MSP and in the Indian scenario has produced a situation of excess production/supply of those food grains. The food grains are subsequently bought back from the farmers by the government at the set administrative price (also procurement price, which must be equal to or above the minimum support price) and kept in government stores under the control of Food Corporation of India (FCI). Some of that is then distributed to sections of "poor" people through the public distribution system (PDS) and the rest is kept as a buffer stock. The creation of buffer stock is based on the "importance of building up a stock of foodgrains, normally rice and wheat to provide *food security* to the country. It is a reserve stock which can be drawn upon at the time of crop failure." (Economic Survey 2000–2001, 92–93). Hear our policy makers:

> The basic objective of the agricultural price policy are to assure remunerative prices to the farmers, to even out effects of seasonality and to provide price and market incentives for diversification of agricultural products to meet consumer needs, besides ensuring stability in consumer prices. Food supply management has been the cardinal element of agricultural price policy, and the Government has been fairly successfully in achieving self-sufficiency in basic staple food—rice, wheat and sugar. (Economic Survey 2000–01, 93)

Unfortunately, in the last decade, food grains have been alarmingly accumulating with the FCI because of good food-grains production courtesy of excellent weather and low off-take from FCI stores. This mismatch between production and distribution means that accumulated food grains have started to rot. Also, the entire process of food supply management via the price and cost support involves a host of subsidies, which are lumped together under the rubric of food subsidy. The food subsidy in India has increased from Rs 2850 crore in 1991–92 to 9200 crore in 1999–2000 (Economic Survey 2000–01, 96). Thus, due to the functional problems as well as budgetary concerns associated with the food supply management, some, especially certain NEP proponents, have as a result called for scrapping the above system of providing security to the farmers and "poor" people either entirely or partially. In line with this thinking, one of the important components of the current phase of NEP is on reforming what is called food supply management in India.

However, notwithstanding the problems at the operational level, the problem at a more fundamental level is that the entire focus of Indian policy makers on this issue seems to be on the production aspect captured by a notion of self-sufficiency that is defined not in terms of consumption but in terms of output production deemed sufficient to take care of the population. Whether produced food grains actually reach the people or not is not part of the discourse on development at this level. That is, once the minimum per capita food-grain production is achieved, it is de facto assumed that the distribution problem is automatically taken care of. This we find disturbing.

Amartya Sen's work on famine as representing some sort of entitlement failure at the collective level has propelled an international institution like the FAO to redefine food security not in terms of simply production and supply of food but also in terms of access to it (Osmani 1995, Fine 1997). This aspect of access has to be integrated into the conception of food security, and its operational success/failure cannot be judged outside of that criteria. Food security, as part of the so-called food supply management, is meaningless otherwise. Thus, the functional failure of food supply management in India is an integral component (a symptom) of the *idea* of food security, and this *idea* must also be questioned. We do not see that happening with the NEP proponents. As if illustrating a case of the misplaced notion of food security as seen by Indian policy makers, while so much food grain is accumulating (seen as a success story of food security—in fact, too much success, which paradoxically is also the source of the problem and hence should be curtailed or expunged—from the Indian policy makers' perspective) a large population in India is suffering from hunger. This phenomenon is exemplified by the poor off-take of the accumulated food grains from FCI godowns when, according to official figures, over one-third of the population is living below the poverty line and, more starkly and perversely, the phenomenon is epitomized by recent reported deaths due to hunger in the state of Orissa. This again represents a coordination failure—failure to connect the different networks of the economy—in this case the failure to transfer the food grains to the poor, to give them access to food grains that would otherwise rot. But this also shows the face of a regime that allows its people to die of hunger and is content to accumulate food grains. This is a structural failure—a distortion—of another kind as well as a severe indictment of that economics centered on the celebration of the logic and psychic comfort of accumulation. It represents the sacrifice of the most obvious of needs at the altar of accumulation. From our standpoint, we question this more than the functional failure.

All in all, the numerous problems presented above in the new age of liberalization and globalization point to a general lack of a coherent policy for the agricultural sector. This lacuna is currently accepted by no an less institution than the Reserve Bank of India:

> The balancing of the relative emphasis on financial versus non-financial sectors in the process of reform is also engaging policy attention in the context of the medium term. For example, considerable anxiety is being expressed that the poor performance of agriculture indicates that the process of reforms has by-passed the

agricultural sector while there has been considerable progress in the financial sector. It is argued that in countries where agricultural reforms were started in the early stage of the overall reform process, the potential output of the economy as a whole has moved upwards. Thus, there is a need to clearly spell out the reform objectives and destinations while carefully accelerating the pace of reforms in several of the non-financial sectors. The legal and institutional changes to enable policy reform would no doubt command attention. (RBI, 2001)

Similarly, another supporter of reform candidly admits,

Thus, overall, it appears that India has taken rapid strides towards globalizing the economy since the 1991 reforms, but the larger part of this remained restricted to the industrial sector. Agriculture experienced a lot of hiccups in trade liberalization, and within agriculture the cereals group remained largely insulated from world markets. The reluctance to open up the cereals sector appears to stem from the issues related to food security. . . . In the case of cash crops, the approach seems to be to allow imports if there is a net deficit and allow exports if there is a comfortable surplus. Trade is still taking place as a "residual" between domestic demand and supply *rather than as a policy instrument* to integrate domestic agriculture with world agriculture, and so to optimize the use of resources. (Gulati, 1999, 129–130)

And this more than ten years since the inception of the NEP. However, through the different policies taken during these ten years, we can discern the transition logic as visualized by the policy makers/government. It wants the agriculture sector to replicate the industrial one—that is, to be a dynamic capitalist sector, producing on a mass scale within a system that makes the aspect of *need* a secondary consideration. From our dual ethical standpoint of exploitation and need, that is the worst of all outcomes and hence to be opposed tooth and nail.

Finally, while we have downplayed the role of growth, that too is not unimportant by the logic of overdetermination. Along with the other factors discussed in detail until now, growth is similarly important. This is especially true if we analyze the overdetermined relation between the agricultural and industrial sector in the context of NEP and its projected consequences. While it is true that the liberalization process may increase the efficiency of agricultural enterprises as claimed by the government, this could simultaneously have an adverse impact on the unemployment scene. As competition forces the adoption of cost-effective new technologies, there will be a shift toward capital-intensive technologies, leading to a fall in employment in agriculture. This should not pose any problem if the excess labor is absorbed in the industries and services sector. However, the condition is that the rate of growth in these sectors has to be fast enough to absorb the newly created mass of unemployed and that the benefits of growth must be distributed. By distribution of benefits of growth, we mean that with growth sufficient employment will take place in goods and services sector in the urban area. This is an important point, since, as in agriculture, modern firms producing goods and services are also using capital-intensive technologies and shedding labor force with a much lower intake rate in new ventures. Where will all of these excess unemployed people go?

If one adds the existing mass of unemployed people to the growth problem, the scenario can become pretty bleak. It must be understood that in the case of India even a 1 percent shift in population comes to a huge number in absolute terms. Thus the rate of growth of the modern industrial sectors has to be very high over a long period of time.[8] According to some NEP proponents, the targeted growth should be around 10 percent (Bhagwati 1998, 38), which would imply a higher industrial growth rate, and not the usual 6 percent, which Bhagwati pointed out was a relic of the prereform regime. Ten years is a long time to assess the performance in this regard. As Appendix Table 9 indicates, India's real GDP has grown by a meager 6.4 percent in the last decade, which is well below the targeted rate. But more important, industrial production—to be the motor of growth under the NEP—slowed to an annual average growth rate of 6.6 percent in the postreform period from 7.8 percent in the 1980s. To make matters worse, in the first four years of the Ninth Plan period, that is, up to 2000–01, industrial production only grew at 5.6 percent per annum. Given the continuing slowdown in the Indian economy along with the impending global recession, it is likely to clearly remain well below the target growth of 8.2 percent per annum set for the Plan period 1997–2002 or Bhagwati's target. In lieu of interlinkage of the dynamics of agricultural growth to be supported by continual industrial expansion to absorb the labor force released from the agricultural sector, the persistent industrial stagnation could pose a serious long-run problem for the very logic of the NEP. The effect of any such disproportionality could have serious consequences not only for the class processes in the agricultural sector but also for the household sector therein.

Also, the present globalized postmodern stage demands that a person have a certain level of education and technical proficiency to have any chance of getting employed. The products, which are becoming more specialized and differentiated, need to be produced by capital-intensive technologies with learning by doing (along with R&D) as one of the chief

sources of innovation. It is difficult to imagine how the surplus population, constituting mostly the illiterate 40 percent of the population, will
meet the challenge (of staying on the cutting edge of competition). The
other source of employment for this potentially displaced populace is
working in the unorganized sector in jobs such as hawking, selling food,
and so on. This avenue does not look attractive in the long run since globalization is putting a severe strain on the unorganized sector (directly
through competition or indirectly through the process of displacement,
that is, primitive capital accumulation), and also since it is difficult to
imagine how so many people could be absorbed into this sector. And if one
adds the urban nightmare that could be created as a result of this population shift, the situation may indeed end up as an urban catastrophe. Thus,
the government's policy of making the agricultural class enterprises efficient may exacerbate an already severe unemployment crisis. By the very-
logic of the NEP, a lot hinges on how fast the Indian industrial sector can
grow and how quickly the population could be trained to meet the challenges of the newly emerging globalized world. The success or failure of the
liberalization policies rests to a large extent on those two counts.

All in all, the pushes and pulls of the New Economic Policies are
predictably or unpredictably changing the types and forms of the class
structures of the agricultural farms with predictable and unpredictable
overdetermined and contradictory effects on the other sectors of the economy, thereby changing the social totality that is India in important ways.
The government defends its policies by pointing out that these changes in
class structures are going to lead to the efficiency and competitiveness of
Indian farms and to general prosperity in terms of increase in GNP per
capita, higher employment, and decreasing poverty. However, the New
Economic Policies will have distinct effects for different types of farms: the
NEP itself needs to be differentiated into many other headings. Indian
agrarian society develops in a contradictory and uneven manner, being
fraught with different kinds of discontinuities, failures, contingencies, and
differences. Because India's social totality is decentered, the transition process of these farms will be complex and uneven. Not all farms will survive
in their present form, and the changes will not always be to the benefit of
the existing set of appropriators. As a result of the government policies and
increased sensitivity to market signals, there will be some farms that will
benefit with increased production and income, but there will also be farms
that will be put at a great disadvantage. It will also have a tremendous effect
on the dynamics of employment prospects, poverty, and concentration of
wealth. Because of the disparate changes in class structure, the government
policies (if the changes are accompanied by the problems we mentioned

above) may end up increasing the rate of exploitation, poverty, and unemployment under a tendency toward a growing concentration of capital unless corrective measures are taken. That is where radical politics has to intervene. To devise a comprehensive agricultural policy that integrates institutionally the differences within agriculture and its dynamics with the impact of globalization that is upon us, that seeks not efficiency as the end but a nonexploitative productive arrangement and fair distribution of the surplus or movement along those directions as, for example, indicated by our political matrix over development in Chapter 7.

Transition of Firms and the Private Capitalist Class Structure

During the present phase of the liberalization policies, when the government is reducing its role in the economy and opening its borders for more open competition and trade, private capitalist enterprises are having to adapt to these changes. The reduction of the capital gains tax, excise and tariffs, the opening up of the financial markets such as insurance and banking, the opening of markets for products hitherto protected for the state enterprises (especially in the capital goods sector) to private capitalist enterprises and getting rid of the licensing policy, and so on are producing changes that are re-creating both the internal and external conditions of existence of the fundamental class processes. Changes in firm technology (or in Marxist terms, the organic composition of capital), management structure, the form of the labor process, the form of supervision, the enterprises' relationship with the government and financial institutions, their relationship with enterprises in other countries, the newer forms of marketing, and so on are fast changing the face of the existing capitalist enterprises. It should be noted that, where the type of appropriation is private, capitalist enterprises are rarely transforming themselves to other types of class structures, such as, for example, the communal class structure. Rather, capitalist enterprises are changing their form, each in their own distinct ways.

While multiple class changes like these are taking place, the effect of all this on the macro scene has been more focused. In this context, the government policies leading to the transition process of capitalist enterprises have been subjected to many criticisms. The principal criticism has been that the government action is leading toward a process of deindustrialization (Economic and Political Weekly Research Foundation 1994, 111–134). While the charge of deindustrialization following the NEP may seem to be an overestimation and premature in 1994, statistical figures do lend some credence to it with regard to some sectors, such as manufacturing and mining—overall, enough to cast serious doubt on the success of reforms in the industrial sector initiated over ten years ago.

Figures in Appendix Table 9 show that industrial production, which had been increasing at a rate of around 8 percent in the 1980s, fell below 7 percent in the decade after the liberalization policies were initiated. As Appendix Table 2 indicates, the drastic drop in the growth of capital goods and basic goods is of particular concern. To some extent, this sluggishness in the growth of industrial production can be attributed to the government's slow but sure detachment from the capital and basic goods production, and the structural adjustments associated with any reforms of this magnitude. However, ten years is a long time, and the private sector was supposed to have substituted the government by now, especially in light of the boom that drove world industries in the 1990s. Alas, the promise of a deluge in investment and high growth never materialized. Furthermore, the story looks grimmer if we discount the dramatic rise in the industrial growth rate in 1994–95 and 1995–96 where this growth rate was principally driven by the phenomenal rise in consumer goods production, especially consumer durables. Recent indications point to a return to the initial sluggishness of industrial growth, which is overdetermined by multiple reasons such as the saturation of pent-up (consumer) demand, world recession, and slow growth rate of world trade at the beginning of the new millennium, the bearish capital market, and political instability associated with the direction of reforms and in South Asia in general. By the reformers' own account, the success and failure of the NEP should be judged in terms of the industrial growth, since it is with regard to this sector that the NEP was initially conceived and its details laid down. By that very account, to say that the NEP in India is in a state of crisis is a serious understatement. NEP proponents often talk in terms of political impediments, blaming those for the failure to implement some of the policies. This defense, as and when made, is an excuse covering up for the policy maker's poverty of basic economic understanding. Even by mainstream standards, optimization is performed subject to constraints. To forget the obvious political constraints that guide any decision making in India and then blame the outcomes on the presence of those political constraints is an example of willful ignorance. A different way could be to change the political constraint itself in favor of reform but that again must lay down the mechanism of integrating the political into the very constitution of the NEP. That is, to create a hegemony in favor of the *idea* of the NEP. However, we are not surprised by this failure to grasp the mutual constitutivity effect of the political and economic, since it is a testimony to the methodological underpinning of working with autonomous and independent spaces—economic and political—with self-reflective and self-constituting knowledge emanating from those spaces.

Having discussed the overall scenario following the liberalization policies, let us now focus on the changes in and across the firms that are being propelled by the NEP. These changes are transforming the very face of India's development process in a qualitative manner than could simply be comprehended by unilaterally looking at the macro transformation of the industrial sector.

Some Far-Reaching Changes

In addition to the above-mentioned overall macro-level changes taking place, there is absolutely no doubt that the New Economic Policies (by changing the conditions of existence) are clearly leading to changes within a multitude of private capitalist class structures. Meeting the global challenge has meant a shift in the focus of private enterprises toward global competition. The goal of such enterprises now is to generate, sustain, and deepen the competitive advantage in their respective commodities. This has meant restructuring at the level of firms hitherto not attempted. Three important points need to be mentioned.

First, survival in the current context means that the new phenomena of global and not simply local demand should fundamentally guide the decisions and actions of any firm. Consequently, competition is also globally played out. Domestic and international rivalry over the market size (both domestic and international) as well as increasing buyers' demand for product differentiation means that technological innovation, new product turnover, and flexibility in adapting and changing the production and distribution system as well as their restructuring have to keep a frantic pace. Competition and pressure on per unit cost has led many firms to resort to outsourcing and piece-rate production while only producing or assembling the final products at their site (Harvey 1989, Porter 1998a, 1998b).[9] With such hyper-competition, changes within and across firms are becoming a dynamic and continuous process.

Second, all of the above-mentioned changes are having a seismic effect on the labor market. With the process of globalization and the advent of hyper-competition, the emphasis is no longer on a body of permanent workers each doing specialized activities in producing a final product (as was the case with Fordism) with a lifetime guarantee of employment, but on a differentiated workforce that is multiskilled, flexible, and disposable. The old employment contract based on what Jack Welch, the C.E.O. of General Electric, called "a paternal, feudal, fuzzy kind of loyalty" enabled the employers to pay less and demand loyalty in exchange for lifetime guarantee of employment. Amid the process of globalization with a different kind of demand on workers, the concept of the old employment contract is disappearing. As two foremost management scholars aver, "In such conditions, the old contract is not just nonviable; any effort to pretend otherwise is immoral" (S. Ghoshal and C. A. Bartlett, 1997, 284). Consequently, in many instances, we are witnessing not only the disintegration of the twentieth-century proletariat as we knew it, but also that of the meaning of the labor contract and labor process that underlies the mechanism of surplus labor performance and appropriation. This change is not being purposefully achieved by a conniving "capitalist class" but is the result of global competition and other complementary factors; and it must be located and (politically) faced at that level. No doubt, capitalists in India are today united in their call for the establishment of a fully flexible labor market so that they can hire and fire at will depending on the conditions imposed by competition. They retort that this action of cost-cutting is imperative for the firms' survival. The government's recent decision to repeal the old labor laws announced in the 2001 budgetary session of parliament testifies to the change that is currently under way in this direction. This is bound to have a profound effect within the fundamental class process of firms. Since already many firms have started operating within the context of the new form of employment contract even before it becomes legally effective, old forms of capitalist exploitation, and with them the class structures, are being transformed into new forms.

But this leaves some important questions unanswered: What happens to the people rendered unemployed? What happens to the conception of a surrogate social safety net that underlined the previous labor contract? These are not mere hypothetical questions but ones that are currently being played out with a vengeance in the transition process of the Indian social totality. Even though no data are currently available on this, and mainstream economic thinking would label such concerns as sociological and ignore them (as they are now doing), management scholars such as Ghosal and Bartlett (1997) and Ghosal, Bartlett, and Moran (1999), henceforth called GBM, have been incisive enough to see through this problem as one to be faced by the present-day firm as well.

Theirs can be reinterpreted as a postmodern approach to the conception of firm/enterprise where they, as in postmodern Marxism, though of course from a different standpoint, see enterprise not as an economic organization but as a social organization—not as private capital but as social capital. Thus firms do lots of things beyond simply maximizing profits as they are assumed to do in the neoclassical framework. In their scheme, firms that operate simply on a market basis, as individual and autonomous agents hunting only for profits, do not create any value but rather prevent others from creating value and hence are destructive of social welfare. The firms' vision in GBM's new framework is to maximize value for society and they go on to illustrate that companies—such as ABB, Motorola, GE—that are following this new philosophy oforganization have grown in recent times while others following the old philosophy have perished.

This new vision of enterprise as social organization calls for a new labor contract between the employee and employer that GBM says is the only way for industry to survive in the long run following globalization and the age of hyper-competition. Earlier we pointed out that globalization and the hyper-competition it has brought along has been seen by firms—including most Indian firms—as a pretext for increasing appropriation (and rate of exploitation) by simply downsizing and cutting labor cost. GBM contend that this obsession with operating efficiencies is bound to be self-destructive for any firm and represents a perverse pathological syndrome. This immoral view of labor completely glosses over the *need* aspect of employability (the necessary material and psychological conditions enabling a person to seek a job that in Third World countries, in the event of little social insurance, amounts to literally surviving by doing so), which is a social problem whose severity has become transparently acute in the present juncture. In the current scenario, if a worker—specialized in one activity as under the old contract—is fired, it becomes very difficult for that person to find a job; and in a country such as India with such high disguised and open unemployment, the effect is compounded. In this regard, as per GBM's vision, firms must take the (social) responsibility of continuous education and development of the workers (by creating their own universities, upgrading the knowledge and skill of workers, and allowing them freedom to innovate even if that may not be immediately beneficial to the firm, and so on) in order to enable workers to enhance their value to others. Thus, competition may compel a firm to fire a worker (that, too, as the last resort) but that worker because of the skill upgrade and flexibility that he has acquired in the previous firm is employable elsewhere. This way the firm can meet its social responsibility to fulfill the newly developing employable needs of people. Otherwise, cost-cutting by downsizing without creating the institution to meet the employable *needs* of workers will have disastrous social effects and ultimately lead to industrial extinction.[10]

We observed earlier that the Indian firms are caught in the grip of downsizing and cost-cutting syndrome, as if this represents the only form of survival and growing in the age ofglobalization and hyper-competition, and that too without any thought about the question of employability. As pointed out earlier, the Indian government seems to be agreeing and its labor reform package is a living testimony to this belief.[11] While the Indian government seems to be emphasizing the incentive and efficiency effects of labor market reforms, the need issue of employability is not even in the ambit of its picture.[12] This presents an attempt on the part of the NEP proponents to take the transition process into the pair {exploitative classes, unfair distribution} which is more intense than in previous times. From a Marxian point of view, this represents an important class and development loci of struggles, both converging in this case to be carried out within firms as well as at the more macro level. Movement to any other direction from this pair will be preferred, hence Marxists might have to ally with others including capitalists (such as those in the small-scale sector, as we will make clear in the next section) who understand the problem to fight the current NEP policy on this important issue.

Third, new geographical clusters are forming for specific industries depending on the advantages that a cluster throws up for a particular industry (Porter 1998a, 1998b).[13] Thus the information technology industry is clustering around the Bangalore-Hyderabad-Chennai belt along with smaller clusters in Kolkata and Delhi. An engineering cluster is forming in the Mumbai-Pune belt, a financial cluster exists in Mumbai, a leather and engineering clustering can be found in Chennai, and so on. Enterprises tend to concentrate on such clusters because there are positive externalities of a different kind emanating from a cluster that has great impact in lowering unit costs. Quicker disembodiment of knowledge from rival firms within the cluster along with the possibilities of sharing knowledge; ability to monitor the suppliers so that they keep up with the speed of supply as well as the high quality standard; easy accessibility to a specialized labor force for firms (since the labor force specialized in the product flocks to the cluster) thereby reducing the firm's search cost yet making it possible to maintain the highly skilled workforce; efficient and easy transportation system conducive to the product; business environment conducive to the growth of the industry; advantages from research and other institutes specializing in the product that tend to grow around the product belt; greater government attention to the problems (infrastructure, political or otherwise) of the product, since so many enterprises are concentrated on a particular area—all of these are important benefits emanating from the cluster. Firms that do not belong to the cluster, thereby missing the multiple positive externalities are disadvantaged by higher unit costs due to the above-mentioned factors and by the sluggishness in change and adaptability through innovations and learning by doing. In other words, subsumed conditions of existence for a specific product or service tend to be more fundamentally friendly under clusters than otherwise. Today because of the multiple changes following globalization and the NEP, India is witnessing a re-clustering of its industries as well as formation of new clusters, some of which we have already mentioned. New clusters are being formed around new products (for example, the so-called sunrise industries, such as information technology). Thus, new areas are becoming industrialized while some old ones are being re-clustered. These are all new growth belts in geographical terms. In other old belts, we are seeing the demise of the clusters and with it the process of de-industrialization in those areas. This has to do with the fact that the products dominating the clusters are becoming noncompetitive or the government is reducing or cutting altogether favorable conditions of existence provided so far for those products. This has been the case with steel and coal. The closure of coal mines and steel mills testifies to the demise of the industrial clusters in the areas around the Jamshedpur-Dhanbad-Asansol belt in Jharkhand and West Bengal. The major firms in this belt are government-owned (TISCO is an important exception) but supported by thousands of private firms producing ancillaries for the major firms. The government in line with its NEP is no longer willing to intervene to bail out the major firms and in fact is currently fast closing down some of them. The NEP, along with the process of globalization, are then producing not simply changes within and across class processes but are producing a shift in the geographical pattern of the process of industrialization via the dynamic formation of new clustering, re-clustering, and de-clustering. This implies a new geographical reorganization of the industrial map and that of the social totality of India.[14] This then adds further into the process of class differentiation as well as the unevenness of the class transition in India and its heterogeneous character.

As revealed earlier, the industrial growth rate in years following the initiation of the process of liberalization turned out to be moderate in comparison to the expected take-off rate. Some critics have pointed to the continued sluggish increase in output as stemming not only from the cutback in public sector investment, but also from the tepid response of the private sector to fill the gap; subsequently, they have expressed the fear of a retarded industrial sector. And with the current recession threatening to drag on for some time, the future is indeed a challenging one for proponents of the NEP. A lot will depend on whether the conditions of existence (demand creation in domestic and world market, relative terms of trade of Indian goods vis-à-vis the goods produced in foreign countries, international competitiveness of Indian firms, evolution of a vibrant capital market including reforms in the banking and insurance sectors, political stability, social stability, global demand for Indian products, etc.) that are supposed to drive the process of industrialization turn out to be conducive to creating a vibrant industrial sector or not. However, what is certain is that the New Economic Policies (by changing the conditions of existence) are clearly leading to immense changes within a multitude of private capitalist class structures. The clear changes in these class structures' conditions of existence are bound to produce changes in their form as well. A new set of heterogeneous private capitalist class processes in the industrial sector is emerging in India amid the process of transition in the industrial sector that is complex and uneven.

Transition and the Small-Scale Sector

The influence of government policies on small-scale industries has been especially far-reaching.[15] The small-scale industrial sector has played a critical role in the Indian economy. As of 1998–99, the total number of small-scale units in India was 31.21 lakhs; its value of production amounted to Rs 5,27,515 crores, which is roughly 40 percent of the value added in the manufacturing sector, contributing to 35 percent of the total exports in 1998–99; and by 1999–2000 this sector employed around 17.850 million people (Economic Survey 1999–2000, 2000–2001; also see Appendix Table 3).

The small-scale enterprise sector is a configuration of capitalist and noncapitalist class structures (notably independent and communist class structures). According to government figures, the Khadi and Village industries, where one would expect to find a large number of "traditional" noncapitalist enterprises, produce output worth 34,900 million rupees and employ around 5.55 million persons (Economic Survey 1994–95, 116). If one adds the noncapitalist enterprises in the urban sector, then the figure for "traditional" enterprises will be much higher.

While the government has avoided a comprehensive reform package for this sector, it has adopted policies that are aimed at bringing the products of the small-scale enterprises under the excise net, thereby broadening the government's tax base and reducing the tax differential between small- and large-scale units, and opening the market for some products that had traditionally belonged to the small-scale industries to brand name enterprises of the organized private sector. These new policies are intended to make the small-scale industries more competitive as well as to allow the big industries to make forays in the products hitherto dominated by small-scale firms. The government is also committed to providing technical, marketing, and credit support for small-scale industries without the current policy barring the large firms from entering. Along with, and resulting from, the changes in these conditions of existence, increased competition and possible gains from export are producing a transformation of the class structures of these small-scale enterprises.

The opposition to the NEP with regard to the small-scale sector has been directed to three fronts. First, it has been pointed out that the tax policies will reduce the competitive edge of small enterprise vis-à-vis the organized private sector. Second, the reduction in tariff and custom duties for imported inputs will reduce the cost of production of the organized private sector, thereby making it possible for the latter to out-compete the small enterprises. One of the two reasons alone, or both of them together, may lead to a demise of many small-scale industries such as what happened in case of the paint industry (Economic and Political Weekly Research Foundation 1994, 129). Third, because of the expansion of the tax base, many analysts fear a sharp increase in the incidence of corruption that, in India, can constitute a substantial amount of subsumed class payments.

However, it would be premature to comment about the fate of the small-scale firms in the long run if we realize that the reform policy with regard to these industries is still in a state of evolution. There is certainly no guarantee that the "traditional" class structures (mainly independent and communist) will disappear. It may very well be the case that they might adapt to the new situation and be able to successfully compete against the capitalist firms—both domestic and international. Thus, we might get a new configuration of class structures in the small-scale sector, probably less in numbers but much more resilient than the old configuration. If one surveys the growth rate of output, employment and exports of the small-scale sector then it becomes clear that an outcome of this sort cannot be ruled out. Average increase in output growth, employment growth, and export growth in the small scale industries from 1991–92 to 1999–2000 have been approximately 8 percent, 4 percent, and 21.7 percent, respectively, which has far outperformed any other sector in the Indian economy during the same period. Even though the present economic recession has dampened the growth in the small-scale sector (as it has for all sectors), the doomsday projection from skeptics, on this front at least, is still far from becoming true.

However, the impending danger to the existence of the small-scale sector following the reform policy of India government cannot be underestimated either. In this regard, we want to highlight in the ensuing discussion the political economy of the small-scale sector within the broader canvas of a desirable society as visualized by the NEP proponents in the domestic and global context.

Currently the government is in a bind as far as the small-scale sector is concerned. This is one area within the industrial sector on which the government has been unable to develop a clear policy. On the one hand, the realization is that the small-scale sector absorbs a vast pool of the employable population and hence serves as a surrogate social safety net. This means that the small-scale sector needs to be somewhat supported and some segment within it to be left out of the ambit of big capitalist encroachment. On the other hand, it is important to stress that the government's role vis-à-vis the small-scale sector is not an exception to create a dynamic capitalist society. Consequently, unlike the pre-NEP interventions in this sector, this time the government wants only successful small-scale units—those that can function without the qualification of any reservations—to survive. The rest should close down:

> There are two main issues in respect of sick SSIs. One is the existence of large number of sick units *which are non-viable* and the other is the *rehabilitation* of potentially viable units. (Economic Survey 2000–2001, 145)

> India is unique in adopting reservation as an instrument for promoting small-scale producers and the policy obviously entails efficiency losses and imposes costs on consumers. Several committees have recommended various degrees of dilution of the reservation policy. Most recently, an Expert Committee on Small Enterprises set up in 1995, has recommended that reservation should be completely abolished and efforts to support small-scale producers should focus instead on private incentives and support measures. (Ahluwalia, 1999, 45)

Furthermore, even when the government supports some of the small-scale industries, the clear preference of current policy makers for larger or "conventional" enterprises can be divulged from the following report on the leather industry:

> Small-scale units still dominate the production base of leather industry. The cottage sector, with its traditional rural artisans, dominates in leather tanning. The Indian leather industry is characterized by several inherent advantages. . . . However, further skill and capacity utilization is constrained to some extent by entry barriers against large scale units in major segments of the industry. (Economic Survey 1994–95, 115)

Or, as one of the policy makers of NEP in India, Montek Singh Ahluwalia (1999) observes:

> . . . a reconsideration of the reservation policy is urgently needed in areas such as garments, toys, shoes, and leather products. These are areas with large export potential but reservation prevents the development of domestic units of the size and technology level that can deliver the volume and quality needed for world markets. . . . It remains to be seen whether this modification will provide sufficient incentive to encourage producers to set up larger capacities to tap export markets. (Ahluwalia 1999, 45)

When the situation seems conducive (the current pretext, for example, is the compliance with the regulations of GATT/WTO calling for certain restrictions to be removed), the government is acquiescent to removing existing restrictions on certain products that debar large industries from entering (such as paints, air-conditioning, garments, toys, etc.), thereby making it difficult for small-scale industries to compete in the market for those products. Overall, with or without restrictions, the government seems inclined to create a competitive small-scale sector that will serve the dynamic capitalist sector (mainly as ancillaries serving the big sector). Yet, as mentioned earlier, the government also recognizes that the overall survival of this sector is also critical for a stable economy especially because of the enormous employment potential of this sector. Hence, despite its professed intention and belief, the government is not allowing the large capitalist enterprises (despite its so-called competitive edge) to enter into this sector en mass. When it does remove certain restrictions it only does so selectively.

We can structure the apparent contradiction (desire to create a dynamic small-scale sector but which at the same time is capable of absorbing huge employable population) emanating from the two extremities of government policy regarding the small-scale sector thus: *The Indian government will preserve the <u>conception</u> of protecting the small-scale sector but will remain flexible regarding the specific commodities it will protect in different time and space.* This amounts to a concession that capitalist class structures will not occupy every instance in the economy even though policy makers would like the noncapitalist units to provide certain specific—fixed—conditions of existence for capitalist ones.

The above interpretation can be illustrated further by exploring the labor market reform currently being put in place by the Indian government. According to the government:

> The contract labour law, as it exists today, makes it impossible for genuine [whatever that may mean—emphasis ours] small-scale entrepreneurs to provide services to industry. A Modern contract labour act should encourage outsourcing of services so that new employment is generated. (Economic Survey 2000–01, 29)

So the secret is out: first, the small-scale sector is to be trimmed to become mere ancillaries to the big capitalist firms, and second, the employability problem is to be taken care of by the small-scale enterprises. Thus, in the broader canvas of the NEP, the small-scale sector is to be a second-class citizen dancing at the dictates of the big capitalist firms and serving as the reservoir of left-out labor force.

In this context, another important question crops up. With the labor market becoming competitive and wages becoming cheaper in a Third

World country, what happens to the family? As a result of being thrown out of the organized sector or as new entrants, the labor force competing with one another will tend to drive down the wage because many small-scale enterprises are simply unable to pay high wages. One can see this trend unfolding in India. So while multinationals and organized domestic firms will continue to pay high wages, a new labor force fed on subhuman wages is being created in the small-scale sector, with official approval, as a fallout of the NEP.

But the NEP must also be seen in the context of the global economy. The global economy after all is an interdependent network of multinational capital, nation-based capital, and noncapital. In this context we ask: Does uniform labor standard (a focal point of furious debate within and outside WTO) mean uniformity at all levels? No—it concerns only labor engaged in multinationals and the big, nation-based capitalist sector and does not apply to labor in the noncapitalist sector or the need-based economy. The proper metaphor for such noncapitalist sectors and need-based sector is colony. Then, what is at issue here is a struggle (though certainly not the only one) between multinational capital and nation-based capital for rights over colonies—for rights over goods produced in noncapitalist and need-based sectors, produced at inhumanly low wages, all couched in honey-coated terms. But, what are subhuman wages? Wages below the value of labor-power. And the value of labor-power is the value of the socially determined subsistent basket necessary to reproduce the laborer and his/her family.

But the small-scale units—those who sell their products to consumers as subsidies, franchises, or outlets of multinationals/big national capitalist firms and supply multinationals/big national capitalist firms the inputs as ancillaries—in Third World countries pay wages to them that can barely sustain a single person. In a large segment of society, to have a family is increasingly becoming a distant dream. Or it—that is, having a family—can be a dream come true if both the partners work. But what about a child—what about the children? "What you get married for, if you don't want children," T. S. Eliot asked in his poem "The Waste Land." Bearing and rearing a child becomes a luxury, a substitute for other comforts for laywomen. Postcolonial (global) capital turns noncapital into its colony and its colony into a wasteland.

The transformation of the meaning of a living wage—from that of the value of the socially determined subsistent basket necessary to reproduce the laborer and his/her family as in Marx, to that of a reservation wage or the minimum basket of commodities required to sustain a single individual (the constraint condition for both firms and individuals in mainstream economics), signals, as we mentioned above, one of the most serious consequences of globalization, hyper-competition, and the NEP. Payment insufficient to reproduce the family (that is, below the value of labor power) was defined as cheating by Marx. For Marx the reason was simple but profound: development of the economy (and the society also) is a long-run process. It involves not simply the present reproduction of the laborer but that of a future workforce as well. How can civilization be sustained if investment is not made for the future reproduction of the labor force? Are we not forsaking future growth and human sustainability in favor of a very myopic idea of present profitability? Are we doing future generations justice by not making this investment? However, we will pretend that the above considerations are unimportant—for the network of the ruling regime comprised of multinationals, big national-based capitalist classes, international institutions (WTO/GATT, World Bank, IMF, etc.), and government. The superhuman families (with a very high level of income) and subhuman families (because they are beasts) will produce enough children for the consumption of capital. But what about the loss of satisfaction of the present individuals who are denied access to the joys of family life because they cannot afford to get married? What about the loss to the couple of not being in a position to bear and rear children because only one of them may be employed? What about the loss of values (sharing system, support system, love chain, friendship chain, etc.) embedded in the concept of family (we are not talking about family values but values of family—two very different things)? Bourgeoisie economists in recent times have emphasized the role of market failures as a reason for intervention either by government or some other third party. What happens if there is a failure at the societal level, at the level of community, at the level of reproduction of families, at the level of reproduction of future workforce? What are we going to do about this failure? Who will bear this cost and how will they bear it? Until now we have expected government to take up the role of a third party. Even Marxists have believed in it. But, as pointed out, government is complicit, is a party, to this process. Its future reproduction itself is tied to the goodwill of multinationals and big domestic capitalist firms. So let us not have any illusions about the "welfaristic" objective of government in the present juncture of history. The third party has to be something else—trade unions, religious/environmental organizations, and so on—or some combination of those who are opposed to attempts to impose this order and willing to take on the regime to demand redemption from this futuristic wasteland. It will mean new realignment of political forces, new ways of visualizing and thinking of developmental politics, and giving meaning to the process/practice of realignment.

The above analysis also makes a mockery of some so-called radical positions in the international arena, such as the one we witnessed in Seattle during the GATT/WTO conference in 1999. The key demand articulated there (and in other forums) is that every worker deserves protection of basic human rights—prohibitions against child labor, slave labor, discrimination, and the freedom to join together with others in a union. The WTO must incorporate rules to enforce workers' rights while environmental and consumer protections and compliance should be required of any new member. National and state laws and regulations concerning public health and the environment must be safe from global veto.

Surely the above suggests a move in the right direction. It will give the global economy a human face. But the slip lies in the surplus meanings of the above demand—in what it negates. One of the points articulated in that demand is to prohibit import of (trade in) goods produced in inhuman conditions, with inhuman conditions having their contextual meanings stated earlier, which means prohibiting trade with the small-scale sector. It is common in the United States and other developed countries to condemn the terrible working conditions in the small-scale sector in the Third World. People in the United States and other developed countries are asked to become enraged about this and boycott the purchase of goods produced in such conditions by small-scale units whose ultimate culmination is banning the goods altogether from entering the border.

But note that it only means banning trade with small-scale sector and not multinationals or organized domestic capitalist enterprise located in the Third World countries. As we described earlier, the latter produces with human wages in human conditions while the former with subhuman wages. But where would the small-scale sector and the people therein go? Far from disappearing, it will become ancillary or tied in some other inferior position to the multinationals/big domestic capitalist firms, and its people will move away from the sight of civilization and suffer severe deprivations. Thus the global dynamics (the complicity—knowingly or inadvertently—of many radicals and trade unions in this cannot be ruled out) and the NEP taking place in India are intertwined in creating new economic spaces and new meanings of those spaces. Radical politics should rethink its demand for a uniform labor standard and instead focus on the international configuration (upholding the concept of a capitalist class-based regime) that is trying to oversee as well as facilitate—by forming a set of rule and regulation—the process that has been let loose by globalization and hyper-competition. It is this process of creating a global architecture that also must become the bone of contention in international as well as domestic struggle.

The above possibility of opening a new frontier for struggle is particularly pertinent since there is an irony in the development story of India as set in motion by the NEP. The irony of the NEP seems to be that capitalist firms—the big ones—are struggling to maintain their dominance while the small firms, including the noncapitalist ones, are far from performing badly. Given that the economy, in our rendition, is decentered and heterogeneous with numerous types of classes, this does not surprise us at all. Earlier we did argue that the recent phase of globalization and liberalization is an opportunity for taking the reform process in a different direction. The stubborn resistance of the noncapitalist small-scale firms in the face of competition along with its employment potential could serve as a political tool to create a strategy of an alternative route to the transition of Indian economy. This is especially true in light of the current trend among many NEP proponents, as seen in the quote by Montek Singh Ahluwalia, to favor the big industries against the small ones and in efforts to turn the small-scale sector into a mere appendage to big capitalist firms. Marxists can turn this shift in policy outlook into a fight against the current rendition of the NEP itself by turning the struggle between the two pro- and anti-NEP camps into a class fight to retain, deepen, and expand certain types of noncapitalist class processes as well as other forms of capitalist class processes (since many small-scale units are capitalists as well), a possibility which we indicated earlier in our matrix for possible developmental politics. This is not to say that class struggles over performance and appropriation in big industries and their distribution and receipt elsewhere should not be carried out but rather, along with the above-mentioned, pitting the small-scale sector against the big capitalist firms could serve as a sharp instrument of engaging combatively against the conception of capitalism as propounded by the NEP proponents and their global partners. The overdetermined effect of such a domestic struggle on the international arena cannot be overestimated.

Transition and the State Capitalist Class Structure

The effect of the NEP on state enterprises has also been far-reaching. In most of the analysis of state enterprises, theorists have tended to call the pre-liberalization state enterprises "socialist enterprises." This naming follows from the traditional way of conceptualizing the difference between capitalist enterprise and state enterprise in terms of property. However, since we conceive class structures in terms of processes of the performance, appropriation, distribution, and receipt of surplus labor along with the conditions of existence of these class processes, our understanding of the state enterprises' class structure is fundamentally different. The pre-liberalization Indian state enterprises closely resemble what Resnick and

Wolff (1993, 94, 95, 2001) conceptualize as state capitalist enterprises. According to Resnick and Wolff,

> State capitalism means that persons within a state apparatus exploit labor in state institutions. State capitalism also has its varieties. . . . State capitalist enterprises may sell their products as commodities, thereby realizing surplus value and then distributing it so as to secure their continued existence; or their products may be administratively distributed with administered prices attached to them. State capitalist enterprises may exist within a predominately private capitalist system. A small minority of state capitalist enterprises may then have to compete with private enterprises in all markets. Alternatively, private capitalist enterprises may be marginalized or delegitimated altogether, leaving most or all production to occur through state capitalist enterprises. (Resnick and Wolff 1995, 212–213)

In the Soviet context (which is largely replicated in the Indian state enterprises), Resnick and Wolff explain that as in private capitalist class process, there too, the worker's labor power were acquired and consumed in return for a remuneration. And after that the surplus labor or its product equivalent was appropriated not by performers of surplus labor but by the Council of Ministers (COM). This surplus product then took the form of surplus value even though the formation of Soviet surplus value was not typically mediated through market. Unlike in the case of private capitalism where technology, resource availability, length and intensity of the working day, and so on, along with the specific conditions of *market* determined the surplus value, in the Soviet case all of the above-mentioned determinants *sans market* were complemented by the *state's method of assigning values* to labor power, resources, and other products in the formation of surplus value. Hence in the Soviet-type state enterprises, exploitation in the process of appropriation is produced with the usage of labor power and as in the case of private capitalist enterprise, the exploited surplus labor/product takes the form of surplus value in distribution via the subsumed class process. Soviet State enterprises are then capitalist even though their form is different from that of the private capitalist enterprises.

The pre-NEP as well as the currently existing Indian State enterprises closely resemble the Soviet State enterprises, though there are certain important differences. As in the case of Soviet enterprises, the surplus labor of workers is appropriated either by a board of directors appointed by the Indian Ministry or the Ministry directly. The big difference is that even before the adoption of the NEP the Indian state enterprises operated in a mixed economy where the market remained a major institution through which exchange was mediated. After the adoption of the NEP, the market has become the dominant institution even though nonmarket forms of exchange still are important especially with respect to state enterprises. Thus certain products of Indian state enterprises, such as the automobiles produced by Maruti Udyog are (and have always been) distributed through the market, while a large number of other state-produced products are not distributed through markets but, as Resnick and Wolff point out, through a set of administered prices. Thus, in the case of India, state enterprises remain capitalist with exploitative fundamental class processes and a complexity of distribution mechanism of surplus through market (as in the case of private capitalist) or nonmarket (as in case of Soviet capitalist) institutions—that is, a complex formation of surplus value through market or nonmarket entities but surplus value nevertheless.

Indian planners made a distinction between the sectors in which private enterprises would be allowed and those sectors in which state enterprises would be allowed. Roughly, private enterprises were given the realm of consumer goods while state enterprises to have sole control over the capital goods sector, raw materials, and the important services sector consisting of the organized banking system, telecom, airlines, railways, and insurance. Thus, the capitalist state sector had a virtual monopoly over its products and services.

The liberalization policies have targeted not only the aspects of these exclusive boundaries of entry and exit to particular industries but are also intent on changing the class structures of the state capitalist enterprises to private capitalist enterprises.

Most of the production and service units that have been previously closed to the private sector have now been opened to different degrees. For example, private enterprises are now being encouraged to invest in infrastructures like power, irrigation, and road construction, the extraction of minerals, oil, telecom, banking, heavy industries like iron and steel, airlines, and so on. Even though new private capitalist class structures are coming up in many such spheres of the economy, the market mechanism has broken down in the case of some capital goods sectors and especially the infrastructure sector. One can witness this phenomenon from the excess capacity in steel, cement, and engineering, while India is in desperately short supply of power, roads and ports, and irrigation canals. There is a point of view gaining currency among NEP proponents that increase in industrial growth depends crucially on the rational pricing of infrastructure products along with government coordination of private infrastructure investment that in turn are essential for industrial growth. On the one hand, they feel the need for the state to detach from pricing decisions in infrastructure products and let those be determined by cost considerations. But attempts to rationally price infrastructure products do not absolve the government from taking part in the economic activities in this regard, since infrastructure investments are huge and profits from those investments are realizable only in the event of other users consuming the product. Such projects require a commitment on the part of other users to use the product (often as an input in order to produce something else) before a private player can even contemplate investment of that magnitude for the specific infrastructure product. This poses the possibility that while there might be a demand for the product (which in turn means that possible projects at the other end may not be happening in the absence of the infrastructure project), it might not be immediately accomplished in the absence of coordination of different sectors. This implies that a third party such as the government should either coordinate the investments in different sectors, thereby increasing the size of the market of those sectors and making the investment feasible, or, when that is not forthcoming, it should take the responsibility on itself to produce the infrastructure commodities (Murphy, Shleifer, and Vishny 1989). While NEP proponents would probably grudgingly agree on the first point, the policy makers have closed their eyes to the latter possibility. By doing so, however, what they fail to acknowledge is that this type of government intervention is desirable because profits in the infrastructure projects do not capture the entire benefits from such projects that a direct or indirect government intervention make possible. The inability to see this point has slowed infrastructural investments in India since private players are not entertaining the idea of investing there for a host of reasons despite attempts to coordinate investment projects by the government. This has been especially revealing in the case of the power sector.

Much has been made of the reforms of the state electricity boards (SEB), which traditionally have controlled both the production and distribution of power. It has been claimed that due to "inefficiencies" and high user subsidies the SEB have run into huge losses. Deficit reduction as per the NEP requires that they be cut. Also, since the states draw power from Central Power Utilities, the loss-making SEBs have increasingly found it difficult to pay back the debt to the central power generation units, thereby throwing the central power system too into a state of crisis. Power reforms drawn by the Indian policy makers call for the unbundling of production and distribution. As per the proposed policy, distribution should definitely be privatized and, whenever possible, private investment in production of power encouraged. This reform has already started but the unfolding results could not be more discouraging. The disaster in the case of the power producer Enron—a multinational giant—operating in Dabhol, the state of Maharashtra, shows that the mechanisms of operating in an underdeveloped country may not be the same as in a developed country. Currently, there are simply no private players willing to invest in power generation and, given the fracas over Enron, it will be too optimistic to pin any hope on investment by multinational corporations (the most appropriate players for investment on such a large scale). If power is as critical as the policy makers make it out to be, shouldn't the government step in to invest to cover up for the market failure? The attempt to privatize distribution of power in the state of Orissa (seen as a test case for the rest of the states) has also ended in a tangle, which has led to a call by some of the private players there to shut down distribution and leave. The much-touted power-sector reform has indeed run into serious trouble in the process of taking off. The policy makers have concentrated on a specific supply side—the fundamental class processes in this context—forgetting that its conditions of existence—the subsumed class processes as well as other nonclass processes such as political risk—too cannot be ignored. The latter affects the fundamental classes, and any framing of a power policy must integrate the two in a coordinated manner. This coordination must not simply include the aspects of production and distribution of power but also those conditions of existence that constitute them.

Another interesting aspect of the liberalization policies is the government's response to what it perceives as a crisis situation in the state capitalist enterprises. This response took two forms. First, state capitalist enterprises are either being phased out or transformed into private capitalist enterprises through the actions of the Bureau of Industrial and Financial Reconstruction (BIFR). One of the tasks of the BIFR is to check the viability of loss-making enterprises including state enterprises and pass a judgment whether restructuring would or would not revive them.[16] If the answer is in the negative, then the government will call an auction to sell the state enterprise. If there are no bidders, then the enterprise will be liquidated. Otherwise, the right to the appropriation and distribution of surplus labor will pass from government hands to private hands. In other words, the state capitalist enterprises would be transformed into private capitalist enterprises.

Appendix Table 6 shows that, as a result of these policies, many enterprises are either being shut down or handed over to private capitalist enterprises. As is to be expected, this has become an extremely contentious political issue. That this is a sensitive issue can be gauged from Appendix Table 7, which shows that government has found it difficult to meet its target year after year.

Second, if the BIFR calls for a restructuring of the state enterprises, then the process of restructuring itself helps in the transition of the state capitalist enterprise from what it was before the restructuring to what it is now after the restructuring. The government's concern and that of the BIFR is to make the enterprises competitive in the domestic and global markets. This is especially crucial in light of the new industrial policies that have abolished these enterprises' monopoly power, thereby opening those previously forbidden product markets for domestic competition and, in light of the open-door trade policies, are increasingly opening these markets to foreign enterprises. The concern over efficiency and profits is producing a host of significant changes—both internal and external—in the ways in which the state capitalist class structures are reproduced. There are two ways in which the restructuring process of existing state capitalist class structures is proceeding. First, the government is restructuring the internal and external conditions of existence (changing the management structure, changing the labor process, changing the goal of the firm, closing its option of using a soft budget constraint, etc.) of unviable state enterprises on its own. The objective is to make the firm run on what is being called a commercial (profitable) basis. Second, in many state enterprises, including some profit-making ones, the equity is being disinvested to finance deficit reduction or shift the resources toward other uses in the social sector, such as primary education, infrastructure, and health. This produces the situation of joint appropriation even though it is only one party (the government or private unit) to whom the right of appropriation is typically delegated. If the government disinvestment of state enterprise equity is less that 50 percent, then the government is the dominant partner in the appropriation of the surplus value produced in the enterprise. In other words, in this case, while the ownership pattern (subsumed class process) is drastically changed, the right to appropriation remains predominantly with the government.[17] If the disinvestment leads to the private players being given dominance in the board of directors, then the right to appropriation passes predominantly into their hands. However, it is important to recognize that changes in ownership pattern and other changes (such as a bank's relationship with the state enterprises, the shift away from the "soft budget constraint" by the government that automatically ensured a state sector enterprise against closure whatever its state of profitability, etc.) are drastically changing the form of these capitalist fundamental class process and, consequently, the class structures of such enterprises. Again these changes have not been easy nor could all the changes the government wants to make happen actually occur because of fierce (class) opposition to them from both within and outside the enterprises. Currently, the government is thinking of ridding the BIFR totally and taking on the total power to take decisions regarding the future of capitalist state firms. In fact, with the disinvestment decisions regarding companies like IBP, Maruti Udyog, and so on, the government has effectively started the process.

There are three criticisms that could be directed at these government policies. First, the state capitalist enterprises have been treated as mere instruments of fiscal policy with the intention of generating more revenue for the government. As a result, the issue becomes not one of reforms of these enterprises but of budgetary concern, ownership, and rights of appropriation. One of the pioneers of Indian reforms confesses,

> Unlike privatization à la Margaret Thatcher, which was driven by the conviction that government control makes public sector units inherently less efficient and privatization therefore improves economic efficiency and is good for the consumers, the policy of disinvestment in India was initially motivated largely by the need to raise resources for the budget. (Ahluwalia 1999, 63)

Here any references to China, as are often made as following a similar pattern of reform with success, are misplaced, since China is following a case of reform of their state enterprises with the sole intention of making them competitive. Furthermore, such reforms are to be backed up by massive government expenditures on retraining of retrenched workers, jobs creating infrastructure projects, and other related activities even at the cost of increasing budget deficits—a very Keynesian solution indeed. Unlike the case of India, the principal concern of the Chinese government is solely growth and employment generation (to compensate in some ways for the fall in employment due to the shedding of the workforce in state enterprises) and not budgetary considerations or ownership patterns.

Second, the disinvestment of state enterprises of non-profitable units will make it very difficult for them to raise capital from the open market. The financial institutions and other investors might be reluctant to supply capital to such loss making enterprises that are shedding off their own holdings.

Our third criticism refers to the extent of corruption involved in dealings related to the transition of the state capitalist enterprise to the private capitalist enterprise. The Indian body politic has been rocked at different times by multiple scandals involving the selling of Public Sector Enterprises (PSE), such as the sale of the Bailadila mine located in the central Indian state of Madhya Pradesh to a private capitalist enterprise for a throwaway price, and a similar case with the sale of aluminum giant BALCO in the state of Chattisgarh, or the telecom scandal in which the then telecommunications minister was accused of receiving a colossal bribe for selling off part of the telecom industry to an unknown company from his home state of Himachal Pradesh. Such ways of selling off public properties, leading often to the transferring of the rights of appropriation to private hands, have created a national political storm.[18] This definitely calls for more transparency in the process dealing with disinvestment and sale of government assets that will have a pronounced effect on the types of fundamental class process.

Notwithstanding the above criticisms, the BJP-led government has made an all-out effort to increase the pace of the disinvestment effort, as can be gauged from the recent announcements in the union budget of 2000–2001 as well as several announcements thereafter. The government has closed down several firms that it owned, thereby making those fundamental class proceeses extinct while it is desperately trying to sell off the more attractive ones to the private players, completely or partly.

Even if the above-mentioned criticisms against the NEP are issues of concern, we should be careful in understanding the changes in the state enterprises as reflecting a transition from one form of exploitative (state) class process to another (private). In the erstwhile state units, those who produced the surplus were certainly not part of any appropriation that took place. In this regard, we find the left's persistent fight for the state enterprises to be problematic. The issue from a Marxian point of view is not the validity or invalidity of the state enterprises but the mechanics of exploitation underlying the particular way in which surplus is being performed, appropriated in a firm, and then distributed and received. The left's insistence on the state enterprises as reflections of socialist enlightenment has been disastrous for its political agenda. It has led to a dangerous political line that has done the radical agenda more harm than good.[19] We are not arguing that one should not fight for a particular state enterprise. There may be multiple reasons as to why one should want to uphold a specific state enterprise against its private transformation. For example, earlier we spelled out the reasons for the need of state investment in the power sector. Similarly, considerations of need may be invoked to support state enterprises. But it has to be contextual, specific to that particular scenario, for special reasons—all of which has to be clearly laid down. Doing this, however, does not amount to the overall Marxian defense of the conception of state enterprise (even in its exploitative form) as a desirable social arrangement in the economic space. In upholding a class-focused analysis of society and its transition, we clearly detach ourselves from such a conflation of state and exploitation and thus from the current left's radical agenda in this regard.

Conclusion

Liberalization policies are directly and indirectly affecting the class structures in the state enterprises, private enterprises (large and small scale), private agricultural farms, household sectors, and service sectors such as banking and insurance that provide critical conditions of existence for these enterprises and farms. They have set in motion a process of transition that is still in progress. Changes in each such specific sector and the overdetermined and contradictory relations between the different sectors are, through a social chain reaction, producing a dramatically changed social totality that is India. The almost "frozen" states of the economic, cultural, and the political are undergoing rapid changes in contemporary India. So, too, are the questions being asked in this era of rapid transformation of the Indian social totality. The hitherto-acceptable ideas of development, progress, the role of the government, the relation between the central government and the state government, the entire cultural milieu, the meaning of democracy, and so on, are in a state of acute transformation. In other words, the effects of the liberalization policies should not be accounted for by looking only at the immediate discernible effects it produces on efficiency and growth but also by the qualitative effects they create among others, in terms of the changed forms of exploitation and need in various sectors of society. The liberalization program is, perhaps unwittingly, opening a space for debate and reconsideration of various aspects of development and transition.

CHAPTER 10

A Conclusion by Way of Opening Up "Other" Spaces

In this book we challenge the thematic of essentialism and historicism underlying the Indian Marxist debates on transition and development and put in its place an alternative class-based concept of transition and development using the thematics of anti-essentialism and antihistoricism encapsulated by the concept of overdetermination. This reconceptualization not only creates new grounds for reviewing the concepts of class, social totality, and primitive capital accumulation but also lays the groundwork for analyzing specific concrete processes of transition and development such as the one discussed in the Indian context. By describing a landscape of alternative developmental practices, it also opens up multiple possibilities of seeking a superior outcome than the ones being currently offered in either the mainstream or the more orthodox radical approaches.

This work is not an attempt to close further discussion of the concept of transition and development. From Derrida, we now know that such a closure is not possible. Writing leads to more writing and to more writing. Our work, like all writing that attempts some form of closure, is full of gaps, absences, and signs of (hidden and sometimes not so hidden) disruption running through the contours of our presentation. Some of these we highlighted in the course of our discussion.

There are certain further implications flowing from our work that we would like to point out:

(i) In the previous chapter, we discussed a broad picture of the unfolding process of transition in India against the background of the liberalization policies undertaken by the Indian government. This class-based description of the transition process needs to be broadened to include a more detailed sector-by-sector analysis of the Indian economy in order to precisely pinpoint the nature of the micro-focused process of transition within each class structure and its articulated effects on the social totality. There is a special need to analyze the economic sector of the household in more detail, something that has been completely glossed over in the Indian debates on Marxism. This micro-focused analysis needs a collective effort. One is reminded of the efforts of the subaltern studies group, which put forth a collective research agenda to make its project a serious undertaking.

(ii) We did create the ground to analyze the political aspect of reform via the concept of hegemony. More concrete results on this awaits further research, though we find the work of Chaudhury (1988, 1994), Chaudhury, Das, and Chakrabarti (2000), and Chakrabarti and Roy Chaudhury (1999/2000), with their concepts of mimicry of overdetermination and synthetic hegemony, particularly useful in contextualizing hegemony, especially in a Third World context, as is found in India. One needs to articulate further the theoretical relationship between development as progress and hegemony. We have discussed the importance of the relationship between primitive accumulation (as well as violence/coercion) and hegemony. The concern of development as progress and its relationship with hegemony and primitive accumulation could be further expanded to enrich our story of the transition of an underdeveloped society such as the Indian one.

(iii) In discussing the issue of social surplus meeting the needs of the people in the chapter on development, the following question was left unanswered: What is the mechanism of extracting this social surplus to satisfy the needs of the people? There is no doubt that the political struggle (violent and nonviolent) to achieve CC and AC with its imbedded ingredient of the spirit of sharing will go a long way toward educating the people regarding the virtue of sharing the surplus at the social level. This could be supplemented by a voting system as the appropriate mechanism in achieving this goal. Chaudhury (2001) perceptively observes,

> If the laws of the market act against of the need economy, counteract that through the operation of the voting system. For the need economy constitutes the overwhelmingly majority in countries like India and therefore can exert political pressure on the state power to tax the surplus economy for provision of funds to finance public expenditure in the need economy. (198)[1]

Democracy is defensible from a Marxist perspective not simply in terms of ethics but as an operational device to ensure the reproduction of the functional spaces of need. Political engagement in a democratic form is one way to extend the milieu of need. It is the instrument of politics of the *world of the third*—the uncanny gaze of need on the world of the surplus.

Reason (surplus) always contains its implicit other—Unreason—(need economy). Pushing Reason to the boundary, we witness unreason: Unreason, in the Lacanian sense, is the small "other" that talks in the language (production, distribution, and consumption) of the "big other." Consequently, the need economy is simultaneously the "other" of surplus/class economy as well as its difference while gender, caste, and so on, are only differences and not others (as is often mistakenly referred to) because they do not register in the same language as surplus. In this context, the need-based economy particularly gives radical democracy a cutting edge over the one propounded by Laclau-Mouffe and their post-Marxist school of thought (Laclau 1990, 1994). They define and understand radical democracy within the context of a totality (Reason). They connect the points of Reason into a singular locus to form either a hegemonic formation or radical democracy as a contestation of that in terms of its differences. We are not denying the importance of this idea of democracy. But we also understand radical democracy to be one dealing with the "other" of any totality. That is, for example here, we additionally understand radical democracy to be politics capturing the encounter of the world of surplus (the totality) with its other—the world of the third/need-based/third space. Specifically, it refers to the mutation of the surplus-based society resulting from the gaze of the world of the third/need-based/third space. This is what gives this democratic engagement its radical content. Radical democracy, in this form, is Marxian politics facing up to the question of development. The contradiction of this Marxian politics is that it may turn against itself—that is, against the nonexploitative class processes. But this may not be undesirable from a Marxian standpoint because this type of transition may lead us to the second existence of expanded communism—the classless arrangement of society.

It is obvious that much more needs to be done to make this idea concrete, and further developments on this could take matters in directions that we have not even contemplated.

(iv) The idea of economically "backward nations" in terms of the development of productive forces—this economistic argument—has been criticized by many postmodernist/poststructuralist theorists, antimodernists, and antidevelopment theorists. Figures such as Mahatma Gandhi, Jayaprakash Narayan, Ashis Nandy, and Vanadana Shiva in the East to Lévi-Strauss, Arturo Escobar, and Stephen Marglin in the West immediately come to mind. The arguments against development policies, those that identify development with increases in the level of productive forces, are often couched in cultural terms. A common criticism is that the development policies are Eurocentric and have had disastrous consequences for the lives of ordinary people in "backward nations." They argue that by decontextualizing and universalizing the social space, the idea of development as progress has been partly responsible for destroying the environment of these countries, displacing people, and turning their traditional life upside down. Many of the aspects that orthodox Marxism considered to be "backward" are now looked at from a positive angle by these antidevelopmentalist theoreticians. Behind such viewpoints lies an inversion of the meaning of "traditional" life. Many of these theorists now see traditional life in a good light and consider it to be either as good as or more civilized than its European counterpart. An example of this inversion is the now famous work of *Tristes Tropiques* by the French anthropologist Lévi-Strauss (1974), in which he celebrates the virtues of the East and decries the West's pride in progress and civility. Progress and Western virtues have only brought sorrow to the East according to Lévi-Strauss and, consequently, it is time for the West to show its remorse. He writes, "if the West has produced anthropologists it is because it was so tormented by remorse" (quoted in Derrida 1976, 337). In a well-known reply, Derrida (1976) criticizes this ethnocentrism as a new device used to constitute the West as a negative of the East that is now rendered pious and good. Derrida argues that the consequence of such an ethnocentric position is an obliteration of the contradictions and divisions within these so-called "good-natured" societies. In contrast, Baudrillard goes to another extreme by announcing that "the countries of the Third World will never internalize the values of democracy and technological progress" (Baudrillard 1989, 78). The West and the East can and will never meet. In this work we have pointed out how Indian Marxists in the subaltern studies school unearthed documents that not only revealed the influence of the West on the East but also brought to light the process through which the values of democracy and technological progress became critical elements in the constitution of modern Indian "nationhood." Further discussion of the NEP also revealed the same. The above statement by Baudrillard reveals a symptomatic postmodernist and poststructuralist ignorance of the Third World, whose likely logical culmination is an occlusion of the Third World as a discursive object of analysis. Sanyal (1995) summarizes well the moral implications of such occlusions of the Third World from postmodernist and poststructuralist discourses on the part of Western intellectuals: sanctioned ignorance (Third Worldism is not our cup of tea, after all) and benign indifference (Who are we to talk about their problems?). Perhaps we can add another to the list: Third World arrogance (Who are you to talk about our problems?). Such moral posturing serves only to freeze any discourse that strives to bypass the boundary of regionalism. It shuts out the West from the East and the East from the West.[2]

This is not to deny that the idea of "backwardness," deriving from a Eurocentric tunnel vision of viewing peripheral countries, has not taken its social toll in terms of the destruction of traditional lifestyles, environment, and other institutions like traditional medicine or village councils. However, simply replacing this tunnel vision with another, one that glorifies the traditional moral boundaries of the village, and thereby effaces the differences in terms of relations of exploitation, need, and power within such societies, is no solution. The problem then boils down to theoretically constructing a social space that is uncontaminated by such tunnel visions.

This social construction of the space of "Third World" or "underdeveloped countries" or "East" is now being debated intensely under the rubric of "postcolonial" theories. However, postcolonial studies are seriously afflicted by the drawback of currently being restricted to the realm of culture. The space of the economic has rarely been touched by this literature, and when it did so it was the essentialist rendition of the economic that was accounted for. This is an enormous gap that needs to be filled, especially against the background of the present situation of the deepening process of globalization. If, as we have argued, the terms "Third World" or "underdeveloped countries" are unhinged from their intrinsic inscription in the concept of progress as visualized by orthodox Marxism, then these terms as used in Marxist development theories become vacuous. Can one then reconceptualize "Third World" or "underdevelopment" from an over-determinist perspective? We have made some headway in constructing a concept of developmental progress within the Marxist paradigm but the answer to the question of distinguishing underdevelopment/Third World from development/First World within this paradigm still remains elusive. It seems to us that this is an important question that needs to be faced by Indian Marxists and Marxists in general. Let us paraphrase our query in the following way: Using an alternative class theory of transition and development, can one produce a social space of Third World countries whose construction does not necessarily entail any prior moral views on backwardness, for or against? This is not to say that there cannot be any moral position on the space that is being produced. However, any such judgment must complement and flow from the construction of this social space.[3]

(v) A major element missing from our work is a comprehensive analysis of the effects of international capital and finance on the transition of class structures, elements that are increasingly becoming interwoven in the presently unfolding scenario of the globalization process. What does the penetration of international capital do to a country's class structure? In what ways does it change the combined and uneven existence of class structures? In a similar vein, since financial structures form one of the conditions of existence of the fundamental class processes, in what way are any changes in the financial structures (as is apparently taking place in India due to the liberalization policies) likely to affect the class structure in question? These are critical questions for a class analysis of transition, since the process of globalization, driven by the twin elements of international capital mobility and changing financial structures (two crucial aspects of subsumed class processes), is bound to produce enormous change in the prevailing class structures. These changes in the class structures, then, are going to affect other aspects in society such as the distribution of income, gender relations, poverty, and unemployment.

While the above research agenda is by no means exhaustive, it does show the different openings that flow from our work. Even if our work has generated as many questions as answers, we consider the production of such questions to be a small but meaningful contribution to the debate on transition and development within Marxism, especially in the Indian context.

Appendix of Tables

Table 1 Gross Domestic Savings (as Percentage of GDP)

Year	Household Sector	Total
1981–82	12.6	18.6
1989–90	17.9	22.0
1990–91	19.3	23.1
1991–92	17.0	22.0
1992–93	17.5	21.8
1993–94	18.4	22.5
1994–95	19.7	24.8
1995–96	18.1	25.1
1996–97	17.0	23.2
1997–98	17.8	23.5
1998–99	19.1	22.0
1999–2000*	19.8	22.3

* Quick Estimates

Source: Economic Survey 2000–2001, Government of India, Ministry of Finance, Economic Division

Table 2 Growth Rates of Industrial Production by Use-Based Classification

Sectors	Weight (Base 1993–94 = 100)	Avg. Annual Growth Rate (1980–81 to 1991–92)	Avg. Annual Growth Rate (1992–93 to 1999–2000)
Basic Goods	35.6	7.4	6.1
Capital Goods	9.3	9.4	5.9
Intermediate Goods	26.5	4.9	9.1
Consumer Goods	28.7	6.0	6.3
(i) Consumer Durables	5.4	10.8	11.2
(ii) Consumer Nondurables	23.3	5.3	5.1

Source: Economic Survey 2000–2001, Government of India, Ministry of Finance, Economic Division

Table 3 Estimates of Female Employment in Organized Public and Private Sectors (Million Persons)

Year	Female Employment in Public and Private Sectors	Total Employment
1990	3.644	26.353
1991	3.781	26.733
1992	3.908	27.056
1993	4.026	27.218
1994	4.154	27.375
1995	4.228	27.525
1996	4.426	27.941
1997	4.637	28.245
1998	4.774	28.166
1999	4.829	28.113

Source: Economic Survey 2000–01, Government of India, Ministry of Finance, Economic Division

Table 4 Percentage Share of Public Sector in GDP, Saving, Capital Formation and Final, Consumption Expenditure from 1980–81 to 1985–86 (at Current Prices)

	1980–81	**1981–82**	**1982–83**	**1983–84**	**1984–85**	**1985–86**
Gross Domestic Product	19.8	20.9	22.8	22.6	23.8	24.9
Gross Domestic Saving	16.2	21.5	22.6	16.5	14.7	14.1
Gross Domestic Capital Formation	42.5	42.5	48.6	45.1	48.3	44.8
Final Consumption Expenditure	11.7	11.9	12.7	12.7	13.2	14.4

Source: CSO: New Series on National Statistics with 1980–81 as Base Year, New Delhi, Department of Statistics, Ministry of Planning, Government of India, February 1988, Statement 20

Table 5 Estimates of Employment in Organized Public, Private Sectors, and Small-Scale Industries (Million persons as on March 31, 1999)

Year	**Public Sector**	**Private Sector**	**Small-Scale Industries**
1990	18.772	7.582	
1991	19.057 (1.52)	7.676 (2.21)	12.980 (3.6)
1992	19.210 (.80)	7.846 (2.21)	13.406 (3.3)
1993	19.326 (.60)	7.851 (.06)	13.938 (4.0)
1994	19.445 (.62)	7.930 (.01)	14.656 (5.2)
1995	19.466 (.11)	8.059 (1.63)	15.261 (4.1)
1996	19.429 (−.19)	8.512 (5.62)	16.000 (4.8)
1997	19.559 (.67)	8.686 (2.04)	16.720 (4.5)
1998	19.418 (−.09)	8.748 (1.72)	17.159 (2.6)
1999	19.415 (.00)	8.698 (.11)	17.850 (4.0)

Source: Economic Survey 2000–01, Government of India, Ministry of Finance, Economic Division.

Table 6 Status of Public Sector Unit Cases Referred to BIFR as on Dec. 31, 2000

	Central Government	State Government	Total
References registered	90	161	251
References Registered Disposals	74	101	175
Dismissed as Not Maintainable	5	26	31
Revival Scheme Sanctioned	20	25	45
Declared No Longer Sick	3	5	8
Winding Up Recommended to the Concerned High Court	13	22	35
Stayed by Courts	1	2	3

Source: Economic Survey 2000–01, Government of India, Ministry of Finance, Economic Division.

Table 7 Disinvestment in Public Sector Undertakings

Year	Target (Rs crore)	Achievement (Rs crore)
1991–92	2500	3038
1992–93	2500	1913
1993–94	3500	Nil
1994–95	4000	4843
1995–96	7000	362
1996–97	5000	380
1997–98	4800	902
1998–99	5000	5371
1999–2000	10000	1829

Source: Economic Survey 2000–01, Government of India, Ministry of Finance, Economic Division

Table 8 Central Government Deficit (Percent of GDP)

	Primary Deficit	Revenue Deficit	Gross Fiscal Deficit
1975–76	0.5	1.1	4.1
1984–85	1.6	1.8	7.5
Average Sixth Plan	1.2	1.1	6.3
1985–86	2.0	2.2	8.3
1986–87	2.8	2.7	9.0
1989–90	2.3	2.6	7.8
Average Seventh Plan	2.1	2.6	8.2
1990–91	2.8	3.3	6.6
1991–92	0.7	2.5	4.7
1992–93	0.6	2.5	4.8
1993–94	2.2	3.8	6.4
1994–95	0.4	3.1	4.7
1995–96	0.0	2.5	4.2
1996–97	−0.2	2.4	4.1
1997–98	0.5	3.1	4.8
1998–99	0.7	3.9	5.1
1999–2000*	0.8	3.5	5.5
2000–2001(BE)	0.5	3.6	5.1

The budget deficit is the difference between total receipts and total expenditure, both revenue and capital. The revenue deficit denotes the difference between revenue receipts and revenue expenditure. The fiscal deficit is the difference between revenue receipts plus certain nondebt capital receipts and the total expenditure including loans, net of repayments.

* = Provisional and BE = Budget Estimates.

Source: Economic Survey 2000–01, Government of India, Ministry of Finance, Economic Division

Table 9

Item	2000–01P	1999–2000P	1998–99	1997–98	1996–97	Average	
						1992–93 to 1999–2000 (8 years)	1980–81 to 1989–90 (10 years)
1. Real GDP (% change)	5.2 (R.E.)	6.4 (Q.E.)	6.6P	4.8	7.8	6.4	5.8
2. Industrial Production (% change) #	5.1	6.7	4.1	6.6	6.1	6.6 &	7.8 $
3. Agricultural Production (% change) @	–6.5	–0.7	7.9	–5.7	9.3	2.6	5.2
4. Gross Domestic Saving Rate (% of GDP)	..	22.3	22.0	23.5	23.2	23.1	19.4
5. Gross Domestic Investment Rate (% of GDP)	..	23.3	23.0	25.0	24.5	24.4	21.2
6. Wholesale Price Index (% change) ##							
a) Point-to-Point	4.9	6.5	5.3	4.5	5.4	7.6	7.5
b) Average	7.2	3.3	5.9	4.4	4.6	7.2	8.0
7. Consumer Price Index—Industrial Workers (% change)							
a) Point-to-Point	2.5	4.8	8.9	8.3	10.0	8.3	8.9
b) Average	3.8	3.4	13.1	6.8	9.4	8.8	9.1

P, Provisional; .., Not available; *, As at the end of the period; $, Average 1981–82 to 1989–90 (9 years); &, Average 1992–93 to 2000–01 (9 years); #, Base: 1993–94 =100 for individual years, 1980–81=100 as also 1993–94=100 for 8-year average and 1970=100 as also 1980–81=100 for 10-year average; B.E., Budget Estimates; R.E., Revised Estimates; E, Estimated; Q.E., Quick Estimates; @, Base: Triennium ending 1980–81 = 100. Index of agricultural production is based on the latest production estimates (including the latest production figures of tea, coffee and other crops); ##, The base year for the WPI series has been revised from 1981–82 to 1993–94 from 1994–95 onward.

Source: Reserve Bank of India, Annual Report 2000–01

For the Year July 1, 2000 to June 30, 2001

Notes

Chapter 1
Redrawing the Boundary of Transition and Development in India

1. "Khadi" means indigenous cloth. It is a symbol for a cottage-based economic system that is characterized by labor-intensive, village- (and family-) based production and marketing processes.
2. Ranajit Guha and Partha Chatterjee are arguably the two foremost leaders of the subaltern studies group.
3. More precisely, passive revolution of capital can be understood as the process of creating a hegemonic rule of capital over precapital such that capital accumulation can proceed relatively freely without any substantive opposition from elements of precapitalism. The details will be worked out in chapter 5.
4. Metaphysics is a branch of philosophy that concerns itself with the analysis of the nature, production, and structure of being or reality. This is such a vast field that often metaphysics is identified with philosophy itself. According to Butchavarov in *The Cambridge Dictionary of Philosophy*, "perhaps the most familiar question in metaphysics is whether there are only material entities—materialism—or only mental entities, i.e., mind and their states—idealism—or both—dualism" (1995, 489). This aspect of the conceptual presence of hierarchical order and the structure of causality that follows from it is our concern in this chapter and we will return to it in detail later on. There we will show why and how this hierarchical structure in metaphysics might lead to essentialism.
5. What is disturbing, however, is the absence on the part of subaltern studies of any concerted and systematic effort in dismantling the essentialist structure of Western metaphysics in the Indian modes of production debate.

6. The common underlying theme in these theories of transition is their understanding of transition as signifying a movement of society from a "backward" stage to a more "advanced" stage. This theme of progressive evolution of society has been the crux of the Indian Marxian development theories. As we shall explain here and in the next four chapters, the problem of essentialism has a lot to do with the received notions of progress.

7. In these orthodox theories, development of society is associated with its transition in certain historicist directions. Consequently, transition in these theories automatically implies development as progress. This conflation of transition and development means that, for these theories, studying the transition dynamics is as good as negotiating the dynamics of development.

8. The process of rational ordered progression of society moving from a pre-ordained origin toward a teleological ending is what we mean by "historicism" or "historicity." As we shall explain later, historical materialism and the concepts that make up its structure are clearly grounded in the idea of historicism or historicity. It is important to realize that historicism is a trait not specific to the Marxist theories of history but one that is shared by both the non-Marxist and Marxist theories of history.

9. Postmodern Marxist theory refers to a theoretical framework that, using the epistemological concept of overdetermination, analyzes society from a class perspective. Following Althusser, Stephen Resnick and Richard Wolff could claim to be the pioneers of this relatively new Marxian school of thought. We use this term frequently throughout the book in order to distinguish our surplus labor (class) focused and overdeterminist approach to Marxism from other types of Marxist theories.

10. Mahatma Gandhi's reply to the calumny of "incivility" was that "it is a charge against India that her people are so uncivilized, ignorant and stolid, that it is not possible to induce them to adopt any changes. It is a charge really against our merit. What we have tested and found true on the anvil of experience, we dare not change" (Gandhi 1958–, vol. 10, 36).

11. This idea of progress looks rationally at the past from the present (along with some of its fallouts), as is eloquently captured in the following passage by Walter Benjamin,

> This is how one pictures the angel of history. His face is turned toward the past. Where we perceive a chain of events, he sees a single catastrophe which keeps piling wreckage upon wreckage and hurls it in front of his feet. The angel would like to stay, awaken the dead, and make whole what has been smashed. But a storm is blowing from Paradise; it has got caught in his wings with such violence that the angel can no longer close them. This storm irresistibly propels him into the future to which his back is turned, while the pile of debris before him grows skyward. This storm is what we call progress. (Benjamin 1973, 259–60)

12. This is best exemplified by the attitude of the post–Second World War United Nations and leaders of the West, such as the United States's President Truman. The United Nations, "Department of Social and Economic Affairs," had the following message for the underdeveloped countries,

> There is a sense in which rapid economic progress is impossible without painful adjustments. Ancient philosophies have to be scrapped; old social institutions have to disintegrate; bonds of caste, creed and race have to burst; and large numbers of persons who cannot keep up with progress have to have their expectations of a comfortable life frustrated. Very few communities are willing to pay the full price of economic progress. (UN, Measures for the Economic Development of Underdeveloped Countries, 1951)

What is that economic progress and how can it be made a reality? Truman summed it up well when he said,

> More than half the people of the world are living in conditions approaching misery. Their food is inadequate, they are victims of disease. Their economic life is *primitive and stagnant*. Their poverty is a handicap and a threat both to them and to more prosperous areas. For the first time in history humanity possesses the knowledge and the skill to relieve the suffering of these people. . . . I believe that we should make available to peace-loving peoples the benefits of our store of *technical knowledge* in order to help them realize their aspirations for better life. . . . What we envisage is a program of development based on the concepts of democratic fair dealing. . . . *Greater production* is the key to prosperity and peace. And the *key to greater production is a wider and more vigorous application of modern scientific and technical knowledge.* (Truman [1949] 1964)

The sentiments expressed in these two quotations would dominate development policies in many underdeveloped countries for decades. The race between the Soviet Union–supported countries and the U.S.–supported countries became one of matching each other's level of technological growth, industrialization, and wealth criteria. While the two differed on means of implementation, the objectives were not vastly different.

13. We will refer to participants in the Indian mode of production debate as traditional or orthodox Marxists. This name is justified since they followed the Second International version of historical materialism.

14. Let us define forces of production and relations of production. The forces of production reflect human beings' encounter with nature in the production process. The forces of production include instruments of production, raw materials, labor power, the skills in the labor force, technology, and so forth. Labor power is devoid of any specific social content. What is emphasized is the material aspects of labor power (skill, knowledge, etc.) which enabled one to work with the in-

struments of production and raw materials. The degree of technological development provides an index of the degree of development of the forces of production. They are often used interchangeably. In the model of historical materialism, technological development (forces of production) is assumed to be exogenously given and developing progressively over time.

If forces of production emphasize the material aspect, then relations of production emphasize (social) relations between people in the production process. More particularly, social relations of production take a specific form, that of class relations. Relations of production refer to the class relations between the direct producers and the nonproducers. Marx defined class relations in terms of the performance, appropriation, and distribution of surplus labor. Class relations take an exploitative form when nonproducer appropriates the surplus (or surplus labor) from direct producers. More often, such class relations are reduced to either property relations or power relations or a combination of both. For example, Cohen (1978) defines relations of production as relations of economic power that people enjoy or lack over labor power and the means of production, that is, control over the labor process. Different relations of production can be distinguished by the fact that the direct producer may have no economic power, some economic power, or total economic power over his/her own labor power and means of production. Under this definition, the economic power and class relations are derived from the ownership criteria. Thus, the capitalist class is defined as the class that enjoys more power at the level of production, thereby controlling the labor process; this power in turn is derived from the differential ownership of property. In contrast, the postmodern Marxist theory is distinguished by the aspect of the irreducibility of class (processes related to performance, appropriation, distribution, and receipt of surplus labor) to property or power. We shall come back to this later.

15. Hegel divides real history, constituting the subject(world spirit or Reason)-object (nature) duality, into three stages:
    (a) Undifferentiated unity (when man and nature are indistinguishable but man does not know nature);
    (b) Differentiated disunity (when man realizes he is different from nature but cannot conquer it);
    (c) Differentiated unity (when man knows he is different from nature and understands nature completely).

    If world spirit is the essence of history then its negative or appearance is nature. History moves from one stage to another through the mechanism of dialectics. Starting from undifferentiated unity (affirmation), history moves to negate it by differentiated disunity that in turn is negated by differentiated unity. Thus, the law of motion (dialectics) is driven by the Hegelian triad of affirmation-negation—negation of negation. Within each period the world spirit confronts its contradictory other—nature—only to move on to a new higher stage where the contradiction takes a higher form. Each subsequent stage gives a higher understanding of world spirit. This auto-development of world spirit goes on until it attains its true self where it overcomes its contradiction. Here the distinction between essence and appearance no longer holds. Society can see and understand the essence without any mediation from the phenomena. This state of absolute ideal was seen by Hegel as realized in the Prussian state (see Cohen 1978 and Cullenberg 1994 for details).

16. In this literature, the subject is considered to be the same as the ideal while the object is used interchangeably with the material. Thus Hegel's framework is grounded on idealism and that of Marx on materialism.

17. The concepts of dialectic and contradiction in historical materialism are directly appropriated from Hegel. The Hegelian *dialectic* is constituted by a triad-affirmation (of essence), negation (of essence), and negation of negation (of essence). The dialectic from the very beginning to the end is the development of the same essence that represents itself from the lower to higher moments via the alienation of the original simple totality. This simple totality that is driving the complex totality develops by alienating (negating) itself to represent an ever-increasing complex totality. Thus essence always has its negative within itself. This is what we call *contradiction*.

    As one can see, this contradiction is simple, defined as the negativity of the essence. The contradiction does not lead to the destruction of the totality but rather to its supersession. This supersession epitomizes the development of the original simple totality to a new higher form. Each complex totality (affirmation) is contradictory, meaning that it contains within itself the seeds of dissolution (negation) leading to the creation of a more complex totality and also the seeds of the dissolution of that totality as well (negation of negation). The contradictory aspect is captured by the negation of essence. The Hegelian dialectic is law-like and natural. This auto-development of simple original totality, as Althusser (1969) calls it, represented in each successive stage as an ever-increasing complex totality, is the core of Hegelian dialectics.

18. See Cohen (1978, 1983) for a detailed explanation on the aspect of correspondence between different structures of the model. According to Cohen, correspondence between the different structures could be consistently explained by functional explanation. The explanation we have put forward is a functional explanation à la Cohen, though we did not use the term. Readers interested in the details of functional explanation should consult Cohen (1978, 1988).

19. By qualitatively *higher* complex totality, Hegel meant that the essence (the simple totality driving the more complex totality) is closer to its self-realization in this stage of history as compared to the previous one.

20. Communism is the telos because, under communism, scarcity is replaced by abundance and class exploitation disappears. Humanity attains freedom when the essence comes to realize its true self, which is communism. As Cohen forcefully makes the point, "Marxism sees history as a protracted process of liberation—from the scarcity imposed on humanity by nature, and from the oppression imposed by some people on others. Members of the ruling and subject classes share the cost of natural scarcity unequally, and Marxism predicts,

and fights for, the disappearance of society's perennial class division" (1988, vii). Under communism, since scarcity is replaced by abundance, the basis of class exploitation and class itself disappears. Humanity frees itself from both material and social limitations. The forces of production can now develop freely without any social barriers. Each according to his ability following from the condition of scarcity is replaced, in communism, by each according to his need, a change that follows from the condition of abundance.

21. That class is revolutionary, which has the potential to develop productive forces more effectively. That class is in effect predestined to emerge as the winner (Cohen 1978, 1988).

22. Subject positions are defined here as the occupation by an individual of a particular position within the structural complex totality. For example, working-class positions are held in the relations of production by individuals who occupy positions related to performance of surplus labor or absence of ownership of means of production or dominated status in production depending on the criteria used to define relations of production and differentiate classes. The collective of all working-class positions are termed working class where the working-class subject positions are assumed to have a pre-given common interest telescoped in working class. That is, it is assumed that the working class has a homogenous identity distinct from other identities that are produced by different sets of subject positions.

23. The important point is to maintain the rational order of history—movement from undifferentiated unity (primitive communism) to differentiated disunity (class-based society, where capitalism is considered to be the highest stage) to differentiated unity (communism). That is, we can move from slavery to socialism but not from socialism to slavery. The linearity given by the sequence of undifferentiated unity to differentiated disunity to differentiated unity is not to be violated.

24. For a detailed treatment of the same from a historical materialistic perspective, see Larrian (1989) and Howard and King (1992a, b).

25. Marxists in general did not welcome Warren's book because of its explicit Eurocentric tendencies, though we believe that his theory of imperialism as a pioneer of capitalism is perfectly compatible from the standpoint of the orthodox historical materialism.

26. The European countries could move to capitalism quickly because the transition process in European society was from feudalism to capitalism. Rey considered this movement to be natural and unproblematic. It is only the transition from traditional or colonial modes to capitalism that brings about the distortions and hence slows down the trajectory.

27. An important position taken in the Indian modes of production debate was the characterization of Indian society as colonial (see Economic and Political Weekly in the 1970s and 80s). Due to the above mentioned difficulties, this position failed to take off.

28. Much has been written on the Marxian attempt to incorporate aspects of postmodernism. For example, Resnick and Wolff (1987, chapters 1 and 2) superbly document the history of Marxism (following Lenin, Lucas, the Frankfurt School, Mao, Althusser, etc) in terms of the many questions (at the level of epistemology

and logic) which were later raised by postmodernists. But here we ask the reverse question: Can we go from postmodernism to Marxism? This will make clear the influence of postmodernism on Marxism as well as reveal some of the differences between the two especially regarding Marxism's continuing emphasis on its basic tenet—class analysis. This reverse gaze has not been explicitly dealt within the postmodern Marxist literature. Our approach of a postmodern interrogation of Marxism is important in this regard. It ends up by the interrogating not only the methodological structure of Marxism but (implicitly) that of postmodernism as well.

29. We have, in part, used Derrida (1976, 1981, 1982), Culler (1982), and Gasche (1986) to develop some of the arguments made in this section.

30. The reason for our inclusion of historical materialism as a subset of Western metaphysics is linked to the similar structure of causality (that is, of logocentrism which we will define soon) and the idea of full presence or closed totality. According to postmodernist and poststructuralist theories, these are the most fundamental features of Western metaphysics, features that, as should be evident by our discussion in the previous section and this section, are also shared by historical materialism.

31. To understand this hierarchical structure is a fundamental tenet of deconstruction.

32. An example of this more sophisticated argument can be found in Althusser (1969) who, while talking about the complex determination of social entities, ends up reducing their existence to the development of forces of production in the last instance.

33. Marx (1990) made a distinction between absolute surplus-value production process and relative surplus-value production process. This distinction is essentially based on the relative level of labor productivity, which for Marx is crucially linked to technical progress and innovation. The absolute surplus-value production process refers to the capitalist production process, where there is a tendency to increase surplus value through a change in working hours. This is a relatively unproductive labor process with a relatively high level of the value of labor power and the surplus labor time extracted is small. In contrast, the relative surplus value production process refers to a capitalist production process with rapid technical progress to achieve a higher level of labor productivity and, consequently, a larger amount of surplus-labor is available to be extracted. This production process is considered to be more dynamic than the first one. Hence, what we call dynamic relative surplus value.

34. Deconstruction is an anti-essentialist response against the violence of the essentialist structure of causality embedded in the metaphysics of logocentrism or foundationalism. As Derrida points out,

> In a traditional philosophical opposition we have not a peaceful coexistence of facing terms but a violent hierarchy. One of the terms dominates the other (axiologically, logically, etc.), occupies the commanding position. To deconstruct the opposition is above all, at a particular moment, to reverse the hierarchy. (1981, 41)

In addition, deconstruction,

> through a double gesture, a double science, a double writing, put into practice a reversal of the classical opposition and a general displacement of the system. It is on that condition alone that deconstruction will provide the means of intervening in the field of oppositions it criticizes and which is also a field of non discursive forces. (1982, 195)

35. According to Derrida, because there is a lack of full presence, there exists a condition for the existence of supplement. Supplement means something additional. Now this addition could be understood as being conditioned by a certain lack of a presence (as in Derrida) or simply as an extra addition to a full presence (as in Saussure, Plato, or Rousseau). In other words, presence as understood by Derrida is never complete or total as an identity. There is always an attempt to provide full presence or identity through supplementaries but this is all the time subverted. Supplementary leads to more supplementary and to more. Unlike the case for metaphysical thinkers, for Derrida, the lack and the subsequent supplementary is something positive without which the full presence cannot be completed. This is in opposition to the metaphysical thinkers, who consider supplement as a harmful addition to presence and desire an end to its existence.

36. Of course, the moments of deconstruction is integrated within the logic *differance* which resembles greatly the notion of overdetermination even though there are some important differences between the two.

37. The reader will have noticed the short shrift given to an explicit discussion of epistemology here. We will present a detailed account of empiricist and rationalist epistemologies in the next chapter, where we will demonstrate that the Indian mode of production debate is characterized by these two forms of epistemological essentialism. There we will also discuss the relationship between essentialist epistemology (especially its rationalist form) and the essentialist structure of causality.

38. The difference between imputed consciousness as structured by objective class interest and actual consciousness is called false consciousness.

39. Along with the above logical problem, recent historical events in the former socialist countries have also cast considerable doubt on the question of the closed unity of working class and that of the subject at the level of practice. Historical events show that the working class did not consider the Communist party to be their vanguard party, that is, to know their interest. Putting it differently, we can say that the working class has emphatically rejected their projected historical role. This act against its own historical interest is made possible by considerations to other dimensions of subjectivity that imply a dispersion of the entity of the subject. This means that the closed identity of a subject too is not feasible, resulting in the now well-established thesis of a decentered, fragmented existence of subject. The proposition regarding the impossibility of working class and subject position in the context of the problem of the internal identity and external practice will be taken up in detail in chapter 3.

40. Hindess defines actor as "a locus of decision and action, where the action is in some sense a consequence of the actor's decisions. Actors do things as a result of their decisions. We call those things actions, and the actor's decisions play a part in their explanation. Actors may also do things that do not result from their decisions, and their explanation has a different form. This is a minimum concept of the actor" (Hindess 1988, 45).

   In order to carry out decisions and actions, the actor must be able to formulate and execute decisions. Hindess points out that there are two types of actors: individuals and social actors. Social actors are entities like political parties, trade unions, churches, etc. According to Hindess, "The actions of capitalist enterprises or community associations always depend on the actions of others—managers and other employers, elected officers, and sometimes other organizations. We call these 'social actors': each and every one of their actions depends on social relations with other actors" (Hindess 1988, 46).

41. Until now we have shown how anti-essentialism problematizes the concepts of closed social totality and class that underlies the orthodox concept of transition and we have also shown why the essentialist structure of causality describing the logic of transition is flawed.

42. The processes constituting classes are economic processes. Resnick and Wolff makes the following distinction between the economic, political, and cultural: "By economic processes we mean the production and distribution of the means of production and consumption for communities of human beings. By political processes we mean the design and regulation of power and authority in such communities. By cultural processes we mean the diverse ways in which human beings produce meanings for their existences" (1987, 20).

43. Lest it be forgotten, Althusser wrote on overdetermination two years before Derrida wrote on *differance*.

44. In Marxian theories, classes have been often defined not in terms of processes related to mechanisms of surplus labor but to relations of property or power. Furthermore, the aspect of surplus-based meaning of class is reduced to either the property-based or power-based meaning of class. As we shall explain in the next four chapters, this reductionism was a feature of the Indian modes of production debate, where the surplus-labor aspect of class was reduced to property, and of the subaltern debate, where it was reduced to power.

45. Process (an entity in a state of change) and not human individual is the primitive of the postmodern theory. Exploitation is understood here in the context of treating class as process. Exploitation is defined as the process of appropriation whereby the performers of surplus labor are themselves excluded from any appropriation. That is, none of the surplus labor is appropriated by the direct producers. Self- or individual exploitation refers to the process of appropriation whereby the performers of surplus labor can exclude all others from appropriation and therefore appropriates the surplus labor completely and individually. That is, the direct producer appropriates the surplus labor at the individual level. Collective appropriation refers to the process of appropriation whereby all

performers of surplus labor share in its appropriation, and therefore no one is either completely excluded from appropriation or can exclude others.

46. We define "class struggle" as such struggles *over* different issues concerning class processes. Class struggle as the struggle *over* the mechanisms of class processes is fundamentally different from arguing that classes can act and struggle against each other. As we explained earlier, classes as such, representing some homogeneous group of people, cannot act. Such subjectively defined class identity is incapable of formulating and acting on decisions. Hence classes cannot struggle against one another.

The two fundamental political issues that crop up around Marxism are (i) to fight for changes in the fundamental class processes with the goal to end class exploitation in society and (ii) to fight for changes in subsumed class processes in order to transform the conditions of existence that underlie a fundamental class process (see Resnick and Wolff [1987, 1992] for details). Class struggle represents struggle over the fundamental and subsumed class processes. That is, class struggle may happen over the existence, size, manner, and form of appropriation or distribution of surplus labor and over the political, economic, and cultural aspects that are the conditions of existence of the class processes. Nothing in postmodern Marxist theory says that a particular form of class struggle (such as, for instance, struggle over the capitalist fundamental and subsumed class processes) is more important than other forms of class struggle. What Marxist theory does say is that since exploitation is the morally unacceptable social aspect from a Marxian perspective, Marxian politics should emphasize class identities that work for the end of exploitation as more desirable than those class identities that are fighting to keep exploitative class processes intact. Thus class struggles that are undertaken to overcome feudal exploitation inside the household are as much a part of Marxist politics as ending capitalist exploitation inside the capitalist enterprise.

47. Many of the foremost Marxists (Lukacs 1971, 1980; Althusser 1971; Balibar 1994; Habermas 1976, 1987; Larrian 1983, 1994; Bourdieu 1994; Eagleton 1990, 1991; Jameson 1981, 1991; Ziˇzek 1989, 1993, and others) had struggled and are still struggling with issues of class-identity formation and ideology in general. There is an increasing realization within Marxist circles about the insurmountable problem of explaining identity formation in terms of false consciousness, and theorists are now trying to take different routes (Althusserian interpellation, Gramscian hegemony, Lacanian unconscious, Bourdieuan doxa, etc.) to formulate concepts of identity.

48. See Culler (1982) for details.

49. Sheridan Smith, the translator of Foucault's *The Archaeology of Knowledge and the Discourse of Language* made the following comment on the French-to-English translation of *connaissance* and *savoir*: "The English "knowledge" translates the French "*connaissance*" and "*savoir*." *Connaissance* refers here to a particular corpus of knowledge, a particular discipline—biology or economics, for example. *Savoir*, which is usually defined as knowledge in general, the totality of *connais-*

sances, is used by Foucault in an underlying, rather than an overall, way" (Sheridan Smith in Foucault 1972b, 15).

50.   Another critique of the impossibility of mode of production and social formation as closed totality was made by Cutler et al. (1977) where the authors argued that these concepts are based on a rationalist and empiricist epistemology and, hence, need to be discarded. We will refrain from any further discussion on this since it has been a source of detailed debate in Marxist circles for a long time now (see Wolpe 1980 for details). But, despite many reservations we have regarding this work (see Resnick and Wolff 1987), the crucial point that Cutler et al. bring out in their discussion, and which is in line with the argument we are putting forward, is that mode of production and social formation as a closed totality is logically incompatible with anti-essentialist epistemology.

51.   The totality of class processes—fundamental and subsumed—and nonclass processes at a particular site are what we mean by class structure. Capitalist class structure is the entirety or totality of the class and nonclass processes that constitute a capitalist fundamental class process at a specific site. We always use the term "class structure" in the context of a postmodern Marxist class analysis in a micro sense.

Chapter 2
Confronting the Indian Modes of Production Debate

1.   In 1962, the Communist party of India–Marxist (CPI-M) split away from the Communist Party of India (CPI). The former, in turn, split in 1967, giving birth to the Communist Party of India–Marxist Leninist (CPI (M-L)). A major cause of the splits can be identified with disagreements over the issue of transition of India's mode of production. The CPI was a pro-Moscow party that wanted to ally with the bourgeoisie, whom they called nationalist and progressive. The CPI (M) did not consider the nationalist bourgeoisie to be progressive since they were in alliance with the precapitalist elements. The CPI (M-L), which was pro-Beijing, declared the bourgeoisie to be outright comprador. Keeping in line with their different perceptions of the bourgeoisie, they argued for different stages of revolution. The CPI called for an alliance with the bourgeoisie on equal terms to intensify the development of capitalism while the CPI (M) aspired to constitute an alliance between the workers, oppressed sections of the peasantry, and a fraction of the bourgeoisie under the leadership of the working class even though they argued that the objective situation for immediate revolution and an abandonment of parliamentary politics has not yet arisen. The CPI (M-L), on the other hand, called for the abandonment of parliamentary politics and the launching of immediate revolution.

2.   The fury and importance of the debate in India can be gauged from the fact that the CPI (M-L), in keeping with its political line of immediate revolution, launched a violent uprising in the late sixties in which thousands of people were killed.

3. As pointed out in the first chapter, transition in a historicist manner (as per the logic of historical materialism in this case) reflects the progressive development of society. Consequently, in analyzing transition, the participants were effectively debating the development of Indian society.

4. Reality or what is often called the "concrete real," takes the form of data or facts (Resnick and Wolff 1987, 39–52).

5. A crucial underlying feature of this proposition is that economic and noneconomic aspects exist as independent and autonomous from one another. This underlying presumption is important for causal essentialism to be directed from one space (economic) to the other (noneconomic).

6. This form of approximation leads to a reductionism because, resulting from the "findings" pertaining to a limited sphere, a theoretical claim is being made about segments of social space that have not been theorized. The question that remains unanswered in making such a claim is how we know that the untheorized sites are capitalist. This is an unsubstantiated theoretical claim made about the state of the Indian "society" on the basis of the empirical findings. It is to be noted that we are not saying that all approximations (via empirical analysis) are reductionist—far from it. What we are saying is that one can conceptualize "society" (as capitalism or feudalism) and also make a concrete ("approximation") analysis of the limited sites such that the claims resulting from the latter analysis are not conceptually outside of the claims made with reference to the former analysis. Theorists do that all the time and there cannot be anything objectionable to this procedure. The theoretical claims they make with regard to their findings in cases of such analyses are not outside of what hasn't already been accommodated and explained in their theorization of the society. However, in the case we are concerned with here, by analyzing a few limited sites, the concerned Indian Marxists are making a theoretical claim on the status of the "society." "Capitalist" society exists in India because the empirical findings in a limited sphere point to the existence of capitalist relations of production in that sphere. In other words, the existence of capitalism in India is dependent on revealing the "concrete" empirical reality of a few relevant sites, which are then taken to signify the broader, undifferentiated presence of an ideal social totality; in this case that of capitalism. The above empirical procedure is reductionist precisely because of the argumentative leap whereby the actual state of the entire society is considered to be reflecting (and being reduced to) these empirical "findings," thereby displacing the analysis to a different level. That is, the analysis of the complex reality of Indian society, which is the objective of the theorists in the Indian modes of production debate is displaced into the terrain of a search for empirical reality such that, based on those findings, unsubstantiated claims could be made on the complex reality of India.

7. The Indian mode of production debate is characterized by economic essentialism (the economic reflects the mode of production where the only relevant social relations are those of class relations), meaning that in the debate, explanations concerning other aspects of society are reduced to the economic aspect. The problem with such essentialisms, as with most forms of essentialist explanations, is that since these specific social aspects are taken to be the essence (the elements

around which society is assumed to be organized) with the critical explanatory power, all other aspects of society are made dependent and, subsequently, reduced to it. This means that the existence of the noneconomic aspects of society are explained in terms of the mode of production or the economic. For example, for traditional Marxists like Patnaik, the caste system is secondary to the economic and its social existence must be explained in terms of the economic. The caste system exists because it performs certain functions for the economic (relations of production). Once the economic changes (to a capitalist relation of production), the function of the castes (defined only in terms of certain functions with respect to the economic) will disappear and so too will the caste system with it. To reduce explanations regarding the caste system in this way to the economic involves a displacement of the many conditions of the existence of the caste system to a single one.

8. Empiricism, or empiricist procedures, which give a privileged status to the concrete-real should not be confused with empirical analysis. Marxist theory has no problem with those empirical analyses that do not distinguish between the real and the theoretical. Such empirical analyses already have a theoretical component embedded in them, that is, they are constituted by theory. Concepts in theory bring their influence to bear on the empirical exercise so much that the empirical becomes the theoretical as well. What we mean to say is that, under the procedure of mutual determination, the empirical results are as much a part of the analytical core as the analytical results of the empirical core. The theoretical claims made in the latter are not different from and outside of the theoretical claims made in the former.

9. By freedom in the double sense, Marx meant

> . . . free laborers, in the double sense that neither they themselves form part and parcel of the means of production, as in the case of slaves, bondsmen, and co., nor do the means of production belong to them, as in the case of peasant-proprietors; they are, therefore, free from, unencumbered by, any means of production of their own. (Marx 1954, 174)

10. As we shall argue in Chapter six, social totality is decentered and under the decentered concept of social totality, the economy is uneven and dispersed (i.e., it cannot be held together by a particular gravitational force operating at a "deeper" level such as capital accumulation), where each site of the economy is uniquely constituted and hence is different from the other sites. Also because of the assumed overdetermined logic, the economy (specified by class processes) cannot be conceived of as independent of and autonomous from the noneconomic aspects of society. Rather, the economy is constituted by noneconomic processes in such a way that the failure to reproduce various noneconomic processes will create a serious crisis for the reproductive process of the economy.

11. One position taken in the Indian modes of production debate was the characterization of Indian society as "colonial" (Banaji 1990, Alavi 1975, 1982, 1990), where it was argued that the Indian mode of production was an articulatory existence of the colonial mode of production with either or both the domestic capi-

talist mode of production and the capitalist mode of production of the concerned center countries. The colonial mode of production school never took off since it faced three major internal theoretical problems. First, if the modes of production are considered to be independent and autonomous of one another, questions regarding their articulatory existence posed problems that were never satisfactorily answered. If, as in historical materialism, one mode of production develops organically from within another, then it is not clear how two independent modes of production could coexist simultaneously (Wolpe 1980, Foster-Carter 1978). Second, the relatively "peaceful" articulatory existence of two or more modes of production is contradictory to the characterization of the modes of production as antagonistically related (Foster-Carter 1978, Wolpe 1980). Third, because a country has been colonized does not mean that its mode of production can be called colonial (Foster-Carter 1978, Bradby 1975, and Rudra 1990b). There is an ad-hoc-ness in naming these modes in the literature on the colonial mode of production. They do not face and answer questions like "What are the relations of production and class structures in the colonial mode of production" and "How and why is it different from the other modes of production"? For these reasons, the concept of colonial mode of production had a short life span in the debate and, more generally, within the Marxist discourse.

12. In this case, we are considering only the mode of exploitation through usury. If rent (lease-land) is added, then we shall have a sharecropping arrangement where the contending parties are sharecroppers and the combination of the merchant-moneylending and the landlord class. Then the sharecroppers are exploited by the combination of two modes—debt and rent. In the semifeudal setup, however, usury income is considered to be more fundamental for the ruling class because it also helps them to maintain their socioeconomic power over the sharecroppers. In the argument below, when we use the term "sharecropper," we imply that the person being referred to is exploited by the combination of the two sources mentioned above. Similarly, we use the term "landlord "(in conjunction with the sharecropper) to refer to someone who exploits through the combination of the two sources. Here, for simplicity's sake, it is assumed by Bhaduri that the moneylender-cum-merchant class and the landlord class have the same interest, hence they are referred to by one name—the landlord class. Later on, while analyzing Bhaduri's concept of class, we shall show that it is the antagonistic relation between the landlord and the moneylender-cum-merchant class that is fundamentally responsible for producing the class differentiation in Indian agriculture.

13. Bhaduri has displaced exploitation from the labor market to the product market. This also involves a slip from capitalist exploitation to semifeudal exploitation, since, as Bhaduri argues, unequal exchange in the labor market is associated with capitalist exploitation while unequal exchange in the product market is associated with semifeudal exploitation. However, note that despite the slippage, both forms of exploitation take place in the common realm of exchange.

14. The laborers perform work against the consumption loan that they took from the moneylender-cum-merchant class. Often this advancement of money is consid-

ered as a wage but, in fact, it is only a form of debt bondage. Here, the laborer has no option but to work for the moneylender-cum-merchant class.

15. Utsa Patnaik (1976), in a different formulation, also argued that precapitalist elements create obstacles for capitalist development. She blames high rent as the culprit. Very high rent leads to a fall in the rate of profit, thereby discouraging investment in agriculture. Some other theorists, including Utsa Patnaik (1990d) also blamed the lack of effective demand as the cause of agricultural backwardness. All of these arguments carry the same basic message—identifying elements that are obstacles to capitalist development.

Chapter 3
Class and the Question of Transition

1. According to Patnaik, normally, at the analytical level, there is a one-to-one correspondence among the three, though conceptually each is different from the others. The correspondence is such that those who own the means of production will exploit others who do not and will also possess a marketable surplus of product. As she argues,

> In agriculture such as India's, the two poles are readily identified: the landless and near landless, who possess no or little means of production and are therefore mainly or wholly dependent on working for others; and the landlords and capitalists, who concentrate sufficient means of production not to need to labor themselves but live on employing others. (Patnaik 1990d, 196)

In other words, exploitation relations can be reduced to the distribution of means of production.

2. $E = \frac{x}{y} =$ net labor days hired in + net labor days appropriated through rent divided by family labor days in cultivation on the operational holding.

From now on as per Patnaik's notation,

a = labor days hired in (a_1) − labor days hired out (a_2) = net labor days hired in

b = labor days taken through rent (b_1) − labor days given through rent (b_2) = net labor days appropriated through rent.

Hence, x = a + b.

3. Here again, the problem with approximation is that its claims on behalf of something cannot be substantiated. With this empirical approximation, Patnaik is reducing the effects of other aspects of her analytical definition of class to the empirical presence of another element. She claims that this empirical aspect is capable of capturing the other aspects of class involved in the analytical definition. But this claim is unsubstantiated: How do we know that the effects from other aspects of class will not lead to a different explanation of the social phenomenon being explained by the empirical aspect? If it does lead to a different explanation, then how can one claim that the explanation made in terms of the approximated aspect of class is identical to the explanation that could have been

made with the analytical concept of class? Such a claim only makes sense if the other aspects of class along with their effects are rendered passive and reduced to the approximated aspect. Thus this procedure of dividing the empirical from the material helps Patnaik to make a claim on the effects of the other aspects of class without ever having to analyze those aspects.

4. This means that x could be negative and high in absolute value. ($|a| > |b|$) means that hiring out accounts for most of the x value even though here the agricultural laborer cultivates the land. ($|a| \leq |b|$) points to the fact that rent payment is the dominant aspect for the individual as compared to hiring out.

5. It was pointed out that the exchange definition of exploitation is incompatible with the Marxist notion of exploitation as a subset of processes related to the production, appropriation, distribution, and receipt of surplus labor.

6. The class of small peasantry ranges from the poor to the middle peasants. The small peasants include tenants and peasants who hire themselves out along with cultivating their land. Bhaduri does not answer the question as to why all groups of people from poor to middle peasants are lumped into the category small peasantry. He simply takes it as given.

7. For Bhaduri, the accrual of property income on productive investments is a particular form of ownership structure. Property income on unproductive investment is another form of ownership structure.

8. Unproductive investment means "distribution of agricultural output in favor of the investing class at a more or less constant (or even declining) level of output, so that those investors gain even though the aggregate agricultural output may not have increased" (1983, 112).

9. For Bhaduri, the emphasis is never on class collaboration (that is, case I), which blunts potential class contradictions. Structural change requires change in the ownership structure and the mode of domination of one class over another. For any transitional mode of production, like that of India's, one must capture the contradictory relation between the two classes.

10. The interests of different classes are mutually antagonistic when the interest of members of one class is furthered at the expense of members of another class.

11. Also, activities of leasing out or leasing in land and self-cultivation of land, participation in manual labor or abstinence from manual labor, and investment in productive channels and investment in unproductive channels lead to no contradictions.

12. Hence, class per se cannot act or struggle—class as an actor with some form of (subjective) political identity is a logical impossibility. This does not preclude the conceptual existence of class identity and class struggle. In the postmodern Marxian framework, collective action signifying class struggle needs to be socially constructed (and is not automatically given), where class struggle is defined as a struggle *over* the mechanisms of class *processes*, that is, over the existence, size, manner, and form of performance, appropriation, distribution, and receipt of *surplus labor*. Social actors such as the trade unions, political parties, government, and religious institutions can engage in such class struggle and they do, all the time. The political dimension of class in the form of class struggle and the

economic dimension of class as constituted by fundamental and subsumed class processes are distinct even though there is a close relation between the two: class struggle is fought over economic processes related to the performance, appropriation, distribution, and receipt of surplus labor. This class struggle requires as its prerequisite a construction of identity formation around the issues (which signify the context of the formation of identity) of class processes in order for collective action on those issues to materialize. This process of identity formation, however, faces three major constraints (i) the identity of individuals in society is dispersed (via its race, caste, gender, etc., position), (ii) courtesy of our concept of class as a process, the classes are also dispersed such that it is feasible for a worker (doer) to be a shareholder capitalist (nondoer) or for a worker (a doer) in capitalist enterprise to be a feudal lord (a nondoer) in the household, and (iii) like any other social site, the domain of the political is also fragmented, with the body politic being pulled in different directions by considerations of class, race, religion, gender, caste, etc. The dispersed nature of individuals, classes, and the body politic means that class identity (or, for that matter, any identity) cannot be based on preformed subjectivity, interest, or consciousness emanating from the individual's occupation of class position. That does not mean that these entities are not important; far from it. These entities have to be laced on to the process of identity formation and collective action in order for these to originate. That is, they overdetermine or constitute the process of identity formation and collective action. And since class-identity formation is contextually produced (that is, depending on the specific issues related to class processes), its constitutive elements such as interest or consciousness must be considered at those very moments of constitution. In fact, it is at those (contextual) moments that these entities announce their existence. They help in defining the context (placing it, changing it, refining it) as much as they are a product of the context. And in what form these entities will come into existence is the play of politics.

13. In Rudra, an individual can be a landlord and a moneylender, but in terms of classes he belongs to the class of big landowners, since he does not have any antagonistic conflict of interest. As we have explained, using power analysis, Rudra reduces individuals to either the class of big landowners or the class of agricultural laborers. In the case of the class of agricultural laborers, even though small peasants may appropriate surplus labor or engage in independent production, they are lumped together with the class of agricultural laborers because of their lack of power and the absence of any antagonistic conflicts with actual agricultural laborers. Thus what in the overdeterminist class processes are referred to as distinct class positions are, in Rudra, reduced to the two classes divided by the disproportionate amount of power they wield.

14. Patnaik first used this net method approach, one with which Bhaduri generally concurs. Rudra, on the other hand, takes a different route to reduce individuals to one class position: he uses power to perform a reductionism to the same effect. See the previous footnote.

15. In postmodern Marxian class analysis, a particular fundamental class process is constituted by other class and nonclass processes. That is, without these class and

nonclass processes a particular fundamental class process will not be socially reproduced. It is in this sense that a class position that reflects the performance of a social function pertaining to a particular process is socially constituted. The social function of the moneylender (lending money capital for production), landlord (leasing land for production), merchant (trading commodities produced in the capitalist fundamental class process), or state (enacting and enforcing laws conducive to the reproduction of the capitalist fundamental class process)—all of which indicates class positions arising from subsumed class processes—are critical for the social reproduction of the two class positions in the capitalist fundamental class process. The subsumed class positions in turn may require the help from other nonclass processes in order to be reproduced. By overdetermining the fundamental class process, other class and nonclass processes constitute the individual's (class) existence as a performer or an appropriator of surplus value. Individuals may occupy many such class and nonclass positions (related to the fundamental and subsumed class processes) and since each such class and nonclass position is socially constituted by other class and nonclass processes we can say that the individual—as an occupier of multiple class and nonclass positions—is socially constituted.

16. The following characterization of *totality* and *centered totality of a subject* follows Laclau (1988), which more or less captures the basic ideas of totality relevant for the argument we will be making. This characterization of totality is very specific to the arguments made in this section and should be read accordingly.

17. The passiveness of the working class in turn flows from the interest given in the (economic) space from which it is derived. Working-class interest reflects the interest embedded in the space of the economic that is considered to be the essence of such a society. The economic flows into the political as a rule rendering the problem of constitution of the political as relatively unproblematic. The interest generated in the economic is the (true) interest of the working class and that of society as a whole, and that interest should reflect in the consciousness of the working class. Hence the assumption of the working class possessing the knowledge about the role it should play in society and history. In chapter 2, we considered a (Hindess 1987) critique of such a structurally given notion of interest relating working class to the economic where it is pointed out that "true" or "real" interest cannot conceptually exist.

18. This is based on the historical materialist conception of the world as an overall becoming of a project (communism), where all practical events and short-term reality are construed in terms of the overall project. To be aware of such a becoming of the world is to be aware of "reason." Not all social groups possess this reason. Only the working class does. The working class carries the reason (the knowledge of the trajectory of history) within it.

19. The vanguard party was assumed to uphold the pure interest of the working class. As a result the interests of the working class and vanguard party became synonymous. Since the totality of the subject directly translates the objective interest of the working class (the totality), the interest of an individual holding a working-class position should coincide with that of the working class and van-

guard party. The subject is represented by a working class that in turn is represented by the vanguard party. Each necessarily flows from the other, and there is no contingent element involved here. Any dissent or revolt against the vanguard party is a revolt against the working class and its true interests.

20. Recent historical events in the former socialist countries have also cast considerable doubt on the question of the closed unity of the working class and that of the subject at the level of practice. Historical events show that the working class did not consider the Communist party to be their vanguard party, that is, to know their interest. Putting it differently, we can say that the working class has emphatically rejected their projected historical role. This act against its own historical interest is made possible by considerations to other dimensions of subjectivity that implies a dispersion of the entity of the subject.

21. In this context, as we have already indicated, the approach of the postmodern Marxian school looks particularly promising. Their epistemological approach and class analysis takes into account the major criticisms that have been directed against Marxism in recent times. In the Indian context, this needs to be embedded to something like Utsa Patnaik's vision of a disaggregated Indian society. The point is to *explain* the *mechanisms* (which will be reflective of the Marxian focal point) driving the *process* of transition in India (for preliminary explorations of this issue, see Chakrabarti and Cullenberg, 2001).

Chapter 4
Transition and Development

1. As in the case of orthodox Marxism, subaltern studies understood development as a particular outcome of transition of society in certain direction.

2. Who is the subaltern and who is the elite? Ranajit Guha, the leader of the school, defined subaltern as the social group or elements of that group that ". . . represented the demographic difference between the total Indian population and all those whom we have described as elite" (Guha 1982, 8). By elite he meant ". . . dominant groups foreign as well as indigenous. The dominant foreign groups included all the non-Indians, that is, mainly British officials of the colonial state and foreign industrialists, merchants, planters, landlords and missionaries" (Guha 1982, 8). The dominant indigenous groups include classes and interests operating at the all-India level (big feudal magnates, industrialist and mercantile bourgeoisie, and native recruits to bureaucracy) and at the regional and local level (belonging to either classes and interests of the dominant all-India groups or belonging to lower social strata but acting in the interest of the dominant all-India groups). The rest of the population who are dominated by the elite constitutes the category of the subaltern. Guha and the subaltern studies school alternately call these groups "subaltern" or "the people." Given this definition, the peasantry, tribal groups, lower-class and ethnic groups are all components of the subaltern.

3. "New democracy" was a term coined by Mao Tse-tung to theorize the so-called first stage of Chinese socialist society. New democracy refers to a situation where

the workers are not powerful enough to rule on their own and must enlist the support of the oppressed peasants (the overwhelming mass in such societies) and the petite bourgeoisie. This alliance led by the working class must ultimately work for the construction of a socialist society.

4. Ryotwari land settlement was a system in which each peasant's revenue to be charged by the state was assessed separately. Permanent settlement referred to the revenue extraction system where the rent was fixed in perpetuity irrespective of the economic ability of the peasants, and the British administration collected the rent through a group of intermediaries called the Zamindar.

5. But why are peasant uprisings important at all? They are important because during such uprisings the antagonistic form of power relations takes its most pure form, that is, the autonomous domain of the elite and the subaltern becomes clear. A study of these uprisings, then, by turning the relations of power upside down, will reveal the truth about the autonomous domain of the peasantry and its consciousness, a point to which we will return soon.

6. The subset of processes related to class will reveal social relationships that relate to relations of exploitation/nonexploitation. Almost all notions of class in the traditional Indian Marxist literature were construed not in terms of relations of exploitation/nonexploitation but rather in terms of relations of property (see the previous chapter). Relations of exploitation/nonexploitation were reduced to relations of property, and property structure (not class) became the organizing principle of conceptualizing society. In the subaltern literature, in contrast, the meaning of class is also derived from the property structure and exploitation follows from the property structure. Here, however, there is one more step in the reduction process by which the meaning of class is further reduced to power relations. In this section, we will abide by the meaning attached to class by the subaltern studies to review the mechanism through which the meaning of class as surplus labor extraction process is rendered passive by the very act of its usurpation by relations of power.

7. As Chakraborty argues, "class relations express themselves in that other language of politics" where that other language is one of domination-subordination (Chakraborty 1985, 376).

8. We will argue below against such a "class" conceptualization of the peasantry.

9. He will turn out to be an exploiter if he employs labor power. If he works on his own as an independent producer then he is what is often called a self-exploiter (one who appropriates his own surplus labor). In either case, the social relationship entailed by such forms of exploitation would be different from that of the subaltern school. For a class analysis of the various forms of sharecropping, see Kayatekin (2001).

10. In the context of recovering peasant consciousness with respect to India there is a practical difficulty, which arises from the absence of any explicit record pertaining to the undominated zone of peasant consciousness. The peasantry's perspective is not written down in the historical records, so how could one study the history of peasant consciousness? The subaltern studies group looks for the answer in peasant insurgency that have been recorded by official (elite) historiogra-

phers, travelers, and administrators at that time. At times of peasant insurgencies, the relations of subordination are challenged and overthrown. The peasants then move into a zone of undominated practice. By reading these undominated practices, one can bring out the autonomous character of peasant consciousness. One can perform such readings by looking at the elite (official) accounts of those insurgencies. The official accounts are written from the perspective of the elite and reveal their consciousness. Their record of the peasant actions, such as inversion of dominant relations of power (attributed in the official account as a challenge to the ruling order), provides evidence that can be used to construct the autonomous domain of the peasantry and its consciousness. That is how the history of subaltern consciousness is produced in subaltern studies. Guha's work *The Elementary Aspects of Peasant Insurgency* is the most famous of this recording of symbolic inversion resulting from peasant uprisings for the case of India. Since the elite and the subaltern belong to different domains, an inversion of elite symbols (indicators of relations of domination and subordination) is a necessary characterization of the subaltern consciousness. In this way, subaltern consciousness is produced via a mirror image of the subversion of elite symbols.

11. Chatterjee sees the relation between what he calls the narrative of community and narrative of capital as antithetical. We consider the claim of such an antithetical relation to be problematic and, in the section on passive revolution of capital, we will demonstrate that this relation is not universally true.

12. For example, the Titu Mir–led peasant revolt in Barasat, a district in West Bengal, in the later part of nineteenth century, underwent a series of transformations from its antilandlord content to anti-Hindu content to finally anti-British content (Guha 1983). Another study by Gyan Pandey (1984) shows a similar series of transformations in the events that occurred in the 1820s in the *qasba* (locality) of Mubarakpur in the district of Azamgarh in Eastern Uttar Pradesh. There, a struggle between the Rajput landlords and the Muslim weavers changed into a united resistance by the town against outside attack (the British interference in that strife) and back to the internal struggle within a few days.

13. Major proponents of this school are Mahatma Gandhi and Sarvepalli Radhakrishnan, the first president of India, who was also a scholar of considerable reputation (see Chatterjee 1993, 174). However, the person who best articulated this school's thought was Dumont (1970), whose work we shall discuss below. The theories of the caste system that refers to its harmonious aspects are termed as the "synthetic theories of castes" by Chatterjee.

14. According to Chatterjee, the proponents of this position on the caste system hold the view that "The ideal varna scheme (the hierarchical structure in the caste system) was meant to be a non-competitive functional division of labor and did not imply a hierarchy of privilege" (Chatterjee 1993, 174).

15. Dharma or religion, very roughly, means a series of duties that need to be performed without any expectation of rewards or benefits. Looking after one's parents or fighting for one's country or abiding by promises once made are acts of dharma. These duties are performed not because they benefit the performer but because they simply should be performed. Any violation of those duties would be

an act of adharma and any adharma is punishable. For example, the ruler's dharma is to look after his or her subjects (or what are called citizens in the Western world). If the ruler does not look after his or her subjects then he commits adharma and the subjects have the moral right to overthrow the ruler. This is an extremely complicated concept, and any exposition would require a detailed treatment that is beyond the scope of this survey. The interested reader can consult Kane (1974) for a classic account of the meaning of dharma.

16. The aspect of force in dharma is extremely crucial, for it is that force which binds together the existing relations between people by defining the permissible boundaries for any individual's or group's (such as a caste's) actions. People act in a certain way because to do otherwise would be seen as an act of adharma, an act for which an individual or a group could be punished. Rebellion by peasants has to be carried out against the additional burden of an action that violates the dharma (the dharma of the peasants is to obey their superiors). Analyzing the different peasant insurgencies in India, Guha makes a similar point: "This risk (*of peasant revolt*) involved not merely the loss of his land and chattels but also that of his moral standing derived from an unquestioning subordination to his superiors, which tradition has made into his dharma (1983, 9)."

17. We will argue later on that the above way of separating caste and class at the level of production is problematic. The relevant critique of a caste theory of class is not to argue for an independent and autonomous existence of caste and class but rather the reductionism involved in displacing class relations in the production process to that of caste relations.

18. Many peasant struggles in India took on a caste (and religious) form because the issues of land and economy were bounded by the constraint of caste or religion. The lower-caste people or people from a particular religious sect, who normally do not own land, would often challenge the dominance of the landowners, who would come from an upper caste or a different religious sect. Here, a class dimension (defined in terms of relations of power deriving in this case from ownership of means of production like land) of peasant insurgency could easily take on a caste or religious dimension as is evident from the analysis of peasant insurgencies in subaltern literature. This also indicates, contrary to the view of the traditional Marxists, the gridlocked social existence of the institutions of caste, religion, and the economic relations of production. To fail to consider the caste and religious factor in the description of the economic in the context of India is a fundamental error in the endeavour to reveal the complexity of India's social reality.

19. For a detailed analysis of this non-Western notion of equality, see Chatterjee (1993, 173–199, 220–239) and Chaudhury (1992).

20. The problems in conceptualizing the peasant class in subaltern studies are repeated in its conceptualization of other classes (working class, elite class, subaltern class, middle class, and so on).

21. The ontological position of the working class could be taken by any other group, say, the bourgeoisie. We are not concerned with who takes the ontologically privileged position. It is the concept of ontological privilege that we want to empha-

size and question. However, it is also fairly obvious from the text of subaltern studies that subaltern studies theorists do emphasize the group they call the working class.

22. Also, the concept of ideal social totality plays a part in creating a historicist sequence of evolution of society in underdeveloped countries. We will expand on this issue in our treatment of the passive revolution of capital.

23. India's freedom struggle, despite the presence of such a large number of subaltern movements, could not become what Guha called the "national liberation" struggle (akin to Mao's strategy of a Chinese revolution brought about by an alliance of the peasantry and workers led by the working class). This historic failure is attributed to the inability of the working class to transform itself from a class in itself to a class for itself (Guha 1982, 5–8).

24. This is done through the concept of the passive revolution of capital, which we will discuss in the next chapter.

25. Spivak (1985, 1988) proposed a postmodern rendition of the category of subaltern. She theorized the "subaltern" as an adjective that is as a standpoint, in contrast to the more popular version of "subaltern" as subject that we have been talking about. This subaltern space is so displaced that any speech originating in that space cannot be communicated. Using Spivak's model, Chakrabarti and Chaudhury (1996) show that it is possible to carve out an unambiguous name for (working) class within the category of subaltern, and that it is possible to speak from that standpoint. This implies that the subaltern, unlike in Spivak, can speak. Subsequently, the term "subaltern" then becomes problematic as a concept. It belongs to the center (space for working class which is now a subset of the subaltern) and periphery (to which Spivak's subaltern is supposed to reside). The subaltern is everywhere, that is, nowhere. The term becomes so general that its usage loses its bite and its meaning lapses into vacuity. If, for example, one can carve out concrete spaces for center and periphery from a reading of *Capital*, then why bother with the general and abstract category of subaltern. Similar such concrete spaces could be created from, say, gender or caste analysis.

26. The major theoretical writings in this literature are those of Chaudhury (1988, 1991–92, 1994), Chatterjee (1988, 1993), and Sanyal (1988, 1991–92).

Chapter 5
A Marxian Critique of the Passive Revolution of Capital

1. The details of surrogate synthesis will be fleshed out soon in the treatment below.

2. We must begin with a note of caution with regard to the usage of concepts of capital, capitalism, and class in this literature. The division is murky, since the theorists do not define these concepts clearly and, consequently, the usage of them is often not clear. However, these theorists seem to be referring to some received theory of these concepts (that seems to be the reason why they do not problematize these concepts), and we have tried to unpack it from their analysis. Also, we have gained many of these (nontransparent) insights in personal conversations

· Notes

we have had with some of these theorists over the years. Let us refer to this briefly. Capital, defined conceptually as the production of surplus value where labor power is paid at its value, is given a consciousness of which it is fully aware. Capital is aware of the historical trajectory of society and its role in it. More important, for us, the most crucial knowledge embedded in capital is that, for society to progress, capital must accumulate. This teleology (capital accumulation) of society will play a crucial role in theorizing the case of passive revolution of capital in India. This subjectivity embedded in capital is passed on to the owners of capital (capital as a thinking object) who constitute the capitalist class. The capitalist class are carriers of the knowledge embedded in capital. The narrative of capital is also the narrative of the capitalist class. It is also assumed that there are political and cultural institutions (property rights, a concept of equality, etc.) associated with the logic of capital accumulation. These institutions are conducive to and hence serve the process of capital accumulation. Capitalism is taken to be this complex whole (entirety of the economic of capital accumulation, political and cultural aspects) that serve the logic of capital accumulation. Capital is given an ontological social privilege in this concept of capitalism. Often, in this literature, the term "capital" is substituted for "capitalism" since as the essence (dominant explanatory factor), capital becomes the representative narrative of capitalism. This substitution is randomly present in the literature. We have not provided any textual evidence here, because we believe the reader can very easily discern our reading of the concepts of capital, capitalism, and capitalist class in the ample textual evidence we will present during the course of this exposition. The usage of terms like "precapital" and "precapitalism" are exactly similar to that of "capital" and "capitalism"; the only difference being that precapitalism represents the totality of tradition (traditional economic, traditional polity, and traditional culture) driven, as under capitalism, by the traditional economic (precapital).

3.   We call this conceptualization a route from Hegel to Gramsci because these theorists claimed to have read and reinterpreted Gramsci's concept of passive revolution of capital in the light of Hegelian logic.

4.   There might be controversy over whether particulars are treated as autonomous and independent from one another in Hegel. In this description we abstract from this and many other such controversies that deal with the correctness of the interpretation of Hegel. Our intention is not to problematize Hegel but rather to critically describe and problematize a particular interpretation of Hegelian logic as put forward by these Indian Marxists in their endeavor to provide an alternative (to the traditional Marxian school) reading of India's complex social reality. To repeat, in such an interpretation of Hegel, particulars are considered as independent and autonomous from one another. This assumption of particulars as independent and autonomous is taken directly from the subaltern studies analysis. We have already provided ample textual evidence of the way in which this was used in subaltern studies.

5.   We need not go into detail as to why capital and the state are considered to be oppressive by some Marxists. Chaudhury deals with the debate between Miliband, Poulantsaz, and the German school's state-derivation approach to make his

point that this was one of the most influential positions in the debate on state theory. Readers interested in the details should consult Chaudhury (1991–92, 1992). Chatterjee (1993) goes from Locke, Montesquieu, and Hegel to Marx to make the same point. Roughly, the basic idea is that the logic of capital leads to coercion and alienation inside the production process, thus nullifying the bourgeois notions of freedom and equality (which is true only in the realm of exchange). The state, which rules by idealizing the attributes of freedom and equality, must somehow legitimize this aspect of coercion so that the populace does not challenge capital's rule. The state might have to use mechanisms of persuasion in order to legitimize the rule by coercion. Some, like Chatterjee and Chaudhury, will say that this mechanism of persuasion is in fact a coercive mechanism since that is what it perpetuates in the end.

6. For the moment, consider the surrogate universal to be the state. However, as we shall point out, in the context of India, it is something else (nationalism) that is reified, as Chatterjee would say, in the body of the state. That is why we say that the surrogate universal is something more than the state but is also deeply connected to it.

7. Again, the fundamental premise here is that thesis and antithesis are autonomous and independent of one another. Also note that the thesis and antithesis are complexes—complexes of precapitalism (totality of the traditional economic, cultural, and political) and capitalism (totality of the modern economic [capital], political, and cultural).

8. In this literature, the terms "surrogate *synthesis*" and "surrogate *universal*" are used interchangeably.

9. In the case of India, it is to be noted that the theorists of passive revolution of capital are not saying that, under colonial rule, absolutely no amount of expropriation of the land of the peasantry leading to a certain amount of free wage labor has occurred. Their point is that after creating an initial vast reserve army of laborers, there was no fundamental need (for the state and capital) to proceed with primitive capital accumulation in a systematic way. It is in this sense that primitive capital accumulation is considered to be a failure. In terms of the labor market, the capitalist labor market may be complemented by other precapitalist forms of labor markets but that does not preclude capitalism from establishing its rule and the process of capital accumulation as the dominant economic process. Also, they are not saying that primitive capital accumulation will be totally absent in modern India. They are part of what Chatterjee calls the rigor of capital accumulation and cannot be totally avoided. That is, under certain specific conditions (such as the building of dams to provide water at cheap cost for production) some precapitalist communities will be negatively effected by the process of capital accumulation. In this context, the task of the state is to legitimize any such hardship as part of the process of nation building. However, they will not be part of a systematic measure (as taken under the industrial the revolution in parts of Europe or the socialist primitive capital accumulation in Russia) undertaken by the state and capital with the intention of transforming society from one mode of production to another. That option is closed by the passive revolution of capital

that internalizes the protection of communities in its system of rule. We shall come back to this point later.

10. To remind the reader, the Congress party was the leading party that fought for India's independence. Its two foremost leaders were Mahatma Gandhi and Jawaharlal Nehru. What we want to emphasize here is that while the former believed in the economic development of India via the development of the cottage-based system and intervention of a welfarist, benevolent state, the latter was strongly in favor of growth (that is, capital accumulation) through the development of large-scale industrialization. The Congress party and the postcolonial Indian development process (which was dominated by the Congress party) aspired to combine these economic dimensions in the (political) rule of the state.

11. Chatterjee uses the term "community groups" instead of "citizen groups." According to Chatterjee, these are different terms signifying different types of identity. The idea of citizen is a product of Western postenlightenment thought and is not the same as that of community that is specific to precapitalist societies. The former is derived from the narrative of capital and is fundamentally opposed to the (precapitalist) communities that are viewed as backward. In Western thought, citizen groups are not taken as a priori given but, instead, need to be constructed so that the groups are associations of individuals who have joined together of their own free will. Precapitalist communities, like those in India, are fundamentally different. Chatterjee (1983) uses Marx's analysis of precapitalist societies in the *Grundrisse* to theorize his claim that these (precapitalist) communities are autonomous and independent from one another and from civil society. One can consider such a community as a prior whole (to use the Hegelian terminology) and individuals existing as part of the whole. Chatterjee points out that this whole is beyond and above the individuals who constitute it. That is, the individuals exist as social individuals because they are part of the whole (the community). The social is given by the whole (community)—community is the social—and the individual's social existence flows from it. There is no notion of social constructivism of the individual here as is the case in much of Western thought. Because of its autonomous and independent nature, such communities have a pure (inner) consciousness that can be recovered by theoretical analysis (that is, recovering the narrative of the community). Chatterjee's work on caste (1989, 1993) and the peasantry (1983, 1993) poses this possibility of recovering the immanent (*inner*) consciousness of these communities. In other words, he attempts to recover the pure, uncontaminated zone of community and the consciousness it generates. The *outer domain* is that of civil society while the inner domain is, as we mentioned, that of the community. For example, Chatterjee (1984, 1986, 1993) interprets Gandhi's work as a case of a "critique of the civil society"—the outer domain—and an attempt to build a nationalist discourse on the basis of the other narrative—that of the community (the inner domain).

12. Chatterjee argues that this is a different narrative than that related to capital accumulation. In fact, it is fundamentally opposed to the narrative of capital accumulation. As he points out, "The crucial break in the history of anticolonial

nationalism comes when the colonized refuse to accept membership of this civil society of subjects. They construct their national identities within a different narrative, that of the community. They do not have the option of doing this within the domain of bourgeois civil-social institutions. They create, consequently, a very different domain—a cultural domain—marked by the distinctions of the material and the spiritual, the outer and the inner. This inner domain of culture is declared the sovereign territory of the nation, where the colonial state is not allowed entry, even as the outer domain remains surrendered to the colonial power. The rhetoric here (Gandhi is a particularly good example) is of love, kinship, austerity, sacrifice. The rhetoric is in fact antimodernist, antiindividualist, even anticapitalist" (Chatterjee 1993, 237).

13. Chatterjee mentions many types of "rigor" associated with capital accumulation though, save for one (breakdown of communities) he does not discuss them in detail. First, there is the rigor associated with the "lack of freedom and equality within the industrial labor process itself and the continued division of society into the opposed classes of capital and labor" (Chatterjee 1993, 235). Then, capital accumulation can "turn the violence of mercantilist trade, war, genocide, conquest, and colonialism into a story of universal progress, development, modernization, and freedom. For this narrative to take shape, the destruction of communities is fundamental" (Chatterjee 1993, 235). Sanyal (1993) discussing the debate between Scott's (1976) "moral economy approach" and Popkin's (1979) "political economy approach" points out a similar antithetical relation between community and capital: "The controversy highlights the antithetical relation between community and commodity, and how the discursive annihilation of the former is essential for the establishment of the latter" (1993, 128).

14. Chatterjee (1993) gives a detailed account of the concept of "nationhood," as can be gauged from the title of his book *The Nation and Its Fragments.* He studies the fragments (women, elite, peasantry, caste, and religion) of the Indian nation and finds that these groups construct their national identities within the narrative of the community. Yet "nationhood" is bigger than these fragments. It is the identities of all these fragments interrupted violently by the identity related to capital accumulation that, according to Chaudhury, is fundamentally opposed to the communities. This interruption—the unresolved struggle between capital and communities—is India's nationhood that is reified in the body of the state. This nationalism (artificial and, hence, surrogate), as can be contemplated by its very construction, is open to contestation and is consequently very fragile, and yet this nationalism must be reproduced for the procreation of the Indian (developmental) state in the present form. It is important to note that capital establishes its dominance at this level of "nationhood" and not directly at the level of state. As we have already mentioned, a challenge to capital's dominance is a challenge to the Indian "nationhood." However, since "nationhood" is situated in the space of the state, capital's dominance is practiced at the level of the state.

15. On the details of these mechanisms of coercion and persuasion, see Chaudhury (1988, 1991–92, 1994), Sanyal (1988, 1991–92), and Chatterjee (1988).

16. This balancing act between accumulation and welfarism is clearly brought out in this passage of Sanyal:

> Unlike the case of primitive accumulation in Western Europe where the state acted as an explicit power organ of capital in estranging direct producers from their means of livelihood, the poverty eradication programs are now launched by the state. Acting on behalf of capital, the state now explicitly recognizes the need to provide the people of the periphery with entitlements sufficient to meet a certain standard of living. It can be done by transferring a part of the fruits of accumulation to the periphery and giving it out as a dole. . . . The property relations and modes of labor associated with it (that is, the system of production) are clearly non capitalist, and in fact it is somewhat of a reversal of the process of primitive accumulation. While capital's power was used in the process of primitive accumulation to estrange direct producers from their traditional production activities, labor is now being united with the means of labor to revive direct production for meeting a required level of consumption. The tramps were once forced into capitalist labor process; now capital's power is being used to keep them away. (1993, 126–127)

17. Unlike in orthodox Marxism, capital cannot annihilate the other particulars to establish its uncontested hegemony. Here, capital must accommodate the other particulars yet should be able to establish its dominance. Consequently, the construction of capital's hegemony in this context will be different and more complicated. Again, see Chaudhury (1988, 1991–92, 1994), Sanyal (1988, 1991–92), and Chatterjee (1988) for details.

18. While constructing the orthodox concept of primitive accumulation, the treatment below takes into account Marx's major work (1973, 1989, 1990) on this issue.

19. While much of Chatterjee's analysis on community stems from his reading of Marx, our reading gives a different rendition of community in Marx. Far from the community being reduced to the underlying core of property or a combination of such entities, the meaning of community comes out as being extraordinary rich and complex so that until the end of his life Marx was struggling with its meaning. Marx was seduced by the different communal forms that existed in India (and later Russia) which have sometimes been characterized as akin to the Asiatic mode of production or AMP. (see Bailey and Llobera 1981 and Shanin 1983). Bailey and Llobera (1981) succintly and incisively summarise Marx's struggle over AMP thus:

> Marx's development of the concept of a specific social totality, the Asiatic mode of production, spanned a period of thirty decades. . . . In certain writings, particular elements of this totality—property, the division of labour, surplus appropriation, exchange, and commodity production—are treated in detail. However, Marx never achieved a systematic exposition of his theory of the AMP. (23)

There are two points to note in this quote. First, unlike political economy whose detailed analysis finds its sedimentation through the three volumes of Capital (that of course is preceded by two decades of research), nothing of that sort existed with respect to the study of community. From his journalistic writings on India to the Grundisse to *Capital* and *Theories of Surplus Value* to *the Ethnological Notes* and the Russian Mir, Marx was struggling to give meaning to the idea of community. One must try to read Marx's theory of community in the background of the totality of Marx's thinking and to which Marx was struggling to give at least a formal—analytical—closure, albeit unsuccessfully. One can blame time (Marx's untimely death) for having robbed us of his comprehensive analytical view even though there are certain clear signals he left us if we view his analysis of community in its totality. This takes us to the second point. Marx clearly understood community as the overdetermined totality of numerous processes and not just that deriving from property or any other entity. Some of the economic processes are mentioned above in Bailey and Llobera. If one further adds noneconomic processes—such as aspects of faith and religion, caste, etc. to which Marx was fully sensitive to and aware of—the overdetermined totality gets much more complex. As Marx never forgot to re-emphasize it is because of this complexity inhering the overdetermined social totality that such societies endured even when despots, rulers and empires came and went. Quite paradoxically, then, the social totality endured not simply due to the existence of an inner core but because of the very complexity that informed the social totality. To reduce Marx's idea of such a social totality referring to community to that of a simple core like property or a subset of some elements is to seriously undermine the idea of community that Marx was trying to establish. We believe that Marxists have often fallen prey to this kind of reductionism that they have often attributed it falsely to Marx.

20. It is ironic that Chatterjee contradicts his own position earlier in his book (which he then forgets to refer back to) when he writes, "we have the establishment of capitalist relations in agricultural production in which the new forms of wage labor fit snugly into the old grid of caste divisions" (1993, 198). This is a counterexample to the generalized antithetical relationship between capital and community.

21. For the case of India Chatterjee's (as well as Sanyal's and Chaudhury's) position is that capital cannot support a systematic policy of primitive capital accumulation to destroy its "other"—precapital or communities—and consequently must appropriate precapital (communities) via the creation of a surrogate synthesis that legitimizes its rule and the process of capital accumulation. Now capital accumulation will involve a process of primitive capital accumulation or what Chatterjee calls the rigor of accumulation, and it cannot be avoided completely because he sees it as a natural outcome of the process of capital accumulation. But the process of primitive capital accumulation will be subjected to severe limitations. It cannot completely ignore the wishes of the communities who are inherently against primitive capital accumulation and hence capital accumulation. In fact, as an earlier quotation from Sanyal reveals, the welfaristic role of the state can create barriers to the process of primitive capital accumulation. Primitive capital

accumulation fails to become the motive force of society and is not a weapon to be used by the state for the systematic transformation of society. Herein lies the failure of primitive capital accumulation in the passive revolution of capital. Capital cannot rule by openly espousing its own process of origin. Capital and communities are inherently opposed to one another; consequently, any surrogate synthesis will be contested and in constant crisis. India's nationhood is in a constant crisis, trying to balance out the inherently opposed narrative of capital and the narrative of community in such a way that the natural process of capital accumulation is not disturbed or challenged in any fundamental way.

22. In line with the theories we are discussing, we use the term "working class" in the traditional sense as a homogeneous group of people who can act consciously.

23. See Sanyal (1993, 117–130) for details.

24. For Sanyal, primitive capital accumulation is a Third World phenomenon: "The second, and more important, reason why the concept of primitive accumulation needs to be given a proper place in the discussion of the capitalist mode of production is that it can be deployed to problematize Third World capitalism. In these countries, the process of destruction of precapital and the establishment of the capitalist mode as the dominant mode of production remains incomplete" (1993, 120). The logical corollary of the above argument is that since precapital is absent in developed countries, the question of primitive capital accumulation does not arise in such countries. Thus the absence of precapital in developed countries seems to be assumed by Sanyal.

25. There is a difference among the theorists on the question of whether precapitalist communities can be called classes. Chatterjee and Chaudhury do not seem to have any problem in describing such communities as non capitalist classes while Sanyal seems to be inclined toward calling the subjects in these communities nonclass agents. We will return to this point below.

26. As mentioned in chapter 1, we consider postmodern approaches contestable. In this regard, from a class standpoint, we differentiate our position sharply from that of Chakraborty (even though we consider some of the other treatment in his book to be illuminating).

Chapter 6
A Marxian Reformulation
of the Concept of Transition

1. By closed social totality we mean the social reality where the only relevant form of class structure is that of a specified class structure, such as the capitalist class structure. Sometimes a closed social totality is also called a centered totality because it is held together by the adjective that closes the boundary of the totality, the term "capitalist" for instance.

2. Also, from now on when we talk about change from one fundamental class process to another—that is, changes between class structures—we shall use the term change in the "content" or "type" of class structure. Thus, a change from a feudal fundamental class process to another (say, capitalist) fundamental class process

would be signified by the term change in the "content" or "type" of the feudal class structure. In contrast, a qualitative change within one class structure would be referred to as a change in "form." Thus, a change within a capitalist class structure is a change in the "form" of that class structure.

   In postmodern Marxist theory, class structure is given by the articulation of a specific fundamental class process and its complementary subsumed and non-class processes that constitute it. Class structures will vary from one another in both content and form. As mentioned above, the content of a class structure is identified in terms of its fundamental class process. For example, a fundamental class process where surplus value is produced and appropriated is defined as a capitalist fundamental class process. The capitalist fundamental class process in turn is constituted by subsumed class processes and other nonclass processes. If these conditions of existence are not reproduced then capitalist fundamental class process will disappear. The articulatory existence of all such class and non-class processes is what we mean by a capitalist class structure. Similarly, there are feudal class structures or independent class structures, and so on. In other words, class structures represent the wholistic presence of a site with all its different so-cial relationships around class. Class structure (i.e., the subset of processes that forms it) is the form through which relationships take the social dimension in a Marxist theory.

3. We must mention one clarifying point concerning the usage of the terms "social totality," "subtotality," and "totality." When we use the term "social totality," we mean society or a configuration of subtotalities. This infers to a macro-level exis-tence. When we refer to the micro-level existence of class structure, we inter-changeably use the term of either subtotality or simply as totality. This distinction helps to keep the two levels, which are intimately interconnected, clear.

4. Consider the case of a capitalist enterprise with a capitalist fundamental class process that is uniquely constituted by other subsumed class and nonclass pro-cesses. Any change in these subsumed or nonclass processes (leading to change in the effects being produced on other processes) will produce a transformation of the capitalist fundamental class process and the capitalist enterprise. This funda-mental class process undergoes a change since its condition of existence has changed. The capitalist enterprise or capitalist class structure (composite of fun-damental class process and its constitutive effects) has undergone a transition from what it was previous to the change to what it is now after the change. The mutation in the fundamental class process will consequently produce changes in the other processes that it constitutes. However, the effect produced on the fun-damental class process is not the same as the effect produced by the fundamental class process on other processes. These are differing, specific effects producing distinct changes within and between class structures.

5. One can discern similar ideas of enterprise in Cullenberg (1994, chapter 4), Resnick and Wolff (1987, chapter 4), and Gibson-Graham (1996, chapter 8).

6. The specification of these class sets does not directly include processes of prop-erty, power, or income distribution. These are nonclass processes whose specific

constitution of a class set creates a further differentiation in terms of multiplicity of uniquely constituted class structures.

7. "A" is the form of appropriation whereby the performer of surplus labor is able to exclude all others from the process of appropriation and therefore appropriates the surplus labor completely and individually. That is, the direct producer appropriates the surplus labor at the individual level. Class structures that fall under the class sets with "A" are called independent or ancient class structures.

8. "N" refers to a form of appropriation whereby the performers of surplus labor are able to excluded themselves from the process of any appropriation. That is, none of the surplus labor is appropriated by the direct producers. Class structures that resemble class sets with "N" are exploitative class structures.

9. "S" refers to a form of appropriation whereby all performers of surplus labor are able to share in its appropriation, and therefore no one is being either completely excluded from appropriation or can exclude others. Class structures that resemble class sets with "S" are communist class structures.

10. The concept of class sets is similar to the concept of fundamental class process first introduced by Resnick and Wolff (1987) insofar as we differentiate class sets by the manner in which surplus labor is appropriated. The difference from Resnick and Wolff is in terms of the exact taxonomies being put forward. The class sets approach allows a finer differentiation of distinct modes of appropriation than does class process as developed by Resnick and Wolff.

11. The exact number of delineated class sets will depend on the details, purpose, and context of a particular analysis. There is no pre-given number that is always and everywhere correct. Therefore, if one considers other relations to appropriation such as corée labor or profit-sharing schemes, the class sets would be further differentiated. This only goes to show the depth of the micro or disaggregated nature of class-based society. This is in direct contrast to the orthodox Marxian concept of social totality signified by a specific, uniform mode of production.

12. As of 1998–99, the central public sector undertakings in India, comprising 235 central public sector enterprises and many more public sector units, employs 19.415 million people (Economic Survey 2000–01, 135; Appendix Table 5). By contrast, the organized private, nonagricultural sector (organized private sector consists of enterprises with ten or more people) employs 8.6 million people (Appendix Table 5). In a predominantly agricultural country like India, the state sector occupies an important place in the industrial economy, especially in light of its role in critical sectors such as industry, minerals and raw materials, banking, and insurance. Contrary to the claim made by many that this represents an indicator of India's socialist nature because state enterprises are supposed to be fundamentally differentiated from capitalist enterprises and therefore, socialist, we find evidence that India's state enterprise sector exhibits a complex class structure. This can be seen especially clearly in light of the liberalization policies that have caused a state of flux in state enterprise sector. Some of the enterprises are remaining under government control where the state or some agencies appropriates the surplus value; others are joint-private ventures, where the state and the private investors share in the appropriation; and some are being completely di-

vested into private hands. Furthermore, some of the output produced by state enterprises is sold on the market as commodities, while other output is provided in various forms of noncommodity distributions. The point we are emphasizing is that even India's state sector is a complex class structure, with various dynamics pertaining to output decisions, accumulation, worker remuneration, and so on, that can't simply be reduced to the "state" or "Socialism," perceived as an undifferentiated concept.

13. The small-scale enterprise sector employs 17.850 million people (Appendix Table 5). Khadi and Village enterprises, a subset of the small enterprise sector, employ 5.5 million people in India as of 1994 (Economic Survey 1994–95, 115). This sector, sometimes referred to as the traditional sector, is a configuration of many class sets, ranging from those which are exploitative, or independent, or even communist. While there are no exact figures available as to the class status of these firms, most would agree that independent and communist class sets dominate these sectors. Similar results can also be found in other small-scale sectors such as in leather and handlooms.

14. This is roughly similar to Marx's critique of the Gotha Programme (Marx 1977, 564–568)—a program that was drawn up by the German socialists on the creation of a future German communist society. Ferdinand Lassalle and other German socialists argued for a "fair" and "equal" distribution of the "undiminished proceeds of labor" among all members of society. Marx ridiculed the idea of an absolute, universally applicable notion of "fairness" or "equality" and questioned the basis of the statement that the "undiminished proceeds of labor" belong to all members of the society. According to Marx, socialists need to develop their own idea of fairness. He also pointed out that, under "communist society," the "undiminished proceeds of labor" will not belong to all members of the society but will be appropriated by the workers. Furthermore, these undiminished proceeds do not remain "undiminished," since the produce has to be redistributed as subsumed class payments to secure the conditions of existence of the fundamental class processes.

15. For a relatively recent Marxian concept of fairness from a non-postmodern Marxist perspective, see Cohen (1995).

16. In other words, our theory of transition precludes the existence of the oft-mentioned permanent paradise under a system dominated by communist class structures. A society dominated by communist class structures could be as fractured (concretely and ethically) as the one dominated by capitalist class structures. Therefore, the body polity is going to be fractured by confrontations between parties and groups. Democracy (in the broader sense of the existence of an institutional configuration capable of internalizing differences and dissent) flows from our theory of transition.

17. There are two features that distinguish the post-Marxian idea of development as progress from Marxian and other non-Marxist ways in which the same have been conceived. Firstly, non-Marxist development as conceived in terms of the growth of Gross National Product, per capita Gross National Product, or even the Human Development Index has tended to concentrate attention either on the production or on the distribution of resources rather than on the articulatory

existence of the production and distribution processes. On the other hand, postmodern Marxists' emphasis on the distribution of wealth in addition to changing the production process is in opposition to the explicit emphasis on just changing the relations of production and ultimately the mode of production by orthodox Marxian theories. Secondly, the non-Marxian indices do not consider the relation between distribution and production from a class perspective or, as in the case of orthodox Marxists, from class qua surplus labor standpoint. Postmodernist Marxist theory sees both of these aspects as deriving from the interaction between fundamental, subsumed, and nonclass processes. For Marxists, income and income distribution are in themselves vague terms. Incomes are surplus payments distinguished in terms of positions occupied by individuals or groups in the fundamental, subsumed, and nonclass processes. Thus, they are either fundamental class payments, subsumed class payments, or nonclass payments (note that nonclass processes are defined from the standpoint of class processes). Postmodern Marxian analysis regarding development or progress brings this aspect of the overdetermined relations between fundamental, subsumed, and nonclass processes into the forefront, something that is not done by any other concepts of development. This is not to say that the other concepts of development are not important, but, rather, that the postmodern Marxist theory of development has its own unique and distinguishing feature.

18. The details again need to be developed as part of the construction of the concept or concepts of "fairness" under the postmodern Marxist framework, an issue we will take up in the next chapter.

19. Our emphasis on the distribution of wealth in addition to changing the production process is in opposition to the explicit emphasis on just changing the relations of production and ultimately the mode of production by orthodox Marxian theories. The latter, in line with the theory of historical materialism, holds that changes made in the mode of production will lead to a change in other aspects of society, including distribution of wealth. This privileged status of production is rejected in our scheme where production (fundamental class process) and distribution (subsumed class process) are intimately linked to one another.

20. This may involve taking part in macro- or state-level politics, but the point we want to emphasize is that the focus of political attention should also shift to the micro politics, because any policy decisions at the macro level are bound to produce profound but uneven changes in class structures—micro-level changes. Changes here will in turn affect the policy decisions in the macro level. Because of this back and forth passage of cause and effect, any difference between the two levels—micro and macro—becomes blurred. However, since orthodox Marxists have for so long tended to consider class struggles explicitly in macro terms, We want to invoke the term "micro" to hammer home our point of difference as far as the concept of transition and (direction of) change is concerned.

21. This displacement reveals a similar strategy to that of Foucault's micro politics of resistance. Foucault points out that oppressed groups should resist oppression, but he also argued that such resistance would be futile since new structures of power would always replace the old ones. This power game is a never-ending

game of resistance against oppression, even though power can never be ultimately overcome, hence, in this sense, the resistance, though desirable, is futile. Our concept of micro politics, on the other hand, is focused on changing the exploitative class structures of society to nonexploitative ones with the belief that such a change will, via its overdetermined and contradictory effects, produce substantial changes in other class and nonclass processes thereby having a profound effect on society or social totality. Thus while Foucault's micro politics is almost static (that is, stuck in the duality of power and resistance), ours is more dynamic and transformative with macro effects. In this context, Gibson-Graham (1993) argues that the apparent monolithic macro existence of "capitalism" can be decentered in terms of micro-level politics of subversion and resistance.

22. A century has elapsed in which theorists have fought with one another trying to pin down the definition of hegemony. While the differences and controversies are very nuanced, let us bring together certain commonly agreed features to define hegemony at a rudimentary level. We define hegemony as a process directed toward producing adherence/legitimacy for certain type of rule/regime/order by constructing and inculcating a system of faith/belief in the rule/regime/order among concerned agents. The crucial element distinguishing hegemony from other apparatuses of rule is the aspect of the system of faith/belief and not brute force as the medium of holding the rule/regime/order. Faith/Belief system is part of the process through which the ideology supportive of the rule/order is transmitted among agents in society. Not rule over the body but rule over the soul: this is the key principle in understanding the concept of hegemony.

23. Environment within a community is constituted by many elements. The river supplying it water, the air it breathes, the land it tills, the birds it watches, the men and women its members talk to, the forest nearby, the kinship and property relationship it sustains, the variegated class and on class processes it supports, the knowledge/information of the terrain its members have—all of these together constitute a community's environment. This environment is shared because members of the "community" can draw upon this configuration of natural and social network without excluding other members in order to reproduce their life(style) including the economic reproduction.

24. When speaking of compensation, the right question is whether people are getting the value of that irrecoverable shared environment along with the direct cost of land.

25. This way of looking at the economy constitutes a fundamentally new way of thinking about the concept of "development" that we will explore in further details in the chapter on development. One can trace an initial glint of this possibility to Sanyal (1993) though he does not pursue it to its logical conclusion.

26. What is a household and which type of household are our point of reference and the point of departure? Here we basically concur with Fraad, Resnick, and Wolff's understanding of household. They point out that

> Historically, the term "household" has carried many different meanings. Sometimes it has referred to the living space occupied by members of a

family and sometimes also to the family's working space. . . . Our analysis
focuses initially on households that display certain basic characteristics.
They contain an adult male who leaves the household to participate in
capitalist class processes (at the social site of the enterprise) to earn cash
income. They also contain an adult female, the wife of the male, who remains inside the household. They may also contain children, elderly parents, and others, but that is of secondary importance at this initial phase of
the analysis. The adult female works inside the household in the task of
shopping, cleaning, cooking, repairing clothes and furniture, gardening,
and so on. . . . In any case, our analysis of this type will then make possible
a comparative analysis of other types characterizing contemporary households. . . . A consideration of the various non-capitalist forms of fundamental class process discussed in the Marxist literature readily suggests
which form best fits our household. It is the feudal form. . . . The feudal
form is appropriate because it requires no intermediary role for markets,
prices, profits or wages in the relation between the producer and appropriator of surplus labor. The producer of surplus on the medieval European
manor often delivered his/her surplus labor (or its product) directly to the
lord of the manor, much as the wife delivers her surplus to her husband.
(Fraad, Resnick, and Wolff 1994, 5–7)

We take this non-capitalist, feudal household class process as our point of reference and departure because it closely resembles the traditional family in households in underdeveloped countries such as that of India. Later on, we will show
how in light of the overdetermined effect of capitalist class process, the feudal
household class process becomes transformed.

27.   The theorists of "domestic labor" debate were severely criticized on mainly three
fronts: (i) the functionalist explanation of the existence of the household economy as serving the need of capitalism, (ii) their reduction of the specificity of the
household to the mode of production, and (iii) their reduction of class processes
inside the household to patriarchy. In our scheme, we avoid these points of criticism. We consider the site of non-capitalist household and capitalist enterprises
to be two distinct sites of the economy where their overdetermined existence may
or may not be beneficial to one another. However, in line with the specific problem that we are dealing with here, we want to take up a small area: the relation between household production processes and the constitution of the commodity
labor power at the moment of overdetermination between capitalist and noncapitalist class processes.

28.   Some of the ideas developed have been taken from Chaudhury and Chakrabarti
(2000).

29.   The postmodern Marxist school led by Wolff, Roberts, and Callari (1982, 1984);
Roberts (1995); and Chaudhury (1998) broke ranks from the traditional Marxian approach to value theory to solve the transformation problem (while the former's approach abstracts away from heterogeneous labor, the latter two solved

the problem in the context of heterogeneous labor). The break is not related to mathematics but to the conceptualization of the problem. The conceptual approach in traditional Marxism to value theory and the transformation problem has been to take value as independent and autonomous from value form (prices of production) with the philosophical grounding that value—the essence or source—will determine the prices of production: the appearance. Under the traditional Marxian approach, the two equalities—Sum of prices = Sum of values and Sum of profits = Sum of surplus values—will not generally hold except under very restrictive conditions (for example, Morishima [1973] demonstrated that the two equalities hold *if and only if* the economy is on a balanced growth path). The postmodern Marxist approach abandoned this essentialist essence/appearance dichotomy and adopted the nonessentialist standpoint of overdetermination. By their logic of overdetermination, value constitutes the price of production and the price of production, in turn, constitutes value. The epistemological difference for the contrasting formulation of the value equation in the two approaches plays the crucial role in solving the transformation problem in the postmodern approach. In line with this conceptual difference, while in the traditional Marxian approach the means of production and means of subsistence (constant and variable capital) in the value equation are measured in terms of value magnitudes, in the postmodern Marxist approach they are measured by prices of production expressed in units of socially necessary abstract labor time. Given this value equation and the (traditional) price equation, the two equalities follow definitionally in the postmodern Marxist framework.

30. Whether the wage paid to the laborer is the reproduction cost of the family of the laborer or that of only the laborer is a contentious issue. However, here we will refrain from entering the controversy and basically accept the former position, which we believe is held by a majority of Marxists (Marx 1990, Seccombe 1974, 1980, Delphy 1984).

31. Strictly speaking, the subsistence basket available in the market is a semifinished product. Household labor transforms the semifinished consumption basket into a finished consumption basket. Thus, the semifinished products together with the amount of labor time exerted by the housewife inside the household in finishing the entire process constitute the value of labor power. In other words, the process of production of the commodity labor power is a vertically integrated system. The capitalist sells the wage goods in a semifinished form while another tier of production (household production) finishes the product. In terms of the value equation for the labor power, the household does not buy the subsistence basket $\{b_i\}$ from the market but its semifinished form $\{b_i'\}$ at prices p_i. Household labor transforms this $\{b_i'\}$ into the finished goods $\{b_i\}$ fit for household consumption reproducing, in turn, the commodity labor power fit for consumption in the capitalist production process. Thus, the household labor constitutes the value of labor power, the capitalist production process, and consequently, the capitalist class process.

32. The attempt to include direct household labor time in the value equation of labor power creates its own problems. In light of the inclusion of household

labor time, one might, following Chaudhury and Chakrabarti (2000), suggest a value equation of labor power as

$$V_L = \sum_i p_i b_i + a_{oL}$$

where a_{oL} = direct household labor time required to produce one unit of the labor power.

The problem with this equation is that while $\sum_i p_i b_i$ is measured in socially necessary abstract labor time, a_{oL} is in concrete labor time—two incommensurable elements. The solution, then, is to make the two elements commensurable by reducing a_{oL} to abstract labor time. If an adequate measure of household abstract labor time can be theorized, then the next problem is to solve the transformation problem in this more general set (where household is present). Both of these are value theoretic problems that need to be faced by the postmodern Marxist theorists. Confronting these problems is important since they will help us to understand the implications of incorporating household class process into the value theoretic framework, thus strengthening and securing its theoretical foundation within the postmodern Marxist theory. However, this is beyond the scope of this book. Instead we will concentrate on the effect of including household class processes.

33. These historical and moral elements are constituted by cultural and political aspects in addition to the economic aspects. Since we are not concentrating on cultural and political aspects, we suspend any detailed analysis of their constitution of the meaning of the socially necessary means of subsistence. We simply take these aspects and the socially necessary means of subsistence as given.

34. The changes in social perception are actualized only if the economic goods are delivered. There might be a change in the social perception of what is the socially necessary basket of commodities without a delivery of such goods. This produces what economists call the shortage economy. There is a more or less general consensus among economists that the former Soviet Union represented one such shortage economy and that this aspect was one major cause of its downfall.

35. The figures on the gross domestic savings could indicate the trend of expenditures for Indian households. Appendix Table 1 shows that the household savings averaged 18.2 percent from 1991–92 to 1999–2000. The composition of household savings also underwent a drastic change, with savings in the form of physical assets increasing sharply from 7.7 percent of GDP in 1994–95 to 10.7 percent in 1995–96 (principally, real estate), and savings in the form of financial assets falling from 11.5 percent to 8.8 percent of GDP (Economic Survey 1996–97, 4). Further indications of a shift in the consumer investment pattern can be gauged from appendix Table 2. There one witnesses a substantial growth of consumer goods, especially that of the consumer durables. The delinking of control over the import of the parts of these goods (as well as freeing investment from licensing control) certainly contributed to the growth. In other words, a lot of "pent

up" demand on the part of consumers is being met indicating the arrival of consumerism in India, inside households.

36. This transformative aspect of modern technology has not been totally lost on social theorists. In the *Alternative Economic Survey* brought out by opponents of the government policies, Ahooja-Patel (1994), commenting on the politics of exclusion of women, avers that, "At a time when India is being rapidly transformed by imported technologies, it might have been useful to study the social implications of these technologies particularly the manner in which these affect the family budget" (Ahooja-Patel 1994, 122). Because of the general lack of interest in the household as a site of production process, very few known studies exist in this direction with respect to India. The deeper problem with such studies is to conceive of a framework that could unambiguously define the household as a site of production. Our class analytic framework is a first step in that direction, since it is able to identify and name a production process in terms of class processes within the household unit, making it possible to conduct concrete studies on the overdetermined nature of the social existence of a household's class processes.

37. The value (commodity) of labor power includes the reproduction of the entire family of the laborer—the laborer himself, his wife, children, and other family members living with them. Thus, when the housewife is working to reproduce the value of the labor power of the laborer, she is exerting necessary labor to reproduce herself and surplus labor to reproduce her husband, children, and other family members.

38. The Human Development Report (1995, 87–99) emphasizes some of the effects of a housewife's work that cannot be quantified even though their effects (in terms of value being created) on the economy may be far-reaching.

39. We have theorized the point that an individual (housewife or the man of the household) may simultaneously hold two class positions, one in the household production process and another in the capitalist production process such that each provides the condition of existence of the other. The simultaneous existence of two class positions arises from the different positions occupied in the two distinct but related class processes. Even at the moment of specifying the economic in terms of a particular class process (like the capitalist fundamental class process), no individual's social existence can be reduced simply to the position he or she occupies inside that particular class process. That is, the worker as an individual overflows with excess meaning. And we repeat, this follows from our theoretical proposition that capitalist class process is overdetermined by noncapitalist class process.

40. From Appendix Table 3 one can witness the steady influx of women workers in organized private and public sectors as well as case study reports in the newspapers and news journals. All such reports indicate a growing influx of female workers in the enterprises. This is not to say that female workers were previously absent from such sites of the economy but, rather, that as a result of the effects of liberalization, a new mass of female workers who were previously tied only to the economy of the household are now entering other uncharted sites.

Chapter 7
Class and Need

1. As Escobar points out, the race between the Soviet Union–supported countries and the U.S.–supported countries—which dominated the discourse on and practice of development in the Third World—became one of matching each other's level of technological growth, industrialization, and wealth. While the two differed on means of implementation, the objectives were not vastly different. Escobar "tells the story of this dream and how it progressively turned into a nightmare." (4, 1995)

2. Some postmodern Marxists seem to be regarding self-exploitative and communist class process as progressive in contrast to other types of exploitative class process, while others are inclined toward the communist class process at the expense of the self-exploitative. There is an eerie silence on both sides when it comes to confronting each other's position in a systematic manner. One of the tasks of this chapter, though not the central one, is to explode this impasse and develop the detail of the differences. Development of this point is important for the purpose of arriving at a conception of a desirable society in the context of need.

3. Our rendition of need is fundamentally different from the basic-needs literature even though we do consider the latter as a fundamental shift in outlook. Basic-needs approach "focuses on conditions without which human beings are unable to survive, avoid misery, relate to other people, and avoid alienation. . . . Having, Loving, and Being are catchwords for central necessary conditions. . . ." (89, Allardt 1993), even though as Sen (1993, 40) correctly pointed out the emphasis remains on commodities or "Having" at the expense of "Loving" and "Being." Our conception of needs differs from the basic-needs approach in four ways: (i) our notion of needs does not preclude production while the basic-needs is purely a distributional concept, (ii) basic-needs only deals with commodities that address people's bare minimum while our needs approach looks at needs as flowing from certain conditions of being of humans, where the condition is not reduced to that of conditions of poverty even though it does not exclude those, (iii) in contrast to our approach, basic-needs is defined in an ad hoc manner—that is, with an objective basis—and its approach does not differentiate between needs while our concept of need is a dynamic one, and (iv) it hardly says anything about the relation between needs and the surplus economy while our framework points to a special kind of connection between the two.

4. See chapter 6 for an elaboration of the matrix of class set and the process of classification (additionally, see Cullenberg [1992] and Chakrabarti and Cullenberg [2001a]).

5. Resnick and Wolff have talked about two kinds of communist class process—type 1, where "all adult individuals in society participate collectively in that class process as appropriators of surplus labor, but only some individuals (a small number) perform surplus labor" (1988, 21) and type 11, where "only those particular individuals who perform surplus labor collectively appropriate it" (1988, 21). Elsewhere they argue that communist class process is characterized by the

fact that "the direct producers *collectively* perform and appropriate surplus labor" (1987, 309). So the crucial feature of a communist fundamental class process is that surplus labor is performed and appropriated *collectively* in some sense of being shared.

6. In communist class process, not only will the cooked food be appropriated collectively, but also the process of cooking (performance of labor) would have to resemble some form of collective process in the sense of being shared. Thus, for example, husbands and wives might shop together for raw materials and cook the food together. Or, they might take turns (i.e., share) cooking the food. By contrast, in AC's case, the men do not cook at all. This is typical in many Indian families where the men are excluded from the kitchen.

7. While the feudal serf is tied to his environment forcefully by the landlord, members of community are free to leave their environment but may desire to be tied to it.

8. In the context of a hegemonic construction, the theoretical production of this need-based space/third space can also be produced as the outside of a totality (Chaudhury 1988, 1994; Chakrabarti and Chaudhury 1996/97; Chaudhury, Das, and Chakrabarti 2000; and more particularly in Chakrabarti and Roy Chaudhury 1999/2000). The basic idea is that a totality is defined in terms of a contingent nodal point. For example, if the nodal point is surplus labor, then the totality will be around that nodal point. Within that totality capitalist class process and noncapitalist class process become the two contending points around which the mutual constitutivity of the totality can be described that may, in certain instances, give way to a scenario where the capitalist class may emerge (note: not as given but produced) as the dominant (center) space as compared to the noncapitalist one (the margin). This is what we call *mimicry of overdetermination* (Chaudhury, Das, and Chakrabarti 2000; Chakrabarti and Roy Chaudhury 1999/2000). This dominance when it reproduces the faith in an idea (such as the virtues of a "capitalist system" or the New Economic Policy) gives way to its hegemony. But then what about the outside of the totality—the space in which surplus does not operate as the unifying and operational mechanism of structuring production and distribution of good and services? This nonsurplus space of producing and distributing goods marks the possibility of its own totality from an altogether different nodal point. We call that space—the outside space—the need/necessity and sometimes subsistence economy. Even though the two ways of producing goods and services constitute two different totalities, from the standpoint of the surplus, the "other" totality presents itself as an outside space to the surplus one. Within the surplus economy, the capitalist class process can negotiate with other forms of surplus-focused class process but the nonsurplus speaks in a different language. In this context, when the capitalist economic travels beyond the contingent totality (without the surplus ever becoming the operational device in the process) to establish its dominance over the outside—the need-based economy—and when that dominance inheres in the reproduction of the faith in an *idea* we call such instances the *synthetic hegemony of capital*, in order to distinguish them from any other hegemonic structure that has hitherto

been discussed from only within the context of the totality (Chaudhury 1988, 1994; Chakrabarti and Roy Chaudhury 1999/2000). This is a case of hegemony where one space rules over another not by appropriation but rather by exclusion. While the details have been developed elsewhere (see the references), for the moment, it suffices to say that, in line with this approach along with the Derridean, one may also take the need-based third as a theoretically constructed space defined in the context of the surplus-focused economy.

9. When we delineated the household into classes, we did not deal with the case of the economic existence of a household with a single member. This member, if he does not produce surplus for internal (which de facto he does not since there is nobody else to appropriate or share the surplus) or external (which he may very well not) purpose is simply producing to reproduce his need without generating any surplus. In case he generated surplus to be delivered externally (such as handing over food or other things as part of religious duty), this economic activity would amount to a self-exploitative process. If not, then this constitutes a need-based activity and such production activities inside the household as need-based household economic.

10. Marxists have found it difficult to deal with the constitution and allocation of budgets (which is especially important in the context of a developing country like India where government is a major player in almost every walk of life) because of the absence of an appropriate frame to look at it. We believe that the structure offered in looking at social surplus provides a way out. Part of the government income provides a condition of existence for the generation of production surplus (that is, FCP) such as water tax, land tax, service charges, etc., but another huge portion takes the form of social surplus that (through the mechanism of tax or otherwise) are above the amount needed to provide direct conditions of existence of production surplus even though they originate from production of goods and services. This social surplus is explicitly directed at fulfilling the necessities emanating from the need criteria. The struggle over the social surplus is in part a nonclass struggle (at a direct level), but it is also in part a class struggle because how much social surplus is to be extracted, from whom it is to be extracted, and the method of extraction are questions pertaining to the distribution of social surplus produced in fundamental class processes. Here is a case where the need-focused and class struggles converge and get interlocked. In facing the budget allocations, Marxists should therefore highlight the mutually constitutive moments of class and development in their own specific ways.

11. Among the NBA, Arundhuti Roy who joined the movement late remains sensitive to the need for some sort of articulation of class and need struggles even though it is not spelt out clearly in her writings. Medha Patkar, the remarkable leader of the NBA, sees "capitalism" as an evil system even though she and the NBA in general are not clear on which alternatives they want to put in place of so-called capitalism. Through our formulation, we want to create a distinctly different way of conceiving transition and development that the NBA and other social organizations sensitive to social change may find useful.

12. The *Mahabharata* is a great Indian epic.

13. Thereby, the synthetic hegemony of capital is established—a hegemony not by including the outside in the surplus-based totality but by excluding that space via the former's metonymic transfers (NGO's for example) into the outside space. The complex of international agencies, national government, and actors supporting capitalist classes that intervenes in the need-based economy—the synthetic hegemony of capital that it generates—can be sensed in terms of what Ruccio (borrowing from Deleuze and Guattari) so perceptively called—in the global context—the imperial machine "as against either a particular stage of capitalism (Lenin's preference) or merely a political choice (the approach of Lenin's nemesis, Kautsky)." He observes that ". . . the machinelike quality of imperialism gives a sense of the ways in which it has various parts that (often but not always) work together, a set of energies, available identities and categories, that propels individuals and groups, institutions and structures, to enact designs and to civilize those who attempt to resist its apparent lessons, to make them succumb to the naturalized logic. Not a stage of capitalism but rather a machine that energizes and is energized by capitalism at various points in its history. Not a mere political choice available to ruling governments and regimes, although it does include various options: military bombardment or invasion, economic carrots and sticks, cultural hegemony and worldwide news reach. . . ." (Ruccio 2001).

14. In this context, one can read Resnick and Wolff's analysis of Soviet Union in a different light. The problem was not that Soviet planning was pushing down real wages below the subsistence level as was pointed in Resnick and Wolff (1993, 1994, 1995, 2001), but rather that it did not compensate the loss with the expansion of the need-based economy. In fact, the logic of Soviet development based on industrialization through capital accumulation did not allow for that. Consequently the need-based economy was either eaten up or destroyed by the surplus economy. Denial of its "other" can indeed be self-defeating for the survival of a system.

15. In this we agree with Sanyal's (2001) concern over such issues, though he is working from a different framework.

Chapter 8
The Political Economy
of the New Economic Policies

1. It is interesting to note that some intellectuals and media groups that support the government policies are projecting India's transition as a movement from a socialist economy to a capitalist economy. According to this view, India's socialist feature is attributed to the broad involvement by the government (and especially the planning board) in many important aspects of the economy. The government's interference in the input, output, and pricing decisions made in the economy is regarded as an indicator of India's socialist feature. The transition process to a dynamic capitalist economy, it is said, requires freeing these broad sets of decisions from government control. The projection of the unworkable nature of the pre-liberalization Indian economy as socialist is being legitimized by refer-

ence to the collapse of the former USSR economy. This metonymy of references between the two is a powerful tool for selling the government's economic policies to the public, but one that reveals a pattern of deception in the face of scrutiny. It is now well documented (Chattopadhyay 1985, Chakravarty 1987, Chatterjee 1986, 1993) that the pre-liberalization policies of extensive government involvement in the economy were laid out by the National Planning Committee (NPC) in the pre–World War II phase in which many important industrial and merchant houses were involved. The so-called socialist policies were jointly arrived at by the government and business houses where the government's involvement, especially in the capital goods sector, was rationalized by observing that not only was it needed for public welfare and aspects of self-sufficiency, but, more important, it was needed by the private sector, which lacked the economic capacity to undertake big infrastructural investment. The idea was that the government would provide essential conditions of production so that the private sector could gain from it. We are not saying that the socialist policies of the USSR did not have any influence on the policies made by the government or the planning commission, but to reduce the historical origin of such policies to the experience of the USSR is a callous case of false juxtaposition that effaces any contextual inference to the arrival and deployment of such a set of polices. Such analysis results in a simplified projection of the pre-liberalization India as a concerted effort by government to stifle or destroy the private sector. This projection flies in the face of data from every source that reveals that it is the so-called business houses and rich agricultural farmers or landlords who have gained most in the last fifty years of India's independence. By standards of income differences, standards of human development, concentration of property or power, and the extent or degree of exploitation, this so-called stifled group of people who are now being lumped together as the new pioneers of India's development path have gained disproportionately in comparison with the rest of the population. Just as "socialism" can be of many types, so can "capitalism." U.S. capitalism is not the same as the French or Russian capitalism. What many now perceive as "socialism" in the pre-NEP period was nothing but a form of "capitalism." And if we further understand the state enterprises as state capitalist enterprises, which is what they are, as we will explain later on, then the lingering doubt transforms into a verity.

2. The left seems to be stuck in a static notion of the past as something good or at least better than the evolving present. This is a very conservative attitude when all indications are that the present is changing from the past in many important ways. The important thing is to understand the dialectics of change, the process through which history is being created instead of ossifying one's analytical perception in such vague terms as self-sufficiency and self-reliance. Granting for argument's sake that the past may have been "better," we do not see how that alters the changes in the newly evolving present. In addition to many other things, the responsibility of a Marxist or a Marxist party should be to analyze the present evolving situation and take its position accordingly. Holding on to the past steadfastly might have the negative and dangerous effect of leaving the entire discursive field relating to the dialectics of change to be dominated by the

neo-conservatives, as is evidently happening today. For all these reasons, a class analysis of transition is important from a political perspective.

3. We are only including figures until 1985–86 because it was roughly during that period that the first loud rumblings about the "inflated" role of government began to surface (which is what we want to emphasize here), both among the academics and among some politicians (Chakravarty 1987). While the full-blown concrete liberalization policies took effect in 1990–91 after the Narasimha Rao–led Congress (I) party came to power, its intellectual and tentative political basis (we discussed Rajiv Gandhi's half-hearted liberalization attempt in chapter I) began to unravel in the mid-1980s.

4. The government in its reports makes a distinction between organized private enterprises, and small-scale enterprises which is based on the size of the firm (approximated by the value of capital). The private enterprises are considered to be run on capitalist principles (production for surplus value). Thus, they constitute what we call private capitalist enterprises. The small-scale enterprises can be of many types of class structures. It could be a small-sized enterprise run on capitalist principles or it could be independent enterprise or even communist enterprise. There are large numbers of small cooperatives or family enterprises that resemble communist class processes. The independent and communist enterprises are also often called traditional enterprises in the Economic Survey.

5. According to the former finance minister Manmohan Singh, who was the pioneer of the reforms, the root cause of the acute fiscal and current account imbalance was the phenomenal rise in the government's revenue deficit. The target of the reform became the reduction of fiscal deficit by especially curtailing what were called the government's nonproductive expenditures. Appendix Table 8 shows the budget deficit, revenue deficit, and fiscal deficit as a percentage of GDP. The government would ideally like the budget deficit to be around 2 percent, and it has been targeting for a reduction of its deficits every year, but without much success. This overshooting indicating the inability of the government to meet its budgetary considerations symbolizes the difficulties faced by the government in implementing its reform.

6. For the difference between absolute surplus-value production process and relative surplus-value production process, see chapter 1.

7. An important point to note in advance is the assumption of the uniformity of the economic space in articulating government policies. That is, the policies are devised and defended by assuming that transitions in one site would be replicated in all other sites. The government defends its action by pointing out that the benefits of reforms would be universally effective across the economic sites while the opposition emphasizes that problems related to it would be similarly applicable to all sites. As we explained in an earlier chapter, this assumption follows from a holistic concept of totality where transition means a movement from one whole to another requiring in the process that its constitutive parts replicate itself in a more or less identical manner. There we explained our discomfort with such concepts of totality and transition. Given the decentered concept of totality and class-based, micro-focused process of transition, any government policies would

have dissimilar effects on existing class structures, since the conditions of existence (both internal and external) are distinct for each of them. One thing that our class analysis does is to show that each of the policy changes (agricultural, industrial, and so on) designated to have uniform effects produces instead a complex process of change in each class structure such that change in one class structure is dissimilar from and thereby irreducible to change in another class structure.

Chapter 9
Transition and the Class Structure
in the Indian Economy

1. The left-hand side of (a) represents the revenue side of the enterprise while the right-hand side its expenditure required to reproduce the conditions of existence of the components in the revenue side. SV and Σ SC reflect the fundamental and subsumed class processes respectively. ΣSCR reflects the subsumed class revenue positions of the enterprise—that is, any revenue it generates from its occupation of subsumed class positions with respect to other firms. It might include returns such as dividends, ground rents, merchant fees, etc. Reproduction of these subsumed revenue class positions, in turn, requires expenditure or payments for those social positions that will ensure the reproduction of the ΣSCR. Such payments are gathered around the Σ X. Similarly, Σ NCR stands for all nonclass revenues earned by the enterprise, such as return on loans advanced to productive laborers. Σ Y stands for the expenditure or payments required to reproduce the conditions of existence of Σ NCR. An enterprise is a complex site of these multiple sources of class and nonclass revenues and expenditures. In the case of any specific enterprise, one or more components could be absent. Thus, the revenue and expenditure side of the enterprise might possibly be constituted by only the relationship between SV and SC. Indeed, much of the Marxian tradition focuses only on this truncated version of the class analytic equation. However, as equation (a) shows, the enterprise can be even more complexly constituted than what is normally assumed to be. See Fraad, Resnick, and Wolff (1994, 96–111); Resnick and Wolff (1987, 163–230); Cullenberg (1994, chapter 4); and Graham-Gibson (1996, chapter 4) for details.

2. The severity of the crises could vary depending on the difference between the revenue side and the expenditure side. Some crises would be mild while others would be severe. Since the revenue components and the expenditure components reflect the different class and nonclass processes, a crisis would imply that the prevailing form of class structure of the farm will have to change. If the extent of the crisis is mild then probably there will be a few minor changes in class structure of the farm, while if the extent of the crisis is severe then there could be major change within the class structures of the farm. Such changes may lead to change in the type of class structure of a farm or even its closure.

3. An example is the attempt to sharply reduce the fertilizer subsidies by government. As part of deficit reduction, policy makers are determined to reduce fertilizer subsidies, which are bound to seriously affect the constitution of the fundamental class processes that benefit from such subsumed class payments (or transfers). Each year the government sets a target to reduce the extent of fertilizer subsidies, which in practice fails to be reached. This phenomenon is replicated almost every year. Why the government is not able to meet its desired policy prescriptions is a political economy question, and it must be faced at that level. The same is true for subsidies on water and electricity. The unsavory events in Haryana (farmers burning down railway stations, police stations, government buildings, etc.) resulting from the state government's efforts to curtail subsidies on electricity is a grim reminder of the class dynamics flowing from such aspects along with the possibilities of class struggle that might flare up.

4. It is to be noted that inflation has different ramifications. First, it affects different sections of the population disparately since it involves a disproportional increase in the prices of commodities and thereby, depending upon their consumption patterns, will change the purchasing power of different groups of people differently. Second, the change in the relative price structure changes the distribution of money income since increases or decreases of prices increase or decrease factor income as well. Because of the present trend in India, which shows that increase in food-grain prices far outweighs the overall rate of inflation (showing itself in a higher consumer price index for agricultural workers than the increase in consumer price index for industrial workers and nonmanual employees), there are studies (Mehta 1994, Sen 1994, Ghosh 1995, Rangarajan 1999) claiming that the present bout of inflation has adversely affected the agricultural laborers, small farmers, and urban poor. This has lead to a redistribution of income that involves a transfer of income from these sections of the population to those categories of the population who are the producers and/or the sellers of those goods, thereby benefiting in the end those who spend a smaller proportion of their income on primary food articles. These studies also show that increases in agricultural wages are unable to compensate for the price increases and that, consequently, real income has gone down. The situation is worst for the urban poor whose nominal wage has stagnated. And all of this happened when the critical stochastic factor of inclement weather was avoided leading to a steady growth of Indian culture.

5. One reason why private investment may not be forthcoming is the low investment in capital formation by public sector. Certain private investment in capital formation is dependent on government investments in infrastructure such as roads and irrigation. Low public investment may drive out private investment. This complementary relation implies that the nature of public and private investment in capital formation in agriculture is guided by crowding in rather than crowding out.

6. In this context, one must note that it would be wrong to consider only the terms of trade of agriculture vis-à-vis domestic industrial market. One must also, in ad-

dition, take into account the internal terms of trade within agriculture—the change in relative prices of cash crop vis-à-vis food-grain prices. That will open up unknown territories as far as visualizing the effect of the government policies are concerned.

7. A national Agriculture Policy was announced by the government on July 28, 2000, giving credence to our criticism that for a decade since the inception of the NEP, the policy makers' comprehension of the agricultural sector in India involved seeing daylight in bits and pieces. The new agriculture policy, however, is a comprehensive package of some of the recommendations of the pro-reform proponents as laid down in this chapter without integrating some of the probable effects emanating from the contradictory instances of those policies, which we are also trying to point out here.

8. This resembles the scenario presented in Harris-Todaro migration model (1970), where the dynamics of the creation of urban unemployment depended on the difference between the new urban jobs created and the number of people leaving the rural sector in each point in time. However, while in Harris-Todaro this dynamic is sensitive to policy makers trying to change the urban employment rate, here the dynamics relating to the creation of urban unemployment are sensitive to the free play of market forces leading to cost-effective agrarian enterprises shedding off rural workers at a faster rate than could be absorbed in the urban areas. Ignorance of this impending danger signals a failure on the part of the government to comprehend the overdetermined relations between the agricultural sector and the industrial sector. A fallout of this is to miss the point that the character of the future labor market in urban cities and urban city life in general will depend to a large extent on what happens in the agricultural sector. So the problem here arises due to the absence of an agricultural policy by the government that is capable of internalizing the situation rather than the presence of one as in the Harris-Todaro model.

9. In a sense, this marks a churning of history. The modern factory system came into being two centuries ago amid the ruin of production organizations such as family production and guilds. In a curious juxtaposition, today we are witnessing the reemergence of these in different forms in the midst of the disintegration of the factory system and the proletariat as we knew it.

10. This can also be read as a way of constructing hegemony in the new era of globalization and hyper-competition. Previously that hegemony was secured through the old labor contract, but now with its breakdown a new hegemony has to be formulated. The attempt to transform the firms from economic to social organizations in order to account for needs related to employability could be seen as a new development on this front. Even though we do not pursue it here, we see this line of research as leading to innovative and interesting conclusions.

11. If the firm is unable to ensure the employability of workers, then government could through massive retraining programs. This is what China, unlike India, is currently doing to take care of the problem.

12. There is one exception regarding the small-scale sector to which we will come in the next chapter.

13. Porter defines cluster as "critical masses—in one place—of unusual competitive success in particular fields" (78, 1998a).

14. The process of formation and disintegration of clusters is one of the innovative ways in which the changing face of the Indian industry could be telescoped. This analysis is especially useful in capturing the dynamism of the development process in India in terms of its geographical (dis)location and regional pattern of industrial change.

15. "Small" is distinguished from "large" in terms of the maximum permitted value of investment in plant and equipment. It has to be remembered that the government has, from time to time, changed the maximum permissible limit and thus the meaning of smallness.

16. Even private enterprises can go to BIFR and, under certain circumstances, need its approval for closing or restructuring. Until December 31, 2000, the number of references received by BIFR concerning the private sector was 4,324 (Economic Survey, 2000–01, 147). However, the government is currently thinking of getting rid of BIFR and henceforth one of the conditions of existence of firms will disappear. Since the BIFR also dealt with sick private sector units, disbanding it would mean that private firms would now be able to exit at will.

17. But even here the government seems to be currently inclined to let the minority private partner run the firm including overseeing the process of performance, appropriation, distribution, and receipt of surplus labor. An interesting case that is still developing is that of Haldia Petrochemical, a giant project in the state of West Bengal worth over Rs 5,000 crores and recently commissioned. Against all odds, the West Bengal government brought two private partners into the project, and currently there are three parties including the state government that take part in the appropriation and distribution of surplus. However, the project has run into financial trouble from day one. To complete the project in time, the unit needed around Rs 1,000 crores, which it was supposed to raise from the equity market. However, in the year 1999–2000 when this was supposed to happen, the equity market crashed and the potential investors vanished. So the authorities in desperation went to the banks and sought loans of the same amount. Since the interest from this loan was never part of the planned liability of the project, Haldia Petrochemical started incurring losses from day one. Currently, unless this amount is somehow written off, it will be practically impossible to make this project viable. In order to overcome this problem, the West Bengal government began inviting other partners who can buy back its additional debt in exchange for a share of the company. Indian Oil Corporation— the public oil giant in India—has shown definite interest but its proposal has torn the existing three partners of Haldia apart. It proposed writing off the specific debt in exchange for 26 percent share of the company. However, its further demand is that even with minority share it wants the full right of appropriation and distribution of surplus of Haldia Petrochemical. One particular partner

who owns a higher share is not inclined to this proposal, but the other partners including the West Bengal government seem to be for it in order to save the project. This is an example of the earlier mentioned point that property rights do not automatically transpire into rights of appropriation—the two are indeed conceptually distinct even though, as we are pointing out, the former does overdetermine the latter in important ways.

18. The political heat can be gauged from the different nationalist organizations resisting reforms that are sprouting out all over the country. For example, the right-wing Hindu fundamentalist Bharatiya Janata Party has a front organization called the *Swadeshi Jagran Manch* (a nationalist organization), which is organizing and arguing for the creation of an indigenous, self-sufficient economy as against the open-door trade and industrial policies of the government. They are especially opposed to the unrestricted entry of multinational enterprises. It is interesting to note that, in recent times, this front organization has gone against its parent party (the BJP), which, now in power, is spearheading the current phase of the NEP.

19. The case of Kanoria jute mill in West Bengal indicates the faulty understanding of the nature of enterprises among the major parties on the left India. In 1993, the workers of Kanoria jute mill rose up in protest against the management of the mill. In an unprecedented, historical class struggle over the class processes that caught the imagination of the people of West Bengal, the workers and their supporters (which include local farmers and traders, other laborers, artists, writers, etc.) under the banner of Sramik Sangram Parishad (the union leading the class struggle) have, against all odds, continued their undaunted battle against the promoter running the mill for ten long years. Currently, the case of Kanoria jute mill is in BIFR and the union's demand is that they be allowed to run the mill on a cooperative basis, that is, as a communist class process where the direct producers will appropriate the surplus they produce. That is, the Kanoria jute mill workers are seeking a transformation of the enterprise from a capitalist (exploitative) class process to a communist (nonexploitative) class process. One would definitely expect the entire left to be behind such a movement. However, the position of the traditional left parties and their unions, to put it mildly, has been anachronistic. In this context, the state government led by the Communist Party of India (Marxist) as well as the far left parties are bent on depicting the movement as revisionist and opposing it. It is almost incomprehensible to rationalize this form of opposition by the left when at the same time they are calling all-India strikes to save the exploitative state enterprises. This opposition stems from the belief that cooperatives are barriers to the development of society that, as per the logic of historical materialism, seeks capitalist development in the present juncture. Thus, this position could only make sense as part of the big-bang macro theory of transition that, as we pointed out in the earlier chapters, is logically unsustainable. Paradoxically, from the class-based standpoint that we are advocating, the traditional left's position can be dubbed as reactionary.

Chapter 10
A Conclustion by Way
of Opening Up "Other" Spaces

1. Since Chaudhury's focus is explicitly on distribution, he ignores production. It does not matter for him whether the surplus is given by nonexploitative processes or exploitative ones. In this context he writes, "If the nation's monopoly houses and the state industrial sector fails, let the multinationals come" (2001, 199). This is something that we, operating in a Marxian framework with its emphasis on class, cannot afford to overlook.

2. This exclusion has enormous implications for the question of knowledge or discourse as an object of power. One of Foucault's many contributions has been to point out that the deployment of the pen is not outside of the prevailing power structures. That is, a book or a statement is not outside the subject's occupation within a power structure and the production of knowledge by the subject in turn helps in the consolidation of the power structure. It is also a well-known fact that most Third World writers occupy powerful positions and can be considered as part of the elite. Consequently, knowledge production (reproducing the prevailing power structures) in Third World countries will be dominated by domestic elite groups who also maintain intimate connections with the West. The West only hears one voice—that of this elite group. It hears itself through the voice of this elite group, and the East makes itself heard through the same voices. Somewhere in this monologue, the differences within the East and the West get lost. See Chakrabarti and Chaudhury (1996) for details.

3. In addition to being simply a work on transition and development, we also see our work here as a preliminary beginning of a class-based construction of such a social space.

Bibliography

Ahluwalia, I. J. and I. M. D. Little. eds. 1998. *India's Economic Reforms and Development: Essays for Manmohan Singh.* New Delhi: Oxford University Press.

Ahluwalia, M. S. 1999. "India's Economic Reforms: An Appraisal." In Sachs, J. D., Varshney, A., and Bajpai, N. ed. *India in the Era of Economic Reforms.* New Delhi: Oxford University Press.

Ahooja-Patel, K. 1994. "Women: Politics of Exclusion." In *Alternative Economic Survey 1993–94.* Delhi: Public Interest Research Group.

Alavi, H. 1975. "India and the Colonial Mode of Production." In *The Socialist Register*, ed. R. Miliband and J. Savage. London: Merlin Press.

———. 1982. "The Structure of Peripheral Capitalism." In *Introduction to the Sociology of "Developing Society,"* ed. H. Alavi and T. Shanin. New York and London: Monthly Review Press.

———. 1990. "Structure of Colonial Formations." In *Agrarian Relations and Accumulation: The "Mode of Production" Debate in India,* ed. U. Patnaik. Sameeksha Trust, Bombay: Oxford University Press.

Allardt, E. 1993. "Having, Loving, Being: An Alternative to the Swedish Model of Welfare Research." In Sen A and M. Nussbaum. *The Quality of Life.* Oxford University Press.

Althusser, L. 1969. *For Marx.* Harmondsworth: Penguin.

———. 1971. *Lenin and Philosophy and Other Essays.* London: New Left Review.

Althusser, L. and E. Balibar. 1975. *Reading Capital.* London: New Left Books.

Amariglio, J. L. and Callari, A. 1989. "Marxian Value Theory and the Problem of the Subject: The Role of Commodity Fetishism." *Rethinking Marxism* 2 (fall).

Amariglio, J. L.; Callari, A. and Cullenberg, S. 1989. "Analytical Marxism: A Critical Overview." *Review of Social Economy* 47 (4).

Amariglio, J. L. and Ruccio, D. 1994. "Postmodernism, Marxism, and the Critique of Modern Economic Thought." In *Rethinking Marxism* 7 (3).

Amin, S. 1974. *Accumulation on a World Scale.* New York: Monthly Review Press.

———. 1982. "Small Peasant Commodity Production and Rural Indebtedness: the Culture of Sugarcane in Eastern U. P., c. 1880–1920." In *Subaltern Studies I,* ed. R. Guha. Delhi: Oxford University Press.

Arnold, D. 1984. "Gramsci and the Peasant Subalternity in India." *The Journal of Peasant Studies* Vol II (4).

Balibar, E. 1994. *Masses, Classes, Ideas: Studies on Politics and Philosophy before and after Marx.* Trans. J. Swenson. London: Routledge.

———. 1995. *The Philosophy of Marx.* Trans. Chris Turner. London: Verso.

Banaji, J. 1990. "For a Theory of Colonial Modes of Production." In *Agrarian Relations and Accumulation: The "Mode of Production" Debate in India,* ed. U. Patnaik. Sameeksha Trust, Bombay: Oxford University Press.

Baran, P. 1973. *The Political Economy of Growth.* Harmondsworth: Penguin.

Bardhan, P. 1980. "Interlocking Factor Markets and Agrarian Development: A Review of Issues." *Oxford Economic Papers.* Vol. 32, March.

———. 1982. "Agrarian Class Formation in India." *The Journal of Peasant Studies* Vol 10 (1).

———. 1984a. *Land, Labor and Rural Poverty: Essays in Development Economics.* Delhi: Oxford University Press.

———. 1984b. *The Political Economy of Development in India.* Oxford: Basil Blackwell.

———. 1986. "Marxist Ideas in Development Economics: An Evaluation." In *Analytical Marxism,* ed. J. Roemer. Cambridge, U.K.: Cambridge University Press.

———. 1989. "A Note on Interlinked Rural Economic Arrangements." In *The Economic Theory of Agrarian Institutions,* ed. P.Bardhan. Oxford: Oxford University Press.

Bardhan, P. and Rudra, A. 1978. "Interlinkage of Land, Labour and Credit Relations: An Analysis of Village Survey Data in East India." *Economic and Political Weekly* Vol. 13, February.

———. 1980. "Terms and Conditions of Sharecropping Contracts: An Analysis of Village Survey Data in India." *Journal of Development Studies* Vol. 16, April.

———. 1981. "Terms and Conditions of Labour Contracts in Agriculture: Results of a Survey in West Bengal 1979." *Oxford Bulletin of Economics and Statistics* Vol. 43, February.

———. 1986. "Labour Mobility and the Boundaries of the Village Moral Economy." *The Journal of Peasant Studies,* April.

Barrett, M. 1988. *Women's Oppression Today.* London: Verso.

Baudrillard, J. 1989. *America.* London: Verso.

Benjamin, W. 1973. *Illuminations.* Trans. Harry Zohn. London: Fontana.

Bhaduri, A. 1973. "A Study of Agricultural Backwardness Under Conditions of Semi Feudalism." *Economic Journal* 83 (329).

———. 1977. "On the Formation of Usurious Interest Rates in Backward Agriculture." *Cambridge Journal of Economics* Vol. 1, March.

———. 1979. "A Rejoinder to Srinivasan's Comment" *Economic Journal* Vol. 89. June.

———. 1981. "Class Relations and the Pattern of Accumulation in an Agrarian Economy." *Cambridge Journal of Economics* Vol. 11. March.

———. 1983. *The Economic Structure of Backward Agriculture.* London: Academic Press.

————. 1986. "Forced Commerce and Agrarian Growth." *World Development* Vol. 14, No. 2.

Bhagwati, J. 1993. *India in Transition: Freeing the Economy.* Oxford: Clarendon Press.

————. 1998. "The Design of Indian Development." In Ahluwalia, I. J. and I. M. D. Little, ed. *India's Economic Reforms and Development: Essays for Manmohan Singh.* New Delhi: Oxford University Press.

Bhagwati, J. and Srinivasan, T. N. 1993. *India's Economic Reforms.* New Delhi: Ministry of Finance, Economic Division.

Bourdieu, P. 1994. "Doxa and Common Life: An Interview with T. Eagleton." In *Mapping Ideology.* ed. S. Zizek. London: Verso.

Bradby, 1975. "The Destruction of Natural Economy." *Economy and Society* Vol IV (2).

R. Brenner. 1977. *The Origins of Capitalist Development: A Critique of Neo-Smithian Marxism* in *New Left Review,* no. 104.

————. 1985. *Agrarian Class Structure and Economic Development in The Brenner Debate,* ed. T. H. Ashton and C. H. E. Philpin, Cambridge: Cambridge University Press.

Byres, T. 1994. "State, Class and Development Planning in India." In *The State and Development Planning in India,* ed. T. Byres. Delhi, New York: Oxford University Press.

Butchavarov, P. "Metaphysics." In *The Cambridge Dictionary of Philosophy,* ed. R. Audi. New York: Cambridge University Press.

Callari, A. and Ruccio, D. F., eds. 1996a. *Post-Modern Materialism and the Future of Marxist Theory: Essays in the Althusserian Tradition.* Hanover and London: Wesleyan University Press.

Callari, A. and Ruccio, D. F. 1996b. "Introduction." In *Post-Modern Materialism and the Future of Marxist Theory: Essays in the Althusserian Tradition,* ed. Callari, A. and Ruccio, D. F. Hanover and London: Wesleyan University Press.

Cassen, R. and V. Joshi, eds. 1995. *India: The Future of Economic Reform.* New Delhi: Oxford University Press.

Conray, M. 1984. *The State of Political Theory.* Stanford: Stanford University Press.

Chakrabarti, A. 1996. *Transition and Development in India: A Critique and Reformulation.* Ph.D. diss. University of California, Riverside.

————. 1998. "Confronting the Indian Modes of Production Debate: An Unhappy Encounter of a Third Kind." *Artha Vijnana* XL (2), June.

Chakrabarti, A. and Chaudhury, A. 1996/97. "Can the Savage Speak?" *Rethinking Marxism.* Vol 9. No. 2

Chakrabarti, A. and Roy Chaudhury, S. 1999/2000. "Post Colonial Capital's Hegemony: Theorizing the Waste Land of Global Capital and its Aftermath." *Working Paper #5.* Department of Economics, Calcutta University.

Chakrabarti, A. and Cullenberg, S. 2001a. "Development and Class Transition in India: A New Perspective." In *Re/presenting Class: Essays in Postmodern Marxism.* Ed. Kathy Gibson, Julie Graham, Stephen Resnick, and Richard Wolff. Duke University Press.

————. 2001b. "Transition and Development: A Methodological Critique of the Subaltern Studies. *Margins* Vol I, No. II (August).

Chakrabarti, A., Chaudhury, A., and Cullenberg, S. 2002. "Global Order and the New Economic Policy in India: The (Post) Colonial Formation of the Small-Scale Sector." Working Paper: Department of Economics, Calcutta University.

Chakraborty, D. 1985. "Invitation to a Dialogue." In *Subaltern Studies IV*, ed. R. Guha. Delhi: Oxford University Press.

———. 1993. "Marx After Marxism: A Subaltern Historian's Perspective." *Economic and Political Weekly* May 29.

———. 1995. "Radical Histories and Question of Enlightenment Rationalism: Some Recent Critiques of *Subaltern Studies*." *Economic and Political Weekly* Vol. 30 (14).

———. 2000. *Provincializing Europe: Postcolonial Thought and Historical Difference.* Princeton: Princeton University Press.

Chakravarty, S. 1987. *Development Planning: The Indian Experience.* Oxford: Clarendon Press.

Chandra, N. K. 1974. "Farm Efficiency Under Semi-Feudalism: A Critique of Marginalist Theories and some Marxist Formulations." *Economic and Political Weekly* Vol. 9. (1309–31).

———. 1975a, 1975b, 1975c. "Agrarian Transition in India." *Frontier* Vol. 7. No. 28, 29, 30.

Chatterjee, P. 1983. "More on Modes of Power and the Peasantry." In *Subaltern Studies II*, ed. R. Guha. Delhi: Oxford University Press.

———. 1984. "Gandhi and the Critique of Civil Society." In *Subaltern Studies III*, ed. R. Guha. Delhi: Oxford University Press.

———. 1986. *Nationalist Thought and Colonial World: A Derivative Discourse.* London: Zed Books.

———. 1988. "On Gramsci's 'Fundamental Mistake'." *Economic and Political Weekly: Review of Political Economy* 23 (3).

———. 1989. "Caste and Subaltern Consciousness." In *Subaltern studies VI*, ed. R. Guha. Delhi: Oxford University Press.

———. 1993. *Nation and its Fragments: Colonial and Post Colonial Histories.* Princeton: Princeton University Press.

———. 1994. "Development Planning and the Indian State." In *The State and Development Planning in India*, ed. T. Byres. Delhi, New York: Oxford University Press.

Chatterjee, P. and Pandey, G., eds. 1992. *Subaltern Studies VII.* Delhi: Oxford University Press.

Chattopadhyay, P. 1990a. "On the Question of the Mode of Production in Indian Agriculture: A Preliminary Note." In *Agrarian Relations and Accumulation: The "Mode of Production" Debate in India*, ed. U. Patnaik. Sameeksha Trust, Bombay: Oxford University Press.

———. 1990b. "An 'Anti-Kritik'." In *Agrarian Relations and Accumulation: The "Mode of Production" Debate in India*, ed. U. Patnaik. Sameeksha Trust, Bombay: Oxford University Press.

Chattopadhyay, R. 1985. "The Idea of Planning in India, 1930–51." Doctoral diss. Canberra: Australian National University.

Chaudhury, A. 1988. "From Hegemony to Counter-Hegemony." In *Economic and Political Weekly* 23(3).

Chaudhuri, A. 1991–92. "From Hegel to Gramsci: Capital's Passive Revolution." *Society and Change* 8 (3 & 4).

————. *Equality beyond Equality: A Prelude to a Post-Structuralist Reading of Capital.* Calcutta: Anustup.

————. 1994. "On Colonial Hegemony: Toward a Critique of Brown Orientalism." *Rethinking Marxism* Vol 7 (4).

————. 1995. "Towards Closing a Century-Old Debate: Transformation of Values into Prices in a World of Heterogeneous Labours." Forthcoming in *Rethinking Marxism* 10 (1).

————. 2001. "Western Marxists' Commodity Fetishism: Looking for an Exit." *Margins* Vol I, No. II (August).

Chaudhury, A. and Chakrabarti, A. 2000. "The Market Economy and Marxist Economists: Through the Lens of a Housewife." *Rethinking Marxism* Vol. 12, No. 2.

Chaudhury, A. and Das, D. 1999–2000. "Interrogating the Primitive: A Reformulation of Smith's Theory of Value." *Working Paper # 3.* Department of Economics, Calcutta University.

Chaudhury, A., Das, D., and Chakrabarti, A. 2000. *Margin of Margin: Profile of an Unrepentant Postcolonial Collaborator.* Anustup: Kolkata.

Cohen, G. A. 1978. *Karl Marx's Theory of History: A Defense.* Oxford: Oxford University Press.

————. 1983. "Reconsidering Historical Materialism." *Nomos* 26.

————. 1988. *History, Labor and Freedom.* Oxford: Oxford University Press.

————. 1995. *Self Ownership, Freedom and Equality.* Cambridge: Cambridge University Press.

Cullenberg, S. 1991. "The Rhetorical Marxian Microfoundations." Review of Radical Political Economics 23 (182).

————. 1992. "Socialism's Burden: Toward a 'Thin' Definition of Socialism." *Rethinking Marxism* 5 (2).

————. 1994. *The Falling Rate of Profit: Recasting the Marxian Debate.* London: Pluto Press.

Cullenberg, S, Amariglio, J., and Ruccio, D. F., eds. 2001. *Postmodernism, Economics and Knowledge.* London and New York: Routledge.

Culler, J. 1982. *On Deconstruction: Theory and Criticism After Structuralism.* Ithaca, N.Y.: Cornell University Press.

————. 1986. *Ferdinand de Saussure.* Ithaca, N.Y.: Cornell University Press.

Cutler, A., Hindess, B., Hirst, P., and Hussain, A. 1977. *Marx's Capital and Capitalism Today.* 2 Vols . London: Routledge and Kegan Paul.

Delphy, C. 1984. *Close to Home: a Materialist Analysis of Women's Oppression.* Trans. Diana Leonard. London: Hutchinson in Association with the Explorations in Feminism Collective.

Derrida, J. 1976. *Of Grammatology.* Trans. G. C. Spivak. Baltimore: John Hopkins University Press.

————. 1977. "Limited Inc." *Glyph* 2.

————. 1978. *Writing and Difference.* Chicago: University of Chicago Press.

————. 1981. *Positions.* Trans. A. Bass. Chicago: University of Chicago Press.

————. 1982. *Margins of Philosophy.* Chicago: University of Chicago Press.

Dobb, M. 1978a. "A Reply" in *The Transition from Feudalism to Capitalism*, ed. R. Hilton. London: Verso.

————. 1978b. "A Further Comment" in *The Transition from Feudalism to Capitalism*, ed. R. Hilton. London: Verso.

Dumont, L. 1970. *Homo Hierarchicus*. Trans. M. Salisbury. London: Paladin.

Eagleton, T. 1990. *The Ideology of the Aesthetic*. Oxford, U.K. and Cambridge, Mass.: Blackwell.

————. 1991. *Ideology*. London: Verso.

Economic and Political Weekly Research Foundation. 1994. *Three Years of Economic Reform in India: A Critical Assessment*. Bombay: S. L. Shetty, EPW Research Foundation.

Emmanuel, A. 1972. *Unequal Exchange: A Study of the Imperialism of Trade*. New York: Monthly Review Press.

Engels, F. 1980. "Die Bewegungen von 1847" *Deutsche Brusseler Zeiting* In *Materiales para la Historia de America Latina*. Trans. P Scaron. Mexico: Siglo Veintiuno Editores.

Escobar, A. 1995. *Encountering Development: The Making and Unmaking of the Third World*. Princeton: Princeton University Press.

Fine, B. 1997. "Entitlement Failures?" *Development and Change*. Vol. 28 (617–47).

Foster-Carter, A. 1978. "The Modes of Production Controversy." *New Left Review* no. 107 (January/February): 47–77.

Foucault, M. 1972a. *Histoire de la folie a l'age classique*. Paris: Gallimard.

————. 1972b. *The Archaeology of Knowledge*. Trans. A. M. Sheridan Smith. New York: Harper and Row.

Fox, B., ed. 1980. *Hidden in the Household*. Toronto: The Women's Press.

Fraad, H., Resnick, S. A., and Wolff, R. D. 1994. *Bringing it All Back Home: Class, Gender and Power in the Modern Household*. Pluto Press: London, Boulder, Colorado.

Fraad, H. 2000. "Exploitation in the Labour of Love." In Gibson-Graham, J. K., Resnick, S. A., and Wolff, R. D. 2000. *Class and its Others*. Minneapolis: University of Minnesota Press.

Frank, G. 1969. *Capitalism and Underdevelopment in Latin America*. New York: Monthly Review Press.

Gabriel, S. 1990. "Ancients: A Marxian Theory of Exploitation." *Rethinking Marxism* 3 (Spring).

Gandhi, M. K. 1958–. *The Collected Works of Mahatma Gandhi*. 90 Vols. New Delhi: Publications Division.

Gasche, R. 1986. *The Tain of the Mirror: Derrida and the Philosophy of Reflection*. Cambridge, Mass.: Harvard University Press.

Ghoshal, S. and C. A. Bartlett. 1997. *The Individualized Corporation: A Fundamentally New Approach to Management*. London: Random House Business Books.

Ghoshal, S., C. A. Bartlett, and P. Moran, 1999. *A New Manifesto For Management*. Sloan Management Review (Spring).

Ghose, A. K. and A. Saith, 1976. "Indebtedness, Tenancy and the Adoption of New Technology in Semi-Feudal Agriculture." *World Development* Vol. 4. (305–19).

Ghosh, A. 1995. "Economy and the Budget." *Economic and Political Weekly* 30 (18–19).

Government of India, Ministry of Finance Discussion Paper. 1993. *Economic Reforms: Two Years After and the Task Ahead*. New Delhi: Ministry of Finance, Economic Division.

Government of India, Ministry of Finance. 1995. *Economic Survey 1994–95*. New Delhi: Ministry of Finance, Economic Division.

———. 1997. *Economic Survey 1996–97*. New Delhi: Ministry of Finance, Economic Division.

———. 2000. *Economic Survey 1999–2000*. New Delhi: Ministry of Finance, Economic Division.

———. 1997. *Economic Survey 2000–2001*. New Delhi: Ministry of Finance, Economic Division.

Gibson-Graham, J. K. 1993. "Waiting for the Revolutions, or How to Smash Capitalism While Working at Home in Your Spare Time." *Rethinking Marxism* 6 (2).

———. 1996. *The End of Capitalism (As We Knew It): A Feminist Critique of Political Economy*. Blackwell.

Gibson-Graham, J. K., S. A. Resnick, and R. D. Wolff. 2000. *Class and its Others*. Minneapolis: University of Minnesota Press.

Gibson-Graham, J. K. and D. Ruccio, 2001a. " 'After' Development: Re-imagining Economy and Class." *Re/presenting Class: Essays in Postmodern Marxism*. 2001. Ed. J. K. Gibson-Graham, S. A. Resnick, and R. D. Wolff. Duke University Press. Also in *Margins* Vol I, No. II (August).

———. 2001a. " Toward a Poststructuralist Political Economy." *Re/presenting Class: Essays in Postmodern Marxism*. 2001. Ed. J. K. Gibson-Graham, S. A. Resnick, and R. D. Wolff. Duke University Press.

Griffin, K. 1974. *The Political Economy of Agrarian Change* Cambridge, Mass.: Harvard University Press.

Guha, R. 1982. "On Some Aspects of the Historiography of Colonial India." In *Subaltern Studies I*, ed. R. Guha. Delhi: Oxford University Press.

———. 1983. *Elementary Aspects of Peasant Insurgency in Colonial India*. Delhi: Oxford University Press.

———. 1989. "Dominance without Hegemony and its Historiography." In *Subaltern Studies VI*, ed. R. Guha. Delhi: Oxford University Press.

———. 1982–1990. *Subaltern Studies*. 6 Vols. Delhi: Oxford University Press.

Gulati, A. 1998. "Indian Agriculture in an Open Economy: Will it Prosper?" In *India's Economic Reforms and Development: Essays for Manmohan Singh*, ed. I. J. Ahluwalia and I. M. D. Little. New Delhi: Oxford University Press.

Habermas, J. 1976. *Legitimation Crisis*. London: Heinemaan.

———. 1987. *The Philosophical Discourse of Modernity*. Trans. F. Lawrence. Cambridge, Mass.: MIT Press.

Harris, J. R. and Todaro, M.P. 1970. "Migration, Unemployment and Development: A Two-Sector Analysis." *American Economic Review* 60: 126–142.

Harris, N. 1986. *The End of the Third World*. Harmondsworth: Penguin.

Hartmann, H. 1981. "The Family as the Locus of Gender, Class and Political Struggle: the Example of the Housewife." *Signs* 6.

Harvey, D. 1989. *The Condition of Postmodernity.* Oxford: Bkackwell.

Himmelweit, S. and Mohun, S. 1977. "Domestic Labor and Capital." *Cambridge Journal of Economics* 1 (1).

Hilton, R. 1978. "Introduction" in *The Transition from Feudalism to Capitalism,* ed. R. Hilton. London: Verso.

Hindess, B. 1987. *Politics and Class Analysis.* Oxford: Blackwell.

———. 1988. *Choice, Rationality, and Social Theory.* London: Unwin Hyman.

Howard, M. and King, J. 1989. A History of Marxian Economics, volume I. Princeton: Princeton University Press.

Howard, M. and King, J. A History of Marxian Economics, volume II. Princeton: Princeton University Press.

Humphries, J. 1977. "Class Struggle and the Persistence of the Working Class Family." *Cambridge Journal of Economics,* September.

Jalan, B. 1991. *India's Economic Crisis: The Way Ahead.* New Delhi: Oxford University Press.

Jessop, B. 1990. *State Theory: Putting Capitalist States in their Place.* Philadelphia: Pennsylvania State University Press.

Jameson, F. 1981. *The Political Unconscious.* Ithaca, N.Y.: Cornell University Press.

———. 1991. *Postmodernism, or, the Cultural Logic of Late Capitalism.* Durham: Duke University Press.

Joshi, V. and I. M. D. Little. 1996. *India's Economic Reforms 1991–2001.* New Delhi: Oxford University Press.

Kane, P. V. 1974. *History of Dharmasastra.* Vol II. Part I. Poona: Bhandarkar Oriental Research Institute.

Kaviraj, S. 1989. "Bankimchandra and the Making of Nationalist Consciousness: I. Signs of Madness; II. The Self-Ironical Tradition; III. A Critique of Colonial Reason." Occasional Papers 108, 109, and 110. Calcutta: Centre for Studies in Social Sciences.

Kaviraj, S. 1992. "The Imaginary Institution of India." In *Subaltern Studies VII,* ed. P. Chatterjee and G. Pandey. Delhi: Oxford University Press.

Laclau, E. 1971. "Feudalism and Capitalism in Latin America." *New Left Review* 67.

———. 1988. "Metaphor and Social Antagonism." In *Marxism and Interpretation of Culture,* ed. C. Nelson and L. Grossberg. Urbana and Chicago: University of Illinois Press.

———. 1990. *New Reflections on The Revolutions of our Times.* Trans. J. Barnes et al. London: Verso.

———. 1994. *The Making of Political Identities.* London, New York: Verso.

Laclau, E. and Mouffe, C. 1985. *Hegemony and Socialist Strategy: Towards a Radical Democratic Politics.* Trans. W. Moore and P. Cammack. London: Verso.

Larrain, J. 1983. *Marxism and Ideology.* London: Macmillan.

———. 1989. *Theories of Development.* Polity Press.

———. 1994. *Ideology and Cultural Identity: Modernity and the Third World Presence.* Cambridge Polity Press.

Levi-Strauss, C. 1974. *Tristes Tropiques*. Trans. J. Weightman and D. Weightman. New York: Antheneum.

Lewis, W. A. 1954. "Economic Development with Unlimited Supplies of Labour." *Manchester School* 28: 139–91.

Lyotard, J. F. 1984. *The Post Modern Condition: A Report on Knowledge*. Trans. G. Bennington and B. Massumi. Minneapolis: University of Minnesota Press.

———. 1992. "What is Postmodernism?" In *The Post-Modern Reader*, ed. C. Jencks. New York: St Martin's Press.

Lukacs, G. 1971. *History and Class Consciousness*. Cambridge, Mass.: MIT Press.

———. 1980. *The Destruction of Reason*. London: Merlin Press.

Mallick, A.; Chaudhury, A.; and Chakrabarti, A. 1997. *The Impossibility of Equal Exhange*. Mimeo, Department of Economics, University of Calcutta.

Malthus, T. R. 1936. *Principles of Political Economy, Book II*. London: International Economic Circle, Tokyo and the London School of Economics and Poltical Science.

Marglin, S and A. Apffel-Marglin, eds. 1990. *Dominating Knowledge*. Oxford: Clarendon Press.

Marx, K. 1954. *Capital*. Vol I. Moscow: Progress Publishers.

———. 1973. *Grundrisse*. Trans. M. Nicolaus. New York: Vintage.

———. 1975. "Letter to Otechestvenniye Zapiski." In *Marx-Engels Selected Correspondence*, ed. S. Ryazanskaya. Moscow: Progress Publishers.

———. 1977. "The Critique of the Gotha Programme." In *Marx: Selected Writings*, ed. McLennan, D. New York: Oxford University Press.

———. 1979. "The British Rule in India." In *Pre-Capitalist Socio-Economic Formations*, Marx, K. and Engels, F. Moscow: Progress Publishers.

———. 1983. "Marx-Zasulich Correspondence: Letters and Drafts." In *Late Road and the Russian Road: Marx and "the Peripheries of Capitalism,"* ed. T. Shanin. New York: Monthly Review Press.

———. 1989. *Pre-Capitalist Economic Formations*. Trans. J. Cohen. New York: International Publishers.

———. 1990. *Capital*. Vol 1. Trans. B. Fowkes. London: Penguin Books.

———. 1993. *Grundrisse*. London: Penguin.

McCloskey, D. N. 1985a. *The Rhetoric of Economics*. Madison: University of Wisconsin Press.

———. 1985b. *Knowledge and Persuasion in Economics*. Cambridge: Cambridge University Press.

Mehta, J. 1994. "Price and Distribution." In *Alternative Economic Survey 1993–94*. Delhi: Public Interest Research Group.

Mill, J. S. 1875. "A Few Words on Non-Intervention" in *Dissertation and Discussions*. London: Longmans, Green, Reader and Deyer.

Mill, J. 1820. *The History of British India, Vol II, Book II*. London: Baldwin, Cradock and Joy.

Mirowski, P. 1989. *More Heat than Light: Economics as Social Physics, Physics as Nature's Economics*. Cambridge: Cambridge University Press.

Morishima, M. 1973. *Marx's Economics: A Dual Theory of Value and Growth.* London: Cambridge University Press.

Mukherjee, M. 1988. "Peasant Resistance and Peasant Consciousness in Colonial India: 'Subaltern and Beyond'." *Economic and Political Weekly* 23 (41 & 42).

Murphy, K. M., Shleifer, A., and Vishny, R. 1989. "Industrialisation and the Big Push." *Journal of Political Economy* 97: 1003–26.

Nandy, A. 1987. *Traditions, Tyranny, and Utopias.* Delhi: Oxford University Press.

Nehru, J. 1954. *Jawaharlal Nehru's Speeches. Vol 2.* New Delhi: Publications Division.

Newbery, D. M. G., 1975. "Tenurial Obstacles to Innovation." *Journal of Development Studies* Vol. 11: 263–277.

Norton, B. 1986. "Steindl, Levine and the Inner Logic of Accumulation: A Marxian Critique." *Social Concept* 3 (2): 43–66.

———. 1988. "The Power Axis: Bowles, Gordon and Weisskopf's Theory of Postwar U.S. Accumulation." *Rethinking Marxism* 1 (3): 6–43.

———. 2001. "Reading Marx for Class." In *Re/presenting Class: Essays in Postmodern Marxism,* ed. K. Gibson, J. Graham, S. Resnick, and R. Wolff. Durham: Duke University Press.

Omvedt, G. 1982. "An Introductory Essay." In *Land, Caste and Politics in Indian States,* ed. G. Omvedt. Delhi: Authors Guild Publications.

Osmani, S. 1995. "The Entitlement Approach to Famine: An Assessment." In K. Basu et. al. (eds.) *Choice, Welfare and Development: A Festschrift in Honour of Amartya K. Sen.* Oxford: Clarendon Press.

Pandey, G. 1982. "Peasant Revolt and Indian Nationalism: The Peasant Movement in Awadh, 1919–1922." In *Subaltern Studies I,* ed. R. Guha. Delhi: Oxford University

———. 1984. "Encounters and Calamities: The History of a North Indian Qasba in the Nineteenth Century." In *Subaltern Studies III,* ed. R. Guha. Delhi: Oxford University Press.

Parikh, K. S.; Narayana, N. S. S.; Panda, M. and Ganesh Kumar, A. 1995. "Stategies for Agricultural Liberalization: Consequences for Growth, Welfare and Distribution." *Economic and Political Weekly* 30 (39).

Patnaik, A. 1988. "Gramsci's Concept of Hegemony: The Case of Development Administration in India." *Economic and Political Weekly: Review of Political Economy* 23 (5).

Patnaik, U. 1976. "Class Differentiation within the Peasantry: An Approach to the Analysis of Indian Agriculture." In *Economic and Political Weekly* 11 (39).

———. 1978. "Development of Capitalism in Agriculture: I and II." In *Studies in the Development of Capitalism in India.* Lahore: Vanguard Books Limited.

———. 1987. *Peasant Class Differentiation: A Study in Method with Reference to Haryana.* Delhi: Oxford University Press.

———. 1990a. "Capitalist Development in Agriculture: Reply." In *Agrarian Relations and Accumulation: The "Mode of Production" Debate in India,* ed. U. Patnaik. Sameeksha Trust, Bombay: Oxford University Press.

———. 1990b. "Capitalist Development in Agriculture: Further Comment." In *Agrarian Relations and Accumulation: The "Mode of Production" Debate in India,* ed. U. Patnaik. Sameeksha Trust, Bombay: Oxford University Press.

———. 1990c. "On the Mode of Production in Indian Agriculture: Reply." In *Agrarian Relations and Accumulation: The "Mode of Production" Debate in India,* ed. U. Patnaik. Sameeksha Trust, Bombay: Oxford University Press.

———. 1990d. "Class Differentiation within the Peasantry: An Approach to the Analysis of Indian Agriculture." In *Agrarian Relations and Accumulation: The "Mode of Production" Debate in India,* ed. U. Patnaik. Sameeksha Trust, Bombay: Oxford University Press.

———. 1990e. "Introduction." In *Agrarian Relations and Accumulation: The "Mode of Production" Debate in India,* ed. U. Patnaik. Sameeksha Trust, Bombay: Oxford University Press.

———. 1996. "Export-Oriented Agriculture and Food Security in Developing Countries and India." *Economic and Political Weekly,* Special Number, Vol XXXI, No. 35–37.

Prasad, P. H. 1973. "Production Relations": Achilles Heel of Indian Planning." *Economic and Political Weekly* May 12.

———. 1979. "Semi-Feudalism: The Basic Constraint of Indian Agriculture." In *Agrarian Relations in India,* ed. A. N. Das and V. Nilakant. Delhi: Manohar Publications.

———. 1990. "Reactionary Role of Usurer's Capital in Rural India." In *Agrarian Relations and Accumulation: The "Mode of Production" Debate in India,* ed. U. Patnaik. Sameeksha Trust, Bombay: Oxford University Press.

Popkin, S. L. 1979. *The Rational Peasant: The Political Economy of Rural Society in Vietnam.* Berkeley: University of California Press.

Porter, M. 1998a. "Clusters and the New Economics of Competition." *Harvard Business Review.* (November–December).

———. 1998b. *On Competition.* Cambridge, Mass.: Harvard Business School Press.

———. 1988. *Jean Baudrillard: Selected Writings.* California: Stanford University Press.

Pursell, G. and A. Gulati. 1995. "Liberalizing Indian Agriculture: An Agenda for Reform." In Cassen, R. and V. Joshi. 1995 ed. *India: The Future of Economic Reform.* New Delhi: Oxford University Press.

Rangarajan, C. 1998. "Development, Inflation and Monetary Policy." In Ahluwalia, I. J. and I. M. D. Little, eds. *India's Economic Reforms and Development: Essays for Manmohan Singh.* New Delhi: Oxford University Press.

Reserve Bank of India. *Annual Report 2000–01. Year July 1, 2000 to June 30, 2001.* Mumbai: Reserve Bank of India Publication.

Resnick, S. A. and Wolff, R. D. 1986. "What are Class Analysis?" In *Research in Political Economy* 9, ed. P. Zarembka, 1–32. Greenwich and London: JAI Press.

———. 1987. *Knowledge and Class: A Marxist Critique of Political Economy.* Chicago and London: University of Chicago Press.

———. 1988. "Communism: Between Class and Classless." *Rethinking Marxism 1 (1).*

———. 1992. "Radical Economics: A Tradition of Theoretical Differences." In *Radical Economics,* ed. B. Roberts and S. Feiner. Boston: Kluwer Academic Publishers.

———. 1993. "State Capitalism in the USSR? A High Stakes Debate." *Rethinking Marxism* 6 (2).

————. 1994. "Between State and Private Capitalism: What was Soviet 'Socialism'?" *Rethinking Marxism* 7 (1).

————. 1995. "Lessons from the USSR: Taking Marxist Theory the Next Step." In *Whither Marxism? Global Crisis in International Perspective*, ed. B. Magnus and S. Cullenberg. New York: Routledge.

————. 2001. "Struggles in the USSR: Communisms Attempted and Undone." In *Re/presenting Class: Essays in Postmodern Marxism*, ed. K. Gibson, J. Graham, S. Resnick, and R. Wolff. Durham: Duke University Press.

Resnick, S. A., Wolff, R. D., and Ruccio, D. 1990. "Class Beyond the Nation-State." In *Review of Radical Political Economics*

Rey, P. P. 1978. *Les Alliances De Classes*. Paris: Maspero.

Roberts, B. 1995. "Value, Abstract Labor and Exchange Equivalence." College of William and Mary, Department of Economics, mimeograph.

Roy, A. 1999. "The Greater Common Good." *Outlook* (24th March).

Ruccio, D and L. H. Simon. 1986a. "A Methodological Analysis of Dependency Theory: Explanation in Andre Gunder Frank." *World Development* 14 (February): 195–210.

————. 1986b. "Methodological Aspects of Marxian Approaches to Development: An Analysis of the Modes of Production School." *World Development* 14 (February): 212–22.

Ruccio, D. 1991. "When Failure Becomes Success: Class and the Debate Over Stabilization and Adjustment." *World Development* 19 (10).

————. 1992. "Failure of Socialism, Future of Socialism?" *Rethinking Marxism*. 5 (2).

————. 2003. "Globalization and Imperialism", forthcoming in *Rethinking Marxism*.

Rudra, A. 1978. "In Search of Capitalist Farmer." In *Studies in the Development of Capitalism in India*, Lahore: Vanguard Books Limited.

————. 1984. "Local Power and Farm-Level Decision-Making." In *Agrarian Power and Agricultural productivity in South Asia*, ed. M. Desai, S. H. Rudolph and A. Rudra. Berkeley and Los Angeles: University of California Press.

————. 1988. "Emerging Class Structure in Rural India." In *Rural Poverty in South Asia*, ed. T. N. Srinivasav and P. K. Bardhan. New York: Columbia University Press.

————. 1990a. "Capitalist Development in Agriculture: Reply." In *Agrarian Relations and Accumulation: The "Mode of Production" Debate in India*, ed. U. Patnaik. Sameeksha Trust, Bombay: Oxford University Press.

————. 1990b. "India and the Colonial Mode of Production: Comment." In *Agrarian Relations and Accumulation: The "Mode of Production" Debate in India*, ed. U. Patnaik. Sameeksha Trust, Bombay: Oxford University Press.

————. 1990c. "Class Relations in Indian Agriculture." In *Agrarian Relations and Accumulation: The "Mode of Production" Debate in India*, ed. U. Patnaik. Sameeksha Trust, Bombay: Oxford University Press.

Rudra, A., Majid, A., and Talib, B. D. 1990. "Big Farmers of Punjab." In *Agrarian Relations and Accumulation: The "Mode of Production" Debate in India*, ed. U. Patnaik. Sameeksha Trust, Bombay: Oxford University Press.

Sachs, J. D. and Varshney, A., and Bajpai, N., eds. 1999. *India in the Era of Economic Reforms*. New Delhi: Oxford University Press.

Sanyal, K. K. 1988. "Accumulation, Poverty and State in Third World Capital/Pre-Capital Complex." *Economic and Political Weekly: Review of Political Economy* 23 (5).

———. 1991–1992. "Of Revolutions, Classic and Passive." *Society and Change* 8 (3 & 4).

———. 1993. "Capital, Primitive Accumulation, and the Third World: From Annihilation to Appropriation." *Rethinking Marxism* 3 (fall).

———. 1995. "Post Marxism and the Third World: A Critical Response to the Radical Democratic Agenda." *Rethinking Marxism*. Forthcoming.

Sanyal, K. 2001. "Beyond the Narrative of Transition: Postcolonial capitalism, Development and the Problematic of Hegemony." *Margins* Vol 1, No. II (August).

Sarkar, S. 1993. "The Fascism of the Sangha Parivar." *Economic and Political Weekly* 27 (5).

———. 1995. "A Marxian Social History beyond the Foucaltian Turn." *Economic and Political Weekly* July 29.

Sau, R. 1975. "Farm Efficiency under Semi-Feudalism: A Critique of Marginalist Theories and Some Marxist Formulations—A Comment." *Economic and Political Weekly* 10 (13).

———. 1990. "On the Essence and Manifestation of Capitalism in Indian Agriculture." In *Agrarian Relations and Accumulation: The "Mode of Production" in India*, ed. U. Patnaik. Sameeksha Trust, Bombay: Oxford University Press.

Say, J. B. 1968. *Ours Compet d'Economie Politique Patique, Part IV*. Rome: Edizioni Bizzari.

Scott, J. 1976. *The Moral Economy of the Peasants*. New Haven: Yale University Press.

Seccombe, W. 1974. "The Housewife and her Labour under Capitalism." *New Left Review* 83.

Seccombe, W. 1980. "Domestic Labor and the Working Class Household." In *Hidden in the Household*, ed. B. Fox. Toronto: The Women's Press.

Sen, A. 1994. "Agriculture." In *Alternative Economic Survey 1993–94*. Delhi: Public Interest Research Group.

———. 1987. "Subaltern Studies: Capital, Class and Community." In *Subaltern Studies V*, ed. R. Guha. Delhi: Oxford University Press.

———. 1988. "The Frontiers of Prison Notebooks." *Economic and Political Weekly: Review of Political Economy* 23 (5).

———. 1993. "Capability and Well-Being" In Sen, A. and M. Nussbaum. *The Quality of Life*. Oxford University Press (paperback ed.).

Sengupta, N. 1977. "Further on the Mode of Production in Agriculture." In *Economic and Political Weekly* Vol. 12. No. 26.

Shiva, V. 1989. *Staying Alive: Women, Ecology and Development*. London: Zed Books.

Spivak, G. C. 1985. "Subaltern Studies: Deconstructing Historiography." In *Subaltern Studies IV*, ed. R. Guha. Delhi: Oxford University Press.

———. 1988. "Can the Subaltern Speak?" In *Marxism and the Interpretation of Culture*, ed. C. Nelson and L. Grossberg. Urbana: University of Illinois Press.

———. 1994. "Introduction." In *Bringing it All Back Home: Class, Gender and Power in the Modern Household*, ed. Fraad, H., Resnick, S. A., and Wolff, R. D. London, Boulder, Colorado: Pluto Press.

Srinivasan, T. N. 1979. "Agriculture Backwardness under Semi-Feudalism-Comment." *Economic Journal* Vol. 89. June.

Sweezy, P. 1978a. "A Critique." In *The Transition from Feudalism to Capitalism*, ed. R. Hilton. London: Verso.

————. 1978b. "A Rejoinder." In *The Transition from Feudalism to Capitalism*, ed. R. Hilton. London: Verso.

Thomas, P. 1994. *Alien Politics: Marxist State Theory Retrieved*. New York: Routeledge.

Truman, H.S. [1949]. 1964. *Public Papers of the President of the United States: Harry. S. Truman*. Washington, D.C.: U.S. Government Printing Office.

United Nations, Department of Social and Economic Affairs. 1951. *Measures for the Economic Development of Underdeveloped Countries*. New York: United Nations.

United Nations Development Program. 1995. *Human Development Report*. New York: Oxford University Press for the U.N.D.P.

Varshney, A. 1999. "Mass Politics or Elite Politics? India's Economic Reforms in Comparative Perspective." In Sachs, J. D., Varshney, A., and Bajpai, N., eds. *India in the Era of Economic Reforms*. New Delhi: Oxford University Press.

Wallerstein, I. 1974. *The Modern World System*. New York: Academic Press.

Warren, B. 1980. *Imperialism, Pioneer of Capitalism*, London: Verso.

World Bank Country Study. 1995. *Economic Developments in India: Achievements and Challenges*. Washington, D.C.: World Bank.

Wolff, R. D., Roberts, B., and Callari, A. 1982. "Marx's (not Ricardo's) 'Transformation Problem': A Radical Reconceptualization." *History of Political Economy* 16 (3).

————. 1984. "A Marxian Alternative to the Traditional Transformation Problem." *Review of Radical Political Economics* 16 (2/3).

Wolff, R. D. 2001. "The US Economic Crisis: A Marxian Analysis." *Margins* Vol I, No. II (August).

Wolpe, H. 1980. "Introduction." In *The Articulation of the Mode of Production*, ed. H. Wolpe. London: Routledge and Kegan Paul.

Zizek, S. 1989. *The Sublime Object of Ideology*. London: Verso.

————. 1993. *Tarrying with the Negative: Kant, Hegel and the Critique of Ideology*. Durham: Duke University Press.

Index